DEFINING THE POLITICAL

# Defining the Political

Dick Howard
*Professor of Philosophy*
*State University of New York at Stony Brook*

University of Minnesota Press, Minneapolis

Published by the University of Minnesota Press
2037 University Avenue Southeast, Minneapolis MN 55414.
Published simultaneously in Canada
by Fitzhenry & Whiteside Limited, Markham.
Printed in Hong Kong.

Library of Congress Cataloging-in-Publication Number
88 27 836

ISBN 0–8166–1716–3 hc
ISBN 0–8166–1717–1 pb

For my mother, and to the
memory of my father

# Contents

* Both indexes compiled by James Clark.

# Sources

1. 'Out of the Silent Fifties': some material taken up in *The Politics of Modernism*, *Philosophy and Social Criticism*, vol. 8, no. 4, 1981.
2. 'Praxis before Politics: The Problem of Sartre', *Thesis Eleven*, no. 10/11, 1984–85, pp. 189–94.
3. 'The Theory and Practice of Dialectical Theory', originally in *The Marxian Legacy* (London: Macmillan, 1977).
4. 'From Marx to Kant', *Thesis Eleven*, no. 8, 1984, pp. 77–91.
5. 'Another Resurrection of Marxism', *Thesis Eleven*, no. 16, 1987, pp. 69–84.
6. 'The Future as Present', originally in *The Marxian Legacy* (London: Macmillan, 1977).
7. 'D'une nouvelle gauche à une autre', *Esprit*, July 1983, pp. 116–24.
8. 'Esprit', *Telos*, no. 36, Summer 1978, pp. 143–53.
9. 'French Socialism and Modernization', *Telos*, no. 61, 1984, pp. 113–20.
10. 'French Rhetoric and Political Reality', *Philosophy and Social Criticism*, vol. 12, 1987.
11. 'France, Germany and the Concept of Europe', *New Political Science*, no. 14, 1985, pp. 67–94.
12. 'Enlightened Despotism and Modern Democracy', complete version of a text published in *Telos*, no. 33, Autumn 1977, pp. 219–30.
13. 'La révolution dans le Révolution américaine', *La lettre internationale*, no. 9, Summer, 1986, pp. 6–9. German translation in *Merkur* 41 Jahrgang, Heft 3, March 1987, pp. 216–22.
14. 'La république et l'ordre international', *Intervention*, vol. 1, no. 4, March–April 1983, pp. 91–100.
15. 'The Political Origins of Democracy', originally in French as talk to Society for Phenomenology and Existential Philosophy, October 1986; in *La lettre internationale*, no. 15, Winter 1987–8. My translation.
16. 'Ethics and Politics', originally presented to Society for Social Philosophy, American Philosophical Association, December 1986; in *Praxis International*, Winter 1987–8.
17. 'A Renaissance of the Political in the USA?', unpublished; sections translated in *Esprit*, June 1987.

# Acknowledgements

Many friends have read, criticised, and debated the arguments of these chapters over the years. Among them have been Andrew Arato, Seyla Benhabib, Cornelius Castoriadis, Jean Cohen, André Gorz, Jürgen Habermas, Pierre Hassner, Peter Kemp, Ernesto Laclau, Gene Lebovics, Claude Lefort, John Mason, Sigrid Meuschel, Chantel Mouffe, Anson Rabinbach, Ulrich Rödel, Fred Siegel and Joel Whitebook. Editors too have been friends, and discussed more than what they edited. Paul Thibaud and Olivier Mongin of *Esprit* have been constant friends; Jean-Luc Pouthier, Joël Roman, and Patrick Viveret of *Intervention* have helped greatly; Antonin Liehn and Paul Noirot of *La lettre internationale* have given good counsel. Julian Triado of *Thesis Eleven*, David Rasmussen of *Philosophy and Social Criticism*, and Florindo Volpaccio of *New Political Science* have aided me when they could. Paul Piccone of *Telos* deserves a place apart, with no further comment. I should also thank publishers. John Winckler initiated the first edition of *The Marxian Legacy*; T. M. Farmiloe and Simon Winder worked with the second, and saw the unity of the present volume. Terry Cochran of the University of Minnesota Press has a genius for recognising problems of which the author is not even aware, and an ability to make him see what he is in fact trying to do. Thanks also go to James Clark for his work on proof-reading and indexes.

Institutions too deserve thanks. The State University of New York at Stony Brook has been a good employer and a congenial place over the years. Some of these chapters were written while on sabbatical leave with its support; and the entire book was concluded with that support. Other work was done while I was the recipient of a grant from the Humboldt Stiftung in Germany and while I benefited from a grant from the American Council of Learned Societies. The material on the American Revolution was presented at a course at the Ecole des Hautes Etudes en Sciences Sociales.

Finally, there is family of whom it is said that they need no thanks, but they certainly deserve it! And there are parents: this book is dedicated to my mother, and to the memory of my father.

Chapter 1, 'Out of the Silent Fifties', was presented as a panel participation in honour of Herbert Marcuse at the New York Marxist School in 1979. It has not been published previously.

Chapter 2, 'Praxis before Politics', was presented in French to a panel discussion at New York University; it was given in English to the Radical Philosophical Caucus of the American Philosophical Association's Eastern Division in December 1980. It was published in *Thesis Eleven*, no. 10/11, 1984–5.

Chapter 3, 'The Theory and Practice of Dialectical Theory' was presented at Yale University in February 1973; it was published in the first edition of *The Marxian Legacy*.

Chapter 4, 'From Marx to Kant', was presented at an Interuniversity Seminar in Dubrovnik, in Copenhagen in April 1983, at the Hegemony Study Group in London in May 1983, and at the New School for Social Research in December 1983; it was published in two different forms, the first in *Thesis Eleven*, no. 8, 1984, the second in *Les Temps Modernes*, November 1983. A translation of one of these versions appeared in the Belgrade journal, *Theorie*, 3–4/1984. The present version is a collage of these variants.

Chapter 5, 'Another Resurrection of Marxism', appeared under the title 'The Possibility of a Post-Marxist Radicalism', in *Thesis Eleven*, no. 16, 1987.

Chapter 6, 'The Future as Present', was first presented at the Research Institute on International Change at Columbia University in March 1976. It was published in the papers of that Conference, *Radicalism in the Contemporary Age*, edited by Seweryn Bialer and Sophia Sluzar, and reprinted in *The Marxian Legacy*.

Chapter 7, 'From One New Left to Another', was published in French in *Esprit*, July 1983. In translating it, I have restored some of the details left out of that publication.

Chapter 8, 'Esprit', was published in *Telos*, no. 36, Summer 1978.

Chapter 9, 'French Socialism and Modernization', was published in *Telos*, no. 61, Autumn 1984.

Chapter 10, 'French Rhetoric and Political Reality', was published in *Philosophy and Social Criticism*, vol. 12, October 1987.

Chapter 11, 'France, Germany and the Concept of Europe', was written in the summer of 1984 for the journal *World Policy*, which paid for it, paid for its revision, and then decided for unstated reasons not to print it! It was published in *New Political Science*, no. 14, 1985–6.

Chapter 12, 'Enlightened Despotism and Modern Democracy', was edited by *Telos* into the form of a book review in no. 33, Autumn 1977. I have gone back to the original manuscript in reconstructing this version.

Chapter 13, 'The Revolution in the American Revolution', was drawn from a draft introduction to my study of *La naissance de la pensée politique américaine*; it was published in *La lettre internationale*, no. 9, Summer 1986; an edited version appeared in German in *Merkur*, March 1987. I have gone back to the original manuscript in translating this version.

Chapter 14, 'The Republic and the International Order', was published in *Intervention*, vol. 1, no. 4, March–April 1983. A shorter version was edited by *Telos* as a book review in no. 59, Spring 1984. I have gone back to the original in translating this version.

Chapter 15, 'The Political Origins of Democracy', was delivered in French to the yearly meeting of the Society for Phenomenology and Existential Philosophy in Toronto in October, 1986. The French version was published in *La lettre internationale*, no. 15, Winter 1987–88. I have added some new material to this English translation.

Chapter 16, 'Ethics and Politics', was presented to a panel at the North American Society for Social Philosophy at the winter meeting of the American Philosophical Association in Boston in December 1986. It was published as delivered in *Praxis International*, Winter 1987–8.

Chapter 17, 'A Renaissance of the Political in the USA?', was written in French for *Esprit*. I have used the original manuscript in making the present translation.

DICK HOWARD

# Introduction

## 1. A SIMPLE INTUITION

This book is the product of a simple intuition about the relation of philosophy and radical politics. Philosophy investigates the conditions of the possibility of the objects with which politics, or any other aspect of life, is concerned. Philosophy seeks the ultimate ground or foundation of the phenomena it investigates. This constantly renewed search for the roots of the given suggests the radical potential of philosophy. If it is not to be merely adaptive reformism, social change must strike at the basic conditions which make possible the injustices that call for political intervention. Philosophy provides the foundations for such a radical political action; it grounds not only political ends but also the chosen means. The simple intuition thus proposes the philosophical imperative to change the conditions of possibility of injustice; it is the most immediate definition of radical politics. In its simplicity, the intuition is irrefutable, self-evident and all-encompassing. Philosophy explains the necessity of politics; politics as radical makes philosophy necessary.

The immediacy of this simple intuition leaves unanswered the question of its execution. What philosophical method is to be applied in the investigation of the conditions of possibility? How can philosophy be certain of having access to the real problems of society? What if there is disagreement about the problems which demand solutions? How are these to be given priority? If the quest is for radical change of the totality rather than piecemeal reforms, will the adequate philosophy be so abstract that it cannot be put into practice? The list of difficulties could be prolonged at will; immediacy demands mediation in order to realise its truth. Yet, despite the difficulties, the intuition retains its validity. Radical politics, as the young Marx insisted, must go to the root; philosophy is the examination of the foundations of the appearing world; radical politics can be grounded only by philosophy. The syllogism mediates the immediacy of the intuition; the argument can be developed further.

Marx is the paradigm case of the radical relation of philosophy and politics. The young Hegelian sought to turn the dialectic of the completed philosophical System out toward the world; he could not accept the truth of philosophy so long as the society in which it existed was unjust and therefore untrue. The philosophical root of the young Marx's radical politics was defined as 'man' himself; the injustice to be remedied was the alienation and exploitation of men and women. The attempt to elaborate this philosophical politics systematically in *The 1844 Manuscripts* and in *The German Ideology* remained incomplete and unpublished. Two decades later, the author of *Capital* founded his radical politics on a different philosophical root. The condition of the possibility of alienation and exploitation was found in the economic structures of social relations. Their revolutionary transformation was the imperative of the mature Marx's radical philosophical politics.

The debate about the 'two Marxes' can be left aside; both are faithful to the basic intuition about the relation of philosophy and radical politics. The 'man' of the young Marx and the social 'relations of production' which concerned the mature philosopher only appear to operate at different levels of concreteness. Man, insisted Marx in 1843, is 'no being squatting outside the world'. He is 'the world of men'. The social relations of production analysed by the critique of political economy are simply 'relations of men mediated by things'. The world of alienation analysed in 1844 is thematised in 1867 as the reified structures created by the fetishism of commodities. *Capital* explains that there would be no need for theory if essence and appearance coincided. Whatever else he may have been, Marx remained a radical *philosopher*.

The rupture between the 'two Marxes' is said to be consummated in the brief and unpublished 'Theses on Feuerbach'. The final, eleventh Thesis formulates the injunction that philosophers have only understood the world; the point, however, is to change it. This is not a command to activism or political voluntarism. It was given adequate philosophical form by the Frankfurt School nearly a century later. Max Horkheimer and Herbert Marcuse opposed traditional to what they called 'critical theory'. Drawing on Georg Lukács, they argued that bourgeois philosophy is contemplative; it stands outside the world at whose supposedly fixed structures it gazes passively. Critical theory is active; the contemplative separation of subject and object is replaced by a dialectical interaction which makes possible change in both. Understanding the world is possible only through the action which changes it; changing the world transforms the subject whose philosophical questioning of its conditions of possibility inaugurated the critical dialectic that opens the path to radical politics.

This critical reformulation of the simple intuition that grounds radical philosophy provides the mediations that avoid some of the political oversimplifications to which the initial insight can give rise. The simple humanism or moralism implied by the affirmation of 'man' as the root is not tenable. It is abstract and contemplative; it does not explain how men and women came to find themselves in an unjust world, why they would decide to change it, or how the transformation could take place. The apparantly concrete economism or sociologism suggested by *Capital* is also abstract and contemplative; its structural logic does not leave room for the human action which permits the qualitative leap from the realm of necessity to that of freedom. Both orientations are non-dialectical; the lack of mediation is based on the implicit positivism which assumes that the philosopher has direct access to the 'really real' grounds of the appearing world. Both positions oversimplify the relation of the conditions of possibility to the unjust society which they attempt to explain.

The critical theory proposed by the Frankfurt School attempts to develop the missing mediation that vitiates the positivist abstraction which results from the immediate application of the simple intuition. It questions the conditions of possibility of both the unjust world and of the philosophy which can understand its roots. Philosophy cannot exist apart from the unjust world it seeks to change. The contemplative humanist abstraction and the positivist economism are avoided; Marx is reinterpreted on the basis of a dialectic which can be found in both phases of his work. In this mediated critical dialectic, the conditions of possibility are constitutive but they are also constituted. Critical philosophy explains both the world as it is and the world as it could become. Understanding and changing the world are a single project whose necessity is grounded in the very world that makes the philosophical project possible and the political practice necessary. The circle is complete; it articulates the foundation that grounds both radical philosophy and radical politics.

Despite its explicitly political goals, the Frankfurt School's critical theory did not found a new politics. Its creators wanted to be *Marxists* even though the application of their critical theory demonstrated that capitalism had changed since Marx's day. When they investigated the conditions of possibility of the new society which made possible their mediated critical theory, the Frankfurt School thinkers probed beneath the economic appearances to discover the 'instrumental reason' on which they are founded. The result was an historical 'dialectic of enlightenment' which demonstrated that every gain in material social utility has been purchased at the cost of a repression of the free human reason that was the root of its possibility. The progressive dialectic leading toward human liberation whose conditions of possibility Marx had diagnosed in capitalism could no longer be assumed. The conclusion drawn by the Frankfurt thinkers was either pessimism or an eschatological hope that, somehow, Reason would come to recognise itself in, and thus free itself from, its Other. Marxism and critical theory could not be reconciled; radical politics had to seek new forms of action.

The Frankfurt School's critique of instrumental reason became a cultural critique whose political justification was found in the new forms of domination that typify modern societies. The modern injustices that called for political remedy took the form of repressions whose analysis demanded a different political orientation. The conditions of possibility of modern (or 'late-capitalist') societies could still be analysed by critical philosophy. In the United States, Herbert Marcuse analysed Soviet Marxism and capitalist one-dimensional society while grounding his political hopes in the radical eros which those societies repress. In Germany, the second generation Frankfurter, Jürgen Habermas, outlined a theory of the decline of public space, while seeking its overcoming in theories of emancipatory interest or communicative action. The French started from different premisses, but the archaeology of Michel Foucault, the 'deconstruction' of Jacques Derrida, and the 'schizo-analysis' of Deleuze and Guattari were motivated by the same dilemmas facing radical philosophy and its politics. However these are judged as philosophy, they are founded still on the simple intuition that radical politics must change the conditions of the possibility of the modern forms of injustice. But each of these formulations of the simple intuition reduces politics to the immediate result of philosophy, which itself is charged with the task of liberation. The mediation is lost.

The collapse of the distinction between philosophy and politics violates the simple intuition which founded their relation; their conflation distorts both of the poles. Critical theory overcame the positivist and contemplative forms of philosophy, but it did not direct its critique to the political goals it inherited from Marxism. Its analysis of cultural repression is social; politics is treated as simply the external and immediate relation among social forces. The positivism that was overcome in the critical dialectic returns in this *social* theory of radical politics. Politics is everywhere, and for this very reason it is nowhere. The radical philosophy which reveals the social conditions of possibility of this politics loses its critical foundation; it becomes a positivism in spite of itself. The conditions of possibility that it uncovers lie ultimately either at the level of abstraction of the humanist 'man' or on the 'really real' plane of socio-cultural repressions. But radical philosophy cannot be separated from radical politics any more than the two can be identified in the inverse form of positivism; their relation is dialectical. The Frankfurt School articulated this critical dialectic, but in the case of philosophy alone.

The simple intuition has to be reformulated if it is to account for the properly political. The conditions of possibility investigated by critical philosophy define the spatio-temporal framework within which politics can appear. These conditions can be designated by the substantive formulation, 'the political'. The political is neither an abstraction nor a positive thing accessible to empirical analysis. It is real and realised in its effects, but it is not their cause. Its mode of existence is *symbolic*; access to it depends on its public presence in a shared world. Philosophical analysis of the political depends on the dialectic elaborated by critical theory; it is not accessible to the contemplative mode because it is not a fixed essence or an external universal determining the lawfulness of the world of appearance. The political exists only in the process of its definition, but it is not identical to that process. This same dialectical process defines a politics which can satisfy the simple intuition's demand to be radical. Analysis of the political reformulates the conditions of the possibility of politics which the Frankfurt School version of critical theory neglected because its one-sided orientation to philosophy took for granted the Marxist definition of politics.

The chapters which compose this book seek to define the political. They range across theory and practice. The volume analyses phenomena as different as Enlightened Despotism and international relations, the New Left and the dilemmas of French Socialists in power, modernism in the arts and the American Revolution. It considers contemporary and classic philosophers, their dialectics and their deconstruction. The theoretical unity of these essays is suggested by the move from Marx to Kant; their practical unity is defined by the problem of democracy. The traditional problems of the relation of ethics and politics, republicanism and democracy, theory and praxis are treated in a context framed by the history of socialism, the question of Europe and the nature of totalitarianism. Contemporary movements are analysed, past revolutions are considered; a final essay tries to apply the simple intuition to the political possibilities that may emerge from the Iran-Contra scandal in the United States.

In all of this the political is nowhere defined; its status as symbolic is also *originary*, making possible both radical philosophy and radical politics. This will be seen to be only apparantly a paradox.

The range of issues involved in defining the political confirms the usefulness of the simple intuition as mediated by critical theory. The elaboration of the intuition underlines the symbolic status of the political as at once real and yet inaccessible to positive empirical analysis. The symbolic mode of existence of the political does not mean that its analysis is arbitrary. The analysis is philosophical; the concepts it applies can be specified; their origin can be explained. The problems and issues analysed here were not chosen to illustrate a philosophical thesis. Everything that passes for politics does not for that reason alone contribute to defining the political. Before turning to the mediations which amplify the simple intuition, and explaining the contents of this book, a brief biographical remark may help clarify the specificity of the political.

## 2. AN APOLOGIA PRO VITA SUA

The simple intuition led me first to work in phenomenology. The New Left of the 1960s developed a critique of everyday life which seemed more radical than the Marxist 'science' which most of us knew only second-hand. If 'the personal is political', as the movement claimed, political change depends on understanding the roots of social deformations. The idea was straightforward; its phenomenological development was not. I went to Europe to try to figure it out, and discovered Marxism and its history instead. The history could be integrated; it was part of an ongoing attempt to assure human dignity by abolishing the distinction of manual and mental labour and establishing institutions of self-managed social autonomy. Marxism was more difficult. I wrote a book to explain to myself how the young Hegelian became a political economist; but its proposed second volume, analysing *Capital*, was never completed. Adding the more dialectical and critical *Grundrisse* to the account was still not satisfactory. I adopted a compromise solution in the form of the theory of the 'new working class', which seemed to be able to account for the radical practice of the New Left without abandoning the structural rigour of Marxist political economy. The European experience reformulated the simple intuition; I edited and translated a volume of the *Selected Writings of Rosa Luxemburg* and joined Karl Klare in editing *The Unknown Dimension: European Marxism since Lenin*.

The new working class theory was more satisfying politically than it was theoretically. I began to work with *Telos*, whose goal was to develop a phenomenological Marxism. The journal undertook the task of developing the theoretical tradition of that 'unknown dimension' whose Marxist prehistory I had analysed earlier. First Lukács, then Korsch and the Frankfurt school, were translated, debated and sometimes updated. Exciting, and no doubt useful, the project soon confronted the theoretical problems that had lamed the Frankfurt School's syncretism of cultural critique and Marxist politics. The new working class theory was no help; its philosophical basis was another form of the positivism which vitiated Marxism. The critical theory had to be applied to itself. This was when I discovered and was able finally to convince *Telos* to publish Castoriadis and Lefort. Their radical critique of Marxism provided the foundations for *The Marxian Legacy*, in which I first introduced the concept of the political. But that book forgot the simple intuition; the political was defined only in opposition to the inability of Marxism and critical theory to explain the foundations of politics. A manuscript called 'The Return of the Political' followed; but the intuition was still absent and the book was consigned to the file cabinet.[1]

The essays that constitute this book were written over more than a decade during which I attempted to define for myself the concept of the political. A systematic attempt from the side of philosophy finally emerged under the title *From Marx to Kant*. It was prepared by many of the attempts published here.[2] A number of these were first written in French for the journal *Esprit*, whose theoretical orientation I try to explain in Chapter 8. *Esprit* became for me a sort of replacement for that New Left movement within which the simple intuition had taken shape.[3] The other influence behind these essays is the work of Castoriadis and Lefort. The self-critique of Marxism which they elaborated in *Socialisme ou Barbarie* has come to take the form of a positive theory of the political centred around the primacy of democracy. The critique of totalitarianism which they propose does not emerge 'out of the silent fifties' like that of Marcuse; it depends on the concept of the political, which makes evident the democratic roots of the totalitarian temptation. Castoriadis and Lefort are largely silent presences in the present volume; their creative contributions during the past decade are put into context and analysed in the lengthy afterword to the new second edition of *The Marxian Legacy*.

## 3. THE COMPLEX EXECUTION OF A SIMPLE INTUITION

The philosopher cannot pretend to define politics; he or she can question only the conditions of the possibility of a given politics. This philosophical question is not answered by the indication of empirical causes. The roots toward which it is directed are radical; they explain *why* social interests come to recognise their needs as more than particular, and *how* their demands can become a concern of the political public. The 'why' explains the *receptivity* of the social world to political action; the 'how' designates those *particular* issues which demand political articulation. The unity of these two explanations presents the *origin* of the political. As originary, the political does not determine the forms of empirical political practice; the political can only exist in the very process by which, so to speak, politics engenders itself. This reflexive structure excludes any reference to an external cause or normative legitimation. The particular issues which call for political action, and the social structures on which its success depends, cannot be analysed separately from the political framework within which they appear. Such a reflexive and self-justificatory structure characterises *modernity*. The radical political project symbolised by the concept of revolution is modern in this specific sense of the term.[4]

The substantive formulation of the political can lead to misunderstanding. It is not an essence or a universal; nor does it designate an artifically carved-out domain with which empirical science can deal. The political is a *symbolic* presence whose existence as a real absence makes possible political change. This paradoxical generalisation can be elucidated negatively at first. A critical theory which neither contemplates eternal essences nor abandons its truth claim to empirical description is tempted to seek its foundation in the real human praxis which constitutes the social and political world. Such a *constitutive* theory reifies praxis; it assumes that it provides a deeper foundation for the alienated structures analysed by empirical social science; and it claims that this new level of critical analysis is radical because it is founded on the praxical activity of human self-realisation. This Marxist proposal is elaborated philosophically by Sartre's *Critique of Dialectical Reason*. Its sociological implications are drawn by the 'new working class' theory. Its political conclusions define socialism as self-management and social autonomy.[5] That sociology and its politics have lost their relevance during the past decade. The difficulty cannot be avoided by more sociology; the problem is not that capitalism has changed its mode of exploitation since 1973, or that the world system has been altered by new factors. Social praxis is not constitutive; it is the political which gives sense to the sheer positivity of both human praxis and social structures.

This book is concerned with *defining* the political; yet it nowhere defines it. It makes a virtue out of what I have come to recognise as a necessity. Empirical politics makes no sense without a framework which explains its conditions of possibility; but the political as framework can never be defined once-and-for-all. The symbolic status of the political means that it is redefined constantly by the processes through which it is created, *and* which it in turn makes possible. Although all societies have a political dimension,[6] its modern form makes explicit for all actors what its traditional forms revealed only to the inquiry of philosophy. Modernity is inaugurated by the rupture with traditional modes of legitimation; it is defined by the immanence of its own conditions of possibility. The public emergence of the problem of the political in the modern epoch is based on the structural parallels of the political and the modern. The referent of the substantive 'modernity' shares the symbolic character that characterises the political. It cannot be defined by an essence, nor exhausted in any single realisation; it exists only in the works which are constantly defining it, and yet it exists too as the condition of the possibility of those same works. This symbolic structure is articulated as the co-presence of two moments, which I call *genesis* and *normativity*; their unity can be described as *originary* because it does not depend on an appeal to external or traditional forms of legitimation. The political, like the modern, is its own origin because it makes possible the works which are its constantly changing realisation.

My concern here is the defining, not the definitions. This explains the role of Kant and Marx in these essays. *The Critique of Pure Reason* attempts to adjudicate between the conflicting claims of empiricism and rationalism. Empiricism derives normativity from genesis; rationalism presents norms that generate reality. But the definitions are not univocal: if genesis determines normativity, genesis can be said to be itself normative; conversely, the reality generated by norms can be taken as the standard by which the legitimacy of the norms are to be decided. Kant's critical method uncovers a *reversibility* between the poles of genesis and normativity.[7] The 'Transcendental Dialectic' of the first two *Critiques* rationalises away this disturbing relation which becomes explicit only in the third *Critique*. That *Critique of Judgement* is explicitly self-reflective; judgement judges itself, standing as the normative critique of its genetic products and as the genetic explanation of the norms it imposes. This third *Critique* poses the question of the *origin* of the critical theory as modern. It is not surprising that these same categories return in Marx. *The Communist Manifesto* describes the immanence of the modern. The logic of *Capital* is its normative formulation; the historical materialism of *The German Ideology* provides a genetic explanation. Class struggle generates new structures of capitalist development, while the revolutionary culmination of history depends on a normative logic of alienation founded on human praxis. This conceptual reversibility founds the practical dilemma of reform and revolution within Marxism. The 'Marxian legacy' is the experience of the originary structure of modernity which poses the question of the political.[8]

The process of defining is practical as well as theoretical. This aspect of the fundamental reversibility is suggested by the titles to Parts I and II of this volume. Modern theory is political; modern politics is theoretical. The 'Problems of Marxism' which emerge in the examination of 'Theory as Political' return from the point of view of 'Politics as Theoretical' in the practice of both the New Left and of Socialism. The progression within each of these Parts is explained by the difficulties encountered when theory is taken univocally as political, or politics univocally as theoretical. Marcuse's normative (Chapter 1) and Sartre's genetic (Chapter 2) application of a theory to reality neglect the properly political dimension; a critical dialectics must stress the difference between theory and practice while insisting on their originary unity (Chapter 3). The move from Marx to Kant (Chapter 4) proposes the foundations of a modern republican politics which gives the political its proper place while making possible a radical democratic politics based on the primacy of (Kantian) reflective judgement. The abstraction of this political proposal appears to call for a more concrete alternative founded philosophically by the method called deconstruction (Chapter 5). But this 'post-Marxist' proposal renews from the side of politics the conflation of theory with reality; the result is a positivist Marxism which suggests the need to break this political circle by examining politics as theoretical. The assertion of the theoretical primacy of reflective judgement finds there its political implication.

The circle which defines the political nature of theory in Part I is avoided by Part II's consideration of 'Politics as Theoretical' by looking at both the New Left and Socialism. Part II begins from the practice of political movements in quest of their own self-understanding; it then turns to the dilemmas of a political party whose politics is defined by a theoretical platform. The first analysis follows the movement from genesis to norm; the second asks how normativity affects the practice which seeks its realisation. These general theoretical categories are specified in the political questions which focus on *why* social interests come to see themselves as more than simply particular, and *how* their demands become public. The same reversibility which appeared in the analysis of theory returns in the consideration of practice. The New Left of the 1960s was able, for a moment, to make a virtue of this necessity; a new New Left in the 1980s has still to confront it. The French Socialists and radical French theory have not been able either to recognise its necessity or to draw its implications. The French could learn from the New Left model; the new New Left can learn from the European option facing the French. The circle described by the political nature of theory becomes a positive relation of mutual implication when politics is treated as theoretical. This transformation is concretised in the movement within Part II.

Treating politics as theoretical is suggested by the practice of the New Left. The New Left defined a particular political style characterised by its refusal to separate its theoretical goal from the present; yet its critique of everyday life adopted implicitly the standpoint of the political in order to explain why its demands arose and how they can be realised. The analysis of particularity becomes an account of receptivity; the explanation of receptivity points to the particularity of a new politics. My assertion that the New Left slogan, '*l'imagination au pouvoir*', is itself an analysis points to the symbolic nature of the political (Chapter 6). A decade later, in the context of a new New Left, the analysis begins from the lessons of the first account; it addresses a still-developing movement in the attempt to make explicit the political standpoint from which it can understand itself (Chapter 7). The guiding question remains why and how the new movement can manifest the originary structure typified by the earlier New Left. The answer I propose depends on the symbolic presence of the political in the international relations which define the framework within which radical politics specifies the particular issues it opens to debate and the reasons for public receptivity to these demands. This analysis was published in *Esprit*, whose peculiarity as a journal-movement makes explicit the critical theoretical place of the political (Chapter 8). Its history and project illustrate the radical implications of an originary politics: the stress on the newness of the new. It provides also a transition to the second half of Part II, which is concerned largely with French socialism.[9]

The progress from politics to theory within the New Left puts into question the Marxist certainties from which the politics of French socialism begins. Despite May 1968, the French socialists did not draw these lessons; they had to learn for themselves when they came to power in 1981. The need for the modernisation of an archaic economy was confronted with the discovery of social modernity. The Socialists' attempts to adapt their normative platform to the new reality generated by their practice left a divided party (Chapter 9). The failure to find a theory adequate to their politics demands a fundamental rethinking not only of Marxism but of the nature of political theory itself (Chapter 10). Rhetoric and reality have ceased to coincide in French politics, while French theory's attempt to deconstruct and to reconstruct itself can no longer take place outside of the exigencies determined by the exercise of power. The French have been forced to rediscover political theory in the history of their own republican experiments which date from their Revolution. It remains to be seen whether they will come to understand the relation between the political and the republican politics with which they seek to revivify their socialism. Grounds for optimism, and grounds for pessimism, can be proposed. The project in which the political dimension could be instantiated is the construction of Europe. This option can be proposed to the French and to the German lefts for tactical reasons; if adopted, its consequences would make explicit the place of the political (Chapter 11). President Mitterrand has taken hesitant steps in this direction, but the German left has remained as steadfast as most French socialists in equating Europe with the Common Market. The positivism implicit in that approach denies the symbolic dimension of a Europe which could provide the framework for a new politics.

The New Left quest for theory, and the Socialists' encounter with reality affirm the political nature of theory and demonstrate the problems of Marxism. The circle cannot be broken here either; once again, it is originary. Part III, the 'Origins of the Political', makes a virtue of necessity. The reversibility of genesis and normativity remains; the originary structure unites symbolically the two poles separated by empirical reality. The division of Part III into an account of the genesis of the theoretical questions posed in Part I, and an analysis of the practical implications of the normative theory that guided Part II, reiterates the reversible originary structure. The genetic accounts demand normative theory; the normative theory entails practical consequences. The conclusions at which these chapters arrive do not pretend to define concretely the nature of a radical politics; they can claim only to demonstrate its conditions of possibility, whose origin is the political.

'The Genesis of Theoretical Questions' treats the emergence of the orientations that are analysed as 'The Practice of Normative Theory' in the second section of Part III. The phenomenon of Enlightened Despotism appears to be a bastard unification of poles which the French Revolution attempts to right (Chapter 12). But modern Revolution cannot be a real unification eliminating contradiction once and for all; its symbolic character is realised in the practice of democracy, which the French Revolution inaugurates. The antinomy that conjoins enlightenment with despotism expresses the symbolic but effective nature of the political. The phenomenon of political revolution in which so much radical theory depends has to be reconsidered in this light. The American Revolution is the forgotten cousin of the French and Bolshevik models which have monopolised the imagination of the left. If 1789 was a genetic social revolution, 1763–89 in America were the years of normative political transformation (Chapter 13). The American struggle against the British coloniser was based on a political philosophy which affirmed the priority of freedom over arbitrary power. This simple dichotomy could justify the demand for independence, but it was of no help in elaborating political institutions to ensure the newly-won freedoms. The Constitution of 1787 replaced the simple form of direct democracy by republican institutions which, for some, amounted to a counter-revolution. The clash between the republican and the democratic orientations defines the political framework in which American liberalism can be evaluated without reducing the political to its immediate social results.

Enlightened Despotism and the American Revolution define the form in which the modern framework for politics was born; the new nation states which arose in their wake have to define themselves also in terms of an international political order (Chapter 14). Its practical role was suggested already in the discussion of the new New Left (Chapter 7); the theory which would account for its symbolic reality is suggested by the analogy between the domestic 'state of nature' from which modern states are said to emerge and the actual relations among nation-states in the international arena. The reformulation of a 'republican' theory on this basis was suggested by Kant;[10] the dilemmas to which French socialism might seek new answers through the European option point to its practical implications (Chapter 11). The relation between the modern nation state affirming its national interest in international politics and the republican or democratic foundations of that same nation state presents the political in a new light. The academic separation between the study of comparative domestic politics and international relations cannot be maintained; nor can the two investigations simply be conflated. Their relation affirms the originary, symbolic nature of the political. The traditional opposition between republican and democratic politics is overthrown by this recognition; the relation between the national interest and the political forms which permit its determination opens the space for a radical politics.

The premise of radical politics that emerges from reflection on the genesis of theoretical questions in Part IIIA is that 'the' Revolution is an ideological chimera. The *real* unification of genesis and normativity, practice and theory, the social and the political is neither desirable nor possible. Yet this temptation haunts both theory and politics. Its source is the originary tension and the frustrating reversibility of the unstable poles of an explicitly modern society. The temptation takes the concrete form of a critique of formal political institutions, which are said to cloak social exploitation. The desired 'revolution' would replace formal bourgeois democracy by 'real' democracy. This misunderstanding of the symbolic nature of the political explains the totalitarian temptation which haunts democracy. Totalitarianism is not despotism or tyranny; it is a modern form whose conditions of possibility are identical with those of democracy itself (Chapter 15). Democracy arises only when a revolution eliminates the external legitimation of an established social order which must seek its political legitimation immanently. Democratic rights are not essential truths or empirical facts; they are conquests which make possible new freedoms. Democracy can degenerate because this lack of external or normative foundation for the rights of the citizen makes possible the manipulation of opinion. The villain is not capitalism. Capitalism is not identical to democracy; democratic political institutions can make it possible but they can permit also its elimination, or its replacement by totalitarianism.

The foundation of modern democracy is the originary tension that defines the political. The opposition to totalitarianism tends to take the form of an opposition between ethics and politics. A comparison of the French student movements in May 1968 and Winter 1986 demonstrates the inadequacy of this dichotomy (Chapter 16). Democracy is no more the product of ethical imperatives than it is simply an expression of empirical social forces in conflict over the relations of production. The purported opposition of ethics and politics is the result of a contemplative theory which neglects that symbolic dimension of the political which makes possible the originary opposition whose ethical and political poles are fundamentally reversible. This specificity of democracy can be illustrated also by the recent Irangate affair in the United States (Chapter 17). The politics of the Reagan administration is the result and completion of a liberal antipolitics which has dominated the post-war United States. The foreign policy of a democracy puts into question the relation between its basic political institutions and its national interest. The transgression of republican guarantees in conditions which bring explicitly into play the relation of the national interest and the democracy which defines the political character of the nation is not simply a scandal. A similar political conjuncture at the time of McCarthyism became the foundation of the 'silent fifties'. Today, it would be the basis of a renewal of politics in the United States.

This Introduction carries no conclusion, just as this book makes no claim to have defined once-and-for-all the political. The simple intuition is presented; the mediations for its realisation are sketched. It remains to acknowledge my debts, and to begin again.

DICK HOWARD

## Notes

1. I have not given references to the earlier works mentioned here so as not to burden the text. I have cited myself in several of the chapters here, when it seemed appropriate.

2. I should add that another collection of essays from this period, centring around the problem of critical agency, is to be published by the University of Minnesota Press and Macmillan under the title, *The Politics of Critique*.
3. Two of the chapters in this book were published in the 'second left' journal *Intervention*, whose recent demise has led many of its contributors to join *Esprit*.
4. The italicised terms in this paragraph and the succeeding ones are elaborated systematically in *From Marx to Kant* (Albany: State University of New York Press, 1985).
5. This volume was to have begun with a chapter written in memory of Serge Mallet. Rereading it more than a decade later helped me clarify the specific status of the political. Mallet updates the Marxian theory of the revolutionary proletariat; its changed sociological status is seen as the result of the successful struggles which force capitalism to alter its mode of exploitation. Social praxis thus explains transformed social structures in what Lucien Goldman labelled a 'genetic structuralism'. Class action replaces politics; alienated social praxis is to be overcome by the institution of self-management. When the 'new working class' did not seem to fulfill its mission, Mallet looked for its radical replacement elsewhere, faithful to his belief in the creativity of the oppressed. He never questioned this belief, nor the supposition that the political is expressed by class action. The reader will see traces of this sociological orientation in my attempt to understand the 'new left' in Chapter 6, 'The Future as Present'; traces of its theoretical foundation appear in Chapter 3, 'The Theory and Practice of Dialectical Theory'.

   'In Memory of Serge Mallet' was first published in *Telos*, no. 20, 1974, and reprinted in Dick Howard and Dean Savage, eds, *Serge Mallet's Essays on the New Working Class* (St. Louis: Telos Press, 1975). The 'new working class' theory of Gorz and Mallet is presented positively in Dick Howard and Karl E. Klare, eds, *The Unknown Dimension: European Marxism since Lenin* (New York: Basic Books, 1972). A critique of its premisses, and of a contemporary American adaptation, is found in Jean L. Cohen and Dick Howard, 'Why Class?', in Pat Walker, ed., *Between Capital and Labor* (Boston: South End Press, 1978).
6. This is true even for those societies whose political nature is brilliantly depicted by Pierre Clastres under the title, *La société contre l'état* (Paris: Editions de Minuit, 1974).
7. The concept of reversibility is derived from Merleau-Ponty. My own understanding of it depends heavily on the interpretation of Claude Lefort.
8. The new Afterword to the second edition of *The Marxian Legacy* (London: Macmillan, and Minneapolis: University of Minnesota Press, 1987) clarifies this structure which is proposed here in Chapter 3. That chapter was originally part of the Introduction to the first edition of the *Legacy*. The teleology which forms the horizon revealing what I call there 'the praxis within practice', has to be understood as symbolic; it explains the importance of the difference between theory and practice

which I emphasised without giving sufficient attention to its symbolic foundation.

9. For the reader who wonders why there is so little in this volume relating directly to the United States, I should note that much of what I have written for *Esprit* over the years concerns that country. These essays have generally taken the form of notes for the 'Journal à plusieurs voix', or of largely factual reporting, for example, on the birth of neo-conservatism in the US. On reflection, I decided not to include these essays here, although in my original plan they would have constituted a fourth Part, under the heading 'The Politics of the Political'.
10. Cf. Kant's essay on *Perpetual Peace*, discussed briefly in Chapter 4, and analysed at length in *From Marx to Kant*.

# Part I

# Theory as Political: Problems of Marxism

# 1 Out of the Silent Fifties

## WHY THE 'SILENT' FIFTIES?

Politically, there was of course outright repression (McCarthyism, purges in the unions), combined with the material fruits of union gains and 'imperialist' wages. The immigrant, white, cultures were integrated, suburbia was opening as were positions for 'intellectual labour'. The New Deal and the War had combined support for business with social legislation, such that opposition now functioned within a system described as 'countervailing powers' seeking a 'pluralist' consensus in a mass democracy where 'ideology' had no role. Amongst the 'Lonely Crowd', class struggle was replaced by caracterological struggle.[1] The decade closed ambiguously, as Castro and the sit-ins met the emerging Goldwater 'crusaders from the barbecue pits'.[2]

The political silence was amplified culturally in what Dwight MacDonald caustically analysed as 'Masscult & Midcult'. The avant-garde was not only materially integrated; modernism had become part of the curricula of the 'liberal imagination', or joined the market for what Harold Rosenberg was to label 'The Tradition of the New'. Lionel Trilling rejected the 'adversary culture', while others joined Leslie Fiedler in search of the 'real' America, rejecting what they took to have been their elitist 'alienation from the masses'.[3] The decade ended ambiguously, with the publications of *Lolita*, *Lady Chatterley*, and the *Tropic of Cancer* (1958, 1959 and 1960), the beginnings of pop glorification and serialisation of the banal, and Tinguely's self-destroying machine sculpture at the MOMA.

Behind the political and cultural 'silence' lies the decade's incomplete attempt to come to grips with its recent past: the critique of totalitarianism. As far as it went, the critique was significant. Sometimes it went too far; sometimes it did not go far enough. It entailed a rejection of 'utopian' or 'ideological' thought in favour of an adaptive 'realism' or a passive depoliticisation. It put into question the role of any vanguard, and the legitimacy of its political and cultural claims. It led, finally, to a paralysis of the imagination because it was a criticism which was not self-critical. Totalitarianism tended to become an intellectual or metaphysical notion which blocked the investigation into concrete social relations.[4]

After showing the primacy of the political and ideological spheres, the critique stopped short. Marxism was treated as Marx himself had first treated religion, without the further step which dissects the social relations and active desire expressed by this 'religion'. Economic class analysis in this context, without the immanent revolutionary goal, remained uncomfortably close to the pluralist, functionalist modes. To the rebel, the half-way critique seemed to leave only the affirmation of the creative, or absurd, individual in existential nakedness. (I should add that the other possibility for protest was seized by the New Left in the 1960s: taking seriously the primacy of the political as penetrating the entirety of daily life and rooting revolt there. The problems with that approach go beyond my concern here, although it seems that the incompleteness of the critique of totalitarianism explains not only why the older generation could not understand the New Left, but also the failure of the New Left, which rejected the half-way critique without substituting another in its place.)

To complete the critique, the old liberal and Marxist categories – such as politics and economics, state and civil society – had to be re-examined. If totalitarianism and its benign neighbour, mass society, are not in some sense the 'truth' or logical completion of capitalism, if they represent a new historical social formation, then the problems of democracy, socialism and culture must be rethought. An older notion of revolution, modelled on the (Marxist view of the) bourgeois transformation, prevented the critics of the 1950s from addressing the question of historical specificity.

Starting from the question of the historical specificity of modern Western society, I am struck by a convergence between Marcuse's *Soviet Marxism* and his *One-Dimensional Man*. As space is short, I quote the former.

> The value of these statements [the rituals of 'soviet Marxism'] is pragmatic rather than logical, as is clearly suggested by their syntactical structure. They are unqualified, inflexible formulas calling for an unqualified, inflexible response. In endless repetition, the same noun is always accompanied by the same adjectives and participles; the noun 'governs' them immediately and directly so that whenever it occurs they follow 'automatically' in their proper place. The same verb always 'moves' the proposition in the same

> direction, and those addressed by the proposition are supposed to move in the same way. These statements do not attribute a predicate to a subject (in the sense of formal or of dialectical logic); they do not develop the subject in its specific relations.[5]

This same complex is analysed at great length a decade later in the context of Western society. Speech as designation, assertion or imitation is criticised as magical, authoritarian and ritual denial of mediation.

> Abridgement of the concept in fixed images; arrested development in self-validating, hypnotic formulas; immunity against contradiction; identification of the thing (and of the person) with its function – these tendencies reveal the one-dimensional mind in the language it speaks.[6]

Operationalism's identity of name and function, the coincidence of word and concept, tautological definitions, evocative rather than demonstrative commands, identification of person and function through the inflectional genitive or hyphenated construction – these are all seen as rejections of transcendence, history, contradiction, negation.

A further illustration is more political. Analytic philosophy, 'often spreads the atmosphere of denunciation and investigation by committee. The intellectual is called on the carpet. What do you mean when you say . . . ? Don't you conceal something? You talk a language which is suspect.'[7] Explaining the rejection of the 'vagueness' of transcendent universals by analytic philosophy, Marcuse continues:

> To protest against the vague, obscure, metaphysical character of such universals, the insistence on familiar concreteness and protective security of common and scientific sense still reveal something of that primordial anxiety which guided the recorded origins of philosophical thought in its evolution from religion to mythology, and from mythology to logic; defense and security are still large items in the intellectual as well as national budget.[8]

*Soviet Marxism* makes a similar argument with respect to the development of political logic. The nineteenth century critical recognition of the limit of bourgeois freedom transforms the demand for freedom into the need for security, which in turn justifies the increased role of the state which then articulates a security-granting scientific ethics to solve the problems of individual freedom and, ultimately, to render all of society subordinate to politics.[9]

A further overlap forces the question. *One-Dimensional Man* offers an incisive criticism of the 'therapeutic' goals of contemporary social science and philosophy which seek to cure the 'unhappy consciousness'. The same problem is present in *Soviet Marxism*, with the same examples:

> If Tristan and Isolde, Romeo and Juliet, and their like are unimaginable as healthy married couples engaged in productive work, it is because their (socially conditioned) 'unproductiveness' is the essential quality of what they stand for and die for – values that can be realized only in an existence outside and against the repressive social group and its rules.[10]

Even before Stalinism, Marcuse insists, the Russian Revolution did not bring liberation despite Marx's correct completion of the bourgeois-Hegelian synthesis. For example:

> Kollontai, who is considered as the representative spokesman of revolutionary sexual morality, sees in childbearing and child raising a mode of 'productive labor,' and brands the prostitute as a 'deserter from the ranks of productive labor.'[11]

Despite this productivist deformation of freedom, in 1958 Marcuse was still hopeful that lessening external pressures and the growth of the internal economy would permit the dialectic to take yet another turn. His argument is typically Frankfurt: as opposed to fascism's irrationality, soviet rationality is oriented toward a future goal; the cognitive nature of its ethics – which he has shown, however, to be classically bourgeois – permits him to hope for a change from below.[12]

While *Soviet Marxism* is calmly, rationally dialectical in its political hope, *One-Dimensional Man's* faith in the Great Refusal is at times apocalyptic, at times the resignation of the 'hopeless'. Did Marcuse's analysis of totalitarianism, and the revolt against it, change? Did he recognise, for example, that the most effective form of totalitarianism is the 'rational' one built on a science of history for which the future is immanent to the totality? Did this, in turn, change the analytic framework through which he conceptualises Western societies and the possibility of a *democratic* socialism? Does he help us get beyond those *non-concepts* we throw about in talking of 'late', or 'neo' or 'monopoly' or 'state', etc., etc. capitalism? I think not.[13] The reason for my doubt lies in another continuity, suggested by the German title of his last book: 'The Permanence of Art' (translated into English as: *The Aesthetic Dimension*).

Marcuse's attitude was first elaborated in the Frankfurt essay on 'The Affirmative Character of Culture' (1937). And *Soviet Marxism* applies it. Because the state must control ethics in order to realise the immanent laws of the infrastructure, the only possible transcendence is that of art. But Soviet aesthetics is contradictory. It is 'Hegelian' in assuming existing reality to be good and true, such that the end of art is at hand because freedom is realised; but it is also 'Marxist' in recognising that the realisation of freedom depends on political action, into whose framework art must be placed. The result is that stuff called Socialist Realism: keeping art, but denying it the transcending or negative function that makes it art, the result is an art which is not art.

The 'dialectical' optimism of *Soviet Marxism* leads Marcuse to deny that this deformation is due to authoritarianism alone. As with Stalin's late views of language, the Russians are said to recognise the independent function of art which preserves possible negation. Yet, despite this 'dialectical' optimism, Marcuse continues in terms closer to *One-Dimensional Man*:

> But art as a political force is art only insofar as it preserves the images of liberation; in a society which is in its totality the negation of these images, art can preserve them only by total refusal, that is, by not succumbing to the standards of the unfree reality, either in style, or in form, or in substance. The more totalitarian these standards become, the more reality controls all language and all communication, the more irrealistic and surrealistic will art tend to be, the more will it be driven from the concrete to the abstract, from harmony to dissonance, from content to form.[14]

Not only do the Russians reject abstraction, dissonance and formalism; they also attack the 'irrationalism' of bourgeois social criticism which

> acts upon precisely those values which Soviet society must protect at all cost: the ethical value of competitive performance, socially necessary labor, self-perpetuating work discipline, postponed and repressed happiness. Thus, Soviet Marxism, in its fight against 'bourgeois values,' cannot recognize and accept the most destructive critique of these values in the 'bourgeois camp' itself.[15]

This would seem to indicate a difference between 'one-dimensional' and 'Soviet-Marxist' societies, since the former is characterised by de-sublimation and immediate gratification. But Marcuse does not pursue this difference through a questioning of 'irrealistic and surrealistic' modernism in art. Instead, he recalls here Plato's dictum permitting only beautiful, simple and harmonious forms which, 'Communicated through the mass media . . . became welcome tunes accompanying daily work and leisure, nourishment for recreation and relaxation periods.'[16] One wonders, however, whether his later stress on art will pick up the thread.

Marcuse's last two books do indeed take on modernist tendencies in art, but still within the old framework. *Counter-Revolution and Revolt* rejects modernist anti-art tendencies and their political claims:

> The abolition of the aesthetic form, the notion that art could become a component part of the revolutionary (and prerevolutionary) *praxis*, until under fully developed socialism, it would be adequately translated into reality (or absorbed by 'science') – this notion is false and oppressive: it would mean the end of art.[17]

And, in *The Permanence of Art*, he insists that 'The discourse of the end of art belongs today (differently than with Hegel) to the ideological arsenal and to the possibilities of *counterrevolution*.'[18] An instinctive anti-elitism and pragmatism wants to democratise creativity and end the ideological split between art and life. Yet, Marcuse is insistent: 'To interpret this irredeemable alienation of art as a mark of bourgeois (or any other) class society is nonsense.'[19] Indeed, he is willing to admit that 'Revolutionary art can very well become the *enemy of the people*.'[20] Clearly, Marcuse has a very specific conception of art in view.

Marcuse's 'permanence' of art cuts across societal forms. First the capitalist:

> The mocking of inwardness, of 'dissection of the soul' in literature which Brecht interprets as the sign of revolutionary consciousness, is not so far from the scorn of the capitalist toward a profitless dimension of life.[21]

Then, the fascist:

> The negation of the individual, even the bourgeois individual, recalls today the practice of fascism. Solidarity, community are

> not the giving up of the individual; they arise in autonomous individual decision; they are the solidarity of individuals, not of masses.[22]

And, finally, the Russian:

> Cut off from its historical base, socialized without a socialist reality art reverts to its ancient prehistorical function: it assumes magical character. Thus, it becomes a decisive element in the pragmatic rationality of behaviorism.[23]

But precisely this sweeping historical applicability seems questionable.

Marcuse's political argument is that anti-art simply makes the artist unnecessary without at the same time making creativity something general. 'The truth of art,' he insists, 'lies in breaking through the monopoly on reality as it is exercised in the existing society.'[24] By denying itself as art, by becoming reality, art opens itself to cooptation and to control. When it denies form and creativity as something elitist it is only an 'abstract negation'[25] of domination. Taking itself as praxis, as part of history and not its critical transcendence, art is no longer protest against, but part of, the established order. Without that critical transcendence and protest, revolution is no longer necessary. This is a 'classical' or 'bourgeois' Hegelian–Marxist account. Revolution demands a subject, a free individual; and it is only in relation to transcendence that this subject can be constituted. Again, historical specificity is lacking. Moreover, Marx's revolutionary subject was to be constituted in, not before, the revolution.

Marcuse's argument does not in fact take account of the fifties' critique of totalitarianism any more than it confronts its art. His view is strictly Frankfurt Marxist. Without a sociological proletariat the bourgeois subject is to remain the bearer of transcendence and the power of negativity. The 'dialectic of enlightenment' explains the immanence of this revolt of the subject . . . and its failure! Although he occasionally recognises the totalitarian 'politics in command', Marcuse tends to describe this politicisation through a (Lukácsian) reconstruction of the History of Western Thought, of which Marxism would be the culmination, and 'Soviet Marxism' the deformation ready to be righted. He no more *explains* the origins of this deformation than he does the transition from liberal capitalism to 'one-dimensionality'. All that is given is a (quite subtle) History of Ideas. It is for this reason that art is supposed to take over the revolutionary function – or rather, maintain the function that, for classical idealism, it always had.

Marcuse's critique of anti-art modernism is not false; the political and aesthetic dangers to which he points are real. Yet the lack of historical specificity weakens the account. At this point, were there time, discussion would have to turn to the question of aesthetic modernism and the modern. Incorporating the demand for historical specificity, it would confront the question of capitalism and modernism, beginning from the striking description in the *Manifesto* of capitalism's revolutionary overthrow of all transcendent traditions. The first question would be the degree to which modernism is simply the final penetration of the commodity-form throughout civil society, creating a closed 'one-dimensional' world. Yet, the politics of Soviet Marxism is non-capitalist, but also 'one-dimensional' – and opposed to aesthetic modernism, which itself is an avant-garde and generally anti-capitalist movement that appears at the end of the nineteenth century only. Unable to unthread this historical tangle, Marcuse's option is to take a step back to the rising bourgeois individual, as if to *reculer pour mieux sauter*.

Who is this subject on whose individualism and need for privacy Marcuse places so much stress? We are never really told. At best, it is the subject who preserves the power of negativity that permits cognition. But the aesthetic – and the political – relation is an *action*, not just a cognition; it takes place in an *institutional* setting (which, of course, the anti-art moderns want to destroy). Marcuse has no theory of action; and no theory of institutions. Action has become negation, Refusal; institutions are cognitive in effect if not in function. Harold Rosenberg explains this lack by noting that 'Marcuse is committed to the art object; modernist notions of art as action, event, process, communication seem to him distortions of the inherent nature of art.'[26] This, he continues, makes 'Marcuse's position . . . an instance of the intrinsic conservation of the contemporary Marxist outlook on art. In the name of a future new society, it rejects the changing imaginative substance of the present.'[27] Marcuse would of course reply by citing examples like Marinetti's description of the battlefield as art, or the Nurnberg Rallies as a 'communication system'; and his criticism of 'repressive desublimation' would also be invoked. But the problem is that Marcuse's subject is ultimately . . . Marcuse! He is quite explicit about this, although still coy, in the

Introduction to *One-Dimensional Man*. The critic allocates to himself a position 'outside' the criticised – and the result cannot but be the affirmation of an 'outsider' as transcendental and transcendent subject.[28] So much for history, institutions, action!

Because it was not self-critical, the critique of totalitarianism was left with only the vague category of 'mass society'. This *Unbegriff* should have led to a rethinking of the classical liberal categories of politics/economics, state/civil society/individual, for it does not fit their framework. But the critics did not think historically or institutionally; and they had abandoned action when they gave up 'utopian' politics. Modernist aesthetics is more self-conscious and self-critical – and more problematic! Harold Rosenberg's article, from which I quoted a moment ago, is entitled 'Set out for Clayton!' Clayton, you will recall, is that town described by Kafka in *Amerika* where everyone is an actor in a 'nature theater'. Marcuse would of course condemn this naturalism as destroying the possibility of negative thinking, of cognition, and thus of individuation. Yet the significant point about Clayton is that there are no spectators! This is the action-goal of modern art. For it to be the goal of modern society, a theory of democratic institutions adequate to the new social formation we are living is necessary. Neither Marcuse nor the 1950's critics of totalitarianism help here. Attention to the 'permanence' of the modern – and not of the art-object – would be more helpful.

**Notes**

1. Norman Birnbaum, 'David Rissman's Image of Politics', in *Toward a Critical Sociology* (New York: Oxford University Press, 1971), p. 258.
2. Irving Howe, 'The Goldwater Movement', in *Steady Work* (New York: Harcourt, Brace & World, 1966), p. 226.
3. Cf., the now-famous *Partisan Review* symposium, 'Our Country and Our Culture'.
4. The results of this critique are summed up concisely by Irving Howe:

   > the role of terror as an integral element of this new society; the terrifying power of ideology as both the mental equivalent of terror and a means for dominating the total life of man; the extreme atomization of social life, so that classes tend to become pulverized into a passive and an anonymous mass; the consolidation of a ruling elite which appropriates to itself not merely a variety of goods or a monopoly of power but the very possession of the state and its citizens. (*Steady Work*, p. 239).

Howe continues his account by suggesting that after Stalin's death we need to return to social and class analysis. In a further article in the same collection, 'Authoritarians of the Left', Howe condemns those who, following Deutscher, suggest that the Party dictatorship has done for Russia what capitalism did in the West in its first century, thus preparing a revolution against it . . . and justifying its crimes! Howe's point – which Marcuse would have done well to ponder in his account of Russia – is that that century of capitalism was also a century during which the working class educated itself and formed itself actively in struggle. There is no reason to think that the passive, dominated Russian workers will suddenly capture the Idea on the wing!

5. Herbert Marcuse, *Soviet Marxism* (New York: Vintage Books, 1961), pp. 71–2 (henceforth, SM).
6. Herbert Marcuse, *One-Dimensional Man* (Boston: Beacon Press, 1964), pp. 96–7 (henceforth ODM).
7. Ibid., p. 192.
8. Ibid., p. 211.
9. SM, op. cit., pp. 189–90; 193.
10. Ibid., p. 229.
11. Ibid., p. 233.
12. This is the argument referred to in n. 4.
13. One might argue for a change in Marcuse's position in *One-Dimensional Man* insofar as his methodological 'Introduction' stresses not the classical Hegelian–Marxist 'determinant negation' but rather the Sartrean notion of an existential 'project'. In fact, as I argue in the concluding remarks here, this only worsens the situation, setting the critic outside the criticised, and necessitating either pessimism or the apocalyptic Great Refusal of the 'outsiders'.
14. SM, op. cit., pp. 117–18.
15. Ibid., p. 213.
16. Ibid., p. 119.
17. Herbert Marcuse, *Counter-Revolution and Revolt* (Boston: Beacon Press, 1972), p. 107 (henceforth, CRR).
18. Herbert Marcuse, *Die Permenenz der Kunst. Wider eine bestimmte marxistische Aesthetik. Ein Essay* (München: Carl Hanser Verlag, 1977), p. 3 (henceforth, PK).
19. CRR, op. cit., p. 108.
20. PK, op. cit., p. 43.
21. Ibid., p. 45.
22. Ibid., p. 46.
23. SM, op. cit., p. 118.
24. PK, op. cit., concluding chapter, and p. 18.
25. CRR, op. cit., p. 93.
26. Harold Rosenberg, *The De-Definition of Art* (New York: Horizon Press, 1972), p. 248.
27. Ibid., p. 249.
28. ODM, op. cit., p. xiv.

# 2 Praxis before Politics: The Problem of Sartre

At one or another moment, in one or other situation, we have all been Sartreans! Why? What kind of thought could be adapted to so many different historical situations and experiences? Not just in the States, or in the West; Sartre is certainly a figure – almost an Hegelian *Gestalt*! – testifying to the nature of modern politics.

One result of this protean character has been that we are willing to pardon his sins – more usually, to forget them – because they are our own. Each of us will define these 'sins' differently. What we tend to agree on, however, is the goal of 'engagement' by the philosopher. Personally, I began to write this under the effect of Poland; and complete it in shock. I'd like, as I think Sartre would have liked, to talk philosophy with that concrete situation as our backdrop. But I want to stress philosophy.

That we seem to be returning to, or be driven or pushed or shoved into a second Cold War makes a reconsideration of Sartre the more relevant. Not that I think that history is repeating itself, or that I think that Sartre will present me some red thread that would permit a return to the slow path of détente or to go beyond it toward those 'Happy Tomorrows' of socialism. Sartre's life is especially tempting for the intellectual in such a situation. Yet the historical differences of our times, and his, and some of his choices which can only be called erroneous to which I will refer – neglecting, in fact, many others – mean that one has to be rigorous with him just because he does represent our temptation.

To protect my flanks, let me say from the outset that like any great thinker Sartre is not a unity, not an infallible source who neither contradicts himself nor learns from experience or starts anew. The author of *Nausea* and the *Words* also wrote the 'Communists and the Peace'; the 'Voltaire' whom de Gaulle refused to put into jail also lent his name and pen to Castro, Mao and other illusory hopes; the militant who sold the '*Cause du peuple*' and harangued the workers from the Renault plant at Billancourt, continued at the same time to work on his *Flaubert*.

The man Sartre knew that he was also the object-Sartre: like his Jew, he knew he was created by the other. Secular like his Jew, the man Sartre took the risk of falling into – and, I think, in fact fell into – the bad faith from which his existential lucidity could not save him.

Sartre belongs to that philosophical experience of *Gestalt* which Vincent Descombes has brilliantly sketched under the (French) title *Le même et l'autre*.[1] Descombes notes at one point that even though French philosophy was constantly preoccupied and impassioned by politics, it is none the less curious that for all its engagement it never gave birth to a *theory* of politics.

But what about the more than seven hundred pages of the *Critique of Dialectical Reason*? The *Critique* would demand more discussion than it can be given here. To put it in a nutshell, it is an attempt which has no precedent in the annals of the history of philosophy: the effort to found or ground a theory of society on the principle of nominalism! The individual is to be maintained, and yet the unity of the whole is also to be justified without the sacrifice of the individual. The effort is valiant, brilliant, exhausting. It had to fail. One senses Sartre's frustration (to which the conditions of writing, scotch and benzidrine, and the rhythm of composition were not foreign) when he tells us, toward the end, that 'the dictatorship of the proletariat is a contradiction in terms'. If the second volume was never written, this could surely be no accident. The good unity – that 'dictatorship of the proletariat' – would be possible only through the loss of the existential freedom of the individual.

Without going into philosophical details,[2] we can sum up the situation by citing the comment of Pierre Victor (i.e. Benny Levi) in the discussion printed as *On a raison de se revolter*:

> What bothers me still in what you're saying Sartre is that at the beginning and at the end freedom remains the same . . . One has the impression that you have an empty form, freedom, which gets filled up in differing manners.[3]

In other words, freedom has no independent history whereas, as we'll see in a moment, Sartre's Marxist or political phase is based on the premise that history is supposed to lead freely to freedom. It seems that freedom for Sartre is like the grace offered by that *deus absconditus*: you've got it or you ain't!

Let's go back some years, to *Being and Nothingness*. In the chapter concerning the existence of the other, Sartre writes:

> The point of view of pure knowing is contradictory: there can exist only the point of view of *engaged* knowing. This implies that knowledge and action are only two abstract sides of an original and concrete relation.

Here, in a book whose subtitle is an 'essay in phenomenological ontology', is the basis of the political engagement of a generation. Here is the foundation permitting (apparently) the transcendence of the dualism that seemed to divide morality from politics, theory from practice. Here is the starting point of Sartrism.

Let's return now to Sartre thirty years, and plenty of engagements afterwards – this time in his Preface to *Les Maos en France* and in *On a raison de se revolter*. The former *campagnon de route* of the PCF has made his self-criticism; he has brilliantly anatomised and criticised the politics of that 'socialism that came in from the cold' as he called it in his superb preface to the *Trois Generations* of Antonin Liehm;[4] and even though he called Marxism the 'unsurpassable horizon of our times' (in Question of Method), he none the less spent another 600 pages reformulating and rethinking that 'unsurpassable horizon' in the *Critique of Dialectical Reason*. And, finally, a certain pseudonymous 'Epistemon' (in fact, Didier Anzieu) will have made the claim that the *Critique* is the prophecy which announces and describes the path taken in May 68.[5] What, then, has Sartre learned from his engagement, so well grounded in *Being and Nothingness?*

Sartre takes up the experience of the Maoists who went to work at Contrexeville, a factory where one seemed to find every possible form of exploitation and injustice that could possible be exercised against the working class, but yet where, for the past twelve years, there had been not a single strike. Sartre explains to us, and to himself, that this worker passivity is the result of what the *Critique* explained as 'serial atomisation'. Tactically, that means that in order for the Maoist lesson to penetrate, the seriality had to be replaced by a 'fusion'. How could such a fusion take place? From a refusal, a refusal which for the Sartre of Maoism as for the existentialist, could only be accidental since, as he puts it in *On a raison*, 'there is no particular situation which by itself could determine people to revolt'.[6] But leaving aside the practical problems this indeterminism implies, one can admit that once there is a fusion, the Maoist lesson ('*parole*' is Sartre's term) can be heard . . . but the problem is that once there has been such a fusion, that lesson or 'parole' is no longer necessary!

What does Sartre draw from this experience? Obviously, his

analysis concerns the serial situation, not the fusion. In conditions of seriality the activist must support the 'most left' tendency amongst the workers, even if its actions are quite modest. More, the activist must know how to listen to the masses, even the masses who are caught up in seriality. He or she must not have the pretension of being their guide. Finally, the activist must continue to belong to the party, since even if the masses do finally fuse at some point, they are destined to return to seriality, and the party therefore remains as a kind of memory whose presence somehow makes the fusion once again a future but real horizon.

In a word, this is in fact the Sartre that we've always known. Engagement is engagement in the party; freedom – rebaptised fusion – remains an omnipresent and abstract possibility. Theory comes only after the fact, as if to give it a sense or a consecration. The problem with this is that if one has to be engaged, it'd be nice to know what it is that merits our engagement, and why. Sartre himself was engaged, sometimes for the better, sometimes for the worse. How is one to decide which was 'better' or 'worse'? For a long time Sartre, along with the 'mass' of French intellectuals – and 'mass' here is the appropriate term – made the distinction in terms of (capital H) history, progress towards the end of exploitation and war. Such was the measure that decided who was progressive, who was the left. For example, in the *Fantôme de Staline*, Sartre condemned the Russian intervention in Hungary at the same time that he remained a *compagnon de route* supporting something like the 1956 Polish solution – blinding himself to what the Hungarians had done, as well as to the implications of the Polish compromise. (Especially, to the party role continuing.) – Or, to mention another example there is Sartre the Third Worldist, lending his pen to a liberation which he considered historically inevitable but at the same time blinding himself to the problems which the newly free nations will have to confront.

What I'm getting at, in a word, is that the philosopher's philosophical a priori of freedom was replaced by an historical a posteriori for the politician – or, worse yet, in the Marxist period, by the a priori of a 'progressive' history whose sense or direction only the party – or the Soviet Union – was supposed to know or incarnate. The only exception to this situation, to my knowledge, was Sartre's pleas for the Vietnamese boat people, where he refused to opt for that sort of cruel and erroneous style that made him say (in *On a raison*) that someone like Solzehnitsyn had 'nineteenth century ideas' and was therefore 'harmful for development'.[7] But this exception itself was significant, as Paul Thibaud noted: it was at the occasion of a personal visit, accompanied by Aron and Glucksmann, to the Elyseé. The philosopher, Voltaire, who appealed to the universal conscience and attempted to awaken the freedom that sleeps in each of us; he whose hatred of the bourgeoisie was without limits, who said that 'to have power over others is precisely the definition of unfreedom'[8] – this Sartre none the less went to plead with Giscard!

But let's try to understand Sartre not according to his times but our own, since it seems that the temptation is still here. First of all, I don't think that it's necessary to stress that the renewal of something like a Cold War should not lead us to make choices according to that flat and manichaean logic of he whom Claude Lefort stigmatised as the 'progressive intellectual'. Still, it is perhaps worth recalling in the US, the silliness into which that logic led Sartre in the 1950s since one of *our* apparent conquests in the 1960s was the 'revisionist' school of history which rethought the causes of the Cold War. The recent upsurge in the movement for disarmament must avoid the implication of the Manichaean options – because the US opposes Russian action in Afghanistan or Poland we are not forced to side with the Russians any more than their criticism of US mixing in Central America makes the US therefore wrong.

Moving on, however, to what is certainly the most significant phenomenon of our present political conditions – Poland – we can perhaps get a better idea of what Sartrism might mean. In 1956, as mentioned, Sartre praised its mature wisdom, as opposed to the Hungarians who rose. That is somewhat surprising for the 'existentialist'. But it is, on reflection, typical of a temptation for the philosopher who, at the service of what he takes to be the imperatives of History, starts to be 'responsible' to think like a politician. But the philosopher should not be a statesman, especially not in a democracy.

What is happening in Poland? The domination of the party-state over civil society has been thrown into question. New forms and places of social relations are affirming themselves (including the Church, we must admit). What is more, we see there how an experience can give rise to a learning; how freedom can be learned. 1956, 1968, 1976, 1979, 1980; these dates testify to a *Bildungsprozess*, something which, as Pierre Victor noted above, Sartre could never explain.

More specifically, Poland shows three points at which Sartre's faithfulness to Marx lead him to misunderstand his own present. 1) Sartre like Marx never understood the independence and specific nature of the political sphere, preferring to reduce it to a relation of the subject to the world (or the subject to other subjects, who in turn become objects); 2) Sartre like Marx thought in terms of civil society, the 'system of atomistics', as Hegel puts it. His nominalism meant that he could not understand the possible and necessary plural reorganisation of this public sphere; 3) Like Marx – except for the *German Ideology* perhaps – Sartre cannot understand a *Bildungsprozess*, a realisation of freedom that takes place in an institutional experience. Thus, the *Bildungsprozess* remains for Sartre merely a *prise de conscience*.

Another aspect of the genius that made Sartre the master philosopher for several generations consisted, I think, in his ability to sense and to rationalise social novelty. But significantly, the prose in which he expressed this refused to think of itself as 'expression'. Sartre was never an avant-gardist, never a writer. (The comparison of his *What is Literature* with Merleau-Ponty's *Prose of the World* would be interesting on this score. Sartre's theatre, which was never avant-gardist, should be considered here.) Sartre remained attached to this conception of the writer down to the end (despite some flickerings in *Les Mots*). For example, the Maoist Sartre in *On a raison* tells us that 'the philosopher who would express in words what that freedom is will permit the workers to develop a deeper consciousness of their situation. But what one wants, I would have thought is not so much a consciousness of their situation but rather a going-beyond that situation, beyond trade unionism to political class consciousness, as Lenin would say'.[9] When Sartre continues the just-cited passages by telling us that 'it will be the job of the philosopher of (or in) the Maoist society to define morals in terms of freedom', this apparent modernity – which contradicts apparently the totalising temptation of the 'statesman-philosopher' – is the avoidance of responsibility on his part. Sartre here seems to abdicate activist philosophy in favour of the stance of the owl of Minerva, which flies only at twilight, after the fact.

I spoke of Sartre and of his Jew; and I've referred to the actual situation in Poland. I'll conclude quickly by saying that just like his Jew, Sartre let himself be defined by the Other. Worse, he misunderstood that Other. His Other was civil society defined as the system of atomism whose only totalisation can come from a third, the party or the state. Yet what Poland shows is that civil society can develop other forms of sociality which go beyond this atomism. And further, that the freedom which remains always the same in its agonising and impossible anxiety is perhaps that of ontology but not that of politics. Poland shows that freedom can be learned; that it can take a plural institutional form.

One sometimes thought that Sartre was re-learning, beginning anew. I mentioned the Jewish question because, at the end of his last interview in the *Nouvel Observateur* with Benny Levi (Pierre Victor), after a long discussion of just this issue, during which Sartre admits his ignorance of Judaism as a *social* and *historical* phenomenon when writing the *Jewish Question*, Levi asks him: but, in fact, you are beginning anew at the age of 75?

Sartre was always beginning again. That was his virtue and his vice, his charm but his frustrating *naïveté*. I think too that this was built into the structure of his thought, but in a curious manner that made his beginnings *apolitical*. He would only think a posteriori, only argue after the fact, rationalising revolt. His defences of 'our' causes, from Nizan to Lumumba to the Czechs, make us forget his defences of causes somewhat less glorious, be it his Stalinist, Castroist or Maoist phases. Why the blindness? Civil society, progressive history, philosophical dualism would be areas to explore at one level; at a second level, some of Marxism's essential premises are called into question; finally, it seems to me that Sartre is *the* example of the philosophic *rationalization* of political choice, and that this may suggest to us, today, something like the need for a *political* philosophy, not a philosophy that can serve a politics which we choose for whatever 'existential' reasons. It is to the elaboration of such a political philosophy that, I think, a 'radical caucus' should turn its attentions.

## Notes

1. English translation from Cambridge under the banal title *Modern French Philosophy* (1981).
2. See, for example, the chapter on Sartre in my *Marxian Legacy* (New York: Urizen Books, 1977), 2nd edition (London: Macmillan, 1987), with a new Afterword.
3. *On a raison de se revolter*, p. 142.
4. I will refer to Poland here, not to 1968 in Czechoslovakia, because I think Sartre could understand 1968 better than 1980, because the Czech movement was a reform that began within the Party-state whereas the

Polish events come from beneath and significantly ignored the Party altogether, just as they went beyond mere formal restructurings. Poland was a social rising, Czechoslovakia was more formally political; cf. the remarks below.

5. The reference here is to Epistemon, *Les idees qui énbranlèrent la France*, (Paris: 1969) which 'reads' the May 1968 events as if Sartre had anticipated them.
6. Op. cit., p. 139.
7. Ibid., p. 349.
8. Ibid., p. 345.
9. Ibid., p. 101.

# 3 The Theory and Practice of Dialectical Theory

The situation of radical theory is a paradoxical one. As theory, it presents analyses and assertions about the historically specific structures and social relations of the present. Its radical premise, on the other hand, is that the reality which it theorises is contradictory, inhuman and in need of fundamental change. Moreover, if it is Marxian theory, its task is to discover *already* present in this self-contradictory givenness the mediations, the potential forces within the social relations which, once they become (class) conscious, will realise the social change with which they are pregnant. As *theory*, then, radical theory makes positive affirmations about a negative reality, and is consequently a 'critical theory'. As *radical*, however, it is not at first clear what function it plays, since the mediations are already present, though not active, and since the theory cannot be an external intervention of a voluntarist or moralist sort, for then it could not justify its analytic claims. On the other hand, if the theory has no contribution to make, one wonders what the potential world-changing forces are waiting for – why they don't get on with the job.

What is the meaning of the Marxian injunction, in the 11th Thesis on Feuerbach, not simply to interpret but to change the world? On the surface, it suggests that we should not waste our time with theory, but rather get down to the serious business of world-changing practice. This in turn would imply that social contradictions on the strictly material level of physical existence and suffering lead to revolt and social change; and that consciousness of these contradictions springs directly from the material relations, unmediated by any theoretical or social-psychological circumstances. Theory would be a means, a weapon just like barricades or guns, at the service of instinctive practice. But. . . . The history of this century, in its suffering, war and repression, stands like the mocking statue of the Commander sneering at the mechanical materialist Don Juans. We cannot avoid the question: why has there *not* been a truly socialist revolution in this century?[1]

Reading the 11th Thesis as simply an option for practice is inadequate.[2] Closer to Marx's point is the Lukácsian interpretation. On the basis of an analysis of the problems confronting the classical

German idealism in which Marx was formed and against which his own views developed, Lukács tries to show that it was his specific dialectical method which enabled Marx to solve the paradoxes and resolve the contradictions that plagued philosophers and social theorists. The Marxian dialectic differs from its idealist counterparts in that it breaks with the passive, contemplative attitude dependent on a pre-given world which it can know but not change.[3] In the place of the abstract observer – divine Logos, transcendental ego, constitutive subject, value-free scientist, or whatever – Marx sets the already involved, praxical participant in the social process. We are 'always-already-social'. The bird's-eye view, for which the world is a congeries of discrete objects interacting and reacting on one another, is replaced by the living participant for whom the web of objects is an invitation and a temptation, to act and react; the subject is part of the objective world, and the world itself becomes active, subjective. The danger that arises here, to which I shall return in the second part of this discussion, is the temptation to conflate theory and praxis, such that theory becomes only another form of social relations, losing its specificity as theory.[4] If this were done, theory would become superfluous. What is needed is already inherent in the paradox of social philosophy: theory which remains itself, but without remaining in splendid isolation. How is this possible?

I take the 11th Thesis as a methodological injunction which talks about the tasks of radical theory-building, and the nature of theory when seen from a dialectical perspective. What I propose to do here is to present the broad methodological lines that a dialectical analysis must follow, and then to reflect on the nature of a dialectical theory as theory, the type of information it gives, and its function as radical.

## 1. DIALECTICAL METHOD AS CRITIQUE

Let me insist from the outset that a radical philosophy is concerned with the social world. If there is such a thing as a 'dialectics of nature', it certainly cannot be understood in an Engelsian (or, indeed, Hegelian) sense where, for example, when water is heated beyond 212 degrees, quantity is said to change to quality, water to steam. We can consider nature as dialectical only if it is taken as a social category. The Engelsian dialectics of nature is a series of mechanical interactions perceptible to the non-situated and non-participant observer. Ultimately, it must treat nature as a thing, other and unchangeable; and therefore it will find itself confronted with the problem of the unknowable thing-in-itself.[5]

As a social and historical being within a socialised and historical world, the philosopher and his/her object are in a homogeneous medium. The philosopher is a socialised and historical product, actor and acted upon. We did not create the language we speak or the world in which we live. Our world and culture are the creation of humans past and present. Yet we use the language and world to our own personal and social ends, changing them and inscribing our presence in them. The objects we confront are themselves social and historical, created by past and present generations, inlaid with strata of meaning which we learn to reactivate and interpret in original ways, finding new sense in the old, and old sense in the new. The world is presented to us through social and historical mediations into which we were born but which we both preserve and alter by our action and passion. We and our world are defining and defined, individual and social, active agents and passive heirs. No transcendent god or ego can look down and take it all in; only we, in living, give and are given meaning. That is what Hegel meant when he insisted that the key to the dialectic is the notion of 'substance as subject'. It is also what Marx's Feuerbach critique aimed at establishing, and it constitutes the basic position in terms of which philosophy functions as *critique*.

Of course, this supple reciprocity is not what appears to confront us in our daily lives on the soil of capitalism. There, the typical emotion is anxiety in the face of a seemingly self-regulating System; things and people threaten my identity and stand against me as Other; I feel empty, and try to fill out my person and I give it permanence by buying and acquiring commodities. I become the centre of my universe, a world of things functioning according to their own laws which I can at best understand and use but never fundamentally alter. I become an object to myself, calculating how best I can 'spend' my scarce time, preserve myself and control the menace so as to acquire that empty calm called happiness. I do not create meanings in this world, but at best use the accepted value codes to carve out some sense of my person and place in the scheme of things. My passivity is continually solicited by the things around me: this year Chrysler is going to 'sell you peace of mind, so calm down, calm down'; Howard Johnson's motels provide me 'with a friend wherever you go'; *Time* magazine tells me that it is 'the last word in packaging the news'; and the seductive voice from the radio whispers huskily

'Fly me'. From 30 000 feet laser-guided 'smart' bombs are launched on a people struggling for their dignity and culture, while I inch along bumper to bumper on the super-expressway, pushing the buttons to get a better station, different commercials, only to hear them coming out of the music itself. In Sartre's terms, this is the situation of *serial* existence.

Henri Lefèbvre calls our social form 'the bureaucratic society of controlled consumption'.[6] Its tentacles reach out toward the smallest details of the most insignificant moment. Technological rationality, the quantification and calculation that has produced and is continually reproduced by industrial accumulating civilisation has engendered its own justification and created its own meanings. But can this system close itself completely? Were it really a self-justificatory, self-referential, all-encompassing system which created us all in its image, then we wouldn't even be able to talk about it, to pin it down, to bitch about it; we wouldn't feel the anxiety of aloneness, search for identity, crave peace. Like the god presented in the 'free will' argument of the theologian, the system must allow a measure of freedom, if only so that we can recognise it and thus pray to it. But as some theologians also understood, because it must be recognised by us, it is, ultimately, dependent on us, on our belief, acceptance, and submission. This social system, like the god of yore, sets itself the contradictory and impossible task; it demands that the human being be obedient to it, recognise its authority and rights, at the same time that such absolute obedience would prevent it from functioning, since it demands recognition from *free* wills, not ones that are conditioned to believe.[7] The system demands that we feel the need for security, for how else would we keep buying, treat our work as a *means* to get newer and different things, blame ourselves and not it for our discomfort? But can this need be controlled?

It is logically impossible to conceive of a closed, self-recreating and self-perpetuating system. From the inside, it would not appear as a system. To conceive of it we would have to be outside of it – in which case it would not be closed. The continuation of the system, therefore, depends on our *active* acquiescence or internalisation of its norms. Presuming, then, that we're not stupid (and excluding an historicist version of the original sin doctrine, which puts the blame on the Past, or on Nature), the question becomes: how is it possible for us to will actively our own unhappy subjugation?

The question is not how to conceive of some force breaking into the closed circle and liberating us (à la Marcuse . . . or à la Lin Piao).

What we need to know is how it is possible for free beings to create their own slavery . . . for only then can they create their own liberation. Only on the assumption that it is such free beings who are responsible for the creation and perpetuation of bureaucratic capitalism can we ever envision the possibility of liberation. A 'Leninist' message of freedom, elaborated by bourgeois intellectuals, could not possibly touch the masses unless they were essentially free, though temporarily self-enslaved.

What must be accounted for is the *alienation* of the citizen in capitalist society which permits the thriving of a *reified* system in which the things and their impersonal laws rule supreme. How is it possible that the product dominate the producer, the object the subject?

Precisely that which prevents the system from being closed creates the possibility of alienation and reification: the fact that we are created by it and create it, are both subject and object, producer and product. The completion of the system would be its collapse; which is why Marcuse's notion of repressive desublimation in its varied forms of pseudo-freedom is so crucial to understanding the maintenance of capitalism, the failure of revolution. Even if we disagree with the details of Marcuse's argument, he has hit at the conceptual centre of the problem. On the other hand, as the system strives to maintain itself by reducing ever more the spaces for free activity, it must increase the alienation of the subject – that is, make it even more object-like – and increase the fetishism by eliminating all traces of the human project from the objective world. It does so by abstracting increasingly from all human *quality*, reducing the world to the law-likeness of quantitative relations. At the same time, however, that it homogenises for its own purposes, it renders all the more evident the commonality of our collective destiny.[8] This commonality is but the obverse side of the coin referred to at the beginning of this section – that insofar as the world is through and through a social world whose subjects are social subject-objects, and whose objects are social object-subjects, it is our common collective destiny to receive and create social meaning. And, to the common quantitative measure of the reified world, there corresponds on this obverse side a common qualitative measure: human praxis in its varied forms.

The social world (both essentially, and in its reified form) is a praxical world. By praxical (or praxis), I do not mean simply technique, activity of some sort or another governed by laws external to it. Praxical activity is self-regulated goal-oriented activity operating in terms of what Habermas calls an 'interest in freedom'. By freedom here is understood, in the sense of classical German Idealism, the autonomy of the moral subject acting in terms of self-given laws aiming at the overcoming of otherness, of heteronomy. Insofar as this moral subject is an actual, embodied social subject, its autonomy is not caprice (*Willfür*) but rather the social will acting within an historically given situation which it did not choose, and in which the activation of its autonomy is limited by the inherited forms. This is what Marx had in mind when he said that humankind does not begin any new work, but rather consciously completes that begun before its time. The past cannot be simply negated; my autonomy in relation to the world in which I find myself consists in my taking possession of it as mine, eliminating its reified dominance, changing my relation to it.

Insofar as we are embodied beings living in a world that is the collective creation of past and present humans, our activity will be governed, in part, by considerations external to ourselves. Though its common measure is praxis, our world is not transparent. If it were, these considerations would not be necessary; all would be for the best in the best of theory-less worlds, and the dream of the positivist or technocratic utopia would be realised. In fact, the world is shot through with opacity and irrationality, with objects and social relations which have outlived their times and yet remain to haunt the present. We need a concept like Sartre's 'practico-inert' or Merleau-Ponty's 'flesh' in order to account for that thick skin that remains and absorbs human intentionality and praxis long after its own subjective drives have left it. The Sartrean notion of the practico-inert, with its dualist construction, attempts to account for this intersubjective tissue which, in its separation from free praxis both incites and invites to action and at the same time is capable of absorbing it like a sponge, hiding from it its own meaning. Merleau-Ponty's flesh has a similar goal, but strives to avoid the dualism that vitiates the Sartrean concept. it is not important to enter into the nuances here, but rather to stress that this inter-world exists and acts, and that it must be taken into account when we attempt to present an historico-social account of the structure of our alienation and the possibilities of our self-liberation.

Our embodiment, and consequent rejection of either an idealism or a materialism in any simplistic sense, helps account for the possibility of alienation and reification. We are not pure minds, free essences, all-seeing egos. We make love, eat and defecate. Iron bars damned well do a prison make. It is precisely for this reason that we do much of what occupies our time and reveries. And it is precisely for this reason that the bourgeois social 'scientist' can predict our behaviour, that the Skinnerian can operantly condition us, that advertisements seduce us. But not always; not completely. The victory of total conditioning would at the same time be its loss. The bourgeois theorist dealing in the realm of appearances, juggling the surface presentation and searching for a quantitative ordering or pigeonholing, is incapable of providing an explanation for the phenomena manipulated. Theory becomes simply the mechanical reflection and descriptive ordering of a series of phenomena. If one manipulation fails, all that remains is to try another, and still another . . . as long as the subjects let themselves be experimented on. More refined techniques of manipulation can be – and have been – developed. But this only prolongs the agony.[9]

That social practice which appears as other-determined, the result of necessity imposed by my bodily being-in-the-world, has to be understood as praxical as well as practical. Without the continual presence of praxis, alienation cannot be overcome. We can assert that in production there is an element of both, the former being called work and the latter labour. Labour would be action performed under external constraint (either of a personal master, or simply material necessity such as the technique an artist must acquire before he/she can create), while work would be self-definitional, teleological, creative.[10] The precondition of our liberation, then, is the liberation of work from labour, of praxis from constrained practice – *as far as that is possible*. (The last clause implies historical specificity, for work will always demand labour; what can be changed is the *relation* of the two operations.)

Thus understood, the task of philosophy (or theory) becomes an eminently moral one, social and engaged, which consists in uncovering the moments of praxis within a given social and historical structure. It provides the active subjects with that hermeneutic mirror which renders evident to them that which is implicit in their own lives. This evidence, which is nothing other than a socially specific autonomy as opposed to the unconscious heteronomy typical of the alienated world, renders them self-conscious, and thus autonomous social subjects. It does not, of course, eliminate the realm of necessity, nor does it alter the material infrastructure. What it does, as we shall see more clearly in Section 2, is to create the conditions for the possibility of human self-affirmation, and hence for social change. It is not yet a politics, but it is the precondition for political action. And its insistence on the historical situatedness of its problems avoids the reproach of an abstract utopia.

In a word, what dialectical theory demands is not criticism but critique; not an ethical Ought but a mediated movement from heteronomy to autonomy. It is not a question of knowing what we Ought to do, but rather of understanding the stages or mediations by which we move from the inarticulate giveness of the present towards an autonomous opening to the future. We have to transcend the present, and not by imagination alone. We need a principle which has its foot, so to speak, in both the present and the future, the is and the ought; something which is not simply an ideal but actually a material force. Classical German Idealism sought such a principle, for example, in Schiller's *Spieltrieb*, in what Fichte first called Community and later called the Nation, in Hegel's Spirit and finally in Marx's Proletariat. The task of dialectical theory becomes the uncovering and unleashing of this principle of mediation in its concrete historical specificity.[11]

The fundamental principle on which this dialectical analysis operates is that every human practice is also a form of praxis, and that therefore social formations and activity must be understood in terms of the horizon towards which they are moving, their telos.[12] Without a principle of teleology, the analysis can only be positivist, static and descriptive; without such a principle, one remains at the level of appearance, society is atomized and immediacy reigns supreme. The teleological orientation demands that we think in terms of continually created and recreated relations, not fixed and permanent fluxes of atoms. It is an historical and dynamic approach, imaginative and active, not receptive and formal. The *telos* does not exist as a property or thingly aspect of the relations to be analysed; it is their immanent *horizon*, their sense and their potential. It may be an unrealised potential[13] – indeed, it will unrealised unless it is consciously acted upon, and the results of that action within human history will open up a new horizon. It is because each of us, in our daily lives, bumps up against something unexpected, unsatisfactory, incomplete, that we are jarred into recognising that we tend to pass most of our lives unconsciously, happy in the world of appearances where we arrange our lives with more or less agility, like Plato's cave-dwellers. This is not a moral or intellectual weakness, for the fetishised commodity world is the world that we and our fellows inhabit. We can recognise that we are living in the shadow world of appearances only insofar as, being also praxical, we have some, perhaps vague and intuitive, knowledge of the possibilities that lie beyond. We needn't know more about them than that they are possibilities; in fact, they may not even exist – or perhaps if they do not exist now, they will come into existence when, acting as if they did exist, we confront the shadow world in such a way that our *telos* becomes a self-fulfilling prophecy. (This of course is only possible if objective mediations do already exist for us to set into action; otherwise, we would be striving to realise an abstract universal or an abstract utopia – and not a concrete one that is possible.)

The complex play by which praxis and practice combine in creating a world of objects and meanings that we continually reactivate consciously or unconsciously is of course affected by the control of power positions within the society. Whether the economic infrastructure is 'determinant in the last instance', as Engels would have it, is not the central issue. Indeed, we have to rethink the nature of the economic itself in praxical, dialectical terms. Marx's *Capital* is not an economics textbook. Subtitled a 'Critique of Political Economy', it makes sense only from a dialectical standpoint (which also prevents us from taking it as dogma, doctrine or timeless truth). In a letter to Lassalle (1857), Marx presents his task as 'a presentation of the system, and through the presentation a critique of that system'. *Capital* is precisely that paradoxical type of radical theory: a positive presentation of a negative or contradictory reality. By showing that the underlying structures of the capitalist economy are the product of a series of social relations, whose articulation he analyses in a structure which parallels that of Hegel's *Logic*,[14] beginning with the most immediate relations of production (Hegel's Being), passing through the mediation of the circulation process (Hegel's Essence), on to a consideration of the system as a whole (Hegel's Concept), Marx pinpoints the play of social relations that make possible the continuation of the system.[15] The 'contradictions' of capitalism from a strictly economic point of view can be overcome, as Marx himself repeatedly shows.[16] The contradiction which cannot be overcome is that of the system's being fully systematic, of its complete subordination not just of the world economy (as Rosa Luxemburg thought), but of the human beings on whom it depends.

The lesson of Marx's *Capital* for a dialectical theory is twofold. There is, first of all, the famous 'fetishism of commodities' discussion, which is central to the further development, and provides a model for the dialectical hermeneutic which dissolves the appearances, reducing their seeming fixity to a flux of interhuman relations. But, second, this is only possible because of the teleological orientation that enables Marx to go beneath, to uncover the contradictions in a system whose inhumanity is patent. Marx could have remained with a moral critique, as did many socialists at that time and since; he could have simply applied the material uncovered by bourgeois critics against the system, organising opposition as a Proudhonian, Owenist or even Leninist. What he did do in *Capital*, however, was different; it was *theoretical*, not *political* (at least not in the common understanding of radical politics, centered around perceivable acts in a specific arena). He knew that he had to discover the underlying mediations, the forces that could lead the system to transcend itself. And these mediations only reveal themselves to the future-oriented praxical dialectic.

The dialectical theory which is conscious of its paradoxical insertion and the demands that this situation poses to it *remains a theory*. But it is a theory conscious that a successful interpretation of the social praxis and practice that weave the form and content of the historical present is only possible if it includes within its objects their horizon. The interpretation of the world is possible only for those who understand the need to change it by liberating its human possibilities, i.e., its human beings. Theory must therefore take account of praxis and its possibilities, but at the same time must itself remain theory. The theory must be oriented towards changing the world, but it itself cannot pretend to effectuate that change. It operates in terms of a teleology, not a causal analysis, and must take a possible future as operational in its analysis of the present. It was claimed above to have a moral, social and engaged function; yet it cannot be looked at as a means to some pre-given end, but rather must determine and justify its ends to itself. The relationship entailed here is similar to that of language to thought or poetry, where language is necessary to the project but not identical with it, nor merely a means to it, since the poem or thought does not exist except in the language used to express it. The subject who used the language to write a poem is not taking language as a tool or means, but rather needs the language itself to even entertain the poetic project, for which the language is then brought into play.

## 2. THE IMPORTANCE OF THE *DIFFERENCE*

In an early essay, Herbert Marcuse writes:

> When reason has been realized as the rational organization of mankind, philosophy is left without an object. For philosophy, to the extent that it has been, up to the present, more than an occupation or a discipline within the given division of labor, has always drawn its life from reason's not yet being reality.[17]

The first insight of theory – and, incidentally, the condition for radical political practice which implies a break with routine – is that there is more to the world than what appears immediately, that the appearances are deficient in some way, and that they present themselves as they do because of forces which can be uncovered – or, in the case of radical practice, opened for change – by the critical use of reason. Philosophy, or theory, is thus based on the *difference* between appearance and reality, thought and being, the is and the ought, the signifier and the signified. This difference provides its motivation, defines the nature and limits of its interrogation. We can concretise the quest in Marcuse's terms as reason's searching the world in the attempt to reconcile itself with itself; or in Hegelian terms as a cosmic struggle for recognition by an Other which is like the subject; or in the language of the young Marx as the making philosophical of the world and the making worldly of philosophy; or simply as the everyday struggle of humans to live in a human world. The motivation of theory, in short, would be its own elimination.

We must be careful here. Is the goal to impose Reason on an uncooperative, dumb and passive world? Is it to change the world in such a way that the difference is eliminated and Reason no longer has an object? The error in both cases is not simply that of total systematicity but, correlatively, that Reason is treated as a thing, a system of doctrine, which is either to be applied to the world from without or which is nothing but the faithful reflection of the world's structure. Reason (or philosophy, or Theory) loses its specificity and is conflated anthropologistically with the other *things* existing in a monistic or one-dimensional universe. The result, in political translation, is in both cases a form of monolithic bureaucratism, a closed system in which orders come from the top and are imposed by whatever means necessary. While there have been historical examples of the attempt to realise this sort of systematicity,[18] they have always failed for precisely the reasons mentioned previously:

namely, the inconsistency and impossibility of a closed social system, of the reduction of human subjectivity to dead passivity.

If this is the case, what sense does it make to argue that dialectical knowledge is governed by the inherent teleological possibilities of the social world, and that this knowledge is nothing but the self-understanding of its own object and the prelude to the object's self-realisation? The teleology seems to demand an 'end of history', and the claim of the dialectic seems to be that we should let the world be what it can become, a becoming which does not call for our help. This seeming, however, omits the fact that we are part of that world; it is a contemplative, god's-eye view (the *pensée de survol* citicised by Merleau-Ponty). We need to look more closely, first at the nature of the social teleology; then at the kind of knowledge that the dialectic gives us, and its specificity as theory; and finally at the reasons for claiming that this theory, as theory, is inherently radical, that it is positive in its negativity, a critique which avoids the sterility of abstract criticism by continually recreating itself as it transcends itself.

The premise on which all theory rests is the *difference*. This implies that what is immediately given is not in itself complete and satisfactory, and it sets up the task of piercing beneath, uncovering the structure, relations and possibilities which present themselves as the conditions of the possibility of the object's appearing as it does. The task is both negative and positive, regressive and progressive, critical and reconstructive. Simply to begin implies that we have some notion of a truth-horizon, for otherwise the objects would overwhelm us with their sheer positivity, and we would remain passive spectators before a magic-lantern show. That we recognise the difference and commence the task supposes that the objects present themselves in relation to a truth or reality the explication of which is theory's goal.

The telos which must be supposed is the truth. In its nakedness, this statement is shockingly formal, slippery and empty. Concretely, the truth has many incarnations, is lived in many forms, all of which can be reduced to one basic structure: *social* autonomy. Note that I stress social here. The autonomy that is meant is not the immediate self-referential nature of a thing turned in on itself; that would be the empty formal immediacy of a monad. *Social* autonomy is that historically specific situation in which the social individual recognises him/herself in a socially given other, such that the relation that is established is one of *mediated* homogeneity.[19] It is the social situation in which the rigidity of law-like social norms is overcome, the constraints of practice mastered, and social praxis let free in an infinite field of co-possibilities. The truth for a human being is not a state of affairs but an open expanse of playful development, where each achievement sets free new capacities and social variations.

As the horizon of social actions and social formations, the *telos* has no concrete incarnation outside of the historically specific moments in which individual and collective actions continually engender it. In a specific society, or in a given social relation, the same 'objective' formation may or may not be inscribed with the richness of teleological possibility. Actions, attitudes, institutions are contextual, and must be analysed – dialectically – in their specificity. In a given historical configuration, for example, democracy may be simply a form by which those in power manipulate the masses in order to preserve their control; while at another junction, democratic forms can serve to unleash desires and possibilities which lead precisely to the self-affirmation of the masses against the forms of socio-economic domination typical, say, of bureaucratic society. High culture may serve as an alibi in one social moment, while at another it may be the spur of revolt against a system whose quantitative norms impede the human goals articulated in culture. Sexuality, dope, and counter-culture may be progressive in one context, while in another they are the cop-out of resigned individualism.[20]

A dialectical analysis is no substitute for empirical investigation; its discoveries are limited and specific, continually to be begun anew. At the same time, however, the dialectical attitude inflects the style, form and execution of empirical study.[21] It warns us against the attitude which contemplates, orders and categorises the objects of the world as if they were just so much dead matter; and it insists that we recognise our objects as social relations, themselves both objective and subjective. The manipulation of things is increasingly possible for our highly refined scientific techniques. But the very desire to manipulate things supposes that they could well be otherwise without the interference of the manipulator. It supposes that they have other possibilities, a horizon of openness, and, in the case of social relations, the stubbornness that is the greatness of the human animal.

The kind of knowledge that the dialectical analysis yields is obviously not that which the accepted paradigm of the natural sciences demands. It is the subject's knowledge of its, and the world's, possibilities. Thrust forward in its investigation by the difference, the subject is continually seeking to overcome the otherness of its world. We saw that in one sense the achievement of this quest would be the conflation of subject and object, theory and world. Indeed, insofar as the self-consciousness of the social subject involves consciousness of its social world – more specifically, involves the making subject-like of that social world, i.e., involves changing that world – then the self-consciousness which is social consciousness also carries with it the project of changing that world. But this project is self-annulling, and could only be achieved through the cancellation of the difference which made possible the original project. Absolute knowledge, like total dictatorship or total freedom, is possible only when all subjectivity – and hence, knowledge itself – is eliminated.

The knowledge yielded by the dialectical analysis preserves and respects the difference, existing only within or as that differential relation. Its goal is not possession of a thing but the self-understanding of a relationship. Here dialectic and dialogue converge.[22] Dialogue is only possible between two separate but equal subjects who respect their difference while striving to understand it. Dialectic is the means of that understanding and self-understanding in and of the dialogue. The dialectical dialogue takes place not only among humans, but also between them and their world (past and present) insofar as they, as social and worldly, and it, as impregnated with their meanings, projects and praxis, interact more or less consciously with one another. The model of the psychoanalytical dialogue, stressed by Habermas, Apel, Ricoeur and others, provides a useful analogy here.

In stressing the preservation of the difference, and in introducing the psychoanalytic model, I have obviously opened a hornet's nest, alluded to at the outset by the discussion of Marx's 'change the world'. If the difference is preserved, does this imply that we let things be as they are, drawing consolation from knowledge, as for example in Hegel's resigned 'Preface' to the *Philosophy of Right*, filled with phrases of reconciliation, refusing 'to construct a state as it ought to be', finding that 'there is less chill in the peace with the world which knowledge supplies', or envisaging philosophy's 'grey in grey' as not to be 'rejuvenated but only understood'? How can theory maintain itself apart from the world, and yet claim to be radical? And, how can theory affect praxis while remaining distinct from it?

The dialectical stance permits the rediscovery of a horizon of mediations whose material force can exert the physical change which makes possible the self-recognition and self-change towards a maximally free interaction of self-conscious social actors (persons *and* institutions). Theory does not come from outside the system; it is the system's self-consciousness of its own potential, and thus is itself a part of the system. It is historically and socially specific, not a once-and-for-all truth. Its immanence and specificity point to the fact that the object of theory (which is also its subject) is nothing other than daily life lived on the soil of the present. Within that daily life, theory must learn to distinguish the appearance from its horizon; it must understand the forces at work which create the disbalances that permit social movement, entail the growth of self-consciousness and, in fact, are the very condition of the possibility of the theory. In this sense, the locus of theory need not be the printed, or even the spoken, word. In our increasingly homogenised and reified world, we become more and more alike, share a common attitude towards the world and ourselves, an attitude determined or infected by the need of the social system, in all their contradictoriness. The awareness of the difference, the need for theory and the self-consciousness that arises with it, can be tripped off by various forms of praxical striving – exemplary actions of the few, the wildcat strike, the youth revolt against traditional values. What counts is that these triggers not be abstract utopias, off in the realm of phantasy; they must be concrete, rooted in daily life and recognisable to all of us because they spring from a common situation that lies all around us.

Not all praxis is theory; and not all theory is praxical. Nor should this be the case. Praxis that presents itself as, or is taken for a substitute for theory is blind, runs into dead ends, becomes habit or defensive spite, an excuse for the lazy and a denial of the difference. Theory that pretends to replace or even guide praxis is empty, pretentious and dogmatic. Nor is theory related to praxis, or vice versa, simply as the continual movement from one to the other, trial-and-error, redprint and execution. From a tactical point of view (in politics, or in arranging my own life), theory may be totally useless for the immediate tasks at hand, which are determined by an accidental conjunction of events.

Merleau-Ponty once entitled an essay on theory 'Everywhere and Nowhere'. This is the point, the paradox of radical theory from which we began. It has no specific object that would permit us to place it in an organigram of the tasks of society, next to say sociology or physics, above or below making love and listening to music. But, like ourselves, it is everywhere. It is critique; it is the opening of hidden horizons; it is the poetry which gives empirical prose its human meaning. We cannot reduce theory to, nor impose it on, practice. But without that awareness of the difference which is the condition of theory, our action is but dumb habit living in a world of pre-given meaning. In the project of daily life, simply in order to live and love, we do a kind of theory without being conscious of it. This is a first, and necessary, step; but it is not sufficient. Were we to know ourselves in what we do, we would acquire that self-consciousness and human feeling that is the condition of not just revolution but a human social world. Social self-consciousness is that positive built upon a negative typical of an open radical theory that continually transcends itself and realises new possibilities for human relations.

## Notes

1. There have, to be sure, been beginnings. They have been quashed in blood, either by the left bureaucrats (Kronstadt, etc.) or by those of the right (Berlin, Turin, Budapest, etc.). My intention here is not to answer this question, but to look at the nature and role of a theory which might have its place in the analysis of the actual forces at play.
2. Inadequate both as a reading of Marx, and more generally as an interpretation of the relation of theory and practice in the revolutionary process, for its character as an *option* denies any role to theory or to rational choice. In earlier drafts of this chapter, I found myself continually sidetracked into polemics with various 'heresies' – which seemed to add little to the positive discussion. I have tried here to avoid them. The theory-praxis problem in its different concrete forms cuts across the polemical history of the working-class movement, from the famous Marx-Weitling quarrel in 1846, on through to the present. Whatever one thinks about Marx's resolution, or that of Lenin, Luxemburg or Lukács, the significant issue for theory is that the problem returns continually – suggesting perhaps that there is no univocal solution but rather that revolutionary *experience* is that which demands theorisation, precisely in order to go beyond traditional theory. If this is so, the self-conception of theory and its role would have to be redefined. In the present context, this would mean that the 'heresies' against which I found myself in polemic consisted simply in the breaking down of this interchange: separated one from the other, theory and praxis, the political and the economic, are meaningless. This negative judgement still leaves the positive problem: how to conceive their unity.
3. Hegel had already observed that the notion of thought as a re-presentation or picturing of reality was an inadequate and incomplete approach which isolates its objects in an atomistic dance of juxtaposed, but essentially unrelated, parts. The persistence of the visual mode (Hegel's term is *vorstellendes Denken*) entails the static or contemplative attitude towards oneself and the world. It encourages a dualism of subject-object, and hence the rigid separation of theory and praxis. The

critique of the visual metaphor is developed especially in the work of Merleau-Ponty, as I argue in *The Marxian Legacy*.

4. This is the error of the Althusserians' notion of 'theoretical practice', or of the 'production of knowledge', which, if not just a redundancy, is the attempt to analyse theory as simply another form of production governed by analogous laws. The result of this conflation, despite its claim to structural specificity, is monistic and idealistic. The 'structuralist' claim that we need to go beyond the idealist notion of the transcendental or constitutive subject is an important theoretical innovation. However, the 'death of the subject' which it heralds can also be seen as the historical process of capitalist reification and alienation. Useful as an analytical tool, the structuralist position cannot be taken as a satisfactory theoretical whole, cf., the elaboration of this point in 'Another Resurrection of Marxism' below.
5. This is not the place for a critique of Engels' materialism. Among many others, Lukács' *History and Class Consciousness* presents an adequate refutation of the 'dialectics of nature'. Interesting attempts to go beyond this have been made by Ernst Bloch on the one hand, and those using the insights of quantum physics on the other (e.g. M. Kosok, P. Heelan, C. Castoriadis). Bloch recalls that nature has not always been conceived as a static Other, but in the case, for example, of the 'left Aristotleans', is itself a dynamic and utopian principle. Heelan and Kosok attempt to use quantum physics to confront the traditional error of the non-situated or transcendental observer. Castoriadis' ontological reformulations are discussed in *The Marxian Legacy*, without, however, making explicit reference to his use of modern mathematics and physics, which appear especially in 'Le monde morcelé' (*Textures*, 72/4–5) and 'Science moderne et interrogation philosophique' (*Encyclopédia Universalis*, Organon, vol. 23).
6. Henri Lefèbvre, *Everyday Life in the Modern World*, tr. S. Rabinovitch (New York: Harper Torchbook, 1971). Too little of Lefèbvre is available in English. For a general introduction, see Alfred Schmidt's essay in *The Unknown Dimension*, Howard and Klare, eds (New York: Basic Books, 1972). On the theory of bureaucratic society see also the discussions of Lefort and Castoriadis in *The Marxian Legacy*.
7. On another level, the same process is involved in the work situation. The worker must submit passively to hierarchy and authority, must be drilled in the art of self-deprecation and self-hatred so as not to be rebellious and a threat to the control exercised in the most minute aspects of his/her life; but at the same time, the individual worker and the team often find themselves using and inventing all sorts of tricks, not just time-savers but ways to actually make production work, since the rules themselves are often either vague or too constricting. The 'rule book strike', in which rules are followed to the letter, screwing up the production process, is a sign of the contradictory demands placed on the workers: to obey and to be inventive. Cf., for example, Daniel Mothé, *Militant chez Renault* (Paris: Editions du Seuil, 1965), and the theory developed by 'Socialisme ou Barbarie'. It is in this sense that the class struggle is fought every day, and is constitutive of the capitalist

system as such. But, as is seen in the criticism addressed by Castoriadis to the Marxists, this means that the labour theory of value loses its applicability, for the input of labour-power does not produce a constant output in the quantity of labour, which depends on intensity etc. As all capitalists know, the 'falling rate of profit' can be compensated by increased 'productivity' – i.e. by increased intensity of labour through methods of controlling the work force.

8. On the implications of this for the radical project, particularly as concerns the impact of the mass media on the birth of the 'New Left', see my article 'Les communications de masse et la naissance d'une nouvelle gauche', in *Actes du XVe Congrès des SPLF*, 1971, where I argue that the dialectic of Otherness, in which, as all alike the receptors of the media, we become all the same, and hence are open to the acceptance of a common project. This explains in part the success of the 'exemplary action' technique, and the spread of the student revolt of May 1968. More generally, this is the 'socialization of society' whose results, according to Marx, make possible a revolution which would be universal, ending all class domination. See also, 'From One New Left to Another', below, where this point is nuanced, leading to the proposals in Part III.
9. Moreover, as Marcuse notes in his critique of M. Weber (in *Negations*), the bureaucratic rationalisation of the world into manipulable quanta makes it impossible to consider the ends for which the System functions. Weber finds himself forced to introduce the dubious notion of charisma here, and the leader gives way to the Führer, above and directing the bureaucracy. Lukács' 'reification' essay in *History and Class Conciousness* posed this as the problem of the 'thing-in-itself' which haunted German Idealism, and whose solution can only be the end of a contemplative stance taken by a subject standing over against its object. The proletariat, as the subject-object identical, becomes the incarnate philosopher. Though Lukács' political translation of this solution runs into problems, for our purpose here what is important is the relativisation of the subject-object dualism which is necessary if theory is to be able to confront the ambiguity of a non-positive, opaque reality.
10. This same analysis could be carried out in other domains, most obviously in that of language, where the system of signifiers which we use as a code, establishing their referentiality, is constantly revivified, altered and rendered human by the act of speaking on the part of the subject. In our everyday situation, we *practise* language; yet it often comes to pass that this practice becomes a *praxis*, as we mould the language, shape and possess it. In de Saussure's terms, we have the opposition of *langue* (language, the given system in its systematicity) and *parole* (the act of speaking, which is diachronic or historical). Praxis is thus historical, while practice reproduces the given system. The importance of this argument and its implications are developed in detail in Castoriadis' *L'institution imaginaire de la société* (Paris: Editions du Seuil, 1975).
11. The historical specificity must be stressed, as the fate of Marx's theory of the proletarian revolution shows. 'The' proletariat doesn't exist

transhistorically but is constantly formed and reformed in struggles that are a reaction to developments in capitalist production, themselves partially determined by the class struggle. Hence, the importance of the 'new working class' theory, on which cf. my article in *The Unknown Dimension*, op. cit., and S. Mallet, *Essays on the New Working Class* (New York: Telos Press, 1976).

12. For an interpretation of the teleology in concrete political practice, there is no better example than Rosa Luxemburg. See my Introduction to *Selected Political Writings* (Monthly Review Press, 1971). On the antinomies to which this position leads, see the discussion of Luxemburg in *The Marxian Legacy*, which is a critique of the earlier argument.
13. It is a necessary but not sufficient condition. A well-nuanced, but ultimately unsatisfactory – because incapable of dealing with social praxis – account of the logic here is found in Georg Henrik von Wright, *Explanation and Understanding* (Cornell University Press, 1971).
14. Thus, despite the remarks about the 'mystifying side' of Hegel's dialectic, of which Marx speaks in the 'Afterword' to the 'Critique of the Political Economy', he distinguishes between the method of presentation and that of investigation. On the dialectical structure of Marx's *Capital*, see the important work of R. Rosdolsky, *Zur Entstehungsgeschichte des Marxschen Kapitals* (Frankfurt: Europaische Verlagsanstalt, 1968). The problems of such a position are developed most lucidly by Castoriadis.
15. It is important to stress that the first volume of *Capital* cannot be read alone for this reason. Stopping there would lead not just to theoretical error, but to political messianism and unwarranted hope.
16. For example, the limits on absolute surplus value are overcome through the production of relative surplus-value; after introducing the 'law' of the tendency of the rate of profit to fall, Marx follows with a chapter listing various reasons why the fall may not take place, etc.
17. 'Philosophy and Critical Theory', in *Zeitschrift für Sozialforschung*, Bd 6, 1937, p. 632.
18. The attempts to realise Marxism in practice have tended towards this direction, not only in Russia but even – however disguised by Mao's pragmatism and the rhetoric of the 'cultural' revolution – in China. (The only systematic and informed critique of China from this point of view is Simon Leys, *Ombres Chinoises* (Paris: UGE, 1974).) I suggest in the last section of *The Marxian Legacy* that this result is inherent in the *rationalism* that underlies Marx's project, making it the last *avatar* of traditional Western metaphysics – though it would be ludicrous to see the theory as the only cause of this degeneration: would that the bureaucrats took theory even that seriously!
19. Mediation is a central concept. Here, it implies the rejection of any reductionism which would criticise social forms purely and simply because they impose themselves on the individual. Autonomy is not law-lessness or caprice (*Willfür*) as both Hegel and Marx show. We do not want to reject social formations which fall into the realm of plural subjectivity that Hegel calls Objective Spirit – the State and its institutions, language, family, etc. – simply because they are supra-

individual. If we refer to a social institution as alienating and therefore inhuman and to be eliminated, this is not because of its nature as the result of plural social praxis, but rather because it is a product which for specific historical reasons has become a tyrannical and one-sided producer of false or non-autonomous human activity. Immediacy is not the goal of the autonomous individual; rather, the goal is to be the most mediated, the most diverse, having the most tensile strength. Cf., for example, Marx's criticism of 'crude' communism in the 3rd of the *1844 Manuscripts*.

20. On this, cf. the style of analysis used by Herbert Marcuse, for example, in 'On Hedonism' or 'On the Affirmative Character of Culture'. The lesson is important, particularly for those stuck in bourgeois institutions created for the accumulation and passing-on of tradition, as well as for judging the concrete forms that present-day social disorganisation is taking.
21. It's an interesting thought-experiment to ask yourself: as 'socialist' Commissar of Research Policy, what would I fund, and why?
22. Cf. Jürgen Habermas' development of this point, which is a guiding principle of his work. The Afterword to the new edition of *The Marxian Legacy* shows some difficulties inherent in the project.

# 4 From Marx to Kant: The Return of the Political

## 1. CAPITALISM AND MODERNITY

The contemporary 'crisis' of capitalism, which should bring hope to a political left, makes it impossible to deny theoretical difficulties which undermine the very foundation of that left. Neither liberalism, welfarism or Marxism can explain the grounds for an eventual collapse of capitalism, nor can they identify the elements of a new economic system which would replace it. No one can seriously believe any more that the breakdown of capitalist relations of production will give birth to a new socialist mode of production, carried supposedly in the womb of the old order. The conceptual crisis is manifested in lame labels like neo- or late-capitalism, and in the Bahro's widely accepted euphemistic 'really-existing socialism'. The theoretical difficulty has practical consequences. The nature and locus of the 'revolutionary subject' is as uncertain as the goal for which it is supposed to strive. Evaluation of the 'new social movements' is as difficult as is judgement of the political implications of the Polish *Solidarity*. Only with regard to the 'Third World' is an ironic advantage gained: the conceptual crisis makes recognition of complexity inevitable; friend/foe manichaeanism is no longer tenable. Nor is the historic image of linear progress applicable. Nor is the historicist image of linear progress applicable. The rediscovery of democracy as a positive political programme by many Latin American lefts is emblematic of the new situation.

How have we come to conceive of our common social life as dominated by the economy? Of course, the capitalist looks at the world from the point of view of his personal interest; Marx was not the first to denounce the resulting 'Robinsonnades'. When the children of peasants accustomed to living in customary societies had to be transformed into workers, capitalism had to teach them this new world outlook. But the capitalists are not the only preachers of economism; the bureaucrats in 'really existing socialism' legitimate themselves by a similar economic logic. But too many revolts, open and collective as well as silent and individual, witness the irreducibility of man to the machine, of reason to a means–end rationality. Might not a 'Copernican Revolution' ask the preliminary question: what are the conditions which make possible the reduction of social to economic life? Might not such a proposal lead us, as it did Kant, to pass beyond a critique of the laws of nature and of morality to a critique of our faculty of judgement? And could not the result reawaken the radical imagination, making possible a move beyond the present conceptual crisis?

The proposed 'Copernican Revolution' suggests that the economic logic presupposed by both liberal and Marxist representations of civil society cannot be maintained (if it ever really existed). The priority of economic life is not the solution but the problem. The 'conditions of the possibility' of its temporary dominance must be explained. The explanation will have the philosophical structure suggested by the Kantian critique. It will be presuppositionless and self-reflexive. It will be both a positive demonstration and a negative (or 'dialectical') presentation of the antinomies which account for the illusory priority of the economic. The result will be neither a system of philosophy (Hegel) nor its end (Marx). If philosophy is returned to its throne (Kant), politics becomes not only possible but necessary. This interdependence of philosophy and politics is incarnated in Kant's notion of the republic which puts the political nature of society back on the radical agenda.

Marx also entitled his work a 'critique'. This is not the place for comparative philology. My claim is not to restore a true Marx nor to reconstruct Kant's actual intentions. My guiding question is defined by the double crisis: of capitalism and of its conceptual representation. The description of capitalism in *The Communist Manifesto* suggests an empirical and theoretical starting point for the analysis. Marx describes a 'constant revolutionizing of production, uninterrupted disturbance of all social conditions, everlasting uncertainty and agitation' that distinguish the capitalist epoch from all others. 'All fixed and fast-frozen relations with their train of ancient and venerable prejudices and opinions are swept away, all new-formed ones become antiquated before they can ossify. All that is solid melts into air, all that is holy is profaned.' The result is 'man is at last compelled to face with sober senses his real conditions of life, and his relations to his kind'. This critique, unlike the *philosophes* of the Enlightenment who stood outside of the Old Regime, is *capitalism's self-critique*. It has a reflexive structure, and, like the Kantian model, it is presuppositionless. Marx's reconstruction of its conditions of possibility can be accepted or rejected. His replacement of Kant's negative

'Dialectic' by a positive 'revolutionary' politics has more important implications.

Capitalism is defined by its specific difference from other social formations. This difference is articulated in its self-critical secular process. Such a self-critical character illustrates the *structure of modernity*. A 'modern' formation is defined by its presuppositionless procedure which can only be legitimated immanently. The resulting structure is characterised by a conceptual antinomy which can be described by the concepts of *genesis* and *normativity*. Illustrations of this antinomic structure are found in modern art as in modern capitalism, modern philosophy as in modern politics. Modern society cannot be reduced to its mode of production; the productive economic base demands a normative political legitimation. The contemporary crisis cannot be overcome only within the economy; praxis is not identical to production, political judgement cannot be reduced to strategy. Even if political norms are called 'ideological', they are none the less a reality which modern societies must constantly reproduce. The change in the political norms adopted by capitalist societies cannot be reduced simply to an effect of economic reality (although it cannot be separated from it). The interdependence of genesis and normativity provides a guideline for the formulation of a political 'Copernican Revolution'.

The specificity of modernity, and the categories useful for its description, can be illustrated simply from the sphere of art.[1] Four artists, two from the beginnings of modern times, and two contemporaries, serve as models. The paintings of Turner and Pollock stress the formation of the work of art; their orientation can be called *genetic*. The brush of Friedrich and Rothko affects the viewer by means of an aesthetic of totality; their art can be called *normative*. These generalisations are of course abusive; they exaggerate to make a simple point. No artist produces uniformly, or with constant success. Successful paintings are characterised by the fact that neither the genetic nor the normative aspect dominates. The genetic artist fails if he forgets that he is truly painting an artwork; similarly, the normative artist fails if his creation petrifies into an eternal presence of the beautiful. The successful work unites the tension of the genetic and the normative. This 'tension' which is the life of the work can overpower it; it appears as a 'crisis' which threatens the work from within. Modern art is defined by the attempt to fight off the seductive 'perpetual peace' which would overcome the internal crisis which defines the modern. The temptation is omni-present, in the artwork as in the capitalist society defined by the *Manifesto*, because there exists no preconceived or external norm which would define once and for all the good work or society. Legitimation can only be *immanent*.

The Kantian thread guiding this descriptive argument will have to explain why the analogy to art succeeds in describing a more general structure. In the history of philosophy, Kant discovered and articulated the structure of modernity. The 'transcendental dialectic' which concludes each of the *Critiques* illustrates the temptations inherent in the modern tension of the genetic and the normative, which confronted Kant in the forms of empiricism and rationalism. Kant's goal was to unite the genetic and the normative orientations without eliminating their respective truths. Hegel and Marx confronted the same difficulties. Hegel's genetic *Phenomenology* demands as its counterpart the normative *Logic*; Marx presents at once a genetic theory of the revolutionary proletariat and a description of the paradoxical logic of the capitalist mode of production. Between Kant and Hegel/Marx, the world had changed in one fundamenttal aspect: civil society had emerged, and its development tended to be dominated by the economy. Kant too spoke of civil society. His 'Idea of World History from a Cosmopolitan Point of View' defined its creation as 'the crucial problem for the human race'; it is 'the most difficult' and 'will be the last to be resolved'. This is the political ground for my proposed 'Copernican Revolution'. Hegel and Marx presupposed the existence of civil society; Kant was concerned to create it. Such a project demands a *political* analysis. Although his republican theory is not fully elaborated, Kant's philosophy respects the immanence of modernity; this makes it possible to propose a new understanding of modern politics, its relation to civil society, and to its supposed economic foundation.[2]

## 2. MARX AND MODERN PHILOSOPHY

The modern imperative of immanent self-critical justification, and the categories of genesis and normativity, suggest a broad interpretation of Marx's theoretical development. A Remark appended to his philosophy Dissertation summarised his project. The editor of Marx's writings gave this note the apt title, 'On the World's Becoming Philosophical as Philosophy's Becoming Worldly'. This relation of mutual implication entails a double difficulty. Marx speaks of a 'psychological law' which explains why 'philosophy as will turns against the phenomenal world'. But a psychological hypothesis does not provide an adequate philosophical foundation; a modern philosophy demands immanent legitimation. To this problem on the side of the subject is added another from the side of the object. The world must be shown to be receptive to the philosophy which sacrifices its purity to engage with the world. Philosophy cannot be applied to a world which is different from it and indifferent to it; the world must itself possess the normative structures of philosophy. These two difficulties arise from the young Marx's attempt to confront the imperatives of modernity. His first solution is unsatisfactory because it treats philosophy as at once normative and genetic in the process of changing itself and the world. Marx's further development can be seen as the articulation of the structural necessities created by the paradoxical unity of genesis and normativity in a modern philosophy.

The premise of Marx's secondary strategy is the inverse of the first. The journalist returning to philosophy criticises the external relation of the state to civil society. Marx is aware of the danger of a pre-modern reductionism, which would be only the inverse of the application of the 'psychological law'. His notes for a 'Critique of the Hegelian State' were never completed because the simple application of Feuerbach's reductive materialist 'invertive method' was not sufficient. The 'Contribution to the Critique of Hegel's *Philosophy of Right*' was more nuanced. The critique of religion is to be completed by an 'irreligious' critique whose foundation is that 'Man makes religion . . . '. This genetic activity is not psychological; man is not a 'being squatting outside the world', he is 'the world of man'. This completes the first systematic requirement by explaining receptivity; the human world is open to human action. Marx then elaborates the genetic argument to explain the necessity of this possible action within the human world. The 'world of man' is an inverted world which produces the 'inverted consciousness' of religion. Religion, however, is not only an opiate, but also a 'protest against actual suffering'. This active character provides the genetic completion of the argument which the 'psychological law' could only suggest.

The result of Marx's second strategy is the thematisation of the revolutionary proletariat at the conclusion of 'Towards a Critique . . .'. Marx's argument can be interpreted by the framework of genesis and normativity. Marx asks whether 'theoretical needs will become immediate practical needs?' He replies that 'it is not sufficient that thought should seek its actualisation; actuality must itself strive toward thought'. This theory of the receptivity of the world to the normative demands of philosophy is elaborated by the emergence of 'radical needs'. The genetic component then returns. The proletariat is that particular which can and must make universal claims; it is the nothing that can become everything, a praxis with theoretical consequences. Marx's argument is familiar, logical, and rhetorically satisfying. Two difficulties recognised at the conclusion of Marx's own demonstration point to the further development of his theory. They point as well to contemporary difficulties. (1) Marx speaks of the formation (*Bildung*, implying education and not simple material causality) of a proletariat, which he says is an artificial (*künstlich*) process. This distinguishes the proletariat from any naturally given agent (such as the poor who 'are always with ye', or women, races . . .). It poses the contemporary problem of the 'revolutionary subject'. (2) When he asks how the structural possibilities which define the proletarian position will be actualised, Marx has recourse to the metaphor of the 'lightning of thought' (*Blitz des Gedankens*). This has come to imply 'class consciousness'. Little more precise has been said about its nature and source since Marx's metaphorical expectation!

The *1844 Manuscripts* can be read as the unity of the two strategies and the attempt to solve the twin difficulties in actualising the revolutionary proletariat. (1) The first Manuscript accounts for the formation of the proletariat by means of lengthy citations from the classical political economists. This is a normative economic presentation of the logic of receptivity; it is completed by the theory of alienated labour which provides a normative explanation of the class consciousness which would explain the genetic action which completes the systematic circle.[3] The implication of this first strategy is that Marx has not fully abandoned the temptation to derive genesis from normativity. The *Poverty of Philosophy* and the structural crisis-theory (*Zusammenbruchstheorie*) of *Capital* can be understood as the development of this orientation within Marx's later work. (2) The genetic concern with class consciousness is elaborated in the third Manuscript. Marx develops the implications of 'the greatness of Hegel's *Phenomenology*' in his theory of objectivation through labour. This process leads to 'a completed humanism = naturalism and a completed naturalism = humanism'. The movement toward communism shows how the senses 'in their praxis' become 'theoricians'. Its result is that 'the eye has become a human eye, just as its object has become a social, human object derived from and for man'. The result of the genetic process of labour is thus shown to have normative consequences. This second orientation is elaborated in *The German Ideology*, and in those aspects of *Capital* (such as the transition from absolute to relative surplus-value) where class struggle is the crucial factor.

Sometimes Marx appears to combine the two orientations, as for example in the first part of the *Communist Manifesto* where the logic of capitalism is not presented simply as structural and objective but also as practical and subjective insofar as the object described is the unification and development of the consciousness of the proletariat as the subject object of history. Such unifications appear more frequently in the historical writings, expressing what Merleau-Ponty called that '*sublime point* where reality and values, the subject and the object, judgement and discipline, the individual and the totality, the present and the future, rather than colliding came gradually to work subtly together'.[4] These unifying moments recall Kant's attempt to bridge his dualism by the introduction of a 'natural genius' which creates 'lawfulness without law' by an action defined as 'purposefulness without purpose'. The Marxist would denounce this conceptual trick as 'ideology'. That accusation permits a further development of the structure of modernity. Its insufficiency makes clear that Marx's difficulties arose from his awareness of the demands of a modern philosophy.

## 3. MODERN PHILOSOPHY AND IDEOLOGY

The concept of ideology and its critique are often introduced in order to avoid the difficulties entailed by the two strategies which appear to present 'two Marxes'. The critique of ideology is perhaps too familiar. It seems to be based on the applications of the notion of 'false consciousness' developed on the model of the Feuerbachian critique of religion (if not in the simple reductionism of the Enlightenment *philosophes*). This procedure can be criticised doubly. Religion is pre-modern; it expresses a relation of externality between ideas and their material foundation, as Claude Lefort has shown convincingly, Marx does not *apply* the critique of ideology. He does not stand outside the world, pretending to know the structures of the really real, and to enlighten the cave-dwellers about their judgemental errors. Marx's discovery, as Lefort insists, is that capitalism *itself* is structured ideologically. This is the true sense of the Marxian notion of 'critique'. It will permit us to see more clearly why economic capitalism could become a paradigm of modernity.[5]

Two complementary illustrations of the material reality of modern capitalist ideology illustrate the normative and the genetic strategies. (1) Marx describes the formal structure of capitalism in the formula M-C-M′: money is invested in commodities whose combination in turn produces the return of more money. The labour theory of value is the genetic component of this structure. A peculiarity within the normative formula itself is more important. The process continually produces difference, inequality, the new. The constant production of novelty is necessary for the process of capitalist reproduction. At the same time, the novelty must always and again be reduced to identity, sameness, repetition. Capitalism is (in one word) the-continual-production-and-reduction-of-the-new, the unequal, the different. Crises are moments when the reduction to sameness cannot be achieved. Since capitalism has destroyed all traditional forms of life, it can only legitimate itself immanently. Either the gentle process of the production and satisfaction of needs or the normative logic of free and equal contractual exchange can be invoked. This situation becomes an active crisis only when a genetic component is added. The labour theory of value, which in this model provides that genetic moment, is not sufficient to explain a political intervention that would actualize and overcome the latent crisis. (2) The genetic structure is inversely analogous to the normative picture. The worker is 'freed' from tradition and from ownership of his own means of production. He is a commodity whose value is determined on the objective free market. Formally free, the worker is really dependent. Yet, although he is a commodity, he knows full well that his value is determined in a struggle with the capitalist (for higher wages or better work conditions, against speed-ups, etc.). Thus, the worker has daily experience of the contradiction of personal freedom and social dependence. This experience is ramified in the production process itself. The worker enters the factory as an individual, works as a member of a collective, and returns from work as an individual. He experiences the social nature of the capitalist production process. He knows that inequality has no objective or personal basis to justify its existence. Further, the continual application of science to the productive technology shows the worker that the difference among products is only a remake of the old in new wrappings. The worker can share the knowledge of possible technical advances because he is not caught up in the competitive imperatives of capitalist survival. His place in the hierarchy does not depend on political legitimation or wealth inherited from elsewhere. The worker can thus look soberly at reality, uniting with comrades while the capitalists compete with one another and hide reality from themselves. This genetic potential, like the possibility demonstrated by the normative logic of capitalism, needs its complement to become an actual political movement that can overcome the latent crisis.

Ideology is produced only in modern societies (of which capitalism is only one of the possible forms). Ideology is the constantly renewed attempt to unify the process in which the new is necessarily and continually produced. Ideology can take three structural forms: (a) the primacy of the genetic determines the normative; (b) the normative is treated as an essence of which the genetic is simply a mode of appearance; (c) the difference between the two is denied by an identity-logic whose forms were discovered and criticised in the Marxist tradition from Lukács to the Frankfurt School. Ideological illusion is not found only within the 'ruling class' or its politicians. Insofar as capitalism is defined by the formula M-C-M′, the profit (designated by M′) characterises the ideological nature of this mode of production. The new (i.e., the commodity produced) is reduced to the homogeneous monetary form from which the process began. The revolutionary who wants only to abolish the old relations of property, to give labour freedom and dignity, commits also an ideological error. The goal is not to redistribute what already exists; that would not be the negation but the affirmation of the primacy of the economic which defines our modernity as capitalist.

The structure of ideology explains the constant reappearance on the left of debates between reform and revolution. From the genetic point of view, a reformist tactic is legitimated by the premise of an immature proletariat whose political education can take place only through experience. Yet Rosa Luxemburg – hardly a reformist! – argues on the same genetic basis that only active democratic participation in direct struggles can bring about that political education. Lenin counters this position from the normative point of view. He claims that in its immediate struggles the proletariat can develop only a trade-unionist consciousness; it needs the help of the party and its normative theory to become a revolutionary agent. But that putative normative certainty incarnate in the party is separated from the empirical everyday world. In the hands of Kautsky, it can become the justification of a conservatism within the party and the society it rules. The hope of uniting the two poles of modern ideology thus motivates the different political practices which claim to derive their legitimation from Marx. The common character of these positions is clear in the third ideological *Gestalt*. Each attempts to eliminate the heteronomy suggested by the other pole; genesis claims to function normatively, normative logic attempts to explain the necessity of generative practice. The immanence of modern ideology condemns any position which gives priority to a unity that claims to explain difference. The modern structure inverts the classical form: difference is the foundation of unity.

Two political conclusions follow from the concept of modern ideology. (1) The Marxist politics which attempts to avoid contradiction seeks to do exactly what the capitalist attempts in vain. However different their rhetoric, both seek to put an end to history as qualitatively new. This Marxist politics does not understand the implications of the notion of ideology as capitalist reality. This assertion is valid also for the position which begins from the proletariat as the unity of genesis and validity. The glorification of labour is, after all, coterminous with the ethic of capitalism. Marxist and capitalist reduce modernity to the economic logic of civil society. (2a) The theoretical justification of this politics can be itself explained by the structure of ideology. Theory can understand itself as genetic or as normative. As normative it claims to present the truth *about* things; this truth is to be put in the service of revolution. Empirical sociological studies can claim to 'serve' the revolution when parties use their results tactically. This presupposes that the parties know the correct strategic direction. But this separation of the truth about things from the things themselves repeats the ideological paradigm. The normative truth about things applied by this type of theory *for* revolution is necessarily inadequate to the contradictory ideological structure of modernity. (2b) The other option is to treat theory as genetic. Marx's notion of his theory as a theory *of* the proletariat is the best illustration. Its difficulty is apparent when the second part of the *Communist Manifesto* explains the role of the communist. He claims to represent the interests of the proletariat 'as a whole' because he understands 'the line of march, the conditions and the ultimate general results of the proletarian movement'. The result is a metaphysics of History which does away with the particularity of proletarian conditions. Genesis has determined a normative necessity which is separated from the proletarian actors and incarnated in the communist (party).

## 4. 'IF KANT WERE A MARXIST . . .'

The Marxist thinks according to an economic, not a political logic. He imagines an actor, and asks himself how that actor *produces* a society and a history. Of course, he supposes that this production takes place within specific limits defined by the given physical and social conditions. But the fact that these limits and conditions are produced by men implies that these same men are capable of understanding and, eventually, changing them. Such a theory is genetic in its orientation toward history; but it is transformed, without admitting it, into a normative approach. The history that has been produced becomes the measure of a history that is being made. It becomes that knowledge which justifies the *hybris* of Marx's communist who becomes the bureaucrat of History applauding his own speech at the Party Congress because, after all, he is merely the accidental organ through which reality expresses its truth. But the grounds of the development by which the Marxist becomes a totalitarian are not found simply in the ideological *Gestalten* that express the paradoxical structure of modernity. A further philosophical ingredient is necessary. The 'Marxist Kant' makes clear that additional step by revealing *the constitutive temptation*.

The Marxist Kant was presented for the first time in Lukács' *History and Class Consciousness*.[6] Lukács claims that Kant's dualism reproduces the actual dilemmas of the bourgeois subject. This subject is monological; it is unable to know anything but appearances; and it is troubled by a moral will which can be sure only of its intentions, not of its results. This subject is portrayed as attempting to bridge the dualism which is presented positively in the Transcendental Analytic of the first *Critique*. The Third Antinomy of the Transcendental Dialectic illustrates the difficulties of Kant's solution. Free will and determinism appear to contradict one another; Kant's demonstration of their non-contradiction is not sufficient because it shows only the possibility, not the necessity of moral action. The *Foundations of the Metaphysics of Morals* develops the three forms of the categorical imperative as the basis of Kant's ethics. But Kant's argument there presupposes the existence of the free will. Recognising the difficulty, the *Critique of Practical Reason* attempts to found the free will through the Postulates of Practical Reason. The existence of God, Freedom and Immortality are supposed to guarantee that the will knows that its intention can in fact be realised. This certainty makes necessary the merely possible morality of the Third Antinomy and of the *Foundations*. These Postulates are, however, only postulates. Kant adds a further argument in the *Critique of Judgement*. The Genius who produces disinterestedly a purposeless purposefulness and a lawfulness without law is combined with the Happy Chance (*glücklicher Zufall*) that gives Nature a teleological structure. This intuition produced a flourishing post-Kantian philosophical industry headed by Schelling. It is hardly satisfactory systematically. A 'fourth *Critique*' seems necessary to solve the problem of Kantian (or bourgeois) dualism. Its possibility is suggested by Kant's historical writings.

Kant's historical essays articulate concretely the dualism which was the premise of his philosophical system. The short text, 'What is Enlightenment?' presents only a formal answer. The 'enlightened' consciousness whose development Kant portrays is autonomous but empty of content. It is incapable of education (*Bildung*). 'The Idea of Universal History from a Cosmopolitan Point of View', attempts to give a concrete content to this formally autonomous consciousness. In the process, the movement beyond the monological subject begins. Kant's fourth Thesis suggests that 'The means used by nature in order to bring all human capacities to full development is the *antagonism* of men in society'. Kant introduces here the concept of human nature as 'unsocial sociability'. The fifth Thesis goes a step further in giving social form to this antinomic structure. 'The greatest problem for the human species, to whose solution nature forces him, is the achievement (*Erreichung*) of a *civil society* under law.' Kant poses immediately the classical question which today has become identified with Marx's 'Theses on Feuerbach': 'Man is an animal which, when it lives among others of its species, needs a master . . . But where is he to find this master?' The seventh Thesis avoids the question by turning to relations among states as central to the formation of the lawful civil society. This is a genetic development of the notion of 'unsocial sociability' from the fourth Thesis. Kant appears to reason in terms of a social learning through crisis; the costs of war will bring men to recognise the need to regulate lawfully their relations. But Kant does not follow through the implications of this genetic argument. His eighth Thesis adds a postulated normative complement in the form of a natural teleology which is to justify the 'hope' that nature's goals will indeed be realised. Since such a hope is not realisable without praxis, Kant concludes with a ninth Thesis which (anachronistically) recalls Marx. A 'philosophical attempt' of the kind he has proposed is seen as 'contributing to this end of Nature'.

'Cosmopolitan History' brings together the genetic and the normative orientations only syncretically; the 'philosophical attempt' has no real institutional place. The dualism remains in the form of a teleological Nature which coexists with the 'crooked wood' of unsociably social humans. These humans are only apparently part of the natural teleology. The ideological structure of modernity is repeated in the illusory unity whose poles are in fact external to each other. At times, genetic human action explains the normative natural teleology; at others, the normative teleology founds the postulated 'hope' that genetic action will succeed. The mediation is unsuccessful because one or the other moment is treated as *constituting* a unitary structure. This constitutive orientation is another attempt to escape from the dilemmas of modernity which falls into the ideological distortion. It can function normatively, as an essentialism which treats history as a natural teleology overdetermining particular acts. It can also function genetically, as in the phenomenological labour of *The German Ideology*. It is inadequate because it is a premodern structure in which externality replaces the immanent self-critical structure of the modern. Kant himself goes beyond it after 1784.

## 5. '. . . HE WOULD NOT HAVE WRITTEN THE *CRITIQUE OF JUDGEMENT*'

The interpretation of Kant as the philosopher of modernity has textual justification. The first edition of the *Critique of Pure Reason* insists that Kant's era is 'the particular epoch of critique to which all must be subjected'. The second edition adds the need to struggle against every 'dogmatism which pretends to philosophize without first undertaking a critique of its own capacities'. These are only external signs, which could be multiplied. More important is an ambiguity in the title of the critical project itself. What is meant by the genetive 'of' in the title of the *Critiques*? Who does the critique? on whom? on what? From what grounds? Is it the supposed purity that is questioned? Is it its rationality that is doubted? Or, conversely, is pure reason the subject or actor of the critique? In this case, whence comes the object that it criticised? What is its nature? Why does it call for a critique?

These questions are unanswerable from a modern perspective. Neither reason nor its object can be presupposed as a given. Subject and object emerge together (as with the young Marx's philosophy and world). They are not identical with one another. The question of their interrelation appears explicitly only in the *Critique of Judgement*. Its Introduction insists on the systematic place and role of this third *Critique*. Kant begins from 'the divisions of philosophy' and from the 'domains of Philosophy in general'. He describes his work as 'a mediator (*Verbindungsmittel*) of the two parts of philosophy into a whole'. After considering the results of the first two *Critiques*, he concludes with the proposal for the 'unification of the legislation of the Understanding [i.e. of the first *Critique*] and that of Reason [i.e., of the second *Critique*] through the faculty of judgement. The object of the *Critique of Judgement* is also its subject. In this sense, the work is explicitly modern.

The systematic content of the *Critique of Judgement* suggests an interpretation of the antinomic unity of the Kantian project as a whole. The Table of Contents shows already its difference from the other Kantian *Critiques*. The co-presence of an Analytic of the Beautiful and an Analytic of the Sublime corresponds to the co-presence of a critique of aesthetic judgement with the judgement of teleology in nature. The normative natural teleology which functioned constitutively in the 'Marxist' Kant's theory of 'Cosmopolitan History' is given a new status. The function of nature within the account of the sublime suggests that the genetic role assumed by judgement differs from the normative rational imperatives that motivate moral action. This structural peculiarity is given further weight by a comment in the Preface. Kant announces that this book marks the 'end of my entire critical business (*Geschäft*). I will now immediately pass on to the doctrinal'. Kant does not explain what he means by the 'doctrinal'. He speaks of a metaphysics of nature and another of morals (*Sitten*). The 1797 completion of the latter does not make use of the new concept. It could be suspected that, parallel to the transformed status of 'nature' in the third *Critique*, the new 'doctrinal' philosophy will provide a new interpretation of the 'unsocial sociability' that was so crucial to the 'Marxist' Kant.

The systematic Marxian Kant helps to interpret the systematic structure of the *Critique of Judgement*. Its central conceptual innovation is the distinction between reflective and determinative (or subsumptive) judgement. Science and morality proceed according to the determinative judgement; a critically justified law proposes universally valid predicates under which any particular can be subsumed. 'Critique' is the method by which the validity of this universal predication is justified. This critique cannot exist in isolation; its categories cannot be imposed externally on an experienced world which has not been shown to be *receptive* to them. This is the addition which the third *Critique* makes to (the Transcendental Analytic of) the first.[7] The concerns of the young Marx clarify the place of the 'doctrinal' in the Kantian project. Kant must show *which* particulars call for the reflective judgement that moves from the particular to a universal which cannot be presupposed as valid. Determination of these particulars permits the transition to a political theory.

The need for a political complement to critical philosophy was apparent in the formalism of 'What is Enlightenment?' The abstract autonomous consciousness needed content; it had to be able to learn, grow, develop. Kant's rejection of any 'contract made to shut off further enlightenment' articulates this concern. A remark in *Religion within the Limits of Reason Alone* suggests the implications of Kant's new orientation. Kant comments that even if the necessity and the success of a revolution could be demonstrated scientifically and morally, that revolution would still not be justified. Its demonstrated necessity would be based on a determinative, subsumptive judgement whose results would entail the end of history and of enlightenment. This suggests that politics differs from morality because of the form of its judgements. The key to a theory of politics is the reflective judgement that proceeds from the particular to the universal. From this point of view, the *Critique of Judgement* constitutes a 'prolegomenon' to any modern politics.

The Analytic in the third *Critique* provides more than the formal structure of political argumentation. The first two moments of the Analytic of the Beautiful reproduce the co-presence of the genetic and the normative moments. Kant insists that reflective judgements proceed without interest in their object. Correlatively, they do not presuppose a universally valid concept or law. In this way, judgement is not legitimated by appeal to genetic interest; nor does conceptual universality guarantee its normative certitude. After these preliminaries, the third moment of the Analytic proposes a new move from the genetic orientation, while the fourth moment adds to it a normative component. The third moment postulates a 'lawfulness without law' or 'purposeless purposefulness' which unify the first two moments from the side of genesis. This unification functions differently from the proposal in the ninth Cosmopolitan Thesis. But Kant's Genius, like Schiller's concept of 'play' reify this unification ideologically. Its practical function in fact serves only to designate those particulars which call for reflective judgement. As he develops its implications, Kant says that this moment presents the 'exemplary' nature of the beautiful; he treats it as a 'symbol' of morality; and he analyses it as that 'culture' which permits humans to postulate goals which are more than natural.[8] Kant's fourth moment in the Analytic moves from the opposite direction in order to account for the normative receptivity to the reflective judgement. He begins from the need to postulate a 'common sense' that makes the subjective reflection of each individual communicable and acceptable to all. This common sense is described at first in quite physical terms. As the analysis continues, the accent turns toward its 'common' or shared character which is guaranteed by the imperative to 'think in the place of the other'. Finally, Kant argues that this common sense can only take the form of a 'communal' (*gemeinschaftlichen*) sense.

These elements of the theory of reflective judgement – to which must be added, for the sake of completeness, the account of natural teleology, which explains not only the particularity of the third moment but also avoids the temptation of a 'convivial' voluntarism – permit the construction of a Kantian political edifice. The political can be said to be the *doctrinal* complement to the critique within a systematic unity. The political serves to determine *which* particulars make necessary the reflective judgement; the critique serves to explain the receptivity of the world to the categories proposed by the doctrine. The systematic unity of doctrine and critique explains Kant's option for a republican politics. Kant's description of republican institutions is faithful to the imperatives of modernity. It suggests the political implications of the proposed 'Copernican Revolution' at the same time that it explains why the model of aesthetic judgement served to define the structures of modernity, as was suggested by the illustrations from modern art.

## 6. MODERN REPUBLICAN POLITICS

The systematic structure that I have attributed to Kant on the basis of the interpretation of the 'Marxist Kant' is present in the decisive essay on 'Perpetual Peace'.[9] This 'philosophical project' of 1796, which sums up Kant's political thinking, is apparently naïve, unsystematic, and confused. The 'Preliminary Articles' are neither consistently moral nor pragmatic. Their order is not logical, and their relation to the three 'Definitive Articles' is not explained. The Definitive Articles are of such generality as to discourage the practical politician. The text concludes with four supplements, of which a

'Secret Article' (added to the second edition) guarantees the place of the philosopher. These supplementary materials provide the negative demonstration – or 'deconstruction' – of the systematic place of the essay. They repeat, in a non-explicit irony, the path that took the 'Marxist' Kant through the *Critiques* toward the discovery of history. The final supplement suggests the systematic structure of the whole. Kant presents there first a 'critical' theory of what he calls the 'transcendental concept of public right'. Its formulation is negative: 'All actions relating to the right of other men whose maxim is not compatible with publicity are unjust.' This analytical argument is then joined by a 'dialectical' remark which points out that a powerful Prince could let his injustices be known without danger. This comment ends the 'critical' phase of the argument. Kant concludes with a 'doctrinal' proposal: 'All maxims which need publicity (in order not to fail to achieve their goal) agree with right and politics together.' This relation of the critical and doctrinal philosophical moments can be spelled out institutionally in the republican form.

Politics is the art – the *mise en scène* or representation – that presents that particularity which makes necessary a public, reflective judgement. The first consequence of this broad definition is negative. Technocratic-bureaucratic procedures which function by predicative subsumption are antipolitical. A second negative implication needs to be underlined in our post-modern epoch. Not all particulars lend themselves to this form of judgement. Not all God's creation is beautiful! Not every issue belongs to the political arena. The institutional stage of political particularity is the Republic. It is the 'doctrinal' complement to the critical system which shapes the framework that permits the transformation of 'unsocial sociability' from a natural postulate to a communal achievement.

Kant's Republic is opposed explicitly to what he calls 'democracy'. His reasoning parallels the forms of ideology derived from the Marxist account of modern capitalism. As a form of sovereignty, the democratic polity provides normative legitimation of the type 'my country right or wrong'. As a form of self-government, democratic decisions are the basis of a genetic proceduralist legitimation which is a threat to minority interests (such as those of the philosopher, whose place 'Perpetual Peace' explicitly guaranteed). In the form of a small-scale self-managing utopia, democracy unites the genetic and the normative in a unity which implies the end of history. Each of these *Gestalten* is defined by the attempt to put an end to the political.

Such a politics is paradoxical. The republican alternative does not advocate the return to a pre-modern aristocratic formation based on an ideal of civic virtue and self-denying individuality. A modern republican 'civil religion' would articulate the communal sense whose contribution to reflective judgement gives it its historical form. The modern republican institutional frame serves the 'doctrinal' purpose of defining (and delimiting) the objects of political action, providing the guarantee of minority rights that pure democracy can endanger.[10]

The process of representation is the foundation of republican politics. Its philosophical structure is defined by the modern imperative of immanence, and by the centrality of reflective judgement in politics. One contemporary interpretation distinguishes needs from interests.[11] Needs cannot be represented; interests can. This suggests the goal of replacing the politics of (capitalist and economic) interest by the attempt to realise directly (radical and human) needs. The difficulty is that a modern politics cannot assume the existence of needs prior to the process of their representation. This is why Kant's republican politics of representation excludes any 'contract made to shut off further enlightenment'. The republic is explicitly and necessarily historical; the lack of fixed or traditional forms of need makes politics not only possible but necessary. Representative politics does not exclude democratic participation. It succeeds precisely when the particularities it articulates make necessary a *communal* process of reflective judgement. Conversely, the theory which is the inverse identical to the refusal to represent radical needs fails for the same structural reason. It conceives of the state as a 'court' which judges among the competing interests represented before it. This violates the modern imperative of immanence because it can only treat political judgement as subsumptive. As opposed to this perspective, the institutional basis of republican politics is not fixed; its Constitution defines basic rights which cannot be violated without, however, precluding the expansion of these rights. The only requirement philosophy imposes on this structure is that it contain the possibility of its own revision; modernity takes care of the necessity that actualises this possibility.

This republican conception of politics has to be able to defend itself against the Marxist accusation that its formal structures provide the framework within which the capitalist economy can flourish. The 'Copernican Revolution' suggests that both the republic and the capitalist civil society are forms of the basic structure of modernity. This does not explain why the capitalist form has been dominant.

Although it was not his question, Kant's concern with the problem of a revolution which would institute the republic suggests the direction in which an answer might be proposed. The seventh Cosmopolitan Thesis proposed that a 'civil society under law', a republic, would result from international relations among states. The citizens would learn from the relation of their state to others what kind of domestic relations were desirable. Kant's intuition was concretised in an essay by Otto Hintze on the 'origins of the representative constitution'.[12] The relations among the Italian states of the Renaissance, at a time when world empire was no longer possible, made it necessary for each state to be represented to the others by ambassadors. These states did not give up the idea of growth or change. Their representative relations acquired new spatial and temporal possibilities. This led to a new conception of representation, which could be transformed in domestic relations among competing groups.

World politics today suggests a similar structure to the one intuited by Kant. The relations among states, and the 'war' which was to lead Kant's individuals to form a liberal social contract can be compared. The difference is that in relations among modern states individuals are involved in both relations, whereas the simple relations of individuals amongst themselves grounded the social contract. The implication is that interstate relations form a 'republican' or 'doctrinal' framework that determines which particulars are in fact capable of, and in need of, political representation. This determination is not one-sided. The relation of a state to the international environment has the same immanent, modern structure as did the relation of civil society and the state in the classical model of liberal society. The two poles stand in a (*reversible*) relation of genesis and normativity. The danger, in both cases, is the separation of the one or the other moment. This second implication of the 'Copernican Revolution' should not be confused with the kind of neo-Marxism (Wallerstein) which treats the 'world economy' as the basic unit of analysis of which domestic politics can be only the dependent variable. The 'republican' relation among state defines a political, not an economic, structure.

## 7. THE RETURN OF THE POLITICAL

The move from Marx to Kant does not assume that Kant provides the answers that some still try to squeeze from Marx. The 'Copernican Revolution' reformulates the questions that animate contemporary radical politics. It suggests reading Marx from the point of view of the problem of modernity, of which capitalist civil society is simply one possible manifestation. Kant proves a more adequate guide to that structure because his problem, the formation of a 'civil society under law', became for Marx the source of a solution. Insofar as the capitalist form of civil society has entered a period of crisis, Marx's optimism cannot be accepted. Kant's problem returns. If the goal were to 'save' Marx, the means would have to be Kantian. But philosophy confronts its own internal limit here. The emergence of capitalist civil society cannot be explained simply by the structure of modernity. Capitalist civil society is the attempted answer to a properly *political* problem, defined generally by the concept of Enlightened Despotism.[13] That term, which would have surprised Kant without being foreign to his 'Marxist' interpretation, defines a tension articulated across the genetic and the normative moments of modernity. Capitalist civil society attempts to defuse the political tension embodied in that institutional form. Its crisis returns the political problem to the agenda.

The return of the political is not the kind of historicist 'solution' against which Hannah Arendt cautioned. The political was present all along; the economic is but one of its forms. It returns now in its own name. Philosophical reflection is necessary for its articulation. Conversely, its presence makes philosophy a modern necessity. Modern philsophy is inevitably political; modern politics is inevitably philosophical. The poles are united by that fundamental tension which defines modernity. Politics today can lead only to the kind of philosophical reflection typified by the 'Copernican Revolution' and concluding with new questions. Philosophy today cannot neglect the question of its realisation which animated the young Marx. The danger would be to treat either of these necessary modern adventures as simply ideological.

**Notes**

1. I am borrowing the following example from Robert Rosenberg, *Modern Painting and The Northern Romantic Tradition* (New York: Harper and

Row, 1975). The relation between modern art and Marx's theory is suggested by Harold Rosenberg. Cf, for example, 'Set Out for Clayton', in *The De-Definition of Art* (New York: Horizon Press, 1972), and 'The Resurrected Romans', in *The Tradition of the New* (New York: McGraw Hill, 1965), as well as 'The Politics of Illusion', in *Discovering the Present* (Chicago: University of Chicago Press, 1973). (Rosenberg's works are being republished by the University of Chicago Press.) Another approach is suggested by Marshall Berman, 'All that is solid melts into air', in *25 Years of Dissent* (New York: Methuen, 1979). The argument proposed here is developed also in my 'The Politics of Modernism', in *Philosophy and Social Criticism*, vol. 8, no. 4, 1981, pp. 361–86. Reprinted in *The Politics of Critique*.

2. I will be suggesting a somewhat idiosyncratic reading of Kant, justified in more detail in my *From Marx to Kant* (Albany: SUNY Press, 1985). The more typical view is the one suggested below under the sub-head, 'If Kant were a Marxist . . .'. That is the Kant criticised by Hannah Arendt in an otherwise cogent argument which concludes that 'each time the modern age has had reason to hope for a new political philosophy, it received a philosophy of history instead', *The Human Condition* (Chicago: University of Chicago Press, 1958), p. 298n. The Kant who wrote the third *Critique* presents the materials for the 'new political philosophy' sought by Arendt. But this does not mean that the third *Critique* is itself to be read politically, or as politics.
3. The mostly lost second Manuscript suggested a similar normative strategy to explain the genetic action by the proletariat. It offers an economic argument which demonstrates the 'necessary' collision of capital and labour.
4. *Les aventures de la dialectique* (Paris: Gallimard, 1955), p. 12.
5. Lefort's argument is developed in 'Marx: D'une vision de l'histoire à l'autre', and in 'Esquisse d'une genèse de l'idéologie dans les sociétés modernes', in *Les Formes de l'histoire* (Paris: Gallimard, 1978). The relation of Lefort's analysis of modernity and the Frankfurt School's notion of 'immanent critique' needs to be developed, particularly with regard to Habermas' reformulation in his *Theorie des kommunikativen Handelns* (Frankfurt: Suhrkamp, 1982). The crucial point turns around the ability of each approach to move beyond social analysis to political theory. (Cf. the Afterword to the second edition of *The Marxian Legacy* on this point.)
6. The Second International had tried to assimilate Kant to Marx, but its results were always syncretic. Kant was treated as an ethical thinker; Marx was the scientific sociologist. The unity of Kant and Marx was defined by the relation of the first to the second *Critique*. What *that* relation in fact was remained unexamined until Lukács. A representative selection of the Second International positions is found in Sandküler and De la Vega, *Marxismus und Ethik* (Frankfurt: Suhrkamp, 1970). For a discussion, see my 'Kant's Political Theory: The Virtue of his Vices', in *Review of Metaphysics*, 34 (December 1980), reprinted in *The Politics of Critique*.
7. The details of this argument were first presented by George Schrader,

'The Status of Teleological Judgement in the Critical Philosophy', *Kantstudien*, 45, 1953–4, pp. 204–55. I have elaborated them in *From Marx to Kant*.

8. Marx's radically needy proletariat is also a particular that can make universal claims. Marx's error is to treat these claims as scientific, determinative rather than reflective judgements. I will return to this problem in a moment.
9. I can only sketch here what is argued in detail in *From Marx to Kant*, and in 'Kant's System and (its) Politics', in *Man and World* 18: 1985, pp. 79–98, reprinted in *The Politics of Critique*.
10. The republican form proposed by Kant introduces a curious distinction between the functions of executive and legislature that needs explication. Kant's structures show remarkable parallels to the institutional reforms proposed by the revolutionary Abbé Sièyes, The function of the executive is to present to the legislative body those materials with which it is to deal. In Kantian terms, the legislative function is 'critical'; it functions by subsuming under universal forms the particulars which the executive judges reflectively. This executive is not a bureaucracy – although Napoleon's deformation of Sièyes' proposals under the Tribunat could lead to the domination by the Emperor! A modern formulation of this structure would argue that politics is the competition for the *mise en scène* of particular relations which demand to be represented. Politics in this sense can have a *democratic form* within the republican structure.
11. The best discussion of these arguments remains Jean L. Cohen's review of Agnes Heller's *The Theory of Need in Marx*, which was published in *Telos*, 33, Fall 1977, pp. 170–85.
12. *Weltgeschichtliche Bedingungen der Repräsentativverfassung* (1931), in Otto Hintze, *Gesammelte Abhandlungen zur allgemeinen Verfassungsgeschichte* (Göttingen: Vandenhoeck & Ruprecht, 1962).
13. In addition to the essay in this volume on Enlightened Despotism, cf. 'The Origin of Revolution', in *Journal of the British Society for Phenomenology*, vol. 14, no. 1, January 1983, reprinted in *The Politics of Critique*.

# 5 Another Resurrection of Marxism

Marxism is dead. The word has penetrated even the ivy walls. And yet, Marxism is thriving in that same academy. It survives in a traditionalist and in a 'post-modern' guise. The traditionalists live by the adage: 'The King is dead; long live the King.' The mortal body has decayed, but the spirit must be preserved and a new body found. The practice of university Marxism is theory; it is the guardian of the spirit waiting for the new incarnation of the revolution. Marx, who built his revolutionary theory from a critique of Hegel, would be horrified; so are the iconoclasts of post-modernism. Against the universities' political idealism, the Nietzschean spirit rejoices in the death of another god. Deconstructionist philosophy fancies itself a new practice, breaking idols as it joyfully undermines the inherited prejudices of Western metaphysics. But it too, in its own coquettish fashion, makes theory a political practice. Deconstruction fits well the needs of those ensconced in the universities. It is hard to imagine Nietzsche happier with his heirs than Marx would be with the traditionalist Marxists. Post-modernism may be many things, but to call it a politics is to play with paradox. Deconstruction destroys the purity of the philosophical subject and the reality of its object. How, then, can it make positive proposals? At best, it preaches resistance to all forms of domination. Is that politics?

It is easy to make fun of the traditionalism of the university Marxists and to scoff at the antics of the deconstructionists. It would be easy, too, to pick on Laclau and Mouffe's attempt to be at once *post*-Marxist and post-*Marxist.** The traditionalist Marxists ignore the real world in order to preserve and perfect their theory of it; the deconstructionist postmoderns revel in the resistance to a theory whose theoretical impossibility their own theory purports to demonstrate. The bemused spectator, like Hegel's phenomenological on-looker, can let them hang themselves on their inner contradictions. The political philosopher has a different attitude. The post-*Marxist* wonders whether deconstruction is not able to destroy finally the idealism of theory; the *post*-Marxist wants to know what political sense can be drawn from deconstruction in the context of what some call postmodern or postindustrial societies. *Hegemony and Socialist*

*Strategy* has the virtue of explaining the radical temptation of deconstruction by situating that project within the historical learning process of Marxism. This first half of the book is complemented by an account of the basic theoretical moves of deconstruction as illustrated by its application to the problems historical Marxism could not solve. This is provocative. The conclusions to which it leads, suggested by the book's subtitle, 'Towards a Radical Democratic Politics', are frustrating. The difficulty, it seems, is that even here, Marxism is not dead; its spirit remains to blind radical politics to the political history in which it lives and which makes it possible.

## 1. FROM MARXISM TO DECONSTRUCTION

Rosa Luxemburg is the crucial figure for any reconstruction of a non-dogmatic Marxism. She lived the contradiction of Marxism while trying constantly to bring her practice into line with the orthodoxy of Marxist theory and her party's practice.[1] Luxemburg drew from her experience of the 1905 Russian revolution a theory of the 'mass strike' in order to bring together the economic underpinnings of Marxism with the political struggle necessary for the realisation of the potential which the economy generates. For Luxemburg, the mass strike *is* the unity of the revolutionary class, which constantly escapes the strait-jacket of the party or trade unions. But what *is* such a conceptual unity? Anticipating, Luxemburg's insight can be reformulated in deconstructionist concepts: the class is 'overdetermined'; its unity is not literal but symbolic. For Marxist socialists, the problem remains: what makes this overdetermined, symbolic unity a real 'class' structure? In what sense is it revolutionary?

Luxemburg started from diversity to seek unity; her Marxist critics like Kautsky begin from the assumption of unity to explain (away) diversity. They suppose, for example, that the middle classes and peasantry will be reduced to proletarian status. Theory in this context is merely the description of the experience of the proletariat as it becomes gradually adequate to its theoretical essence. Theory describes a paradigm from which temporary deviations are mere accidents. With the end of the economic depression of the early 1890s, this optimism could not be maintained. The nature of Marxist theory had to be reconceptualised in order to save its practical project. Theory and practice were separated in fact; a new sense of theory had to be invented to reunite them.

The formation of a Marxist orthodoxy was one response to the crisis of the pristine Marxism represented by the early Kautsky. No longer the descriptive systematisation of observable tendencies, theory now had to guarantee 'that these tendencies will eventually coincide with the type of social articulation proposed by the Marxist paradigm' (19)[2]. Instead of describing the unfolding of a pregiven class essence, Marxism became a science formulating a future goal (the so-called *Endziel*) which serves politically to unify the diverse struggles and interests which cannot be reduced simply to deviations from the essential paradigm. This justifies the increased role of the party and its intellectuals in the Second International, best known today in Lenin's quite orthodox *What is to be Done?*. Three rhetorical strategies can be employed to preserve this theoretical orthodoxy: argument from appearance, from contingency, or from recognition. 'Appearance' is either artifice (nationalism conceals bourgeois interests) or the appearance of an essence (the liberal state is the necessary political form of capitalism). 'Contingency' argues that the phenomena which do not fit the teleological pattern are merely marginal. 'Recognition' permits the reduction of a complex situation to one that has been encountered previously. In each case, the concrete is reduced to the abstract, the visible to the invisible, the appearance to its essence. The role given to theory by this political orthodoxy is paradoxical: it is more necessary, since the gap between the present consciousness and the historical mission of the class is admitted; but it is based on a determination which makes it merely consciousness of a pregiven necessity.

The emergence of revisionism in this context is not simply the thematisation of the reformist politics based on immediate class interest practised by the party. 'The autonomy of the political from the economic base,' argue Laclau and Mouffe, 'is the true novelty of Bernstein's argument' (30). Bernstein saw that the orthodox expectation that revolution will spring from one central opposition was refuted by the increasing complexity of modernising capitalism. Unification would not result from the homogeneous development of the infrastructure but from the party's political ability to submerge special under general interests in a *Volkspartei*. Within the framework of Marxism, the problem for political revisionism is the same as the one that confronted Luxemburg's mass strike: what makes this pluralist party a class unity? Bernstein's reply was based on a neo-Kantian dualism. He accepted the Marxist 'scientific' analysis of capitalism but attributed the socialist transformation to the intervention of an 'ethical will' which follows non-determinist paths as it learns from its participation in politics. This neo-Kantian Marxism thus unites practical reformism and theoretical revisionism: the reforms provide the evolutionary framework within which the ethical will of the worker and citizen evolve. But this 'solution' postulates a kind of transcendental subject in the form of an ethical humanity increasingly freed from economic necessity. Marxism can no more accept this transcendental postulate than can deconstruction.

The political problem confonted by the Second International can be reformulated as the theoretical demand to avoid the hypothesis of either the economic essence or a transcendental subject. This recalls the deconstructionist critique of 'Western metaphysics' in general. The Marxists were brought by their own experience to realise the weight of this critique. The Russian Marxists confronted a situation in which the bourgeoisie had not fulfilled its designated task within the orthodox narrative. Bourgeois domination was supposed to bring with it the democratic conditions in which the proletariat can organise itself politically. The Russian proletariat had to take upon itself a task which the teleology of History's progress assigned to another class. This disjunction between its empirical reality and its political role provides a first illustration of the practice of political hegemony. But the *concept* of hegemony, which gives to politics an independent role, was hidden because the Russians remained bound to orthodoxy. The historical logic of necessary stages of development meant that the autonomy of the state which was *de facto* assumed in the hegemonic practice could not be thematised. The identification of the class by its position in the infrastructure made it impossible to recognise the changes that its hegemonic practice meant to its own character. The result of this short circuit was Leninism.

Because it did not theorise the concept of hegemony, the Leninist tradition developed a politics of 'class alliance' which had contradictory and ultimately authoritarian implications. Politics was treated as if it were based on pregiven interests which were assumed to be knowable rationally and represented immediately in the action of the party. The communist militant was put in the paradoxical situation of leading a struggle for democratic liberties with which s/he could not identify and which were to be abolished in the 'higher forms of democracy'. Because the revolutionary proletariat cannot exist at the lower stage of development, the 'masses' were to be organised by leaders who incarnate the politics ordained by historical orthodoxy. Vanguardism and Lenin's replacement of political by military theory follow. The party's role is thus determined by theory; it is not based in real social relations. Its theory forbids it from integrating the real social interests it claims to represent in its class alliance. The Bolshevization of the International follows from this orthodoxy.

Different political results could emerge when Gramsci gave Lenin's hegemonic practice its proper theoretical form. The backward Italian South manifested parallels to the Russian situation. But Gramsci did not treat politics as taking place in a field of pre-given interests and pre-constituted actors defined by the logic of History. Without falling back into the scientism of Bernstein's Kantian dualism, he conceived class unity on the 'intellectual and moral' plane, creating a 'collective will' which must become the cement of an 'historical bloc'. Politics must articulate *new* social relations; it is not simply the representation of existing economic interests that are explained by the logic of History. Gramsci's stress on the material nature of ideology followed from this shift. Political actors are not to be defined economistically; they are a 'cultural-social' unity with a single aim based on a common world view. The elements united in action get their identity *only* from this political commonality in which their previous empirical identity is dissolved. This is why Gramsci insisted that the revolutionary class does not take state-power but rather becomes the state. Gramsci's 'war of position' differs from the Leninist military manoeuvres among pre-given forces; his politics is not a zero-sum game on a single, unified terrain of economic class struggle. Gramsci envisages the progressive disintegration of one civilisation while another is constructed within it around a new class core. This is the task which an hegemonic politics must assume.

Laclau and Mouffe stress that Gramsci is still caught within the framework of Marxism even though his politics implicitly goes beyond it. He tries to have it both ways. The political organisation of the hegemonic working class changes its nature; and yet Gramsci thinks that this political articulation is only possible because of its economic position. Marxism must be liberated from 'The Last Redoubt of Essentialism: the Economy'.[3] Once that is accomplished three conclusions lead toward a new theoretical politics. (1) All social identities are relational, and the system of relations is itself not fixed. This means (2) that class boundaries are constantly transformed. Because identities are relational, they are changed by their entry into political action. (3) Hegemony is not restricted to the actions of a privileged actor undertaking tasks which are not prescribed by its own role, as in the Leninist model. The first two arguments lead toward the deconstructionist theory; the third suggests a postmodern pluralist politics that results from the social practice of deconstructionist theory.

## 2. DECONSTRUCTION AS POLITICS

For the Marxist or the *post*-Marxist politician, the relational nature of social phenomena has to be given some sort of real identity. This cannot come from society; 'the social itself has no essence' (96). Its elements themselves do not have a literal identity; they are defined only by their relation to other elements. Identity comes from 'an *articulatory practice*' which must constantly fix differences in the face of the changing relations that constitute the social world. This articulation cannot be the action of a pre-existing subject, nor the product of real social relations. Such a structure is conceptualised by Foucault's notion of a 'discursive formation' as 'regulatory in dispersion' governed neither by reference to a common object, a common way of producing statements, or the constancy of concepts. The regularity itself is the unit of meaning whose analysis must be undertaken with adequate theoretical tools. This conceptual equipment is provided by structuralist linguistics. Structuralism provides a tempting tool-kit and model for social analysis. For example, Benveniste shows that although linguistic meaning is produced by the arbitrary oppositional relation among signs, language itself is not accidental. Its specific kind of necessity is not founded in an underlying intelligible principle but simply on the regularity of the relations among terms internal to the language which has meaning only through the relations it establishes. This linguistic necessity is not a determination because language can never be a complete system. If a discursive system were complete, articulation would be impossible; we could not generate new forms of *la parole* as opposed to the structural imperatives of *la langue*. There must always be something not fully immanent to the system. This 'something' calls for the articulatory practice which gives constantly new structure to the system.

The crucial assumption is that society can be conceptualised as a discursive formation like language. Its elements are defined only relationally. This definition cannot be exhaustive because society, like language, must be open. No identity can be fully constituted, fixed and permanent; 'literality is, in actual fact, the first of metaphors' (111). Every action fixes identities; but these are only temporary 'articulations'. This is why 'society' as such cannot be a valid object of discourse. Dialectics has to be reformulated. Political analysis is necessarily engaged with its object, whose temporary definition by politics changes the system as well. A closed system would fixate identity and end discourse; a fully dispersed system would have the same result because each object would be a fixed essence unrelated to, and thus unchangeable by, any other object with which it comes into contact. Political action, like discourse, is thus always only a partial limitation of the flow of meaning which constantly subverts any attempt to fix meaning. This sets a limit on any politics claiming to take its justification from the logic of History or the material laws of a social science. At the same time, this play of deferral means that there must be always present partial fixations without which the flow of differences and the reconstitution of relational identities would cease. The paradoxical imperative of the Marxist Second International can be reformulated by the structuralist: meanings must be fixed at the same time that their fixity is constantly undermined.

The hegemonic political practice which Lenin undertook and Gramsci sought to theorise is conceptualised by the linguistic notion of articulation. The relational nature of identities which constantly subverts any attempt to fix their meaning creates 'floating signifiers' which lend themselves to the constitution of new identities. The necessary presence of these floating signifiers explains why any discursive formation is 'overdetermined'. As with Luxemburg's mass strike, articulation fixes temporarily points of struggle, which become in their turn floating signifiers for new articulatory practices. The movement between the economic and the political class struggle is the result of the nature of society itself, once it is conceptualised as a discursive formation. Society *is* articulation; as such, it constantly subverts itself, releasing the floating signifiers which preset the possibility of new articulations. Articulation can – but need not – produce hegemonic practice. For example, the constitution of an 'historical bloc' for Gramsci is possible when the old civilisation loses its coherence, setting free elements which can be recombined in a new civilisation. This process is not based on material necessity. The temptation is to conceive of it as the result of action by a subject; but that concept has been deconstructed: the party is itself the result of relational elements that are united by a discourse. If deconstructionist politics is not to be simply arbitrary, this unifying discourse will have to be founded.

The political subject cannot be replaced by or founded on 'objective' contradictions whose resolution is imperative for the continued existence of society. That is only a functionalist variant of the old Marxism. Contradictions are only logical relations within a given totality. Like Gramsci's ideology, the discursive formation is a material reality. Logical contradiction becomes real 'antagonism' in social conditions where 'the presence of the "Other" prevents me from being totally myself' (125). This 'Other', like 'me', is itself relational; if it were fully external it would be indifferent to me, and I to it. This means that antagonism must be internal to the subject (or society). Antagonism 'constitutes the limits to every objectivity, which is revealed as partial and precarious *objectification*' (id.). Antagonism can be defined as a failure in the flow of difference, a disruption of language or of the flow of social relations. Because antagonism shows the limits of objectivity, it frees the participants from the illusion of permanence, making possible the hegemonic replacement – not overthrow! – of a social formation. Because it is internal to the subject (or society), antagonism does not depend on a telos or *Endziel* giving meaning to the self-subverting relational identity (or society). Antagonism replaces contradiction within the deconstructive Marxist arsenal.

This deconstructive social theory appears to cast its nets too wide for any real political practice. All is discourse; there are no subjects and no objects, only 'dispersive regularities'. How am 'I' to judge? Whence come the criteria for action? Two negative examples suggest the radical political potential of the reformulated concept of hegemony. Bureaucratic reorganisation of the social institutions of liberal capitalism according to criteria of efficiency is an articulatory practice like any other. It constitutes an organised system of differences where each function is defined by obligations and powers in relation to others. This articulation is *not* hegemonic because it does not confront antagonistic relations. Bureaucratising is simply the re-articulation of the already-given in a different framework. It does not occur (at least in the change from liberal-market to organised capitalism) in conditions that threaten the identity of the system as such. But antagonism alone does not guarantee hegemonic practice. A millenarian movement which is so radically exclusive that there are no 'floating signifiers' available for mobilisation is not hegemonic. The millenarian opposition is pre-given; the chains of equivalence among its elements do not structure a common *political space* within which the 'discourse' can continue to flow. Thus, the broad definition of 'discourse' is reformulated as a first imperative: politics takes place in, and most conserve, a common political space.

Deconstructionist politics must be democratic and pluralist. Gramsci's 'organic crisis' which weakens the relational system constituting social and political identities, creating floating elements, crises of identity and new antagonisms, is not an abstract formula. It describes the historical transition from a traditional to a modern democratic society. But Gramsci's Marxist stress on the economic subject was combined with the goal of reconstituting society around the traditional concept of 'the people'. Yet, his 'war of position' constitutes new and plural identities within a social space whose elements have lost their external fixity. The identities of the actors change in this 'war', as does that of the society itself. This is not a causal change; its discursive form is metonymical.[4] The politics described does not replace one ruling class by another; that would be 'metaphor', the replacing of one fixed identity by another. Metonymy can be said to operate in terms of a 'democratic' logic. Because no social identity is fully fixed, articulation must be renewed constantly. Power is constituted at 'nodal points' of partial fixation. Its concentration must be attacked; but the struggle against the historically specific nodal points of power is not the basis for a hegemonic politics. The goal is not the elimination of difference. Hegemony is the *articulation* of difference. Pluralism and democracy go together because the metonymical displacement can take place only when (temporary) differences make it possible. Systemic completeness is the opposite of the revolutionary result of hegemonic politics.

The description of hegemonic politics as pluralist and democratic only seems far from the Marxist programme that seeks to end relations of exploitation. Because exploitation is a relation, it is structured by a system of differences. Difference is simply a fact; it is an inherently temporary fixation of identity which is constantly subject to re-articulation in a new discourse. Politics is an articulation; radical politics is 'a type of action whose objective is the transformation of a social relation which constitutes a subject in a relation of subordination' (153). A changed political discourse fixes new subordinations, transforming previous ones into oppressive and (potentially) antagonistic relations. But the deconstructionist cannot attribute this new political articulation to the action of a real subject or the empirical result of changed objective conditions. The advent of modernity provides the deconstructionist with the explanation of the radical force of democratic politics. Modernity destroys the traditionalist society whose principle of identity was given by an external or transcendent signifier. The hierarchical order of accepted relations of subordination gives way to the 'democratic imaginary' founded on the principle of equality. Thus, Tocqueville's expectation of the constant displacement and extension of the demand for equality furnishes the basis for the democratic attack on exploitation.

The concept of a 'democratic imaginary' is introduced in order to provide a principle of political agency in a context from which subjective action and empirical social causality are excluded. The concept refers to the 'symbolic' form of unification of which Luxemburg's mass strike provided a model. Its political justification is provided negatively by the reconstruction of the Marxist dilemmas that led to the deconstructionist theoretical option. Its positive function is suggested by the fact that the central revolutionary demand through at least 1848 centred around democratic gains. Afterwards, emphasis moved to economic demands, then to the social claims for equality which produced finally the welfare state – and the contemporary dead-end of radical socialist thought. The reason for this shift is explained by the presence of a 'Jacobin imaginary' in socialist thought. This Jacobin heritage sought a unique point from which a rupture in the social fabric was to occur. The deconstructionist can predict the failure of the Jacobin socialist project because this image of political action is theoretically impossible. The assumption of a single foundation for revolution neglects the 'syntagmatic' extension of democratic demands to other relations of subordination. Radical democracy must be explicitly pluralist.

The contribution of the deconstructionist arsenal to the politics imposed by the democratic imaginary is suggested by the ambiguity of the project of the 'new social movements', and by the neo-conservative attempt to co-opt their claims.[5] Political philosophy is said to be a crucial element in 'shaping the common sense of the masses'. But why should these 'masses' listen? The deconstructionist philosopher cannot be a new political subject. The new political philosophy can only insist on what is already the case in modern societies – that they remain democratic and pluralist. They are democratic because each individual 'subject position' is constituted through metonymical displacements of the egalitarian imaginary in the syntagmatic chain that is society; and they are pluralist because each individual is involved in many identities, none of which is fixed and hierarchised by an external or transcendental ground. The radical political articulation is to be 'a more complex set of discursive-hegemonic operations embracing a variety of aspects, both institutional and ideological, through which certain "themes" are transformed into nodal points of a discursive formation (i.e. of an historic bloc)' (174–5). Beyond the deconstructive warning against political metaphysics, this generality needs to be spelled out.

Hegemonic democratic politics implies a reformulation of the concept of Revolution. It excludes as an illusory fixation of difference the notion of the seizure of the means of production, the state, or any other 'real' instance. Like Gramsci's war of position, it is immanent and processual; the revolutionary *mise en scène* loses its dramatic actor and decisive dénouement in the discursive public space of democracy. Revolution is 'the overdetermination of a set of struggles in a point of political rupture, from which there follow a variety of effects spread across the whole of the fabric of society' (177). No single identity or social position is unambiguously revolutionary; the state can be a positive or a negative factor; workers' self-management may conflict with ecological concerns of society; the politicisation of the private need not destroy it but may establish new political spaces. This is why the 'new social movements' are ambiguous. Each element in the overdetermined discursive formation must be autonomous and yet the hegemonic discourse articulates them as equivalent without establishing new relations of subordination. This co-presence of autonomy among the actors and yet equivalence among their actions is a contradiction only if each pole is treated as if it were independent such that either autonomy or the results of action is taken as defining 'the' Revolution. That error occurs because the political theorist forgets that each moment functions according to a logic that is symbolic, not literal. Neither pole is a fixed, factual identity; each is constantly reconstituted by hegemonic discourse. Revolution is neither self-management nor the elimination of difference in a 'classless' society.

This description of the hegemonic articulation of pluralist democracy explains why the intervention of the political philosopher is important. The plurality of democratic struggles would result merely in a corporatist competition among interest groups if 'possessive individualism' remains the 'common sense' which defines social identity. The hegemonic discourse differs from the interest-group pluralism which contemporary political 'science' identifies with democracy. Radical politics does not seek to create a coalition based on the equivalence among pre-given *interests*; rather, it aims at a change in the identity of the allies (and thus of their interests). Since all identities are precarious relations, total equivalence never exists; the logic of History invoked by the Leninist is denied. To avoid Leninist results, the autonomy of each of the plural 'subject positions' must be maintained. This stress on autonomy has the positive virtue that it captures a major motivation of the new social movements which the neoconservative discourse tries to hegemonise in its own interest. As pluralist, radical democracy is not simply liberal; but it is at least liberal. If it were only liberal, democracy could articulate only the equivalent displacement of the egalitarian imaginary typical of contemporary Western democracies; it could found no nodal points around which reconstruction could be proposed. The radical politics of deconstructionism cannot be limited merely to critique.

Rejection of 'the' Revolution does not mean the abandonment of utopia. Utopia is an 'imaginary as a set of symbolic meanings' which 'is absolutely essential for the institution of all left-wing thought' (190). This utopia exists in an 'unstable equilibrium' or 'tension' with the need for the 'management of social positivity' (id). The logic of the democratic imaginary does not define entirely the discursive formation that is a modern society. Other logics co-exist with the democratic demand; the state, the economy, even the family have their own, relationally open-ended logics. The political reconstruction cannot neglect these logics, which present both limits and possibilities for the democratic project – or for the jacobin imaginary. That is why the left utopia cannot be a single unified discourse; it is a 'diversity', a 'polyphony of voices, each of which constructs its own irreducible discursive identity' in all domains (191). The result is that 'This moment of tension, of openness, which gives the social its essentially incomplete and precious character, is what every project for a radical democracy should set out to institutionalize' (190). The form of the new institutions, which depends of course on empirical social and historical conditions, corresponds precisely to the unending process of deconstruction. Translated as social analysis, that philosophical position is stripped of its abstract negativity and presented by Laclau and Mouffe as a left utopia.

## 3. THE REVENGE OF MARXISM

The key to this deconstructionist politics is the definition of society as a discursive formation. The assertion is justified by the reconstruction of the dead-ends of Marxism, whose radical project it seeks to maintain by other means. The equation of social praxis with articulatory practice is to result in a political project realising the left utopia. The book's concluding lines shed doubt on the identification of the discursive, the social and the political projects under the concept of hegemony.

> Affirmation of a 'ground' which lives only by negating its fundamental character; of an 'order' which exists only as a partial limiting of disorder; of a 'meaning' which is constructed only as excess and paradox in the face of meaninglessness – in other words, the field of the political as the space for a game which is never 'zero-sum' because the rules and the players are never fully explicit. This game, which eludes the concept, does at least have a name: hegemony (193).

The central concept here, 'the political', is not defined. It seems to refer to a symbolic unification of the kind that existed socially in Luxemburg's mass strike, or which was introduced historically as 'the' democratic imaginary. But the social relations thematised by Luxemburg as producing a political rupture cannot be equated with the political phenomena that produce historically a change in the 'imaginary' which defines a society's self-conception. The mediation is supposed to be produced by the definition of society as a discursive formation. Politics is dependent on this 'society'.

Marxist politics was built on a critique of the 'political illusion' that politics could institute social change. Marx's theory was formulated as the immanent self-critique of historically specific social relations. Deconstruction shows that Marx's heirs were left to cope with the antinomies resulting from this conception of society. Its conclusion was that 'The social itself has no essence' (96). This led to the pluralist democratic project which refuses to hypostatise either society or an independent centre of political action. The democratic imaginary functions instead as that which, in Marx's words, 'sets those petrified relations dancing'. But Marx explained that the dance is occasioned when one 'sings before them their own tune'.[6] Deconstruction rejects the Hegelian overtones of immanent critique in Marx's assertion; they imply that society has an identity within which contradictions are based on fixed positive elements. The hegemonic articulation replaces immanent critique. The temptation is to look for a dance-master, someone or some movement which *performs* the articulation.

But that reintroduces an independent and external agent, which deconstruction cannot allow. How can the 'democratic imaginary' be immanent to modern society, as deconstruction demands, without being reified, as an immanent critique seems to imply? Is it a social, a discursive, or a political concept?

The pluralist democratic project is at once an institutional form and an hegemonic 'articulation'. The latter supposes the former, in the form of a public space that remains always open to 'discursive practice'. The institution of public space depends on the action of the democratic imaginary. It is responsible for the modern emergence of the plurality of social movements which create constantly new identities and delimit new subject positions. This imaginary agent cannot be a subject, still less an essence producing antagonisms as its appearance. Yet this is the implicit motor driving the political analysis. Laclau and Mouffe do admit the existence of 'other logics' when they insist on the need for pluralism. But reference is made to them as self-evident. That is not sufficient. The conditions of their emergence, and an explanation of why, when, and how they become important, must be provided. Such an explanation is implicit in the critique of Gramsci's inability to recognise the democratic implications of his practice of hegemony. Traditional society is organised and fixed by an external source of legitimation. Its demise means that society exists only in relation to itself; only in such modern societies is democracy possible. But the democratic imaginary cannot be identified with this simple *social* change. As Lefort demonstrates, the new structure is defined *politically*.[7]

Although Laclau and Mouffe insist on the specificity of modern societies, their attempt to formulate a theory of 'the political' is premised on a general definition of theory *as* practice. Society, or any 'relational identity', is attributed the same characteristics as the discourse which deconstructs it. This theoretical assumption was justified by the derivation of the deconstructionist project from the history of Marxism. But the identity of society with discourse makes it impossible to demonstrate historical specificity. The plural democracy sought by hegemonic politics turns out to be identical to modern society itself. 'Revolution' is not its transcendence, despite the presence of the utopian imaginary. Politics becomes superfluous, or at best the defence of an already existing democratic social order against 'totalitarian' temptations built into the logic of discourse itself. The reason for this conflation of politics with society lies in Laclau and Mouffe's retention of the Marxist paradigm in spite of their deconstruction of its premisses. They want to show first of all why political theory will be able to change the 'common sense' of the 'masses'. Something like immanent critique is necessary – in this case, the identification of discourse and social practice. Further, they retain from Marx the idea of a *social* revolution – in this case, by identifying political theory with the hegemonic social articulation. These two premisses, which unite the three operative terms of their 'discourse' – social praxis, articulatory practice and the political – remain to be 'deconstructed'.

The attempt to use the concept of hegemony to explain the receptivity of the 'masses' to political theory while rejecting the idea of a political subject is faithful to a basic premise of Marx. A recent essay by Lefort, 'Rereading the *Communist Manifesto*',[8] stresses the means by which Marx's text speaks from nowhere, addresses no one, asserts nothing: the famous 'spector' in whose name Marx speaks is simply the self-critique of capitalism, which needs no theoretical input to be deciphered, and no political input to be transformed. This is not simply a rhetorical device used by Marx's 'discourse'. The power of Marxism lies in just this ability to draw from really existing social relations their own, their immanent, self-critique. But the difficulty is that, implicitly, this immanent critique suggests that the 'really real' social relations can be known, and that they reveal immediately their true meaning if only one knows how to listen. This is the latent positivism that vitiates not only the orthodoxy of Marxism that was deconstructed; it is the positivism that underlies ultimately Laclau and Mouffe's attempt to deconstruct and reconstruct *post*-Marxist society while remaining still post-*Marxist.*

To accuse a deconstructionist theory of positivism, whatever the authors' intention, demands explanation. After all, Laclau and Mouffe refuse constantly to attribute identity to any social relation; each is dissolved, renewed, articulated in the metonymic chain of syntagmatic structures. Literality was rejected as the 'first of metaphors'. But the picture of modern society as a discursive formation is not the only ground for their rejection of social positivity. They cannot do without some direction for the social flux. The 'democratic imaginary' is the agency which prevents the fixation of hierarchical relations typical of traditional relations. But this second explanation of social openness accomplishes too much. It produces a political theory with no proper space for politics. Radical politics becomes the constant attack on any social fixation. This democratic political logic becomes in fact a *social* logic. Its difference from the benevolent anarchy, or joyous nihilism often attributed to deconstructivist politics is not explained. Without the postulated direction of the democratic imaginary, the result would be the (perhaps joyous) positivism of post-modernism.

Just as Gramsci's theory of hegemony remained caught in the implications of his economism, Laclau and Mouffe's contemporary reconstruction of that theory for explicitly modern societies is the victim of an unexamined premise: the priority of 'the social'. They know that they need an explicitly *political* theory 'as the space for this game which eludes the concept'. Yet their hegemonic politics remains caught in the social; it can be accused of positivism in this specifically Marxist sense. Whatever its other virtues, their essay has proven that Marxism is still not dead – and its deconstructive variant cannot save it from its internal flaws.

## Notes

* This essay was written as a review of Chantal Mouffe and Ernesto Laclau's *Hegemony and Socialist Strategy: Towards a Radical Democratic Politics* (London: Verso, 1985).

1. Laclau and Mouffe begin their presentation with Luxemburg's mass strike theory, as I present it here. For their purposes, the choice is well-made. They do not delve deeply into Luxemburg's self-contradictory experience, nor – more surprisingly – into her conception of democracy which led her to criticise the Bolshevik seizure of power. I have made this experience the centrepiece of *The Marxian Legacy*, and of the lengthy afterword to its 2nd edition (London: Macmillan, 1987; Minneapolis, University of Minnesota Press, 1987).
2. Numbers in parenthesis refer to Laclau and Mouffe, op. cit.
3. This lengthy discussion takes place among Althusserians, especially of the English variety. The reader who is not lost within the arcania may wonder why Laclau and Mouffe think it is so important to flog these particular riders of an old horse! The answer lies in Laclau and Mouffe's own adherence to the post-*Marxist* stance, as I will argue below. None the less, their critique of Althusserianism is decisive.
4. For those unfamiliar with the jargon, metonymy refers to identification by contiguity, while metaphor functions in terms of identification by likeness. In psychoanalytic terms, metonymy is displacement while metaphor is condensation. For example, metonymy might identify a rose with a thorn, while metaphor would identify it with a virgin, as D. S. Petrey summarises it.
5. I cannot discuss here the political details of Laclau and Mouffe's

arguments on these points, other than to say that, in general, I find them unobjectionable, and often insightful. The relation of these insights to their theoretical arguments is, for me, unclear.

Claude Lefort, to whom the authors refer favourably but without treating his contribution in detail, has been developing the implications of the 'democratic imaginary' without the aid of deconstructionism (and without restricting himself to Tocqueville). See his *Essais sur le politique. XIXe–XXe siècles* (Paris: Seuil, 1986), and my discussion in *The Marxian Legacy*, 2nd edition (Minneapolis: University of Minnesota Press; London: Macmillan, 1987).

6. The passage appears in Marx's 'Introduction to a Critique of Hegel's *Philosophy of Right*'. The critique of the 'political illusions' is, of course, found in the essay 'On the Jewish Question'.
7. Lefort criticises Marx for assuming that history passes from feudalism to capitalism without taking into account the political mutation represented by Absolutism and the constitution of the *Rechtsstaat*. The birth of the democratic imaginary is thus not a kind of immaculate conception; it too has a history, as well as specific social manifestations. To talk of a democratic and pluralist *politics* simply on the basis of modern *social* structures is an illicit reduction.
8. In *Essais sur le politique*, op. cit.; originally in *Dictionnaire des Oeuvres politiques* (Paris: PUF, 1986), pp. 528–39.

# Part II

# Politics as Theoretical: The New Left and Socialism

# 6 The Future as Present: Theoretical and Political Implications

## I PRELUDE . . . AND FUGUE!

In retrospect, the incoherence of the New Left is astounding. Every shade of political and moral conviction united in single and multi-issue campaigns which brought to awareness the rent fibre of the American Joseph's many-coloured coat. In an immediate sense, it was not a vision of the future but a projection, an identification, that united the critics: identification with guerrilla movements – be they Castroist, Christian or Communist-Trotskyist; identification with Eastern European intellectuals and youth who dared speak out in the stifling world of total bureaucracy; identification with the Vietnamese, Chinese, North Koreans and even Albanians, as well as projection on to the American Blacks, ethnic poor, technological and traditional working classes. Camus was as important as Marx, the Bible as 'On Contradiction', Nietzsche and Freud as Bakunin and Tolstoy. All this lived comfortably (for a time) with the attempt to restructure daily life, to build a counter-culture while at the same time fighting Imperialist-Capitalism as The Enemy.

Today the New Left is in shambles, from Czechoslovakia to the Third World, to our own. We wonder what in fact it was. Dropping out, returning to God or gods, to the earth or the drug-dazed sky? (Or, too often, crushed by the bureaucratic state, be it FBI, CIA, or USSR!) It is difficult to conceive of the Marches on Washington, the solidarity of building occupations, the intensity of the minute. When Leonard Woodcock calls his UAW troops to Washington, it seems as incoherent as Gerald Ford's economic experts – though perhaps more traditional. The New Left rose like a meteor, burned itself out, ecstatic. What happened? What traces remain? What did it mean? Benign neglect has replaced the Civil Rights Movement; Allende is dead and the only 'progressive' regimes in the Third World are military; the war has temporarily ended in S.E. Asia, but the Middle Eastern situation has worsened; the invasion of Czechoslovakia confirmed the most dour anti-communist convictions; and the Lin

Piao escapade coupled with Nixon's visit demystified China. Unless you're a believer in the Breakdown Theory – which the New Left never was – it's certainly not comforting to read the economic statistics for the US today.

Because it rose so quickly and catalysed so many hopes; and because it died so pitifully and seemed to leave nothing in its place – the New Left presents an enigma, rich in suggestions for the interpreter. The following remarks should be read under a series of *caveats*: (1) They do not claim descriptive completeness, nor is each illustration or suggestion coupled with a stock of references; each of us will certainly be able to provide our own. (2) The description that is offered is conceptual and historical at once, trying to make clear *post festum* the choices that were often made quite unconsciously. My goal is to offer a *framework* for a general interpretation. The guiding thread is that the New Left was neither 'necessary' in some causal sense, nor 'accidental' in an existential-irrationalist world. It represents our society's own self-interpretation. (3) This implies a kind of reflexive sociology to whose presuppositions I can only allude in this essentially descriptive account. This over-general approach seems to have the virtue of proposing discussion, not blocking it off with 'facts'. Hence, I shall be less concerned with what the New Left said and/or envisioned than with what it did and the meaning of its activity for our understanding of our present situation. (4) I will be starting from the premisses of Marx, adapting his method to the present, and then using the structure of that present – including the lesson of the New Left – to criticise Marx. This does not lessen the importance of Marx; nor should it be interpreted within a Manichaean friend/foe context. I write as a participant, reflecting on the New Left experience as my own, concerned with the spirit more than the letter; and attempting here to learn something about myself and my society as well as the meaning of my – of our – work in the present.

## 2. PROBLEMS OF DEFINITION AND OF METHOD

If anything is clear, it is that the New Left was hardly a united phenomenon. The term may be one of those 'sponges' ridiculed by C. Wright Mills. On the other hand, it has its usefulness. It forces us to look beneath the empirical to the structural conditions which the category reflects and defines, however inadequately. It demands that we analyse in such a way that the unity and sense of our object emerge in the analysis itself. We cannot fly above our object, assuming that it has already been defined; we are looking for the *new*, and hence our method must permit it to appear.

It is not generally helpful for an historian to speak of a 'New' Left practice in opposition to the 'Old'. If we were to think of the Old Left as characterised by the Leninist 'party of a new type', for example, this labelling of the New Left would prove deceptive. After all, anti-Leninists of the non-Social Democratic type were strong enough to lead Lenin to write 'Left-Wing Communism: An Infantile Disease'; to give Stalin reason to defile and disfigure the person and work of Rosa Luxemburg: and to be partially at the root of the sacrifice of Spain to Franco and his minions – to mention but three cases that come immediately to mind. In this sense, the 'New' Left is an old phenomenon.

Nor is it historically useful to distinguish a New Left from an Old Left theory of capitalism and its revolutionary potential. From the moral and liberalist utopia of the Port Huron Statement to the radical rhetoric of the Weatherpeople, Progressive Labor and assorted company, the path was back to Marxism – but if the first time was tragedy, this time was a farce as well. Encountering practical and theoretical problems – to be discussed in a moment – much of the New Left took the facile path back to 'science', a kind of compensation for the 'sins' of its moralistic past and a way of countering its academic enemies on their own terrain. The Marxism that was adopted was mostly of the crudest sort, mechanical in its sociology, metaphysical in its ideology. It is not surprising that, even within its own frame of reference, it made no really fruitful contributions here. As opposed to this, if we think beyond the context of the United States, the German SDS, (Sozial Demokratische Studentenbund) for example, was probably the most scholarly political movement in recent memory, basing its new tactics and style precisely on a rereading of Marx.[1] The same was true – at least partially – elsewhere, from France to Czechoslovakia.

If we try to use the criterion of 'vision of the future' as a *differentia specifica*, we get only a bit further from the historical stance. If anything characterised the New Left *as an everyday practice*, it was its denial of a vision of the future, its insistence on living today in the everyday, incarnating the new social relations in the here and now. The 'old' idea of sacrifice for the future, making the revolution for one's grandchildren, or awaiting the maturation of the contradictions, was ridiculed. This was perhaps one reason for the New Left's anti-Leninism. It certainly had something to do with the youthfulness of most of the participants; but youth is not a sufficient explanation, any more than is psychology, for a political practice.

The question of vision immediately entails that of ideology. Marxism itself of course emerged from the discovery of the function of ideology, first as a mask of the real (critique of religion) and then as the structure of the real itself (critique of capitalism). Marxists like to talk about 'scientific socialism', to distinguish themselves from 'utopians' of various orders. This is certainly consistent with Marx insofar as what really galled the Founder was not the goals of the utopians, but that their theory and practice hurt, not helped, the good cause.[2] But the Marxists, from Engels on, tended to make 'scientific socialism' an ideology – now in the sense that it was not just a refutation of disguised and misguided positions, nor solely a guide to practice; it was also to be an ideology in the explicitly 'religious', faith-giving, sense. Ideology justified the sacrifices and trials here in the capitalist present; and – however vaguely – promised the socialist future.[3]

If the Old Left had a vision of the future and an ideology – in the double sense – the New Left's immediacy and concern with the everyday today acquires a structural importance. Certainly, New Leftists threw around the term ideology; and periodically were convinced that one was needed. Its lack, however, speaks loudly. Marx *discovered* ideology as a structure of the real; he did not run around accusing others of being subjectively ideologists – as his continual writing of 'Critiques' indicates. He did not oppose a true to a false ideology, nor a 'really real' revealed by science to a false representation of it. He turned to the structure of the real in order to read its sense as ideology.[4] The everyday practice of the New Left is consistent with Marx's theoretical practice as ideology-critique: making the world speak the contradictory structures and imperatives which present themselves as fixed, permanent and natural. Neither moral criticism based on values externally derived or justified, nor scientific comparison with a true and a false, a good and a bad society: Marx's theory and the New Left's practice aim, as Marx put it enigmatically in 1843, at 'bringing those petrified relations to dancing by singing before them their own melody'.

My methodological premise, therefore, will be that of Marx's ideology-critique. To relate the expression to the expressed, signifier to signified, in a unitary structure; to try to read the New Left as a phenomenon without prejudicing the analysis by pretending either to know the real or to know what the real ought to be. It is not a question of judging. Accepting its disparateness, refusing to privilege the 'subjective' or the 'objective', the attempt will be to see what the New Left has to tell us about our society and the kind of revolutionary project it engenders.

## 3. INTELLECTUAL ROOTS

While all the New Lefts can be understood as oriented by and around Marxism, the salient features reside in the ways in which they deviate from the model. Since the movement in the United States was the least affected by Marxism in its formative stage, these 'deviant' sources expressed themselves most purely and profoundly here and are a reason to concentrate on the US.

There is a further reason to concentrate on the United States as typical. The New Left existed as a 'movement', which affected far more persons than those who were organisationally affiliated with it. Its open structure permitted many to feel themselves a part of the movement, to empathise with it and to learn from it. Particularly important to all the New Lefts were the vast protest movements that grew up in the US – first the Civil Rights Movement, then the University Reform and Free Speech Movements, and finally the movement sparked by opposition to the Vietnam War. Most striking in this *movement-character* is that the moral stance predominated over the strategic revolutionary orientation. The lack of organisation of these multifaceted movements typified also, to a large degree, the revolutionaries whose causes they supported. Particularly in the case of Vietnam, the role of *revolutionary will*, individual courage and willingness to be sacrificed, were impressive. It was inevitable that a certain *voluntarism* characterise the intellectual, organisational, political and tactical stance of the New Left.[5]

This voluntarism, which typified the climate in which the New Left functioned, coloured its choice of theorists. In the US – though nowhere else to my knowledge – the Camus of *The Rebel* played a crucial role. Where he was replaced by Sartre, it was certainly not the Sartre of 'The Communists and Peace', nor the author of the *Critique de la raison dialectique* (finally translated after fifteen years!). Of course, the existentialist tradition opened on to the Anarchists on the one hand, and the holy, mystical and self-sacrificing populists on the other. Moral issues, such as those portrayed in Camus' play 'The

Just Assassins', dominated the discussion of means/ends – rather than the concern with strategy and tactics, the organisational question, social structure, the proletariat, and the like. When historical issues – from the Russian terrorists to the classical anarchists – arose, they were treated as part of the existential present. There was no historical consciousness, as the metaphors and images chosen by New Left writers indicate.

This existential voluntarism helps us to understand the two areas where the New Left in the US developed its own theoretical contribution. Psychology became important. The often quite astute structural criticisms of capitalism raised, for example, in *Walden II*, made no impact: Skinner was the goat; Rogers, Fromm and an areopagitica of pop psychologists became the common currency. Freud was not taken seriously; at best, one borrowed some rhetoric from 'Civilisation and its Discontents'. Wilhelm Reich came into his own only later; and even where he did it was his more idealistic side that dominated over the heavy mechanism of his 'dialectical materialism'. It was in this context too that Marx made his first entry as the theorist of an ill-defined 'alienation' stripped of its original connection to the structure of proletarian labour, closer to a Heideggerian fundamental ontology than to a concrete sociology. Overlaid as it was with an existential voluntarism, this psychology could immediately and easily adapt itself to the drug culture. At the same time, however, as it fled beyond, the stress also turned to the *critique of everyday life*. This theme, central to the New Left, will be treated in more detail below. For now, it is important to recognise that the turn to the (right-wing) libertarianism of a Szasz, to psychiatric liberation movements, and most importantly to the small group – fundamental to the rise of the Woman's Movement, whose importance cannot be overstated – stemmed from an intellectual – often, seemingly, an anti-intellectual – stance which was not arbitrary. The 'getting into your own head' arose from a movement of social concern whose models of revolutionary voluntarism were consciously movements for social change. Fanon struggled with Camus; the reform of everyday life with the flight to drugs; social change with personal salvation.

The second intellectual contribution of the New Left lay, paradoxically, in the domain of the very history which its voluntarism tended to neglect. Significantly, it was not History with a capital H that was interesting; it was the existential history of the everyday. This was typical of most of the movements. However, the United States was again unique in its choice of object. Where the Germans, for example, chose to unearth forgotten episodes and movements of their revolutionary history – the various oppositional groups during the Weimar period in particular, or the Opposition within Russia – the turn in the United States was to local history. There were of course the 'revisionist' radical historians of the W. A. Williams school and *Studies on the Left*, whose intellectual role was crucial in the debunking of myths, from the Open Door through the Progressive era down to the origins of the Cold War; there were fundamental studies like those of Green or Snow on the way we were mystified about China; and there were important attempts to revivify the specific American revolutionary tradition, from the Wobblies through the great strike movements which marked the advent of the United States as a world capitalist power. But far more important were the pathbreaking works on the structure of daily life – from the slave plantation to the northern city, from the gangs of the mid-nineteenth century to the relation of work and community in the twentieth. This concern with the existential and everyday, which owed so much to the work of E. P. Thompson, showed the juxtaposition of political activity with intellectual practice – and most significantly, it was conducted (for the most part) in an a-Marxist, often a-theoretical or agnostic vein. The 'anti-intellectual' stance of the New Left was not, therefore, a rejection of thought and analysis, but a putting into question of a kind of Enlightenment rationality whose 'dialectic' Adorno and Horkheimer had exposed years before in a little-known volume.

In short, the 'intellectual roots' of the New Left were largely a rejection of the traditional, rationalist views; they were part of a political practice, a social regrouping, and a personal will and moralism. None of this is the stuff of which 'ideologies' are made, at least not politically effective ones. This was to present a problem – not a problem that arose from the material itself, nor even one that emerged necessarily from practice. The attempt was very American; very much in *our* tradition of natural law.[6]

Although the Vietnamese were a model of voluntarism, they also claimed to be Marxists; so did the Chinese; and so did many participants in the movement, feeling the need for science, the passion to *make* – not just *live* – the revolution. Marxism entered – a mysterious doctrine, sanctified, accompanied by a priesthood, sects and holy books. It was a disaster; a weapon in the hands of potential leaders, a cudgel to beat the individualist, and a theory for a nontheoretical movement. Of course, it was a deformed Marxism; and of course, there was much to be learned from Marx. But it came from the outside – as Lenin and Kautsky might have wished – and it was not natural. The guilty adopted it, learned its rhetoric and style . . . or slunk away. Defining the movement atomised it; single issues became just that. The height of absurdity was reached at a California conference bringing together the black and white movements to 'fight fascism': the fundamental text was Dimitrov's Speech on Fascism to the 7th Congress of the 3rd International in 1935!

## 4. SOCIAL ROOTS

In retrospect, the introduction of Marxism as ideology into the New Left helps to clarify a fundamental feature of its development. One can look at the history of the American SDS (Students for a Democratic Society) as the *search for the revolutionary subject*. Not consciously at first, but ever more so, an essentially student, largely 'middle-class' group attempted to shake its guilt-feeling by identifying its actions with those of the classic oppressed groups. First it was civil rights, then the liberal-labour coalition within the Democratic Party, then the various Third World peoples, and finally – and fully incoherently – a 'proletariat' defined in terms of a combination of Imperialism theory and Marxian orthodoxy. The history of the New Left can thus be conceived as a history of self-denial, with the resultant loss of its own originality.[7]

Marxism as ideology is not the same as a Marxian analysis of contemporary social relations. From the latter perspective, for purposes of simplification, it might be argued that three events symbolise the changed social relations from which the New Left emerged. There was the post-1956 face-lifting in Russia, whose importance is manifest not only or simply in the open 'revisionism' and power politics revealed in the Sino-Soviet split but, more importantly, in the consecration and open emergence of the bureaucracy as a new class operating in a new social formation.[8] Second, there was de Gaulle's assumption of power through a playing off of the landed and colonial capitalists against the modernisers in order to end the Algerian war and open France to a new, state-dominated capitalism.[9] Finally, there was the Kennedy tax-cut, whose counterposition to Hooverian fiscal orthodoxy marked a 'fiscal revolution', and symbolised a new conception of the relation of society and the state.[10] These three symbols, notwithstanding archaic remnants such as the Berlin Wall, Castro's revolution or Sputnik, consecrate a change that restructured the globe.[11]

Broadly speaking – though the Russian case is somewhat different – the historical struggle of the working class had resulted in the paradoxical success crowned by integration into a system of countervailing powers sharing a common interest in 'delivery of the goods'. This class struggle operated not only through the formal mechanism of the strike; it was not always a conscious 'class' struggle, and certainly not led by a Party, but rather was the everyday guerrilla warfare of production relations. In Marxian terms, it forced the capitalists to increase the production of relative surplus-value, i.e. to introduce technological advances on an ever-greater scale; and at the same time, the increased intensity of labour was achieved through a variety of technical and socio-psychological means. Its results were manifold. More skills were demanded of labour-power, which meant increasing the length and quality of education; which was also necessary to prevent youthful (and other) unemployment due to the decreasing number of productive jobs; which in turn meant that since more and more goods were produced, an ever-greater sales force of parasites was necessary, credit purchasing became the rule, and the role of the unemployed and underemployed, as well as the ethnically underprivileged, increased; which meant in turn the increased responsibility of the state in the sphere of scientific innovation, labour training, investment credits, and social legitimation; which in turn restructured the colonial-imperial system and changed the relations of the 'capitalist' and 'communist' worlds. With all this arose a series of 'objective' and 'subjective' contradictions – between state and private capital, skilled educated labour and routine tasks, demand for worker participation and need to make every minute count, client and state, production and distribution, as well as the tension between work and leisure, formal democracy and actual powerlessness, scientific rationalisation and creative experience, education and job training, etc.

One could go on describing features; and one could debate the degree to which they are *really* differences that make a difference. The New Left's existence – though not necessarily its self-understanding – suggests a mode of analysis. Capitalism is a mode of social relations predicated on the production of surplus-value profit. It doesn't matter what is produced, nor how it is produced; to make a profit producing shoes or bibles is equivalent. Whether you accept the labour theory of value and its implications, or choose to reason commonsensically from the standpoint of the individual capitalist, the implication is that the worker is crucial to the endeavour. If the worker will work more for less – longer hours or more intensively – the capitalist profits. The result is a class struggle, which manifests itself in a series of adaptations in the productive process. From being a crafts-person, whose personal skills or training are central to production, the worker becomes simply a cog. This is the classical proletariat, trained on the job, immediately replaceable, and fully dominated. Its situation is explosive; it is de-fused only through the formation of unions which defend its most immediate interests. Able only to 'cash in', as it were, on the crisis of the 1930s and the War, this proletariat found itself restructured by the pressure that it itself put on the capitalist. Production processes changed, new technology was introduced, group dynamics were restructured. A 'new working class' emerged. Not that the 'old' one was eliminated or its situation altered; simply, it was no longer the vanguard, the locus of the most advanced forms of struggle, the seat of felt contradiction and the source of an impulse toward the *positive* restructuring of society. The 'new working class' is an ill-defined, hermeneutic device, not an empirical statistic. The suggestion is simply that capitalism develops new needs, and that its reply to them points to a new structure.[12] The point is not Veblen's, Burnham's or Galbraith's – to mention only those. It is not a new permutation of an old set of relations, social goals and norms. It is that *capitalism as a total experience changes*: its imperatives are different, its social relations modeled after a new principle, its norms in flux.

The suggestion is that capitalism has changed (as has the Russian system). We can begin to account for that change in terms of the class struggle and the profit-imperative. But this means that, once it accounts for the new, the old theory, self-destructs, so to speak. The experience of the New Left witnesses this. What was fundamental to capitalism has disappeared: the free labour market, the establishment among fully independent partners of free contracts, and the domination of production over consumption.[13] Not that the contradictions on which it was based have disappeared, or become less crying or cruel – to the contrary. The point, however, is that the logic of the present social conflicts is determined differently – by the logic of *bureaucratic rationality*. Such a logic is of course not foreign to classical capitalism. Weber saw its implications very early. But Weber did not go far enough in his analysis of it, and studied it in its own terms: though he knew and discussed the role of the political in its institution, Weber did not see that this rationality is the ultimate result not of the logic of the entrepreneur, still less of the Protestant spirit, but rather of precisely the politics of the class struggle. In a favourite Marxian metaphor: 'its victory is at the same time its loss'. Better: its transformation. The phenomenon of the New Left pushes us to analyse this transformation.

## 5. TACTICS, THEMES AND PRACTICE

The New Left considered itself a *movement*. Save in the phase of its ideological phantasies, it never saw itself as the expression of the proletariat; and certainly it never claimed to be a political party in any traditional sense. Its success as a movement, and its failure once it sought to limit and define itself, testify to the correctness of this self-understanding. Given its intellectual nature and sociological insertion, it could not have been anything else. The smoothed-over capitalism whose conflicts have shifted does not permit a frontal attack: it offends everyone, but not in the same manner. A new series of issues open; but they open in series, in seriality, and their unity becomes a problem. The unification which – eventually – poses the question of the nature of the social totality did push toward Marxism as the immediately available explanation. That didn't work. It could, and did, lead to other approaches on the level of social theory. On the level of practice, the movement form made possible a unification of the differences, however unstable and fragile.

The themes around which New Left practice centred are well known. From civil rights and anti-war through community organisation, women's and gay rights, to the drug culture and student power – they can be unified around the concerns with *daily life*, and the *autonomy* of the *person*. These were lived, felt issues which demanded immediate responses. They could be communicated, it seemed, through the counter- and the mass-media. The speed at which the movement-as-feeling or attitude spread testifies to the society's ripeness. It witnesses the homogenisation that resulted, covering the differences while making them all the more explosive. If the theories of the Frankfurt School, or Marcuse's writings, appeared to express the New Left, it was because of a – perhaps old-fashioned in its Frankfurt formulation – recognition of the ever-present need for autonomy in all spheres of daily life.

If we ask why these themes could take as they did, the above sociological description, guided by the practice of the New Left, provides a key. Bureaucratic capitalism, Marcuse's one-dimensional society, Adorno and Horkheimer's 'dialectic of enlightenment', point to a common structure, a unity in difference: *a modernity which hides from itself its own origins* – in a manner analogous to the way Marx's ideology critique in *Capital* points to the role of the fetishism of commodities. The tactics of the New Left are significant in this regard: from Berkeley to Berlin, from Warsaw to Washington and Paris to Prague, the tactic was the deed, the confrontation, the direct action. The goal was to unmask the power relations hidden by the apparently smoothly functioning machine. *The tactic unmasked the power lurking beneath bureaucratically rationalised social relations, uncovering the new structure of domination in its most intimate resting place: daily life.* This tactic was not just the result of a philosophical or moral existentialism, nor the practice of desperados and outsiders; it was sociologically rooted, and points to the core social structure. That the New Left was able to discover this makes its experience all the more important.

The tactics, themes and practice of the New Left reflect a further aspect of the present social structure: its use of the immediate, the here-and-now, the pseudo-personal to cover over the root *historical* structure and *origins* of the system. 'In no epoch has one talked so much,' writes Claude Lefort.[14] Everything is present, open, available – from the ski-vacation of 'our' president to the local porn shop; from the starvation in the Sahal to the napalm in Vietnam or the Near East; from *Psychology Today* to the *Intellectual Digest*. The everyday is trivialised and thus stolen; domination is rationalised in our scientific belief systems. God is dead because we don't need her any more; we are our own gods – and hence all the more vulnerable. One can leap forward into a new whose novelty is already structurally old, vain and predictable like the changing of fashion; or one can turn for anchorage to an ideal derived from the dead past. The system has conjured the risk of change by making change its principle. It seems to have created a closed world, a system, with no outside – Hegelianism with feedback loops.

Drawing this lesson, implicitly, the New Left committed suicide. It was incapable of imagining its own insertion or role, and fell back on the old models. It moved backward, groping for certainty and denying itself.

This need not have been. The stress on the immediate, on

experience, on the personal and the communal, implicitly posed a forward-reaching demand: that of self-management in all spheres of life, self-activity and self-representation. *This lesson burst forth in May 1968*! No one started it; no one planned it; no one consciously wanted it. Yet it spread like a prairie fire: *l'imagination au pouvoir*! Sure, it was crushed and de Gaulle re-elected; but that doesn't make it the less important. February to October 1917 – if we want to remember those dates – was an extended learning process; revolutionary consciousness is not achieved overnight. The old is tenacious, the new fragile.

As an organised, self-identified movement, the New Left is dead. Its practice and its themes are still with us, in communities, groups and issues. If we turn now to some aspects of its vision, the implications of its life-style-as-practice, we will be able better to understand our present and its possibilities.

## 6. IMPLICATIONS AND QUESTIONS

From its intellectual roots to its themes, tactics and practice, the New Left represented a *critique of the political*. Not just a critique of politics, politicians and the irrationality of their imperatives; the New Left rejected the political as a form of mystification – an imaginary community floating in the clouds, as the young Marx puts it. The New Left critique of representative democracy is far more than a critique of the political from within its bounds and premisses (as is, for example, the 'Marxist' debunking of formal democracy). It is the critique of a mode of life, a form of self- and social perception. The implication is that it is in *daily life*, in 'civil society', to use the consecrated term, that change must occur.

It is worth noting, however, that the a-political politics of the New Left is a *rediscovery of the path of the young Marx*, from the critique of the Hegelian state through the discovery of the proletariat and the phenomenon of alienated labour. As Marx looked back at the French Revolution, so the New Left – when it looked back at all – saw that the revolution must not only destroy the political bonds that limit and narrow, but must revolutionise the sphere of personal interest and egoism. It would seem that the New Left could have followed Marx (in 'On the Jewish Question') in citing Rousseau:

Whoever dares to undertake the founding of a nation must feel

> himself capable of changing so to speak human nature and transforming each individual, who is in himself a complete but isolated whole, into a part of something greater than himself from which he somehow derives his life and existence, substituting a limited and moral existence for physical and independent existence. Man must be deprived of his own powers and given alien powers which he cannot use without the aid of others. (*Social Contract*, Book II, Chapter II)

What emerges from the critique of the political as the constant theme and tension is, paradoxically, the *politicisation of daily life*, the over-determination of every activity with a political sense, the denial of the private and the individual. As a sociological critique of contemporary bureaucratic capitalism, this stress is rich in potential. It discovered and uncovered a manifold of experience heretofore unthematised and ignored; society and socialisation were experienced as a unified process, each the horizon of the other and each the critique of the other.

There was an unbearable tension in this turn to civil society and its politicisation. Not simply the tension with the individualistic, existential and anarchic roots of a movement based on moral will; the Rousseauian stress on 'transforming the individual' implies a deprivation of one's 'own powers', which is hardly consistent with the New Left's original impulses. Yet the internal logic of its approach drove the New Left towards Rousseau – towards Lenin and a certain Marx as well – creating a tension which would become a rupture. Activism, spontaneism, immediacy and the lack of taboos, along with more overtly negative phenomena like anti-intellectualism, drugs, and the continual strain of becoming an individual through the collective, fitted together so long as development and success did not demand reflection and analysis. With the first failures, as the movement slowed down, the poles began to separate. Society had been conceived as the relation of one to one; the future society would be one of dyadic communication; and the properly social was felt as 'alienation'. At the same time, however, experience pointed to the role of the *totality*. Not simply that community organisers found that you can't create 'socialism in one community', or that each single issue group found itself forced to go beyond its issue by its very successes: the demand for totalisation appeared in the very immediacy of civil society, of daily life and immediate experience.

The *politicisation of daily life* which appeared so apparent and effective a perspective implied the *destruction of everyday life*. Concern with the individual and the everyday led to the totality; but the route back remained barred. The particular and the universal were conflated and collapsed, each losing what was specific to it. The psychological effects were of course disastrous. But more important here, the image of the political changed. It was through this door that a Marxian orthodoxy implicitly mediated by Lukács re-entered. For all its sublety in analysing the phenomenon of reification in the daily existence of the proletariat, Lukács' attempt led of necessity not simply to an *ouvrièrisme* but directly to the Leninist Party as possessor and incarnation of the totality. Though most did not read Lukács, their logic followed, or recreated, his – and returned to the old politics. Those who remained with the original impulse of the New Left encountered another set of problems.

*The politicisation of daily life is an attempt to remove the mystery, to render society transparent to itself, to end history in the present.* This position is of course the identical obverse of the orthodox, which removes the mystery through its science, understands the present in terms of a necessary future, and sacrifices the present to that future. Making the totality, the political, present in the immediacy of daily life permitted a critique of that everyday experience, and guided attempts to restructure it in terms of what Trent Schroyer has called 'utopian enclosures'. From food co-ops to day-care centres, from small-grouping to ethnicity, the attempt was to transform the single issues into total social solutions through the transformation of the individual experience. As a form of critique-in-action, this led to an important reconsideration of the nature and role of *power* in society and social relations. At the same time, it opened a critique of the *technological rationality* of strategic action which structures our society. Here, Marcuse, Habermas and the Frankfurt School struck the theoretical chord.

While the experiments still continue, their internal logic poses problems. On the one hand, the above considerations of the social roots of the New Left suggest that in the blabbermouth society, critique of this sort is precisely *essential* to the *masking* of the social divisions. The turn to the immediate, the small group and closed community naturally (not socially or politically) defined, conceals as well as reveals. It may be a personal necessity, but precisely the stress on immediacy turns it inward and limits its thrust. The identical opposite, which stresses the totality's presence in the immediate, is in fact dealing with a representation of the totality which it attempts to incarnate through the creation of what Claude Lefort calls 'a new social type: the militant'. If you must always incarnate the totality in the everyday, you *become* it, denying your particularity and your experience – and the totality is in fact lost. The quest for the totality in the immediate, whether through the dyadic group, individual consciousness, or the representational imagination of the militant, tends towards a new form of totalitarianism – which, to its credit, most of the new Left conscientiously attempted to avoid – but only at the cost of either the incoherence of its projects or the psychological integrity of its members.

The politicisation of daily life is not, however, a wholly negative phenomenon: it points forward – to a redefinition of revolution and to a rethinking of the nature of society and its political structure. Explicitly, the New Left stressed and harped on two central themes, without which the notion of socialist revolution is a contradiction in terms: *the end of the division of manual and mental labour, and the notion of self-management*. The striving for the immediacy of dyadic communication – whatever criticism it calls forth from one standpoint – recognises that the element of power and domination in personal relations must be eliminated. Power and domination are exercised daily in a society structured in terms of the exacerbation of the division of labour; not consciously, but of necessity, our languages are different, our self-conceptions limited, our horizons blocked, and sub- and super-ordination distort communication. This *is* ideology as the structure of our bureaucratic society. It can only be overcome with the elimination of the structured divisions which affect the individual to the core, and are crystallised in that division of manual and mental labour. At the same time, the notion of self-management becomes central; it is the issue of control and power, but also that of personal relations. Self-management – *not only in production but in all spheres of life* – is the central theme of the New Left, and essential to its vision; but the vision is not one of a future which teleologically affects practice in the present; it is a vision which bureaucratic capitalism itself calls forth, as it increasingly socialises society, making all dependent on each, and yet dividing them at work and in leisure. Self-management and the end of the division of manual and mental labour as the goal of a revolution are already inscribed as demands in our present while they are still denied in the everyday. This is why the New Left's tactics of immediate action and provocation met with such success. Where the success turned sour, it seems, was when the question of totalisation emerged and, as such, either separated revolution from present activities (the Leninist view) or distorted the present by over-determining it (the group *as* future).

From this perspective, the New Left opens on to a *changed sociology of contemporary society*, and a *critique of Marxism*. Not simply a critique of the simplified and vulgarised Marx of the apologists. It is obvious enough that capitalism has changed; indeed, Marx himself can account for these changes. What is more important is that the New Left is a critique in action of *Marx as the last Hegelian*, of *Marx the rationalist*. Of course, there is the myth of the proletariat as the Subject-Object of History, an inverted materialist form of the Hegelian *Geist* or, seen politically, his bureaucracy. Of greater import is the critique in action of Marx's linear view of History, of History as the Progress of Humanity towards its Self-Realization through the elimination of Otherness. Capitalism is not necessarily the antechamber to the socialist reconciliation; nor is it doomed to collapse through its own inner 'logic'. The class struggle will not come to fruition when 'X' millions are unemployed, any more than revolution can be organised as a societal *coup d'état*. The increased role of the state, not simply as collective capitalist but as distributor of legitimation through its relation to its clients, throws into question the absolutising of the infrastructure, which is inherent in the orthodox analysis. Human relations are certainly not independent of their material substratum; but the latter is not to be taken in isolation, as the 'really real' on which all else sits. Marx's analysis of *laissez-faire* competitive capitalism is limited to a specific case where the universe of meaning of the society is structured around accelerated reproduction through a free market – including the labour market. Such was not the case in pre-capitalist societies; and it is true today only in the vaguest manner. Marx spoke of four constitutive elements of human being: production, consciousness, language and community. The latter three appear ever more central as liberal capitalism veers towards bureaucratic capitalism. The result is the re-emergence of daily life as a sphere of contestation, and the need for a renewal of sociological analysis. Marx was perhaps not so much wrong as he was misunderstood – though the misunderstandings are inherent in the scientised self-understanding he had of his own work.

The most pressing problem which emerges from the consideration of the New Left's vision is the changing role of the political. The move to civil society as the place of the political has been seen to be paradoxical and insufficient – or worse, to contain the seeds of a new totalitarianism. The old politics, on the other hand, is all the more bankrupt in that even its formal legitimacy hinged on the now-surpassed structure of liberal capitalism. At a first level, the New Left can be seen to reopen the domain of the political as it has traditionally been conceived since the Greeks *invented* democracy: as the dimension in which the *good life in the City* is elaborated. Politics is neither science nor technique; the politician is neither planner nor administrator. The slogan of 'participatory democracy' takes on its full sense here. Politics is not the sum and substance, the totality, of everyday life; it is and must remain different. At the same time, it cannot be isolated in its difference, either determining directly daily life from on high or being the simple addition or representation of the atoms which compose the social. It is the locus of Power, *the place where society represents itself to itself*; but at the same time that it is constitutive of the form of the society, it is constituted by and dependent on the society itself. Neither identical with, nor separate from the society, the political is not for that reason simply nothing: it is a *process* which is unending – and whose end could mark only the advent of a totalitarianism – in which the society and its members seek to define and structure their relations. In its concern with the good life of the citizens, it is universal; in its dependence on and relation to the individuals, it is particular and open to change.

What then would revolution mean from a New Left perspective? *L'imagination au pouvoir* is not a slogan but an analysis! – a programme. Power is not to be occupied; to think that one could – or should – seek to seize the reins of state is to be the victim of an illusion. Centred upon the demand to occupy the place of power, revolutionary activity becomes a question of adequate means to a given end, a technological equation neglecting the human material one wants to serve, and denying oneself one's own particularity. Through its experiments, however successful or however incoherent, the New Left points to the dimension of the political process in which the good life is put into question and developed. The forms of language, consciousness and community take precedence over any unilateral determination of society by production and reproduction. They are the universals in terms of which the particulars structure their relations. In today's bureaucratic capitalism, the question of rationality, and with it, that of legitimation, is the locus of political debate and practice. This cannot be 'seized' or 'occupied'. But it is none the less the centre from which the manifold variety of empirical struggles, from the traditional workplace to the community and the classroom, spread. These latter have, and will continue to have, a surface resemblance to those predicted by the orthodox theory. But they find themselves in another context, and wear a different meaning. To treat them in the old manner would be to neglect the change, and to return to the time-worn patter.

The implications of this 'revolutionary politics' for the New Left theory are first of all found in its critique of the 'Old Left'. The Old Left politics – despite some glimmerings found in Marx – are caught within the bourgeois system of representation. Power is conceived as a *place* to be occupied; society is seen in economic metaphors; practice is taken to be the production of an object. The goals are determined through a means–ends rationality; and success is defined in terms of an adequation of theory and practice, ends and means, plan and realisation. *It is this rationality which the New Left has put into question.* History is not a linear process, an empty objective space within which we move, guided by a teleological vision of the Good. The visual metaphor is destroyed; Cartesian rationalism with its 'clear and distinct' ideas and causal thinking falls by the wayside, not to be replaced by an irrationalist existentialism or some qualitative physics. The *process* of the political is archetypal: it points to the implications of the particular in the universal, and vice versa; to the inseparability of subject and object, thought and reality, mind and body; and most importantly, it signals to us the danger of thinking that we could somehow possess the truth or totality as a thing to be held and caressed in our hands.

The New Left foundered because it was unable to recognise and realise both its own sociological insertion and the implications of its critical project. It fell for the image of having (or being) the totality: either returning to an orthodoxy of Marxism-Leninism, or turning inward to the ideology of dyadic immediacy. To founder is not, however, to fail. The New Left may be dead as an *organised* movement – but then it never really lived as such. It lives on in all its contradictoriness because the structure of bureaucratic capitalism based on the division of society forces the emergence not only of traditional revolts, but of new ones as well. If the New Left has anything to teach us, or itself to learn from its own experience, it is the dangers of objectivised 'success'. Perhaps the 'failure' was inherent in the project; not because the project was wrong-headedly conceived, but because it can only structure itself in terms of the redefined political. The future of the New Left – its own, and the one it (however implicitly) conceived – is still with us in a project which was not engendered in the heads of the theorists, but structured into our society itself.

No explicit tactic or theory emerges from the New Left. Yet whatever we do, and however we conceive ourselves, the structures that the New Left revealed, the imaginative tactics it applied, and its openness to experiment and self-criticism, cannot help but be of influence. This is no small tribute to its vision.

## Notes

1. For example, the early SDS leaders, and their present-day heirs, engaged in detailed rereadings of Marx. See, e.g. Michael Mauke, *Die Klassentheorie von Marx und Engels* (Frankfurt, 1970); Oskar Negt, particularly the essay 'Marxismus als Legitimationswissenschaft', introducing the Deborin-Bucharin, *Kontroversen über dialektischen und-mechanistischen Materialismus* (Frankfurt, 1969), and Hans-Jürgen Krahl's work on the *Grundrisse*, in *Konstitution und Klassenkampf* (Frankfurt, 1971). Recent work in Germany has concentrated itself around what amounts sometimes to a 'Marx philology with revolutionary intent', reinterpreting the 'logic' and the 'dialectic' of *Capital*.
2. On Marx's attitude to the utopians, see the fundamental reexamination by Miguel Abensour, 'L'histoire de l'utopie et le destin de sa critique', in *Textures*, 73/6–7, and 74/8–9. Abensour stresses a '*nouvel esprit utopique*', which breaks both with the rationalist-technocratic schemas and with the empty and pious eschatology of utopia as an abstract universal.
3. An example is found in a 1912 sociological survey: a 29-year-old metalworker states, 'I am not without hope, for one who is so filled with socialism as myself believes in a liberation like a new Evangel'. Or a 39-year-old metalworker, who states that 'It was the political and trade-union movement which first gave a goal to my being, a content to my life'. (Citations from Grebing, *Geschichte der deutschen Arbeiterbewegung*.) One could cite Dietzgen, Engels, Gramsci and so many others to a similar effect.
4. Cf. Lefort's analysis discussed in *The Marxian Legacy*, and in "From Marx to Kant" in the present volume.
5. A possible third reason for concentrating on the United States – its position as leader of the capitalist world, where presumably the contradictions, co-optations, etc., are most advanced – is questionable. Particularly as concerns the role of the state, one could look to the examples of France, Britain or Scandinavia as models. This is not the place to debate which country is the 'vanguard of capitalism'.

6. As Jürgen Habermas has pointed out, our very moralistic natural law tradition, defended with the eloquence of a Tom Paine and the passion of Everyman, follows a Lockean notion of natural reason incarnating itself through the labour of the individual. Where the French tradition of Rousseau or the Physiocrats saw natural law rationalistically, as what ought to be – and what had to be imposed on society – the Anglo-American tradition saw it as already existing, lived in the everyday but deformed and deviated by the intervention of the state. Ours is a tradition of anarchic capitalism, of existentialists carving out their world from day to day. But it is not possible to hark back explicitly to that tradition; it was smothered under its natural results: the monopolies, the consumer society, the interventionist state. Natural law anarchism was not enough.
7. This is not to propose a psychologising interpretation, or to suggest the correlative reductionism. The argument is sociological, posed in terms of social structure and the nature of sociality, as will be seen. It helps to explain the mess in which the remnants of the New Left find themselves – from Jesus freaks to gurus, to the resurging 'Leninist' sects, to the withdrawal into drugs and/or communal ventures.
8. Cf. the lucid analysis by Claude Lefort, 'Le totalitarisme sans Staline', first in *Socialisme ou Barbarie*, 14, 1956; now in *Eléments d'une critique de la bureaucratie* (Geneva-Paris, 1971).
9. See the analyses of Cornelius Castoriadis in *Socialisme ou Barbarie* at the time, as well as those of Serge Mallet in *Le Gaullisme et la gauche* (Paris, 1965).
10. The term is taken from the title of Herbert Stein's useful work (Chicago, 1971). The analysis, of course, differs from his.
11. I omit reference to the Chinese Revolution and its aftermath, or to the succession of ex-colonies assuming independence in one or another manner. Not that these are unimportant: simply that their symbolic dimension can only be understood in the mirror of the productivist, bureaucratic capitalist countries.
12. On the 'new working class' theory and its implications, see the translation of Serge Mallet's writings, *The New Working Class: A Socialist Perspective*, edited and translated by Dick Howard and Dean Savage (St. Louis: Telos Press, 1976).
13. Marx predicts this in the form of state capitalism. Simply, Marx didn't see its implications for the structure of the wage-labour/capital relation, and expected the old contradictions to persist in an unchanged manner. This is not the case, and explains the error of 'state capitalism' theses which propose to explain Russia through a kind of Marx-reading. Cf. the discussion of this problem by C. Castoriadis in *The Marxian Legacy*.
14. The references from Claude Lefort are to his article, 'Esquisse d'une genèse de l'idéologie dans les sociétés modernes', in *Textures*, 74/8–9, a slightly altered version of which appeared in the *Encyclopédie Universalis* under the title 'L'ère de l'idéologie'. On Lefort, to whom this interpretation is deeply indebted, see *The Marxian Legacy*.

    In the context of this argument, it is worth referring also to the former colleague of Lukács, Belá Fogarasi, whose article on the function of a communist newspaper was translated in *Radical America* some years back. Fogarasi points out that it is not so much in giving us false news or hiding the news from us that the capitalist press exercises its ideological and mystificatory function – on the contrary, we have perhaps too much of it! What is missing is the context, the sense and meaning of the news that we get.

# 7 From One New Left to Another?

I will begin with the *experience* of the new international movement which was born from the NATO 'double decision' of 1979, from the warlike rhetoric of Ronald Reagan and, for many, from the Soviet invasion of Afghanistan. The short existence of this movement has been marked by theoretical and practical interventions, of which some should be noted here. On the left, there was the Appeal by the British historian E. P. Thompson, published under the title *Protest and Survive*, and Thompson's theoretical analysis of what he calls 'Exterminism, the highest stage of civilisation,' which attempted to go beyond the wooden Marxist theses to open a debate which has continued across national borders. In more apolitical milieus, there was the success of Jonathen Schell's *The Fate of the Earth*, which continued and crystallised the work of scientists, doctors, religious leaders and women who have left the household frame. The debate provoked by the Declaration of the American Catholic Bishops, and the support of the Freeze on nuclear arms by former high-ranking Defense Department officials in the US strengthened this movement. To it must be added the election of the German Green Party to the Bundestag after a series of debates which left their mark within a Social Democratic Party held tightly by Chancellor Helmut Schmidt at the time of its Munich Congress in 1982 but now shaken once again by ecological and especially pacifist groups. Finally, one should note a non-event which will determine more than all these phenomena the future of the new movement once the date of the installation of the missiles has passed: the incapacity of this movement, which has no institutional form or designated leaders, to reply to the Coup of 13 December in Poland puts its future in question.

I stress the experience of this new movement for a methodological reason. I admit the importance of classical political analyses. The critique that can be directed at the new movement on the basis of such analyses are well known, especially in France where the critics do not always understand the use that can be made of them by a neo-conservative or 'liberal' Right which, everywhere except in France, feels threatened by the new movement. That right-wing use does not mean that the critiques are invalid. The call for a General

Strike against the placing of US Pershing missiles in Germany by the popular Socialist Mayor of Sarrebrücken, Oskar Lafontaine, will have no more success than did the self-righteous declarations of the Socialist International on the threshold of the First World War. Lafontaine's proposal that Germany leave NATO in the event that the missiles are actually installed is no more realistic than is the unilateralism of the platform of the British Labour Party. Proposing such measures is not only naïve but politically dangerous and simply stupid. But despite these critiques the movement exists, mobilises new activists and brings them to political engagement on the basis of serious questions and good intentions. This is why the movement has to be analysed on the basis of a methodological imperative which refuses to treat the movement from outside, or in terms of a theory; rather, a theory must be elaborated on the basis of the movement itself.

## 1. THE EXPERIENCE OF THE NEW LEFT

I have the impression of reliving recently the optimistic and naïve atmosphere which characterised the New Left of the 1960s. Indeed, the present movement in Germany can be seen as an offspring of its New Left. That experience was already international, even though its different manifestations and its goals were adapted to the conditions and traditions of each country. But the rapid success of that movement was followed by a decline which puts into question the validity of the experience. The reasons for the failure are not simply the result of external circumstances. Beyond the return of Gaullism after May 1968, beyond the invasion of Czechoslovakia in August of that year – an August which saw also the riots in Chicago and soon the election of Richard Nixon – there were contradictions and fault-lines within the movement itself.

The analyses, modes of action and goals of the New Left were defined first of all by the negation of the classical political Left. Against the politics of the politicians, spontaneity and innovation were valued; democratic participation at the base implied the rejection of all forms of hierarchy. That critique of politics determined also the social analysis proposed by the movement. The accent was on the critique of forms of bureaucratic domination rather than on class struggle. The practical impact of the Frankfurt School critical theory is explained by its denunciation of bureaucracy and critique of 'one-dimensionality'. At the same time, the very breadth of this critique, to which corresponded an everyday practice, could lead to a Third Worldist anti-imperialism for which the West as a whole was the enemy. The revolutionary goal was imagined in a vague and apocalyptic manner, when it was not defined simply in terms of action, as a kind of 'permanent revolution'. This might explain the fascination with Trotskyism, to which some succumbed.

The negative self-definition also implied a positive conception. First and above all, the movement substituted itself for the party as the subject of politics. Political actors defined themselves by their immediate and direct participation. The universal but abstract formulations by politicians were replaced by a particularism whose effect was to extend the sphere of politics to daily life. One of the often-heard slogans was the title of a book by Henri Lefèbvre: the 'Critique of Everyday Life'. Another explained that 'The personal is political'. From this it followed that expertise, which politicians claimed to monopolise, was replaced by the appeal to public opinion; science tended to be identified with bureaucracy in a rejection of any distinction between manual and mental labour. In a word, the New Left brought about an extension of the sphere of the political, its subjects or actors and its objects. One could say that the classical sense of the political replaced bourgeois politics. The latter concerned itself with the administration of an already given social state; the former wanted to change society as a whole. The New Left tried politically to define the social whereas bourgeois politics lets itself be defined by the existent society.

The New Left did not think in these theoretical and historical terms, which I attribute to it retrospectively. Action acquired its definition as a process. It worked for a while, but it couldn't last. Once politics reasserted itself, the heterogeneity of the actors and their goals, from which the movement had drawn strength, began to pose problems for its internal functioning. The extension of the political to private life imposed on each the weight of a political discouragement and of an intolerant moralism which had not existed during the rising phase of the movement. A moral attitude is universalising, and thus reductive; it is basically antipolitical, tending to impose everywhere certitudes which cannot be debated. Joined to an anti-institutional and participatory attitude, this leads to a romanticism or to an irrationalism which rejects the gains of modernity. In the face of these depoliticising trends, some rediscovered Marxism in its 'Euro-Communist' form while others continued to denounce the too-evident misdeeds of imperialism in the Third World since they could not find at home the terrain for their own action.

This schematic description concerns France only partially. But it joins with France at a fundamental moment, when the critique of totalitarianism began in earnest. The New Left criticism of social relations determined by economic or bureaucratic rationality was incarnated in the extension of political participation to daily life. It thus discovered the structure of what can be called 'civil society'. The same opposition and discovery were the basis of the French critique of totalitarianism. There is one difference, at least at first view: the critique of totalitarianism led the French to rediscover also the virtue of institutions, and especially of the law. The result is that they are now giving new weight to political liberalism, both as a critique of voluntarist tendencies within the socialist-communist government of the moment, and in an international conjuncture strongly influenced by the new movement against nuclear mega-armament which does not take seriously constitutional forms.

French antitotalitarianism and the new movement appear at once to converge and to diverge. The convergence appears more clearly when it is recalled that the New Left began historically from the Civil Rights Movement in the US. That movement sought forms of action (for example, the sit-ins or the freedom marches) which began from a situation of particular wrong in order to find the legal and moral forms which it made necessary. In so doing, it put into practice another aspect of liberalism and of civil society; it was not founded on the respect for the established legal procedures, but it did not reject the importance of law. The reasons that the New Left prolongation of the Civil Rights Movement did not develop further the implication of *this* kind of liberalism would demand a different analysis. For our purposes, the important point is that the results of the critique of totalitarianism, those of the practice of the New Left, and those of the present international movement which picks up the mantle of the New Left, can be united around a concept of 'civil society'.

## 2. NEW MOVEMENT, OLD THEORY

In order to analyse the new international movement as a political project, one must get rid not only of a certain conceptual baggage but above all of an attitude or perspective. This is what is proposed apparently by the essay of E. P. Thompson, which gave rise to a debate which has been published partially in the collection, *Exterminism and Cold War*.[1] The basis of Thompson's original article was that exterminism, as the 'highest stage' of our civilisation, is the moment at which the soviet and capitalist systems converge. When he returns to the argument three years later, at the conclusion of the published debate, Thompson is far more nuanced, particularly after the Polish experience.[2] Before, he seemed to take up the old theory of the 'convergence' of the soviet and capitalist systems; now, he claims only to be able to demonstrate that the two systems are driven by a logic which goes beyond either of them and which they do not implement consciously. The crucial point remains the fact that the symmetrical analysis of the two systems as united by an exterminist or by a bureaucratic logic does not permit the elaboration of a positive politics. It does not take into account the implications of the Polish experience, and the fundamental role played there by the law. The question is, why can Thompson not innovate on the conceptual level?

The debate around Thompson's thesis is suggestive of the difficulties faced by the new movement. In some cases, the aims are those of the politician, seeking to put action into a theoretical frame that permits the author to suggest the correct direction, the apt analysis, the necessary slogans. For example, the leader of the Italian PDUP, Lucio Magri, says he is expressing 'our' attitude, which is formulated on the basis of what the movement 'is' even though it may not be conscious of its true nature. This explicitly external analysis is developed at length by the functionalist Marxism of Mike Davis. Thompson's reply to Davis gets quickly to the point: 'In preempting the schema, we preempt also the permissible questions.' A similar functionalism, which claims to be able to explain everything, is often applied in this volume, for example by those who see a convergence of interests between the movement and German 'capital' which wants to continue its *Ostpolitik*, or those who claim that the Politburo want to use the movement to divide the Atlantic Alliance. This functionalism takes a curious form in Mary Kaldor's contribution. Beginning from the 'often remarked' fact that 'a world government is the utopia of the multinational corporation', she analyses the 'mode of war', the 'relations of war', and the like according to a Marxist scholasticism based on the analysis of the commodity at the beginning of *Capital*. This 'dialectic' changes nothing fundamental in Kaldor's position.[3]

Other ways of denying the political originality of the new movement appear in the replies to Thompson. The most pernicious is exemplified by Noam Chomsky and Fred Halliday. Both admit the existence of the movement in order, quickly, to take from it its content by making it merely the manifestation of a 'new cold war' which, in its turn, is supposed to be the expression of true struggles which take place in the Third World where, according to Chomsky, one finds 'the true signification of the cold war'. Halliday is more subtle insofar as he tries to stress the 'newness' of the present Cold War. But the difference makes no difference.[4] The same technique is applied by Balibar and the Medvedev brothers: the movement is reduced to the *expression*, the product or the symptom of either a social structure or an historical logic. The image of the clock stopped at five minutes before midnight, reproduced internationally on the covers of weeklies, expresses the same type of thought on the part of supporters of the Freeze: the situation forces our hand, we are able only to recognise and to react to its demands.

Thompson's insistence on the *newness* of the so-called 'exterminist' present expresses an important insight. Yet his own attempt at explanation has the same reductionist orientation. The movement is seen as a reply to the Cold War which, in a word, is an absurd monstrosity: 'The Object of the Cold War,' says Thompson, 'is the Cold War.' The author of *The Making of the English Working Class*, which demonstrated the self-constitution of a political class, and the author of the fierce denunciation of structuralism in *The Poverty of Theory*, seems to base his argument on the logic of one of those infamous 'structures without a subject' which he ridiculed not so long ago. The political translation of that analysis is an existentialist voluntarism which is simply a form of that 'zoological politics' for which Castoriadis criticised the movement. A strictly moralist argument like that of Marcus Raskin would be preferable to such an antipolitical politics.

Rather than locking up the movement within a theory, it is more useful to begin from the movement to search for its theory. The title of Thompson's original essay, parodying Lenin's thesis on imperialism, has the virtue of insisting on the novelty of a present which cannot be simply deduced from its past. Although Thompson's analysis fails, his intuition remains. A politics founded on a social theory can only reproduce the politics of the politicians or the bureaucrats. A sociological analysis, be it structuralist, functionalist or simply descriptive, cannot open up toward the project of a 'civil society'. It is more useful to work from within. Does the movement itself point to a political form which would permit the structuration of a modern civil society?

## 3. SOCIAL MOVEMENTS AND LIBERAL POLITICS

The Polish experience and that of the New Left took the form of a movement. This concept can be analysed in terms of experience. The Civil Rights movement invented forms of action which were characterised by the *mise en scène* of a specific injustice. The tactic plays on the relation between the law and the specific forms of injustice which violate it. Success is not defined simply by the formal or procedural correction of the injustice; success is achieved insofar as other people are involved in other actions, creating in this way a *movement*. The relation *and* at the same time the distinction between the particular and the universal explains how the movement produces a public space where a debate can take place. Other forms of action against racism, for example the Black Muslims or that of Malcolm X, did not find the same resonance. Similarly, at the beginning of the (American) war in Vietnam, certain forms of public resistance against the draft lead to others. The use of law distinguishes these movements both from a sociologising politics and from a politics that claims to put into practice an absolute morality. The difficulty that confronts the new political actor is to know *which* particular case is able to unleash this process. The other difficulty is to avoid dispersion once the first goal is attained.

Rather than present a thesis which defines and classifies the present movement, it is better to start from descriptions and internal critiques of its functioning. The critiques addressed to the Greens by the German left journal *Freibeuter* (Nr. 15) are useful. Thomas Schmid finds two difficulties in the political platform statement of the Greens. On the one hand, there is a false odour of communitarianism which coexists with that high-flying rhetorical tone which is characteristic of former Marxists. Schmid condemns the mixture of polemic and invective which produced a document that he characterises as 'jacobin' and 'pedagogical'. The critique of what Schmidt denounces as 'the lie of participatory democracy' (*Basis-Lüge*) is elaborated in the same issue under the title, 'Concerning Alternative Movements' Fear of Individual Maturity (*Mündigkeit*)'. Ernst Hoplitschek analyses critically the anti-individualist programme and practice of the Greens, whose quantitative egalitarianism is said to be based on a refusal to admit the specific importance of individual abilities. The result is that its politicians 'never speak in their own name' in order to avoid alienating the democratic base. Similarly, the attempt to formulate a *Philosophie der Grünen* by Manon Maren-Griesebach is criticised for its overstress on the participatory base community which neglects the hard institutional realities of modern societies. The only essay in this 'left' journal that nuances the negative image is Norbert Kostede's 'Mixtum compositum. The Cost of Governability', which points out correctly that the old politics is hardly a satisfactory basis from which to criticise the new.

These critiques of the new movement recall the worries expressed by Tocqueville about democracy and its revolutionary tendencies. 'One acquires easily the habit of sacrificing particular interests and of tramping on individual rights in order to arrive more quickly at the general goal that one seeks'.[5] The French, who have rediscovered Constant and Tocqueville in their intellectual inheritance, are seeking in that liberal politics an antidote to the excesses of democracy. They oppose the primacy of freedom and individual rights to its equalising tendencies. Germans and Americans are shocked: they recognise here what in their countries is called *neo-conservatism*. As opposed to traditional conservatives who generally turn toward a supposedly better past, the neo-conservatives are wed *sociologically* to their times on the basis of a realism which in no way excludes more traditionalist moral or political stances. In the wake of the authors of the famous Trilateral Commission report, they propose to limit social democracy in order to save a political democracy which is supposed to be one of the results of that very social democracy which has become a threat to itself.

These same concerns are expressed within a French left that is disillusioned by the experience of political power. One of the authors of the Trilateral Commission report, Michel Crozier, used the same approach in a recent issue of the 'second left' journal *Intervention*[6] to criticise Marcel Gauchet's analysis of the political possibilities of the CFDT as more than just a trade union. According to Crozier, the May 1968 movement did not advance democratic practice; France still has no democratic culture. The old left which came to power in 1981 is therefore not counterbalanced by a second strategy (unless one is referring to a supposedly liberalised old right). Crozier concludes that the second left must give up the 'disastrous myth of self-management', that it must reflect realistically on the bureaucratic element that enters into all human co-operation, and that it must admit that 'the right is not evil'. This is not false; but it is abstract and negative.

It is not sufficient to provide prudential advice to a movement which is attempting to create a civil society. Whatever the standpoint of the critic, the movement's contribution to a public debate concerning hitherto excluded domains has to be treated postively. The question is, by what means, and to what degree, can this goal be attained? It is not sufficient to add together or to juxtapose Tocquevillean sociology and liberal political logic. The crucial move depends on the mediation by the law which makes possible a politics which can give an institutional form to a movement which, without institutions, will explode or implode.

As in the 1960s in the US, the appeal to the law is crucial. Law is of course understood here in the sense of *droit*, or *Recht*; it alludes to the moral foundations as well as to the positive institutions of the law. The goal is to expand the domain of participation by a *mise en scène* of the particular in a way that makes clear that this particular is none the less the concern of everyone. The crucial tactic here is *civil disobedience* – a concept that is more accurate than the simple notion of 'non-violence', which does not refer to law and which usually is presented as a panacea. Such a tactic can give rise to a political development insofar as it appeals to a law which goes beyond positive law. Such a 'law beyond' can be a constitutional form, in the case of the US or Germany; it can be a more fundamental law in the case of Poland.[7] In all events, such a mediation transforms liberal politics which is no longer defined by its opposition to social democracy. It permits the constitution of a civil society in which that opposition will no longer be valid.

## 4. INTERNATIONAL CIVIL SOCIETY

The contemporary movements are international in a different sense than those of the 1960s. Not only do we see similar movements in different countries; the objectives of the different movements are given a unity by the context of East–West relations. This makes it more important than ever that the questions that were unresolved in the 1960s find a solution. The political responsibility of the present movements is greater.

In order for the legal mediation to take the form of a democratic international politics, one needs principles that make possible the designation of those problems around which public opinion can be mobilised. Insofar as a movement is egalitarian, activist and naïvely universalising, that is not easy. Politics is the art of distinctions and differences; it plays with time. Movements, on the other hand, like democracy, stress the immediate. This explains the inability of democracies to develop a foreign policy. They don't make war, for example; they undertake crusades on the basis of a messianism that does not permit strategic retreat and which is always ready to fall back in a disgusted cynicism. (Such an orientation may also explain why the US cannot conceive of its European allies as equal partners, as the editors of *Der Spiegel*, along with the Peace Movement, complain constantly.)

If it is not to fail and to disappear like the movement of the 1960s, the antinuclear movement will have to be not simply pacifist; it will have to take on more complex goals. There are signs of this in German domestic politics, where the peace movement is simply one element in a development of 'citizen initiatives' (*Bürgerinitiativen*) that began before the question of NATO missiles ever arose. These movements fit the 'civil rights model', combining citizen mobilisation with the appeal to law, and to the extension of legal protections (*Verrechtlichung*). The rise of the Peace Movement has for the moment overshadowed, and at the same time united, these separated and local initiatives. Their further development is suggested by a recent article[8] by the leftist Social Democrat, Günther Gaus. The former diplomat reprints his speech at the 1981 Berlin Congress of the SPD, in which he attacked the German acceptance of the NATO double decision under the ironic title, 'Peace cannot be More Beautiful'. The beautiful peace proposed by Gaus was a return of the American nuclear umbrella. In a Postscript added to that speech, Gaus explains that he received from Chancellor Schmidt the reply he had desired: the Americans will never do that. Hence, concludes Gaus, Europe must take on its own political unity, learning to fend for itself. Gaus' European option could draw together the strains that make up the present movement. But it is precisely this positive potential that makes the failure of the German left to react with other than cynical 'political realism' to the Coup in Poland so discouraging.

These critiques of the new movement by no means support the haughty stance adopted by the 'left liberals' who dominate the Parisian scene. They must admit that the movement that they call 'pacifist' is a challenge to them. Will they be able to recognise in this new international movement the political issues capable of mobilising the citizenry, the questions that could be the occasion for public opinion to form a practical judgement and to give itself the form of a movement? Will their defence of the rights of man become the basis of an international civil society in the same way that the reference to lawful right played that role in the creative period of the 1960s? The 1960s were an optimistic decade; we are living in a pessimistic climate whose reality the movement cannot deny. Perhaps great social transformations are born not from poverty or 'austerity' but from prosperity and those 'rising expectations' so loved by American sociologists. The new movement has arisen in an atmosphere of fear, anguish, and perhaps a civilisational crisis whose dimensions are moral, religious and rational. None the less, what is remarkable is that today, when the great religious moralities are no longer valid and when the universal morality of philosophy concerns only a few, one sees a renaissance of moral thought. But this time, morality cannot avoid the political because the international situation forces its attention. It is that necessity which justifies what might be called the optimism that underlies my analysis.

**Notes**

1. Edited by the New Left Review (London: 1982), the volume contains Thompson's original essay along with replies by Mike Davies, Raymond Williams, Rudolf Bahro, Lucio Magri, Etienne Balibar, Roy and Yhores Medvedev, John Cox, Saburo Kugai, Marcus Raskin, Noam Chomsky, Alan Wolfe, Mary Kaldor, and Fred Halliday. Thompson concludes the volume with a reply, under the suggestive title 'Europe, the Weak Link in the Cold War'.

   The different facets of the debate unleashed by the new movement are more evident in the journal *Telos*, which translated articles by French and other critics, as well as the internal debate within the German movement. (See especially no. 51, Spring 1982.)
2. One might note that Thompson's reply is often the speech of a politician anxious to preserve the adherence and coherence of his troops. His gentility toward the Medvedev brothers, for example, is frustrating. When he turns to the zany romanticism of Bahro, he limits himself to a brief remark concerning their disagreement about 'industrialism' as the root of all evils on both sides of the Cold War. This sort of sacrifice on the altar of the politics of the movement is hardly sufficient.
3. Kaldor does not return here to her better known thesis concerning the

'baroque' nature of modern arms. That thesis is well-summarised in an interview with John Mason, in *Telos*, op. cit. One need not be a Marxist to be a functionalist, as is evident in the attempts by those who see the roots of the movement in the search for an identity (especially in the case of the Germans, but more generally in the context of a modern state which is unable to mobilise affective support). This position is well-criticised by Sigrid Meuschel's article on 'German Neo-Nationalism', in the present issue of *Esprit* (and in English in *Telos*). One might add the remark of Seyla Benhabib: 'To accuse the present German peace movement of nationalism is the same as accusing the person who asks a question of affirming the truth of what they question.' (*Telos*, op. cit., p. 154).

4. Halliday's argument can be sketched briefly. As opposed to the Cold War of 1947–53, the present Cold War is marked by: the erosion of American nuclear superiority; a new wave of Revolutions in the Third World (after the calm from 1962–74); the birth of a new militarism in the USA; the 'political involution' of what the author calls prudishly 'post-revolutionary states'; and the accentuation of inter-capitalist contradictions. There is nothing to deny in these affirmations – that is why the analysis is pernicious – but such facts do not form the basis for a politics; at best they are to be integrated into a strategy, which is not the same thing.
5. *La Démocratie en Amérique*, vol. II, 4, 7.
6. No. 3, mars-avril, 1983.
7. In the French case, it seems to me that republican tradition serves this function. See my essay in *Intervention*, 'La république et l'order international' (No. 3, mars-avril, 1983). (This essay is reproduced in the present volume, which also suggests a further development of the role of constitutional law in France; see 'French Rhetoric and Political Reality'.)
8. In *Kursbuch*, No. 71, März, 1983.

# 8 *Esprit*

As the new director of *Esprit*, Paul Thibaud finds himself in an enviable, yet difficult and complex situation. Nearly half a century's tradition is a mixed blessing. The journal can call on contributors whose horizons extend beyond the tentacles of Paris, to the provinces, Europe and the Third World. Its reputation assures it a far-flung readership and influence as well. Tradition can, of course, easily become habit and govern expectations: that is the danger that Jean-Marie Domenach successfully confronted when he took over the directorship from Albert Beguin in 1957; and it is now Thibaud's problem in different social and political conditions. But the particular tradition of *Esprit* is a help here. From its foundation in 1932, *Esprit* has been socially and politically engaged against what it calls the 'established disorder'. Anchored in the French Catholic milieu – although many of its important contributors have been non-Catholic and non-religious – the journal has remained unique among Parisian intellectual reviews because of its attachment to ongoing struggles throughout France due to its national implantation, which gives it a movement character.[1]

But increasing secularisation may be drying the springs from which *Esprit* drew so much and so many of value. Further, May 1968 transformed the co-ordinates within which radical-critical activity can take place. *Esprit* is at an organisational and intellectual turning point. By looking at how it got there, and what it wants to do, I hope to show that we should, however we can, help *Esprit* to turn the corner. I want to argue that what one gets from the pages of *Esprit* is not so much an understanding of French (or Parisian) intellectuals as it is an image of France: its hopes, fears, possibilities and illusions.[2] The reason for this lies in a specific attitude or methodology, which *Esprit* has developed from its radical Christian political engagement – although one may come to this stance today by a different path.

Before turning to the historical and theoretical antecendents of *Esprit*, a specific and unique aspect of its content, present from the outset and continuing, which points to its movement character, should be mentioned. Many readers turn first to the 20–30 page section of every issue called the 'Journal à plusieurs voix'. On double-columned pages, one finds short essays – factual, ironic, engaged or simply points of information. The brief, pointed essay is rooted in a conversational genre that often works by counterpoint. In this case, the 'many voices' that constitute this section have actually spoken much of what we read. There is a weekly meeting at the office of *Esprit*, attended by 10 to 15 regulars and varying numbers of passers-through Paris (foreign and French). One talks informally about what is going on, what one thinks is important, what is bothersome or promising for the future. Here, being in Paris helps. There are visitors from all corners of the world, friends of the review or travellers returning. New ideas are brought, experiences confronted and deepened. At times, the discussion could be imaged as that of a nineteenth-century 'salon', with all its *préciosité*; at others, it is more like editorial meetings deciding the week's assignments; at still others, a political group elaborating strategy and evaluating its activities. Crucial is the feeling of collegiality and the sharing of an attempt to reveal the originality and yet typicality of the *event*. It was Merleau-Ponty, himself a member of an *Esprit* support group before the war, who wrote that 'there is often more truth in a small event (*fait divers*) than in a philosophical tome'. This could serve as the motto of the 'Journal à plusieurs voix', with the addendum that this style of writing engages the reader as participant in a way that edifying or scientific prose can never approach. This engaged style of intellectual work, and the stress on the event, are constant features of *Esprit*'s engagement.

This stylistic feature explains, in part, how *Esprit* has been able to retain its personality while following and remaining engaged in a rapidly transformed social and political half-century. If, as good intellectuals, we ask after the theoretical premise underlying this attitude, we find it in the specific Christianity which Mounier elaborated as the theory of 'personalism'. Mounier's theoretical writings would need a separate essay; and I confess to finding those that I have read far less interesting than the action that is *Esprit*. Mounier's predecessor, in theory and in practice, was Péguy. In both cases, Christianity becomes a faith and action built on the paradox of the *Incarnation*. We secularised moderns might find it easier to think this paradox with Heidegger's notions of the finitude of *Dasein* and its consequences; or to elaborate its political implications with Hannah Arendt and the theory of the Republic. For the person of faith, Christ incarnate is witness to the necessary tension of being human, which is the tension that we too experience as political actors:

the polarity of witness and efficacity, of dirty hands. The tension is not one of good vs. evil spirit vs. the flesh (as it might be for the Manichaeans or even for Augustine). It arises in the Incarnation because flesh cannot be abstracted from the spirit; flesh and spirit are not mutually exclusive, they abide in One. The moral is clear: the material (or the political) is not in principle evil, for as part of God's creation it is purposeful and potentially, but never actually, the embodiment of the holy. Faith in the Incarnation thus makes problematic rendering to Caesar, just as it does blind obedience to the established Church. There is and can be no 'good society' on finite Earth, where purity is impossible; and yet the task is to work for its advent. The intellectual aspect of this is very close to what the phenomenology of Merleau-Ponty aimed at: neither a rationalism-spiritualism, nor an empiricism-scientism is adequate to present the event (or advent) in its singularity. Seeking to preserve this singularity leads to the anti-bureaucratic, anti-exploitative politics that we shall see emerge over the years of *Esprit*'s development.

From the outset, *Esprit* was searching for a 'third way' to combat the 'money society' that it called the 'established disorder'. The Church hierarchy in France had demonstrated its complicity with disorder at the end of the nineteenth century, in the struggle against lay schooling, and in the Dreyfus affair. For Mounier and his group, this complicity is not inherent in Christianity; and one side of the journal's task was defined as wresting free the spiritual from its institutional form. That did not mean, however, returning to a pure spiritualism, for the purity of spiritualism could lead only to the implicit complicity of a pure consciousness that closes its eyes to the evils of the material world in which it is none the less embodied. *Esprit*'s engagement in the socio-cultural and political events of the times did not reject the spiritual in favour of efficacy, however, as Nizan's option for the Communist Party was urging so many at the time. Nor could the choice be that of the 'progressive Christian', who separated worldly and spiritual activity and worked with that same Party; for that is another manner of denying the message of the Incarnation. Mounier's paradoxical task demanded the maintenance of both poles: spiritual witness with a continual concern for efficacity. When *Esprit* was founded in 1932, Mounier's first struggle, against his friend Déléage, was to ensure that *Esprit* remain a journal, a place of reflection and communication, and not a political movement *per se*. Only in this way, he thought, could the spiritual have the necessary practical influence without wholly immersing itself in practicality.

If one were to trace the history of *Esprit*'s political choices, treating the journal-movement as if it were an organised political formation, one would be as often disappointed by its naiveté as one would be excited by its prescience.[3] In the pre-war period, *Esprit* developed some important insights. The rejection of the secular complicity of the church implied first and foremost that the movement *Esprit* could not claim, any more than could the church, to hold the truth of economic and political life. Our own 'church' cannot come with its 'good' doctrines to replace the corrupt one. (This is a lesson that continually aided *Esprit* in its relations with the Communist party, and in its analysis of the 'socialist' experiments elsewhere. From the outset, a critique of totalitarian pretensions was a part of *Esprit*'s basic attitude.) On the other side, however, it is not simply the church that is responsible for the established disorder; and thus, the attack on liberal individualism and economic exploitation cannot be limited to a demand for formal equality and material well-being, but must entail the creation of a reconstituted community (and not the return to a glorious, romanticised, past). While aspects of the Russian experience were tempting, it had to be rejected not only for its crude materialistic philosophy, but also because putting off the happy future for a present of sacrifice was not consistent with Mounier's personalist Christianity. But not all conclusions could be drawn from theory alone. Although he was friendly with Victor Serge, Mounier could only partly share his analysis of the Russian experience at this time. And although *Esprit* published E. Borne's attack under the title 'Stakhanovism and the working person' in March 1936, it was not until the love-hate collaboration with the French Communist Party after the liberation, and the struggles for decolonisation, that a clear view of Marxism in theory and in practice began to emerge. Condemning the Moscow purges, Mounier refused to equate Stalinism with Marxism (even though, like so many of his generation, including Sartre, his knowledge of Marx's texts was vague). Although in the early 1940s, N. Berdaieff wrote several essays on Russia for the journal, no reckoning was drawn – leaving the way open for a period of 'philo-communism' during and after the Resistance. A final aspect of *Esprit*'s pre-war politics was the sharp rejection of liberalism at the time of the Popular Front, and especially with its refusal to aid the Spanish Republicans. Liberalism's theoretical respect for the free individual was again and again shown in practice to be a sham, an atomism of the means with no view of the (spiritual) end.

The negative process by which *Esprit* set about defining its own position gave rise, in fact, to little substance from the viewpoint of social or political theory. Mounier was tempted by the approach of de Man's *The Socialist Idea*, which tried to go beyond the sterile dilemma of reformism vs. revolution by integrating the rising middle classes and stressing the role of governmental fiscal policies in establishing an almost medieval notion of the just price and the just wage. But *Esprit*'s anti-romantic and anti-parliamentary stance and Proudhonist sympathies made the group suspicious of the statism and spiritual idealism in this programme. *Esprit*'s anti-bourgeois and anti-materialist attitude opened it up toward the new phenomena with which de Man was concerned; but its voluntarism forbade any structured politics. For example, an issue of June 1936 was devoted to women, who were characterised as 'spiritual proletariat . . . who have remained outside history'. Nothing seems to have come of this, however, for it was the movement, not the goal's realisation, that was vital. Work groups were established throughout France (and, to a degree, abroad: *Esprit* was subtitled 'International Journal, French edition'). To avoid attracting authors only in search of personal glory, all were to take part in the menial tasks as well. Politically, despite its generally pacifist sympathies, *Esprit* was among the few publications that took a public stance against the Munich Accords. Yet, with the war, the defeat and establishment of the Vichy regime, *Esprit* remained more a movement and an attitude than a theory or a party.

The *Esprit* group's role during the Resistance is only of peripheral interest in our context. Winock's history provides ample detail for those interested; and it shows, as one might expect, the kind of distortions and quarrels to which, with the Cold War, its role was subjected. More important is that, with the liberation, *Esprit* devoted increasing stress to political matters, and adopted what Winock calls a 'philo-communist' attitude. Sympathy with the communists was rooted not so much in an abstract anti-capitalism or a theoretical convergence of views as it was in the *experienced fact* of the fraternal and sacrificing *community* established during the Resistance. This was the spiritual side, a unity of the idea of socialism and the real efficacity of struggle. The other side was more political. The personalist philosophy had to be de-purified; the temptation to absolutisation to be avoided. Thus, Mounier polemicised against Camus and *Combat* for their purism; and Domenach supported the need for a 'political justice' after the Liberation. Without consciously sacrificing its original attitude, *Esprit* could assert, from the pen of Jean Lacroix, that 'we will not make our revolution without' the communists, since their trust in the communists was based on an ethical admiration for their solid activity as a determined minority held together by its communal faith.

*Esprit*'s period of philo-communism did not pretend to justify itself with reference to Marxian theory. It was an *activity of bearing witness* that tempted them, for it fitted their own self-image. To this was added, of course, a visceral rejection of the 'American way of life', which seemed to embody all the evils of atomised individualism and the domination of money over any collective values. And, finally, in this early phase, there was the communist support of de-colonisation. This political attitude based in the shared *ethos* of a movement, paradoxically, made it easier for the *Esprit* group to move away from its supportive stance when the wave of purges and then revolts broke out in Eastern Europe.[4] Still, although Mounier had called in February 1947 for the creation of that 'socialism with a human face' that became a living slogan 20 years later in Czechoslovakia, the Cold War and its intrigues, which established a false but psychologically real friend-or-foe community, made the break difficult and painful.

*Esprit*'s period of philo-communism enjoined it to return to Marx's own texts. *Esprit* played an important role in that Catholic rediscovery of the humanist young Marx – not yet stigmatised by Louis Althusser as the root of all deviations! A special issue was devoted to the theme 'Open Marxism vs. Scholastic Marxism', in which such communists as C. Roy, Remo Cantoni, Georges Mounin, Marcel Prenant, Maurice Caveing and Jean Momarchi wrote alongside Jean Beaufret, Walter Dircks, Father Chenu, Christopher Hill, Francis Jeanson, Henri Desroches, M. Collinet and Jean Lacroix. In his summary article, speaking for *Esprit*, Lacroix attempted to draw together Proudhon and Marx, each correcting and complementing the other. However theoretical this debate may appear in retrospect, it was its political side that outweighed whatever theoretical contribution to a 'science of revolution' might have emerged.

*Esprit*'s basic theoretical or personalist stance seemed at the time to prohibit an elaborate, structural theory of revolution. In Christian terms, it had to maintain at once the poles of transcendence and of incarnation; in intellectual terms, it could neither give itself entirely to the play of material forces, nor fly above them at the level of theory. For a time, this tension led to a kind of Lukácsian theory of the proletariat as the revolutionary subject-object of history. Winock describes this attitude toward 'the proletarians: new barbarians to be baptized, and new chance for Christianity'. Later, he cites a letter from a participant, F. Goguel, who describes a 'mystique of the proletariat' that seemed to inspire the journal at this time. It was, of course, at this same period that the worker-priest movement began to take root in France.

While the temptation and mystification of the proletariat is obvious, what is important is that *Esprit* did not succumb. The constitutive tension of Mounier's personalist Christianity of the Incarnation was as opposed to absolutising the temporal as it was to separating the absolute from the temporal. Once can no more judge the real in terms of the ideal than one can understand the real apart from the ideal. Mounier continually rejected attempts by 'progressives' to justify their political strategy by reference to the Absolute; and just as strongly opposed those who would suggest that this meant that the means can be justified without reference to that Absolute. While this may sound like a truism, the history of *Esprit*'s political engagement demonstrates again and again that only in this manner can one let the *event* appear in all its originality. Only when one sees this originality of the event can one respond to it intelligently and humanely. The need to preserve the priority of the event implies a politics deeply rooted in anti-bureaucratism since the bureaucrat is defined precisely by a subsumptive mentality that excludes the presence of the originality of the event. Intellectually, it implies a rejection of both rationalism and empiricism, a stance akin to that of phenomenology.

The years that followed Mounier's sudden death in 1950 were marked by a basic fidelity to the attitude that had been worked out across two decades of engagement. Precisely for that reason, there ensued a series of gradual changes as the Fourth Republic staggered along, the Third World entered the world stage, and Stalinism's barbarity was revealed by its own proletariat. Under the directorship of Albert Beguin, *Esprit* continued its work, maintaining itself as a place of reflection and a movement open to the event. When Beguin suddenly died in 1957, a 'new series' was inaugurated under the direction of Jean-Marie Domenach, who had joined Mounier during the Resistance and had worked with the journal since the Liberation. The editorial that began the 'new series' started with the significant assertion that where Beguin's task had been to continue, without pretending to replace the work inaugurated by Mounier, now there was the need for more than continuation. A new generation, born of the Resistance and liberation, was taking over; its task was to stand on its own feet.

Domenach's essay, 'Esprit, New Series',[5] tried to define the direction that he wanted to give the journal. He began with the differences between his situation and that of Mounier in 1932. Most important was that the innocence of Mounier's generation was no longer possible: it had been lost in the Resistance and the struggles that followed it. The failure of communism was shown in all its nakedness in 1956; the new wave of resistance seemed to be centring around the anti-colonial struggles. The failure of past actions and ideals called for a more serious labour of reflection, an end to facile syntheses. Domenach recognised the specificity of personalism, and the chief problem it had not yet resolved: 'As opposed to Marxism, personalism doesn't carry with it its sociology.' This need for sociological concretion, to which *Esprit* would devote much of its energy, did not mean, however, that the analytic intellect was stressed at the expense of the spirit. Sociology cannot be practised at the sacrifice of the person. Thus, while Domenach saw Lukács' reading of the proletariat as correct, emerging from it is a kind of revenge of Hegel and the nineteenth century: the individual is replaced by a collective form. Not only does the idea of the vocation of the proletariat to be the 'consciousness of society' pose theoretical problems; the attitude of the French proletariat toward the struggle in Algeria indicated that the proletariat does not in fact function as the theory said that it should. More, if one part of the society is said to represent the totality of society, this eliminates the rest, and poses a dangerous basis for a totalitarianism. Rejecting the idea of a universal, revolutionary class, Domenach observed that 'in the society of comfort itself, new proletarians emerge as the organisation becomes the more perfect: those who are ignored, rejected, unintegrated – physically or mentally ill, the aged, inmates of asylums and hospitals, lost children and young delinquents.' He went on to point to the changed nature and role of labour, and to insist that intellectual labour too is affected by this change. A collective elaboration is necessary; and such a collective project reaffirms the old idea that if the truth is to be known, the person knowing it must be worthy as well. For this reason, *Esprit*'s movement-character was seen as still vital.

The concluding section of Domenach's article is titled 'Reformists, Revolutionaries or Franciscans?' It seeks to reaffirm, in the changed conditions, the project begun by Mounier. The term reformist has become vague as neo-capitalism has made socialism an ever-less direct antithesis. The charge of reformism is important only insofar as it forces socialists to make more clear and precise their understanding of the content and the means of achieving socialism. Furthermore, as neo-capitalism transforms the old structures, the question of power comes to take precedence over that of property. Revolution, therefore, concerns 'control, administration . . . education at least as much as political overthrow'. The 'Franciscan' element is maintained in order to retain the constitutive tension of the Christian project. Domenach writes of it in terms of 'an easy friendship with nature, with machines; a manner of playing with things rather than appropriating them'. All of this, finally, returns to the central theme: 'It is necessary to describe the event in its novelty.' Any other approach – Marxism on the one side, bureaucracy on the other – dissolves the event, and with it, the human personality.

Domenach remained director of *Esprit* for 21 years. He maintained the breadth and depth of its concerns, opening up to new directions in the analysis of social and political tendencies as well as to cultural change. It was during this period that the nature and role of the French intellectual began to change. Where the traditional intellectual was a literary person who took a political stance from the standpoint of the moral universal, the 1960s saw the emergence of the social scientist. *Esprit* tried to keep abreast of these new developments, with special issues, interviews, and round-table discussions. A central figure in this aspect of the journal's work was Paul Ricoeur. At the same time, in keeping with his goal of developing a personalist sociology, Domenach opened the journal to sociologists like Alain Touraine, Michel Crozier, Serge Mallet and Daniel Mothé. Sectoral analyses were published, and issues devoted to specific problems. Some of the ideas of 1968 were anticipated, for example, by the younger Michel Crozier's 1957 analysis of participation, or Serge Mallet's new working class perspective, or Daniel Mothé's sociology of work.

1968 was a halfway point, and perhaps a turning point, in the directorship of Domenach. It took *Esprit*, like everyone else, by surprise. That generation that Domenach had wanted to stand on its own feet may have grown a bit too comfortable; and its ties with the Gaullists, many of whom, like Edmond Michelet, were compagnons from the Resistance, may have been a bit too close. None the less, after the period of hesitation, *Esprit*'s basic attitude before the event stood up; *Esprit* made the turn. The years of disarray of the Left that followed and which reached their heights and depths with the unity and rupture of the Common Programme, posed new problems. Many of these are described by the new director, Paul Thibaud, in the text that follows.[6] 'Thibaud is not of the generation of May in a genealogical sense; he had begun writing for the journal while Beguin was still director, and was its general editor under Domenach (while being formed, as well, through co-editorship of the clandestine *Verité-Liberté* during the Algerian struggle). There is thus a continuity of the *Esprit* tradition, coupled with an opening to the post-May generation. Domenach felt the need to broaden his own work, after more than 30 years with *Esprit*'s day-to-day activities. With Thibaud, we can hope for that famous 'change in continuity'.

Thus far, under Thibaud, the rubrics into which the journal's contents are divided have remained similar: major articles, the 'Journal à plusiers voix', a series of shorter essays called 'Chroniques', and a book review section (which seems a bit less 'literary' than in the past, although literature is still the dominant subject). A 'review of reviews' section has been added as an occasional feature, to focus on either a special issue of a journal or on a new journal, or on an important foreign journal. Many of the old authors are still present, but new ones have begun to appear. The ecumenical aspect remains, as do the contacts with the provinces, on which more stress is being placed through attempts to hold public meetings and discussions involving *Esprit*'s editors and collaborators. (Some of these, as in Paris, too, are held jointly with other journals, *Silex* in Grenoble, for example, or *Libre* and *Faire* in Paris.) The 'Internal Bulletin' has reappeared regularly, reporting activities, printing projects still in elaboration, and serving to bring in new followers (its existence is announced in the journal; it can be ordered at a cost of 5 francs). Regular work groups are meeting in the areas of philosophy, culture, politics and history; and summaries of their meetings appear in the Internal Bulletin. All of this appears to be a return to the journal-movement approach of Mounier; and some of it had begun again already at the end of Domenach's directorship. Finally, for those who may have known *Esprit* at one or another period, a change in format should be noted: from the severe tome of the past has emerged a multicoloured, illustrated series of covers; inside too one finds some illustrations, and even a cartoon or two, as well as a bolder typeface and less demanding visual presentation with more editorial subtitles. This is, of course, a concession to the market, since the growing numbers of French journals are competing on the same news-stands as before, and *Esprit* is attempting to gain a new audience as its old one from the days of Mounier increasingly passes away.

More difficult to evaluate is the changed intellectual thrust of the new direction. To read *Esprit* regularly remains an education, with coverage ranging from foreign and domestic politics across the arts and sciences (including poetry and translation) to the minor fact. If there is a change here, it seems to me to lie in the increasingly self-critical stance which reflects *Esprit*'s own self-questioning. It is important to note that this self-questioning is not the same as that which has recently overcome so many French intellectuals in the wake of the *Gulag*: it is not the breast-beating and abstract negation of an earlier position that thought that it had the key to the world and world history, and which now sinks into a nihilism hidden within a rhetoric of revolt. Mounier's engaged personalist Christianity saved his successors from this extreme of French intellectual self-abnegation, as we saw. It is for this reason that *Esprit* has found itself publishing essays by Castoriadis, Lefort, Gauchet and those editing the new journal *Libre*, as well as analyses from self-management theorists like Rosanvallon. The critique of totalitarianism undertaken by *Esprit* had begun already in 1932, when Mounier realised that the criticism of the established Church meant that one could not, in turn, establish a new church. This attitude has continued in recent issues: in Cadard and Chen Ying-Hsiang's presentation of the power struggles in China, Lavau's analysis of the historiographical distortions by the French Communist Party and in a series of essays on religious sects, as well as through the publication of documents on Poland, Czechoslovakia and the Hungarian minority in Transylvania. Or, on a more 'engaged' level, this has taken the form of analyses of the ecology movement (Mongin), the problems within the French left (Julliard, Thibaud, Castoriadis and Rosanvallon), and a series of hefty criticisms of the knee-jerk leftism that appeared in France at the time of the suicides of the Baader-Meinhof group in Germany.

A key to *Esprit*'s changed stance is the new subtitle of the journal: 'Change Culture and Politics'.[7] The guiding idea seems to be that we must conceive of politics as a form of culture. In a sense, this is a logical development of the early stress on the event in its originality. The difference appears first of all insofar as the analysis of the event seems to take a less party-like or tactical orientation than it did in the past. The idea of a 'logic of emancipation' and the notion of self-management in all spheres implies that one focus on those activities that, at one or another cultural level, are seeking to restore the dimension of community. The guiding idea here is that the 'logic of emancipation' cannot be the result of abstract analysis. The events that *Esprit* analyses are seen as social experiments. Their originality lies first of all in their democratic character. Democracy is not conceived of as a method through which social harmony and unanimity can be achieved. The goal is not to create (or to see created) a society without contradictions. Rather, democracy is liberating in the sense that it is an arrangement that permits and demands difference; the democratic community is a community of persons who are constantly in a position to redefine their relation to the collective.

The 'Working Program' published in No. 4 of the Internal Bulletin, shows the direction this questioning takes as a systematic programme. Recent articles in the journal illustrate the idea as well. Jeanne Favret-Saada's ethnography of the nature of French peasant beliefs in sorcery, the long discussion and debate concerning the innovative community mental health practices in the small mining town of Monceau-les-Mines, the discussion of the Canadian firm Tricofil as a new 'LIP', or the analysis of the failure of technocracy in the Aquitaine region – to mention only these – are illustrative. To these are joined more historical and theoretical presentations, such as Philippe Ariès' essay on family and the cities, the structures of scientific practice today, or Louis Dumont's remarkable historical-ethnographic essay on the birth of the modern conception of the individual. Nor is Marx neglected, as indicated by Hyppolite Simon's attempt to draw from Marx's confrontation with Hegel a 'logic of emancipation' separate from the political state.

To conceive of politics as a form of culture does not, of course, mean that the activity of the established state and political parties are to be simply neglected. In addition to the analysis in the 'Working Program', the essay by Olivier Mongin in this issue of *Telos*[8] points to the kind of understanding of the relation of the state (or politics) and civil society that is typical of *Esprit*'s approach. Political questions, in the narrow sense, are not neglected, nor can they be. Obviously, foreign affairs, the question of nuclear deterrence, the Third World, Middle East, Horn of Africa, Southeast Asia, etc., are presented and analysed, as are actual events in France. For, once again, it must be stressed that *Esprit* is a general journal, a French journal – and not an organ of pure theory. For the same reason, the journal still publishes poetry (and a special segment in January 1978 on the 'Crisis of Poetry'), short stories and literary analysis. The stress on the different, which is necessary for a functioning democracy, does not imply that one can simply neglect the common established disorder we all live.

Thibaud's task on assuming the directorship is thus a triple one, as I see it. First, to retain the movement-character of the journal, letting neither its practical activities nor its nature as a place of reflection take precedence. Second, as Domenach had already suggested in 1957, to continue to provide the sociology of personalism, and to do so through the continued stress on the originality of the event. Third, to maintain *Esprit*'s role as an actual, immediate political voice in French cultural and political life. As I said at the outset, I think this effort merits our support. We foreign readers of *Esprit* will find in it not only a general education, not only information or a sense of French cultural-political life. We find too a theoretical reflection seeking to come to grips with problems that we share with the authors, and attacking them from a perspective similar to our own. And we find the attempt to make this reflection concrete through the presentation of actual, ongoing social and cultural developments. In short, we can learn from this journal.

## Notes

1. In 1971, at a *Telos* conference in Buffalo, André Gorz was asked to represent *Les Temps Modernes* on a panel discussing the role of left journals. He justified his refusal by remarking that *Les Temps Modernes* was no longer a radical journal but rather an institution! While the remark is somewhat anachronistic at present, since the editorial board of *Les Temps Modernes* has been joined by a number of younger, more activist 'veterans' of the post-May realignments and rethinkings – such as Claire Etcherelli, François George, Pierre Goldman. Pierre Rigoulot and Pierre Victor – it is still the case that one does not go to that journal to get an understanding of the ongoing social and political dynamic of contemporary France. Whether *Les Temps Modernes* will disappear with Sartre and de Beauvoir, as Gorz thought then, or whether it has taken a new lease on life remains to be seen. For the present, I think, Gorz's judgement still holds; because of its manner of functioning, which is not independent of its lack of a social and political base, as well as the weight of its past, *Les Temps Modernes*' only tradition is an 'existential' lack of roots that will no doubt condemn it.

2. This is not to say that the journal is solely national, nor anti-intellectual. It does take up the issues raised by the intellectuals, in the world of theory, culture and politics. And it is continually concerned with the ongoing world situation. 'Parochial' would be the last term one would think of applying to *Esprit*, as the list of special sections and issues indicates. My point is that when foreigners read it, they get a sense not just of a common intellectual project, or a similar political project; they also come to feel and understand the specificity of the French context.
3. Michel Winock's *Histoire politique de la revue Esprit*, 1930–1950 (Paris, 1975), on which I rely for much of the following, is more than just that kind of chronicle. On the other hand, it is less than an analysis, since it explicitly neglects the socio-cultural reflection which occupied much of the journal's space. A well-schooled historian, who has used unpublished materials and interviews with many of the participants, Winock seems to me to have cut short the range of his work by not asking the more 'pedagogical' question: how could such a journal-movement survive; why did it maintain its influence; and what are the implications of its basic stance for us today? These, of course, are my questions – but without Winock's excellent work, and occasional observations on this score, I could not ask them so clearly. Winock's tendency is to point frequently to the tension between witness and efficacity, to indicate that an engaged spiritualism entails an ambiguity between short-term and long-term goals, and to suggest that it was, somehow, the genius of Mounier's person that bridged the gap. By taking his history beyond 1950, and posing what must be Thibaud's and our own question, I hope to show that there is something more involved.
4. One might compare *Esprit*'s situation with that described by Dominique Desanti in *The Stalinists*. Once a philosophy of history is added to that personal experience of community, the rupture becomes the more tortuous, the circumlocutions and rationalisations become necessary defence mechanisms, and one becomes truly a Stalinist, the member of a counter-Church with its own iron-clad orthodoxy.
5. Published in *Esprit*, 25e année, no. 255, novembre, 1957, pp. 468–84. (Citations in the following paragraph are from this article.)
6. The 'Working Program of *Esprit*' was published with this essay in *Telos*.
7. The following text appears on the first page of each issue: "The totalitarian imposture has finally exploded. And now, it is as if our world had lost its future: the decomposition of capitalist societies no longer announces anything. This truth leads to disarray: for us, it is an opening, the occasion to invent something else.

   'First of all: to renew critique. And, when we denounce capitalist speculation and deception, no longer to have as our horizon that good society where the professionals of well-being would have free play. To stop protesting against exploitation in order better to forget domination.

   'The rich and the powerful don't only exploit the poor; they prevent them from living. If exploitation has power over its victims, it is because autonomous modes of life are destroyed. In a society that is atomized (*défaite*), large commercial, cultural and political organizations propose or impose a product, a service, an obligation for each aspect of life.

Thus, the people becomes a public; the resident, a user; the citizen, a consumer; the worker, a tool.

'The false technical rationalization fails in the details; each of its operations fails to reach their goal. Productivist activism only knows how to put off its failure. Revolts break out on the margins, but this system in which we no longer believe still determines behaviours and demands. By reflection, by experimentation, we must find an alternative to it. We don't believe in a society 'without contradictions' and without a State, but in a society of diversity and conflicts where the capacities of analysis, management and critique which the organizers and clerics have taken over are returned to the common life.

'The transformation that we want in culture, politics and religion presupposes that intellectuals change their way of working; that they walk in the world without blinkers and without catechisms; that they get rid of their clericalism, their concern with themselves, and no longer consider themselves as the vanguard of a good power, as those who determine the sense of life.

'To recognize the limits of reason, the force and the value of conflicts; to combat the separation of experience and competence – this is to give a body to this simple proposition: democracy is a future.'

8. 'Questioning Politics' was printed in *Telos*, no. 36.

# 9 French Socialism and Modernisation

*Il faut choisir l'avenir contre le passé quand le passé est vide d'avenir.* F. Mitterrand

## 1. REALITY PLUS MODERNITY EQUALS WHAT?

No social movement carried the French Socialists to power in 1981; and contrary to 1936, none emerged to support or push further its action. Three years and three policies later the government was confronted by the largest demonstration in post-war history. More than a million Frenchmen came in the name of freedom of education to protest against the modernisation of an educational system whose foundation was laid by Napoleon! The protesters were not concerned so much with the details of the reform but its very principle: state-controlled and uniform educational practices. That these millions misread the government's proposal is no more relevant than the charge that they were manipulated by the opposition (or the Church). This inability to build support for modernising projects has roots that are French, others that are socialist, and still others that are found in all modern democracies.

The Socialist victory was actually the defeat of Valery Giscard d'Estaing. De Gaulle's long-time Finance minister had been elected in 1974 on a platform of modernisation with a human face. His early years were marked by impromptu suppers with modest families, visits to prisons and other bureaucratic institutions, and even – an ungallic first – a photo of the President in his swimming shorts. They were also characterised by a refusal to begin the adaptation to the post-1973 world economic slowdown. Giscard continued a policy of rapidly modernising French industry in which the state played a key role. The inevitable reckoning with this reality replaced the human face; a new Prime Minister, Raymond Barre, replaced the gaullist, Jacques Chirac. The new strategy was to force-feed market-liberalism into the listless economy while Giscard, to avoid the heat, assumed the Presidential *hauteur* that De Gaulle's institutions permit. The domestic repercussions of the return to the market were not long in coming. Two foreign policy *gaffes* sealed Giscard's unpopular fate – the diamonds given him by the bloody African dictator Bokassa, and the meeting with Brezhnev despite the invasion of Afghanistan.

The phenomenon of election-as-rejection is not specific to France. But Mitterrand is not Reagan or Thatcher; he was elected as a socialist (and a non-appeaser). Still, the militant posturings and nationalisations of his first year in power gave way in June 1982 to a devaluation of wage-freeze which was followed, in March 1983, by a politics of 'austerity' (and another devaluation) which would surprise neither Reagan nor Thatcher (who find nothing to complain of in Mitterrand's Atlanticism either). This 'Barreism without Barre' is directed since July 1984 by Laurent Fabius, a well-bred young technocrat (and Giscard look-alike) whose credo of '*modernité*' has replaced the old-style socialism of Pierre Mauroy and his motto of '*changement*'. Eighteen months remain until the elections. Success in the 1986 Parliamentary depended on demonstrating a new equation: socialism = modernity + reality.

The French socialists don't put it quite this way. They are socialists. Austerity is said to be 'conjunctural'; it is a 'parenthesis' in a steady course. The party claims to have retained its socialist 'essence' despite the difficulties of its dialectical 'existence'. The union with the Communist Party was the sign of this fidelity. Now that the Communists have left the government – as a result of their own internal power struggles following their fall to only 12 per cent of the voters in the June European elections – the reshuffled cabinet returned Jean-Pierre Chèvenement and his CERES-Marxist faction to play this symbolic role.

The socialists are also French. Bitter pills like the industrial restructuring in the Lorraine or the refusal to aid the bankrupt giant Creusot-Loire are justified by the rhetorical identification of the Left with French nationalism which dates from the French Revolution and the Resistance. The international struggle for markets has transformed the class struggle into the struggle for modernisation. Again, if for different reasons, socialism = modernity + reality.

But the problem is not only French or socialist. This is apparent in the disarray among the intellectuals. The socialist concern with *égalité* has been replaced by a flirt with *Liberté*. One finds Hayek strewn together with Rawls and Nozick on the pages of erstwhile 'Left' journals. Liberalism has become as confused and confusing a label as Marxism once was. *Liberté* tends to be identified with privatisation. The appeal to the market covers the rise of technical managers whose power increases because their role cannot be admitted by the new rhetoric. The two most interesting journals, *Esprit* and *Intervention* seem to have made a virtue of necessity. Sociology and politics have been subordinated to philosophy. Debate focuses, for example, on the difference of 'left and right-wing liberalism', questions the relation of democratic and republican institutions, attempts to break free of the gallocentrism typical of French thought. Probing received wisdom instead of dishing out new *verités* suggests that the search for questions has replaced the demand for answers. The French and the Socialists are joining the rest of us. They may have the advantages of the late-comer due to their own idiosyncrasies.

## 2. THE ROAD TO POWER. FOR WHAT?

François Mitterrand was an extraordinarily successful politician of the parliamentary Fourth Republic whose stalemated system de Gaulle replaced in 1958. This (non-socialist) leader of a small party had manoeuvred himself into one Ministerial portfolio after another in the rapidly changing governments of the Fourth Republic. His career was not an unfamiliar pattern, in France or elsewhere. Mitterrand managed finally to shake his nickname, 'Le Florentin', by his continual denunciation of the Fifth Republic as 'a permanent *coup d'état*', as he titled a 1964 book. He began a new career by adopting the ideology of socialism to the changing conditions of modernising France.

French socialism had reached its nadir in the early 1960s. Local bastions remained in the North (which produced Pierre Mauroy) and Marseilles (whose Mayor was Gaston Deferre), but the barons were feuding. Progressive Catholics were swept up in the Gaullist wave (Jacques Delors, for example, served in the Cabinet of Chaban-Delmas). The after-shocks of Budapest weakened the Communists, and the end of the Algerian War eliminated a unifying issue. Mitterrand set about rebuilding. The institutions of the Fifth Republic served his aims. The opposition could triumph in the Presidential Fifth Republic only by rallying around a single leader. When the Russian invasion of Czechoslovakia ended the hope for a Euro-Communist revival, socialism was the only game in town. Mitterrand had positioned himself well. He used the 1970s to create a new coalition.

The new Socialist Party was a coalition of leaders and factions divided by ideology but united by the quest for power. The founding Congress at Epinay in 1971 federated the remnants of Alain Savary's traditional socialists, the regional groups of Mauroy and Deferre, and the Marxist ideologies of Chèvenement's Centre d'études et de recherches marxistes (CERES) under the direction of Mitterrand's Convention des institutions republicaines. The next step was to formulate a Common Programme with the Communist Party. This permitted Mitterrand to make a credible showing in the 1974 Presidential elections.

Mitterrand's electoral coalition was given a needed activist base when the 'self-management' orientation from the small Parti socialiste unifié (PSU) led by Michel Rocard joined it in 1975. At the same time, socially concerned Catholics, such as Delors' club 'echange et projets', began to participate. This forged links to the CFDT trade union which had been revivified under the leadership of Edmond Maire. The 1977 municipal elections brought socialist victories and the expectation of left success in the 1978 parliamentary battle. The three currents, which continue to exist formally within the Party, were now clearly defined. The majority Mitterrandists (including the Mauroy, Deferre and Savary factions) were momentarily allied with the 'self-management' orientation led by Rocard. The CERES was a minority representative of doctrinal orthodoxy.

There were two worms in this electoral apple. Michel Rocard identified the more fundamental problem in a speech to the 1977 Party Congress in Nantes. He spoke of a conflict between 'two cultures' which divided French socialism: a centralist and a self-management orientation. Rocard identified himself clearly with the latter, which has come to be known as the 'second left' and includes the trade unionists of the CFDT. The immediate consequences of the presence of these two cultures was revealed by the second worm. The Communist ally had not profited as it expected from the coalition; it seized an occasion shortly before the parliamentary elections to reject the Common Programme. This gave Mitterrand the occasion for a tactical manoeuvre to eliminate the threat to his personal power posed by the growing popularity of Rocard (who remains today the most popular politician in France). At the Party Congress in 1979, Mitterrand allied himself with the CERES-Marxists on the grounds that the Party needed to regain credibility on the left. The Rocardians were limited to 21 per cent of the Party executive. The results were felt in the first year of socialist government.

As with Ronald Reagan, Mitterrand took his electoral victory in

1981 for a popular mandate. To the surprise of many, his platform began to be implemented, literally. Communist support was not necessary, but four communist ministers were selected. Nationalisations, the reduced work week at no cut in pay, a fifth week of paid vacation, increased minimum wage and social benefits followed one another rapidly. The press spoke of a 'state of grace', neglecting its own responsibility for the uncritical acceptance of this economic orthodoxy.

The results were not surprising: a temporary wage freeze in June of 1982 accompanied a first devaluation; a second devaluation in March of 1983 stressed the need of a 'politics of austerity' for a France which could not deny that it is part of the world market. Much had been accomplished elsewhere, in judicial reform, cultural politics and especially decentralisation, but the economy came to dominate the debate. Electoral defeat followed electoral defeat; municipal bastions conquered in 1977, and older fiefdoms, fell. Some, like the CERES and the Communists said that the government should have stayed the orthodox course. But the French economy does not have the weight that supported Reagan's kind of economic voluntarism. Chèvenement left the cabinet when his protectionist-nationalist proposals were rejected; the communists remained.

The dilemma confronting the French socialists is how to translate the economics of 'austerity' into a politics capable of mobilising French opinion. Austerity means attacking entrenched positions — inflation-adjustment to wages, social security and health care benefits, decreased subsidies for public transportation and the like. France may or may not have more such bastions of privilege than the other Western democracies; the problem, in any case, is familiar. Those who stand to lose from the changes appeal to 'acquired rights' and to personal freedom of choice and contract. When it is socialists who are doing the cutting, this oppositional 'liberal' rhetoric has a ready market. And so it was that millions were mobilised to demonstrate for freedom of (educational) choice on 24 June.

Mitterrand had to regain the initiative. The Florentine reappeared. A thinly disguised attempt from the Elysée to float a centre-left alliance in the European elections was roundly defeated, as were the socialists (and communists). The demonstration came a week later. Stone-walling did little good. Mitterrand unveiled the secret weapon of the Fifth Republic: he called for a referendum! In fact, for a referendum permitting the President to go over the head of Parliament to propose to the people measures concerning 'public liberties' such as educational reform. The stratagem was apparently brilliant – what could the opposition object to? – but potentially dangerous: could one imagine another President calling a referendum on immigrant workers, for example? What are public as opposed to private liberties? Before discussion could begin, however, a second move offset the stratagem. The Prime Minister was replaced, and the communists departed. The referendum was never held.

What next? The new government has pledged to continue the recovery-through-austerity which has shown some results (despite unemployment figures of some 2 500 000). The communists' departure may bring more strike activity, but the power and support of the unions is limited. The opposition is divided among supporters of Giscard, Chirac and Barre; more important, it is uncertain how to relate to the new right wing National Front movement of Jean-Marie Le Pen which received 12 per cent of the votes in the European elections. The new dynamics of the situation were unintentionally revealed in the nearly identical headlines that greeted the new cabinet in the left-leaning *Libération* and the right-oriented *Le Quotidien*: 'Mitterrand Prime Minister'. Giscard reacted to adversity by withdrawing to Elysian *grandeur*. Now, the Florentine has put himself on the line – but for what? For self-preservation, say the cynical. But the interplay of his socialist rhetoric, French politics, and a modernising democratic economy may produce unexpected results over the longer term.

## 3. THE END OF MARXISM AND THE POSSIBILITY OF SOCIALISM

My Marxist friends are devotees of what Hegel called 'the cunning of reason'. They used to call it the logic of history or the dialectic, but that was refuted by the Gulag. Still, old habits die hard. Their temptation is to write off the French experience as another illustration of socialists doing the capitalists' dirty work. The working class is again the victim of politicians who prefer power to principle. Socialist rhetoric, communist participation are the appearance; austerity politics, praise of the market and rehabilitation of the entrepreneur are the reality. And the frosting on this cake: Mitterrand's Bundestag speech in favour of the Pershings, and his unblushing Atlanticism.

The Socialist Party's Marxists take a different tack. Their attitude recalls the behaviour that got the British Labour Party into such trouble. The CERES-faction presented a counter-project at the Party Congress at Bourg-en-Bresse in October 1983. It warned against a free market liberalism imported because of France's place in international competition and its internal backwardness. It condemned what it calls the realism that simply 'administers' the crisis on the grounds that this implies that the crisis is something inevitable. The CERES proposes a voluntarism which combines economic proposals with the necessity to prepare for the 1986 elections. France is said to need 'un grand projet', which liberalism, realism or modernism cannot offer. A 'competitive devaluation', protectionism, and a new 'St.-Simonian alliance' are the '*projet*' which will stimulate greater productivity in adversity while also bringing voters to the defence of the courageous but beleaguered party. The logic behind these proposals is very French if not particularly Marxist. Revolutionary images of *la patrie en danger* are evoked by this Jacobin appeal . . . with its Gaullist overtones.

The CERES' analysis is revealing because it notes correctly that it is only restating the platform which brought the Socialists to power. It highlights a neglected aspect of French-style socialist politics. French socialism had never confronted the difficulties of government. It participated in coalitions, had an occasional minister, and one brief moment of glory in 1936. Absolute powerlessness, like absolute power, corrupts. The victim loses touch with reality. He lives in a dream world where everything is possible. The political result is the voluntarism and nationalism that were apparent in the first year of socialist government. Socialist Keynesianism accompanied by nationalisations superbly ignored France's place in the world economy. Similarly, it expected the enthusiasm of the now-sovereign masses to pay for the new social measures gaily voted. The masses, however, acted like modern consumers, spending their new benefits on goods which depressed French industry could not supply with sufficient speed. Inflation increased as the trade balance worsened and the franc weakened. This was not predicted by the Socialist plans.

French socialism has been a culture of opposition since the foundation of the Third Republic more than a century ago. This explains the ideological passion that characterises French politics. The cultural attachment of the '*peuple de gauche*' is electorally crucial. This century-old tradition explains some of the incongruities of socialist politics, for example the maintenance of Pierre Mauroy as Prime Minister despite shifting policies, or the abortive educational reform. The openly pragmatic horse-trading that characterises American politics is inconceivable within the French socialist culture of opposition – although its practice is hardly unknown. The invocation of ancesters like Jaurès or Blum has none of the ritual piety that characterises the 'party of Lincoln' or even the legacy of FDR.

But the very fact that the socialists are now in power means the symbolic end of the Third Republic; it marks the irrelevance of the ideological passions that dominated French history. The situation is, classically, dialectical: the ideology that served for the conquest of power is no longer relevant once power has been conquered. The government needs a link between itself and the population in order to avoid the appearance of arbitrariness that made the issue of *liberté* an opposition theme. The 'Union of the Left' was a political operation; it was not a 'popular front', arising from the working class (or classes, as some would have it). The parties to this union can either justify to the population the measures of the government, or they can attempt to represent the interests of their constituents. The trick would be to perform both functions simultaneously. The party majority (and CERES) are attempting this trick by appealing to the '*peuple de gauche*'. But the demographic change that has accompanied French modernisation condemns this tactic to failure.

## 4. SOCIALIST RIGOUR

Another solution has been proposed, taking into account the impossibility of recreating the old symbolic politics. Some 5 per cent of the delegates at the 1983 Party Congress at Bourg-en-Bresse supported an alternative motion titled, 'Regain Political Initiative by a Proper Use of Rigour'.[1] The thrust of their criticism is seen in a pre-Congress letter to the delegates from Party secretary Lionel Jospin. He attacks particularly the proposal's suggestion that the crisis be treated as a positive lever to transform the pre-modern remnants blocking French development. Jospin worries about the electoral implications of the call for self-criticism and admission of error; this would dismay the '*peuple de gauche*'. Jospin also finds 'false and caricatural' the assertion that the Party has neglected its base in favour of internal power-plays, and that 'autonomous action other than propaganda work has been timid'. The Party secretary clinches his case with the suggestion that the proposal emanated from 'another Left' whose vision might be laudable, honest and even interesting, 'but since we are here in the First Left, there is a problem'. To put a nail in the coffin, Jospin added a footnote citation from Michel Rocard disavowing the proposal.[2]

The details of the Motion are less important than its selfconscious attempt to force the Party to recognise the new situation created by its own actions. Many of the proposals have a familiar ring, despite an occasional gallic flourish. The authors insist that the 'reversal' in direction is not just a 'parenthesis' in an otherwise steady course. They polemicise against demands that the state intervene to aid 'temporarily' weaker industries by financial or tariff policy. The French lack of entrepreneurial spirit is blamed on the expectation that the state will always eventually come to the rescue. The 'proper' use of rigour means attacking the legacy of corporatist privilege, entrenched position or 'acquired rights'. This creative destruction will make possible applications of the socialist principle of self-management in an economy undergoing rapid modernisation. Proposals for job-sharing and the reduction of the work-week (*not* with full compensation) highlight another aspect of modernity neglected by the traditionalist socialists. Work is no longer definitional of character; nor is work in itself a social good. There is no reason to produce useless jobs; youth is aware of this, as is the bored typist. The problem is not unemployment *per se* but rather new kinds of employment. This aspect of the 'proper' use of the crisis recalls themes that emerged in the critique of the society of abundance. The objection to that 'new left' critique has to be answered here: can it be made *politically* feasible?

The Motion claims not to be an oppositional statement. Its purpose is not to propose another volley of new laws and institutional transformations from on high. The task, rather, is to give content to the legislation already initiated. For example, the laws on decentralisation have only begun to transform the inherited Jacobin tradition. This transfer of power meets resistance from entrenched privilege which can only be overcome by the mobilisation of the new publics who will benefit from the new possibilities. Similarly, the Auroux laws giving workers a voice in shop life will degenerate into another source of union bureaucratic power unless those directly concerned are mobilised. The same is true concerning tenant rights, new measures permitting small co-operative industries, and the like.

The authors of the Motion knew that they represent a small minority of the Party. Their proposal is clearly part of a longer term strategy discussed in their bulletin, AGIRS (A Gauche pour l'initiative, la Responsabilité et la Solidarité). The fidelity to the government's programme is the tactic of the Emperor's New Clothes. The appeal to new publics and a self-management politics applies a similar tactic. The first is directed down, the second up. But tactics are effective only in the service of a strategy. In the old days, this was the achievement of socialism. Modern French socialist power has put it into question. The seeds of a new definition are implicit in the intellectuals' gropings; Mitterrand's simple or cynical attempt to preserve power may make them explicit.

## 5. MODERN SOCIALISM?

The one point on which French socialists (but not Communists) agree is foreign policy. Americans are surprised to hear Mrs Kirkpatrick's distinction between totalitarian and authoritarian governments in socialist mouths, and to see it in socialist actions. The distinction is not without its use, in the proper context. It took the French a long while to realise what was self-evident to American democrats; the so-called 'Solzhenitsyn shock' has been the butt of justified mockery. But the same concepts can conceal quite different interpretations because they are rooted in quite different experiences. French attitudes toward Russia (as they have insisted on calling it since de Gaulle taught them the relevance of classical diplomatic thinking) are not determined by ideology alone.

The French concern with totalitarianism is based on an analysis of their own society. The number of Frenchmen who have passed through the Communist Party is staggeringly high. This experience cannot be the result of a personal aberration or accident. If the 'best and the brightest' of the French were drawn to the communist line, they conclude, this could only be because of some dangerous potential within democratic capitalist societies themselves. This is what concerns the socialists who, finally, came to understand the nature of totalitarianism.

The French wax quickly philosophical, but the point is simple enough. Modernising France will upset the life-patterns of millions. It will generate material as well as psychological insecurity. The Welfare State, socialist or capitalist, comes to the rescue. The danger, of course, is that its intervention creates a class of persons who will never be able to free themselves from what Kant liked to call 'self-incurred tutelage'. This danger is magnified when the state is controlled by a party which dispenses security in order to keep itself in power.

The influence of the critique of totalitarianism can be seen in the warnings of the oppositional Motion at Bourg-en-Bresse, as well as in the 'silence of the intellectuals' from which the Socialists expected ideological legitimation. The near-adulation of Raymond Aron by left-leaning intellectuals, and the popularity of the journal *Commentaire*, which he founded, are a sign of the times. Former socialists identify themselves as 'lib/lib' – liberal libertarians. Historians who had searched for lessons in the phases of the French Revolution are now studying nineteenth-century liberalism and its peculiar French variants. Regis Debray, former Guerverrist and now Mitterrand adviser, has just published *Power and Dreams* to justify *realpolitik* as real socialism. The recently deceased philosopher Michel Foucault published the continuation of his theory of sexuality eight years after the first volume. The new volumes reveal a new philosopher: it is as if, like the French socialist, the speculative dreams have learned the lessons of rigour and realism. The preservation of liberal democracy has become a prime value for these socialists who have learned that it can never be taken for granted. The question now is whether the defensive posture can become also a positive politics.

The implications of the critique of totalitarianism come together with the self-management orientation to define a political *attitude*. The attitude is defined negatively by the end of two great myths that paralysed French political thinking. The end of the Third Republic means the end of a religious-ideological quarrelsomeness that made France a caricatured insular nation. Economic necessity and the internal political evolution point unavoidably outside of the hexagon. But the opening toward the world depends on overcoming the myth of a socialist utopia. The economy again favours this tendency, but politics is ambivalent. If the party persists in its appeal to the '*peuple de gauche*', all bets are off . . . save the certain victory of the opposition in the parliamentary elections of 1986.

Two variables bear watching in the 18 months that remain until the elections. The 12 per cent who voted for the right-wing National Front movement (whose slogan in the European election was '*Les Francais d'abord!*') are not the renewal of a 1950s anti-modernism. They have two potential political roles: their threat could serve the

Socialists as an alibi for not reforming themselves; or they could serve the Florentine Mitterrand by driving a wedge between the honest centre-right and the hard-right. This latter option would revive the failed attempt to create a centre-left government in 1986; it would be a 'left' variant of what Giscard had tried previously. Mitterrand would appeal to the European sentiment which has begun to take root in France, especially among the modernist, realist 'second left'. This strategy could also permit the Socialist Party to undertake the needed self-re-evaluation, paralleling *mutatis mutandis* the Bad Godesberg Programme which brought the German SPD into modern politics.

The equation 'socialism = modernity + realism' is not inspiring; it will not bring the masses into the streets. But it is just the conception of politics as militant demonstration in the name of higher values that the Socialist experience has overcome. Will the Emperor admit that he is naked?

**Notes**

1. I will be relying here on documents from the Congress made available to me by Jean-Pierre Worms, socialist Deputy from Macon and one of the authors of the Motion. I interviewed Worms twice during July, 1984. The interpretation offered here is of course my own, based on numerous informal conversations with participants currently known as the 'second left'.
2. Rocard's case would make an interesting study in itself. The representative of the 'self-management' wing within the party opposed the electoral alliance with the Communists prior to the 1981 elections. Mitterrand outmanoeuvred him and won the Party designation. Rocard's popularity dictated that he participate in the new cabinet, but without real power to threaten Mitterrand and his allies. He was the powerless Minister of the Plan, and is now Minister of Agriculture. He seems to have decided to sacrifice principle to power, playing the waiting game rather than enter into opposition. His former intellectual allies drew the conclusion and founded the journal *Intervention*. Among his political allies, the 5 per cent who supported the Motion at Bourg-en-Bresse have been excluded from the regular luncheon meetings at the Ministry.

# 10 French Rhetoric and Political Reality

## 1. POLITICAL OR INSTITUTIONAL CRISIS?

The conflict between a socialist President and a coalition of right-wing parties who now control Parliament is said by some to threaten the foundations of the Fifth Republic which stabilised, finally, French political life after 1958. The short-term perspective remains fluid, dominated on the one hand by a public opinion which prefers 'cohabitation' to an institutional crisis, and on the other by politicians jockeying for position in the Presidential elections which must take place by May of 1988. Everyone has their trump card; the problem is when to play it. A sketch of relations among what the French call 'the political class' suggests, however, that things are not so simple. Why should the continuation of de Gaulle's institutions define a *socialist* politics? Although François Mitterrand spent decades of bitter opposition to the Fifth Republic, as President, the socialist leader has adopted a Gaullian pose in the name of the national interest. Although the institutional question is not identical with party politics, analysis must begin with the immediate choices in order to make sense of the implications of the institutional structure within which the political day-to-day takes place. Only then do questions of theory take on their full sense.

The line-ups are reasonably simple. On the Right, Raymond Barre's refusal of cohabitation is based on the expectation of its failure; Giscard d'Estaing expects his co-operation to be rewarded after the same failure; while Prime Minister Chirac expects to use the machinery of power (and the mayoralty of Paris) to advance the candidacy of a successful administration, perhaps lamed by the Socialist President. There are a few odd balls in the right's equation, notably the rising star of François Léotard, using his Ministry of Culture and Communication to advance his own cause. More important are the representatives of that 12 per cent of the population who supported the far-right National Front of Jean-Marie Le Pen. Without them, the Right's parliamentary majority becomes a slender reed of several voices, federated for the moment by governmental power but loyal to their respective leaders. Ambitious plans for privatising not only firms nationalised by the Socialists but some taken over after the war, and privatisation of one (or more) of the national TV stations could provide grounds, or pretences, for division within this spectrum unified by a quest for power without a common goal for its utilisation. Mitterrand's strongest card is his ability to set the date for the next elections, and the canny Fourth Republic politician baptised 'Le Florentin' will live up to his name. But the author of the *Prince* also wrote the 'republican' commentary on Livy's *Discourses*, an historical fact not without theoretical implications.

As to the Left, the Communists represent a dwindled faction only as large as the National Front. Their decline has been continual, and will no doubt continue. Attempts to reform the party from within have been met with old-fashioned Stalinist stolidity, and exclusions. The party controls still a good bit of patronage, in part through its CGT trade union affiliate (which controls the large social funds of state-owned utility companies and railroads). Its other course of patronage, municipal control, has been decreasing although not as rapidly as the national representation of the party. A single-figure electoral score can be expected in the next elections. That leaves the Socialist party in a dilemma. The Socialists did far better than had been predicted in losing the March, 1986 parliamentary elections. They are now the largest single party in French politics. But there is no chance that they will become a majority party. Even if an alliance with the Communists were plausible on ideological grounds – which it is not – the Right would still hold the majority. How are the socialists to represent their large but none the less minority electorate?[1]

The difficulty for the French socialists is not unfamiliar to Northern European Social-Democratic parties whose 'opportunism' used to provide a kind of foil against which the French could measure their own faith and console themselves for the purity of their powerlessness. It would be tempting to say that the French will have to undergo a 'Bad Godesberg' in order to find new bases for their politics. The analogy, however, fails on two counts. The German SPD is presently revising its own programme under attack from political purists on its left. More important, the 1959 Congress at Bad Godesberg was intended to make the SPD a party capable of governing; but the French have already shown that they can govern, perhaps better even than their capitalist predecessors. The French dilemma does, however, depend on a theoretical revision, one concerning their 'socialism' and perhaps another concerning the institutions of the Fifth Republic itself.

## 2. FRENCH SOCIALISM AS THEORY

French socialism is often identified with its theoretical products. The 'higher' forms are well-known. The decline of Sartre's existential Marxism into a politics of Third Worldism and then 'Maoism', was countered by concrete political proposals such as Gorz's revolutionary reformism and Mallet's theory of a 'new working class'. The sociological combination of these into a theory of post-industrial society by Touraine suggested a new politics built around 'new social movements'. The structural Marxism of Althusser and Poulantzas was a passing phase which seems to have more disciples in England than in France. May 1968 was followed by a wave of theories which dropped the reference to Marx and to socialism in favour of new forms of freedom, thematised as micro-politics by Foucault and rhyzomes by Deleuze-Guattari. For the more literary, the deconstructionism patronised by Derrida became the theoretical orientation for a new politics of immediacy, desire, and perhaps community. For the more political, the critique of Marxism developed by Castoriadis and Lefort in *Socialisme ou Barbarie* was the stimulus for rethinking the roots of radical politics. This important contribution was vulgarised in the mid-1970s by the critique of totalitarianism presented by the 'new philosophers' as the basis for a new politics – or, rather, an ethics replacing politics and history by sheer moral choice.[2] This orientation to a politics of 'human rights' seemed typical of the short circuit by which French theorising after May 1968 eliminated the question of politics (or replaced it under the vague concept of 'the political').

The decline of 'high' theory has a political parallel. French left politicians make a virtue of their theoretical purity, whether they belong to the Socialist or the Communist parties. This began to change in 1972, with the attempt to formulate a 'Common Programme' of the Left. On the one hand, the Communist Party had managed to control the popular outbursts of May 1968, only to be shocked when the Warsaw Pact crushed Czech 'socialism with a human face' in August. The Party at first condemned the invasion; then, with the retirement of Waldeck-Rochet, the new leadership under Georges Marchais set about supporting Czech 'normalisation'. But the Czech hope for reforms gave rise to a 'Euro-Communist' orientation, within and increasingly outside or excluded from the Party, which kept alive the idea of a liberal communism.[3] This hope may have been stronger on the side of the new Socialist Party, led by François Mitterrand, which had replaced the moribund SFIO whose ideological rigidity and practical opportunism had destroyed its credibility.[4] The Common Programme was a political platform but also a theoretical affirmation of faith. It was updated and reaffirmed in 1977, and appeared to furnish a unifying position around which the 1978 Parliamentary elections could be won. At that point, for reasons about which one can only speculate (including Soviet wishes), the Communists broke the alliance. The Left was defeated in the 1978 elections; the decline of Communist support began, accelerated by the Russian invasion of Afghanistan in 1979, which the Communists defended as the 'modernisation' of a feudal, religious and barbarous nation!

The belief in the political efficacy of theory apparently died when François Mitterrand was elected President in 1981. The Communists had not supported his candidacy, running Georges Marchais against him in the first round of the elections. Mitterrand's platform was an elaboration of the old Common Programme, but without the apparatus of theoretical justification; he called his programme simply the '110 Propositions'. Upon election, he set about to implement these proposals, with the aid of the Communists, whom he brought into his cabinet for tactical reasons. Despite its electoral support, the new socialist government was unable to catalyse popular energies. Measures such as nationalisations, a slightly reduced work-week and an additional week's paid vacation, increased minimum wages, and other 'safety net' provisions may have been taken for ideological reasons; or they may have aimed simply to avoid the kind of popular mobilisation that accompanied the Popular Front government of 1936. Attempts by the Minister of Culture, Jack Lang, to use anti-American and Third Worldist rhetoric to attract allegiance drew widespread ironic criticism, and were subsequently dropped. The attempt to increase state power over the private sector in education was an ideological sop to the faithful which was met by massive demonstrations that led to the resignation of the Minister of Education, Alain Savary. Meanwhile, the attempt to reflate unilaterally the economy brought successive devaluations, the institution of an 'austerity politics' directed by Jacques Delors, and eventually the resignation of the old-time Socialist, Prime Minister Pierre Mauroy, who was replaced by the young technocrat, Laurent Fabius. The most popular government official by the end of the Socialists' five years of undisputed power was the Minister of Justice, Robert Badinter, whose humanitarian policies had little 'socialist' ideological content. Defence and Foreign Policy, meanwhile, continued the 'Gaullist' tradition, tilting toward the American side on the strategic nuclear plane, against it in Latin America, while acting independently in the African ex-colonies (and in the Greenpeace Affair).

What can socialist theory say about this French experience? Does it illustrate the bankruptcy of pragmatism? Or does the experience put into question the theory that was supposed to guide, or at least to legitimate, socialist practice? A debate at the 1986 Socialists' Scholars Conference in New York made clear some of the theoretical premisses still embraced by socialists.[5] The speakers reassured each other that since we were 'among socialists' we would all agree that the five years of socialist government had been a failure. The theory remains true, regardless of the actions of those claiming to be in its service. On that assumption, analysis could take two possible directions: it could draw lessons for tomorrow; or it could seek to cheer the troops by showing that the failure was not the fault of socialism and its theory. Or, it could ask whether revision is necessary for precisely the reasons that led Eduard Bernstein to propose his new theoretical frame to explain the actual practice of pre-War socialism under Goethe's slogan: 'It should dare to appear as that which it *is*!'

As a political platform socialism proposes immediate practical measures on the basis of a theory which gives them coherence as part of a broader social transformation. This means that theory is crucial to socialist politics. It means, too, that 'socialist experiences' elsewhere are important for convincing people of the coherence of the theory. Daniel Singer worried that the French 'failure' would be adduced as yet another proof that socialism doesn't work; France would be another empirical disproof of the theoretical argument of Marxism. Singer's tactic for the defence of socialism was to take the offensive by analysing critically the three self-justifications French socialists might offer. The French 'failure' would thus be only the refutation of a false theoretical project; the truth of socialist theory would remain untouched. The first justification could stress that, for the first time in French history, a socialist regime maintained itself in power throughout its term of office. But, replied the theorist Singer, this was possible only because they did the capitalists' work for them. Second, the Socialists could say that they brought archaic French industry and society finally into the twentieth century. But Singer's true socialist theory easily demystified this claim: the Socialists, again, only did the capitalists' work. It follows, on a positive note, that the Mitterrand years were not a defeat of democratic socialism; they proved only that 'social democracy', operating from the top-down, does not work. Democratic socialism remains the telos of history. The 'continual revolt from below' expected by the Socialist Scholars presumably will reappear, as the theory demands.

As a political scientist, Mark Kesselman seemed to feel the need to build models to house the reality he investigates. He proposed three conceptual models of socialist transition, which co-existed in the French socialist practice after 1981: liberal democracy, social democracy, and democratic socialism. For Kesselman the socialist, these represent a progressive series, a logic of history which practice has to realise. The French practice of liberal democracy was pronounced most successful, with decentralisation, reform of the penal code, and decentralising the means of mass communication serving as example. But, alas, these liberal reforms operated from the top-down, in the good old 'Jacobin' fashion. The French Socialists' theory had mocked the Northern European practice of social democracy; yet when they came to power, the Socialists learned to practise its modest reform programme. But as opposed to the Northern Europeans, whose pragmatic reformism had brought concrete if not theoretical satisfaction in the form of strong trade union support, the rhetorical French Socialists had no interested social base on which to rest their case when the economic crisis hit them. The result was their 'austerity politics' which meant, asserted Kesselman, that they 'got serious, responsible, i.e., conservative'.[6] This lack of a social base meant also that the democratic socialist component of their programme, ensconced in lyrical appeals to '*changer la vie*', was without effect. The political-scientist-as-socialist theorising the course of History thus proposed a fourth model to understand this failure without putting into question the stagist development; Kesselman called it 'socialism without the workers' or 'state-capitalist socialism'. This is a 'deviation' whose overcoming demands 'a certain radical impulse' that would permit a correct articulation of the three stage model of socialist development.

The plausibility of these theoretical justifications of true socialist theory depends on the fact that the French Socialists themselves adhered to a theory-guided practice. Their aim is to defend the *concept* of socialism against the 'detractors' – in this case, the 'reality' of the French experience. Kesselman worried about the danger for socialists in the United States who – like the French – have a project but can't mobilise the masses to support it. Singer's rhetoric was more captivating: he had a good story to tell, an historical narrative with familiar actors, turns of fate, and a message of hope. He is a clever man; he had a tempting target and a willing audience: who could disagree with the need for democracy in any socialist transformation? Once his story line was established, and at least the major characters in his play accepted, the plot was easy to follow. The story line was the advent of socialism; the characters included the capitalists, imperialists, workers and other familiar faces; the plot was less clear, but it didn't seem to matter: perhaps betrayal – as when Singer attacked the 'political crimes' of the Mitterrand regime! – perhaps stupidity, perhaps outside intervention, sometimes even the wrong ideas. Yet changes in the plot that the debator had to admit grudgingly on occasion as the audience intervened, suggest the need to rethink the story line and the characters.

The difficulty of replying to Singer's story, or to Kesselman's stage theory of History, points to a practical, empirical problem. One might ask, what really is meant by socialism, by working class, and the other characters acting in this story? But that's too general a question, at least at this level of analysis of a concrete experience. One might make the reflex move taught by critical theory since Marx, trying to develop an immanent critique of what has occurred, drawing the positive from the dross of the negative. That's still too theoretical. So is the more political, or polemical, line which suggests that just this faith in a sense of History and an immutable Theory underpins the various varieties of Stalinist practice (including the Trotskyist version to which Singer seems to adhere). The paradox is that by defending the purity of Socialist Theory any real practice is condemned to the status of a 'deviation' due to the press of real exigencies. The difficulty results from the fact that socialist theory, in whatever guise, provides answers to any and all questions simply by expanding its theoretical compass, or by ruling out as incidental, accidental, or unimportant details that can not be subsumed within its plot.

Another type of reply to the defenders of the Faith has come from within the French left. This critique is often neglected or misunderstood; some are too theory-bound to hear it, while others dismiss it as falling outside the pale of socialism. Singer brought up the point polemically in replying to some who criticised his story. He called them 'new philosophers'. The label is pejorative because the new philosophers, Singer explained, have all become neo-conservatives. But that is American language, taken out of context and applied polemically. It is true that since the 'Solzhenitsyn shock' of the mid-1970s, some French former leftists have taken the critique of totalitarianism to the extreme of rejecting any socialist project as a threatening utopia which destroys particular freedoms while adopting Rousseau's famous injunction to 'force them to be free'. But this is the extreme. The French anti-totalitarian left calls itself 'lib-lib' *libéraux libértaires*. This libertarian option is rooted among other things in the post-May 1968 experience; it attempts to thematise civil society as the space of political transformation. This does not fit the label 'conservative'. Conservatives generally stand against the increase in the space for democratic self-affirmation. French anti-totalitarian support for, and analysis of, the *Solidarity* movement in Poland was not based on the simple anti-communism that animates the American neo-conservatives. Nor is the liberalism of the 'lib-libs' a simple option for free-market capitalism. In the French tradition, which goes back to Constant's critique of the French Revolution, liberalism refers to *political*, not to economic liberalism. The new political questions posed from within the critical French left have to be treated in context.

The first issue of the 'second left'[7] journal, *Intervention*, suggested an analysis of the prospects for the newly elected socialist government which still rings true. Its editor, Jacques Julliard, titled his essay, 'Mitterrand: Between Socialism and the Republic'.[8] He stressed the fact that Socialists had never held power in France. This meant that their socialist theory had never met the test of reality. For this reason, the theory could remain impervious to any refutation by experience. The theory had the status of an imaginary future, a guiding star, and a critical lever from which to move the present. In French history, this function paralleled the imaginary role of the French Revolution, and the 'true' Republic which it never attained. The Socialists' experience of power, Julliard suggested, would demystify this theory; and this would 'complete' the French Revolution, in imagination if not in factual measures (since socialist Theory can never be simply identified with any set of given empirical measures). In this way, the advent of Socialist power made possible a new beginning for French politics. It challenged the left to invent a new project.

Nearly five years later, in the issue of *Intervention* preceding the March parliamentary elections,[9] Julliard's voice was more subdued. 'The issues of March', as he defined them, came down to the choice between two moderate policies, the one stitching the 'safety net' more tightly than the other. This hardly seems to be the new politics he had expected. Indeed, six months prior to this discussion, in an issue devoted to the 'The End of a Cycle in the Life of the Left', Julliard had denounced the idea of a political programme, rejected the 'pedagogical' politics that tries to tell people how to live their lives, and stressed a 'reduction in the field of conflict' within society. This sober and sombre perspective, although not necessarily an inaccurate description, leaves open the question whether *this* is the adequate basis from which to conceptualise that 'new politics' that the Socialists' experience in power was supposed to put on the agenda. Does theory really have nothing to offer?

## 3. FRENCH THEORY AS SOCIALIST

French social theory, at least in this country, has come to be inseparable from the French version of philosophy which passes under the label of deconstruction. This is due not only to American 'litcrit' departments adopting what our analytically-trained philosophers reject. It may also be due to our finding ourselves in a political situation characterised by choices no more exalting than those Julliard describes. Our 'post-moderns' may well be stuck in the same unpleasant situation as the French post-socialists. We turn to 'high' social theory. The deconstruction of metaphysics proposed by French philosophy parallels the disintegration of the socialist imagination that was supposed to guide political practice. Deconstruction argues against any 'foundational discourse', be it idealism or empiricism, let alone Marx or Hegel, Freud or Heidegger. Borrowing Heidegger's notion of the 'ontological difference' (between Being and beings), and radicalising it with Saussure's insistence that the meaning of a sign is 'diacritical' (since signs refer only to other signs, never to 'reality'), deconstruction sweeps away the debris of certainty. In the place of the Hegelian–Marxist idea that the path and the goal are constituted together historically, the new approach denies both path and goal. This seems to result in a nihilism for which anything goes; no answers are forthcoming from the deconstruction of the old questions. This does not disturb the deconstructionist; the existence of answers would imply that History has a sense, a foundation or a *telos*, which is just what deconstruction denies. The responsibility of deconstruction, its paradoxical seriousness, is to restore playfulness to its rightful place, in both senses of the term. Play, right and justice are said to belong together. At this point, the residual pragmatism of socialist theory rebels.

It is sometimes forgotten that philosophy as deconstruction tried first to remain within the socialist framework. Although Althusser's *For Marx* is not usually thought of as part of the deconstructionist movement, the basic concepts and methods it applies, and the 'humanism' and Hegelianism it criticises in attempting to restore a Marxist 'science', were minted at the same mill which has served Derrida, Foucault and the others. Althusser's debt to structuralism, to Lacanian psychoanalysis, and even to Heidegger are evident. The Introduction to *For Marx* makes explicit the political framework of its project. Althusser criticises those 'philosophers without works . . . [who] made all works political' by the simple division between bourgeois and proletarian science. This was due to the fact that the French bourgeoisie had been revolutionary, drawing naturally to its banner the most advanced thought of the time. Opposition to bourgeois domination therefore took on the instinctively anti-intellectual form of *ouvrièrisme*. Althusser laments that his generation of Marxists 'spent the majority of our time as militants when we should have defended also our right and our duty to know, simply to study in order to produce'.[10] But what Althusser produced, under the label of 'over-determination', could not mask the orthodoxy of Marxism's 'determination in the last instance' by the economic. This last remnant of the 'real' remained to be deconstructed.[11]

What happens to politics when reality is eliminated by deconstruction? The line of attack proposed by Althusser suggests that the illusion of reality – for example, the supposed 'subject' of which humanism is the 'bourgeois' theory – is an ideological product blinding political actors to real social relations. Althusser's theory of the 'ideological state apparatuses' presented in *Lenin and Philosophy* elaborates this perspective. The difficulty is that *everything* becomes ideological from this point of view; 'Marxist science' is the study of the production of this ideological veil. But when everything is ideological, nothing is ideological; the anti-metaphysical stance of deconstruction becomes simply a long-winded, jargonesque *positivism*. Reality is reduced to a single plane of existence attainable by the methods of science. This difficulty confronts, ultimately, the non-Althusserian political versions of deconstruction as well. The micro-politics, rhyzomes and other self-congratulatory rebellions of the particular against the weight of the universal are trivially true, and politically and philosophically false. It is of course true that subsumption of the particular under a universal destroys the uniqueness of the particular claim. But is particularity somehow good in itself? The universality of particularism, atomism, becomes anomie, the loss of social coherence, and the impossibility of politics. The universality of particularism is privatisation at best; at worst, it is what the 1950s decried as 'mass society'.[12]

The concept of deconstruction applied by Derrida has other potential implications, some of which were decorticated at a ten-day meeting at Cérisy-la-Salle. Two quite different papers addressed its political implications.[13] Gayatri Spivak drew from Derrida's critique of Western logocentrism the implication that the return of the excluded Other – women, the non-Western world, the victims generally of capitalism – puts into question the domination imposed by rationality and its economic institutions. Deconstruction's aim should be to open up thought to this excluded element whose presence will overthrow the inherited domination. Jacob Rogozinski proposed a more radical deconstruction: that of the notion of revolution itself. Revolution, with its supposition of an *arché* and a *telos*, is a form of political metaphysics; Marx's attempt to overcome such constitutive differences as that between state and civil society by the creation of a unified and transparent society is nothing but the completion of metaphysics on its own grounds. One needs either a radically different politics, or a politics whose function is to preserve the differences that make thought – and freedom – possible. Inclusion of Spivak's excluded Other is thus only another metaphysical remnant. But the deconstruction of 'revolution' seems to leave no perspective but empirical social engineering tinkering at reforms of the status quo.

A 'deconstructionist politics' which remains true to both deconstruction and to politics has to make a virtue of necessity – or, in philosophical jargon, to ontologise its own embarrassment. Deconstruction becomes itself a politics. Politics is defined as the constant 'deferral' (Derrida's *différance*) through which one practical reform fixates difference only long enough to ensure its 'subversion' by another reform in an indefinite process, which Hegel would call a 'bad infinite' but is here labelled 'play'. This politics precludes the metaphysical utopia of a reconciliation of each with all, and with nature, in the guise of an End of History. Clothed in philosophical language, this sounds more impressive than its humble realisation, which – if it is not the intellectual elitism of a 'new class' falsely generalising its own concerns to all of society – could be simply a meliorative, pragmatic and falsifiable everyday community association seeking to make things work. Such pragmatism is no more the intention of the deconstructionists than is the similar pragmatism finally espoused by Julliard's 'second left' version of post-socialism. The deconstructionists may claim to be the philosophical prophets of a new politics. For the politician, however, the result is simply the pragmatics of everyday life raised to theoretical dignity and rhetorical splendour.[14] Perhaps the deconstructionists are still too much the philosophers, while the politicians are trapped by a reality whose institutional forms they cannot put into question. The parallel failures of socialist politics and deconstructionist philosophy suggest the need for a different approach.

## 4. THE RETURN OF POLITICAL PHILOSOPHY

The contemporary French political debate is marked by a concern with ethics as the at once particular yet universal and practical domain from which a post-socialist and post-deconstructionist theory could emerge. Emmanuel Levinas, and the Czech phenomenologist and Speaker for the Charter 77, Jan Patocka, are the oft-cited if little-read banner-carriers. This turn to ethics can be translated facilely into a politics because of the ambiguity in the notion of 'right' – which connotes both individual and socio-legal (as well as pragmatic) measures. The most important implication of this ambiguity is that once deconstruction has shaken any and all transcendental, empirical or even subjective foundations there remains only the appeal to judgement as its own self-foundation. The English title of a recent dialogue between Jean-François Lyotard and Jean-Loup Thébaud, *Just Gaming*,[15] draws the radical conclusion from this assertion. Lyotard's deconstructive imperative is said to be inherent in the nature of speaking itself: *il faut enchaîner*, one can never stop the wheel of discourse without falling into reification, illusion or ideology. The most tempting, and dangerous way to end the langauge game is to give it a foundation, a realisable goal, a cause and an effect. This explicitly paradoxical argument for the primacy of ethical *judgement* without foundations has socio-political implications.

Lyotard's philosophy is not just gaming; keeping the game going is *just* gaming, a practice generating a rule which permits legitimating (or criticising) what are apparently mere pragmatic choices by disconnected actors. A practice which excludes further practice is illegitimate. A judgemental 'practice generating a rule' governing further practice can be expressed in Kantian language: it is the schematism, which Kant's first *Critique* called 'an art hidden in the depths of the human soul' and which the third *Critique* thematises as the art-work which, as 'lawless lawfulness' or 'purposefulness without purpose', creates its own standards, the rules of its own justness. The analogy between foundationless, deconstructed French philosophy and French socialist politics which can appeal only to a judgement which cannot be grounded by external criteria explains the role of Kant in recent French political philosophy.[16] To this analogy between theory and practice are added two other motives for the return to Kant. If the Hegel–Marx 'completion' of the history of philosophy is deconstructed, the return to the 'Copernican Revolution' that inaugurated that path seems like a good research hypothesis. Further, contemporary discussions of modernism/post-modernism that have replaced the older and exhausted socialist themes have been conducted largely in the sphere of the aesthetic, where Kant's critical system reaches its conclusion in the *Critique of Judgement*.[17]

The dilemmas of translating a pure theory into practical reality which confronted the 'Socialist Scholars'' analysis of French socialism recall Kant's distinction between the noumenal and the phenomenal realms. A simple step from this initial dualism would suggest that socialism is only an Idea of Reason which can never be realised but which must constantly be maintained as an ideal. Indeed, the attempt to translate such an Idea into reality must fall victim to the Kantian 'Transcendental Dialectic' which shows it to produce an inevitable antinomic structure. Kant's Transcendental Dialectic can be called the first deconstruction. Its implication is apparently that the only rational stance for practice will be guided by the purity of the ethical Ought. This could lead to the 'new philosophers'' rediscovery of the virtues of an abstract liberalism. Or, if the moralism of the categorial imperative is itself deconstructed, as Kant himself proposes, the result could be a kind of conservatism[18] which insists on the complexity of the real against social-engineers who want to reform it and democrats who want to increase democratic participation. The same position could lead to the kind of post-modern 'neo-pagan' politics of Lyotard. None of these approaches is satisfactory *as a politics*. They have been viciously criticised in a recent polemic against what is called *La pensée 68*. The polemic can be left aside here;[19] the theory that underlies it is more serious.

The deconstructionists were not the first to see the importance of the Kantian Transcendental Dialectic. Fichte developed his own philosophy from the results of Kant's Dialectic. The necessity which produces the antinomic structures opposing, for example, freedom and necessity is not simply the result of the pretensions of Theory to incorporate itself in the world and the world in itself. The antinomies are not just critical; they have a positive, constitutive implication. Ferry draws the contemporary implications of this approach in his *Philosophie politique*. He constructs a 'system of the philosophies of history'. Two polar positions are possible from the side of the object: the Hegelian logic articulated as a 'Cunning of Reason', and the Heideggerian phenomenological deconstruction of any historical necessity. To these objective poles are added two further possibilities which stress the subjective factor: Marx's action based on knowledge of historical necessity, and the liberal market-maximizing autonomous subject. Ferry's own proposal is the unification of all four poles in a 'dialectical' Kantianism which gives each its necessary place while denying to any the possibility of totalising the others. This schema is then applied, with the help of Alain Renaut, in the third volume of *Philosophie Politique* to the question of the political implications of the new French moralism: can the 'rights of man', which all want to defend against 'totalitarianism', furnish the basis of a politics?

A politics of human rights must define these rights. Ferry and Renaut point to the obvious oppositions, which become for them antinomies. The liberal notion of rights as freedom-from (*droits-libertés*) is opposed to the socialist notion of rights that demand state intervention for their realisation (*droits-créances*). The theoretical foundation for this distinction lies in the antinomy between a rationalist assumption that some form of the Cunning of Reason will lead from individual action to social results and an ethical-practical assumption which demands intervention by the Will (in the form of the state). Ferry and Renaut examine the historical emergence of human rights politics, first in the French Revolution, then in the debates during 1848 concerning the right to work, and finally in the early twentieth century socialists' inability to guarantee social welfare without threatening individual freedom. A first antinomic development opposes Sièyes' concept of the Nation to Constant's insistence on the place of 'modern' private freedom. This is followed by a second, double antinomic development which shows the identical theoretical intent animating the apparently opposed positions of Marx and Proudhon (both of whom want to dissolve the opposition of society and the state) as opposed to the radical liberalism of a Hayek, whose implicit supposition of a Cunning of Reason drawing together the individual monads is easily denounced. The unification of these schematically opposed positions is suggested by the dilemmas facing the democratic socialism of Jaurès and Blum. The Republic is taken to be the institutional form which unifies all three antinomic structures.

Ferry and Renaut's political project elaborates the passage 'From the Rights of Man to the Republican Idea'. The Kantian knows that an Idea can never be realised completely. In practice the Idea functions along two axes, paralleling the antinomic structures that underlie any political theory of human rights. The freedom-from that liberalism seeks to guarantee is the premise for the existence of a human community within which individuals can seek to realise those freedoms that *do* demand intervention for their realisation. The full realisation of these latter can never be assured because their fulfilment depends on contingencies such as the real wealth of a given society at a given moment. This does not imply a political relativism. The status of the Republic as an Idea of reason means that it is itself a universal value of a type that does not fall victim to the historicist assumptions criticised by classical natural law theorists such as Leo Strauss[20] and by the tradition of deconstruction. But the function of the Kantian Idea is not the same as the reflective judgement which is the key to the third *Critique*. Either the Idea of the republic is constantly present – in which case politics is eliminated; or judgement is the central focus – in which case, the deconstructionists' dilemma returns. The critique of the ideology of 1968 opts for the former.

Whereas Ferry begins from philosophy to propose a politics, Claude Lefort's interpretation of the rights of man shows why philosophy is necessary to political analysis. Lefort reminds us that the issue arose from the critique of totalitarianism. The critics had to wage a two-front campaign, against the Marxists for whom only economic rights are real, and against the moralism of the new philosophers. Lefort agrees with Marx's criticism of the humanistic defence of 'abstract man'. Yet the same alienation hidden by this abstract ideology is present in totalitarianism, whose denial of the rights of man is based on the action of a state which not only rationalises exploitation within civil society but interferes in all forms of socialisation. Totalitarianism, not bourgeois democracy, is the completion of what Marx called the 'political illusion'. Its extreme form was expressed by Stalin, who explained in 1931 that the state must be reinforced in order to create the conditions which permit it to 'wither' into society. Such excesses suggest that while Marx was not wrong to denounce the exploitation masked by liberal rhetoric, his debunking of this ideology in order to make visible the social reality behind alienation is incomplete. The reduction of politics to social relations is challenged by its realisation in totalitarianism. The experience of totalitarianism renews philosophical reflection.

Lefort returns to Marx's critique of bourgeois humanism in 'On the Jewish Question'. Marx himself is a victim of ideology; his analysis of the Declarations of the Rights of Man neglects the concrete social relations that these rights establish. The freedom to do whatever does not harm others which Marx attributes to the bourgeois, egoistic monad separated from others and seeking protection from them is also the affirmation of 'the freedom to do whatever' – it is a liberation from the constraints of monarchical, hierarchical society. Marx does not see the new, positive relations which this freedom makes possibly by creating a public space to which access is in principle unlimited. His criticism of the separation of private and public life neglects Articles 10 and 11 of the Declaration which guarantee freedom of opinion and the right of communication. These are not the rights of isolated monads; they are the right to create new social relations. These rights suppose a distinction between knowledge and power, which cannot be identified in an omniscient state. Marx's criticism of the right of security as 'bourgeois' neglects the prohibition of arbitrary arrest and establishment of the presumption of innocence. These guarantees imply that power and law cannot be conflated in an omnipotent state; they protect the possibility of criticising those exercising power. The attempt to conflate power, knowledge and law leads to totalitarianism; their separation, guaranteed by the rights of man, opens the adventure of democratic politics, which cannot be identified with capitalism.

Whereas Marx wanted to replace the political forms of human rights by 'real democracy', Lefort insists on the specificity of the political dimension. 'Man' has rights by virtue of a triple paradox. Society is ideally one, yet it cannot be incarnated in a single body; as a result, no mode of activity can be forbidden by an external agency claiming to act in the name of the whole. Further, the rights which belong to 'man' are given by no one; no power ratifies these rights, which are self-declared and have constantly to be reaffirmed. Finally, these rights as individual are 'transversal'; my exercise of them depends on your presence. The 'abstract man' with no social determinations whose rights are declared is thus man as indeterminable and as historical. Rights can be increased; acquired rights support demands for new ones. This implies a new relation to politics. The plurality of rights means that they cannot be regrouped into one platform enacted by a single agency. Rights cannot be guaranteed by a state; the separation of power and society is not something to be overcome through the creation of 'real democracy'. That is the totalitarian temptation. Democratic politics are based on the antinomic structure expressed in the triple paradox of the rights of man. Lefort stresses the political dimension of the multiplicity of new demands for rights that have emerged since May 1968 – in sexuality, the family, children, women, prisoners, farmers or lawyers. Even demands coming from more traditional socialist approaches, like the right against arbitrary dismissal, combine 'the idea of a legitimacy with the representation of a particularity'. This unity of universality and particularity – which Ferry situated in the republican institutional form – typifies for Lefort a democratic politics. In the present context, its institutional form remains to be specified.[21]

## 5. A NEW REPUBLICAN IDEOLOGY?

Ferry's republican return to Kant seems to exclude practical politics, while Lefort's democratic theory apparently has no institutional framework. Lyotard suggests a mediation by stressing the place of judgement within the republican politics. The first two *Critiques* were based on what Kant calls 'subsumptive judgement' which begins from the existence of a universal and gives sense to the particular case by fitting it under this pregiven certainty. This type of argument is illustrated by those Marxists for whom the sense of History is already known. They can subsume empirical cases, like the French socialist experience, under the laws of historical development – and find them lacking, deviant, or worse. This was Daniel Singer's tack at the Socialist Scholars Conference. On the other hand, the third *Critique* analyses 'reflective judgement', which begins from the particular and seeks to articulate a universal law which gives it its sense without thereby denying the particularity from which the action began. Reflective judgement is social or communicative action; it cannot suppose that its hearers already know the laws to which it appeals; it must bring them, in a kind of dialogue, to mutual understanding. Aesthetic judgement is Kant's model – there are no a priori laws of beauty – but political judgement follows the same path when it refuses historical (or technocratic) a prioris.

Lyotard does not reduce politics to judgement. The same subject is judging in both Kantian forms of judgement. This means that the universal is not absent from its repertoire. The particular which calls for reflective judgement is one which *resists* subsumption. Reflective judgement is not a-historical and decontextualised; it emerges at specific moments, when previous unities are threatened and the old rules seem no longer to apply. Politics must determine those particulars which call for reflective judgement. Such non-subsumable and autonomous particulars are what Lyotard calls a *différand*.[22] Not *every* particular object can be called 'beautiful', nor can *any* situation become the basis of a politics. Lyotard illustrates his argument in an interview with *Intervention*.[23] Each individual occupies a variety of positions or roles. To these correspond specific discourses which take account of particular constraints. There need not and should not be perfect consistency among the actions taken by a single subject. For example, Lyotard as citizen supported actively Algerian independence while Lyotard the political philosopher criticised the kind of institutions emerging in liberated Algeria. To think that there can be some '*grand récit*' uniting the discourses of an individual, a society, or History is to put an end to the (Kantian) project of Enlightenment, and with it, to political thinking.

Lyotard claims that the republican institutional form makes possible a new politics freed from the Marxist imagination of a realised humanity reconciled with itself. Like Kant, he rejects democracy as an institutional form because it confuses the question of authority with the source of legitimacy. There is no reason why the majority (or *le peuple*), just because of its quantitative superiority, should be ipso facto correct. This is not the elitism of philosophy. The republican form institutes a plurality of discourses. 'Reread Pascal: popular opinion is uncertain and unstable. But at the same time, the people are right because that instability is faithful to the heterogeneity of language. The idea of the general will thus makes no sense; it is absurd and dangerous to confuse it with the universal will.'[24] Republican politics is not based on the ethical ought which applies to individual behaviour. The political question is what do *we* want to be, who are *we*, how are *we* together? Within the republic, this question is premised on our common being as citizens whose freedom and rationality is the condition for asking it. But it is a question which can never have a definitive answer because – as opposed to the democracy where the common will can be thought to be incarnate – the 'we' or Idea can never be occupied or realised. Lyotard's republic emerges as the result of that 'continual revolt from below' which the Socialist Scholars consider to be 'the real socialist struggle'.

Lyotard's stress on the political structure of reflective judgement seems to provide the necessary supplement to Ferry's institutional republican philosophy. Yet his argument remains abstract. When he turns to the concrete, Lyotard falls into the kind of positivism typified by the nihilism of deconstruction. For example, he explains that 'A baby cries, and there is a politics to be undertaken. The manner in which one responds is a micro-politics: there are rules, but these are plural and one can change them; the correct one is not certain.' A page later, Lyotard recalls Sade's famous aphorism: 'One more effort, Frenchmen, to be republicans'. He explains that 'Republic does not mean democracy. The effort should be understood as extending the Idea of citizenship even to the erotic.' This 'discourse' is unsatisfactory. If all particulars are equal, and all actions generate appropriate rules, political judgement has no place. The 'new politics' called for by Julliard's second left rejected the pedagogical model which gave to the state the responsibility for moulding social life. Lyotard's 'just gaming' draws the extreme conclusion by rejecting politics altogether through the sleight-of-hand that makes it simply another element within society. Like Ferry's abstract Idea of the universal republican form, this solution is an empty ideology.

## 6. THE RETURN OF THE POLITICAL

The French 'lib-libs' appear to Anglo-Saxon eyes as a gallic version of the neo-conservative critique of the social-democratic welfare-state. Republicanism appears to represent a formal institutional frame which, as Marx taught us, hides the material realities of exploitation. But Lefort's critique of Marx cannot be forgotten. His reply to a French neo-conservative, Pierre Manent, clarifies the political implications of his argument. It may be that the increase in 'rights' has brought a growing penetration of society by the state in order to guarantee those rights. Yet the welfare state is not totalitarian. Recognition by the state of 'the right to have a right' legitimates the possibility of questioning the status and extent of rights within a given historical situation. It guarantees 'the legitimacy of a debate on the legitimate and the illegitimate'. It means that rights are not fixed from some independent source of power, law or knowledge; they are produced within a public space. If the welfare-state appears to limit that space, it is also true that this state is constantly under pressure to admit new rights. The neo-conservative or 'republican' practises an elitist politics in the guise of a 'realism' which wants to prevent interest from interfering in politics. Lefort's point is that when interest becomes political, its character changes: it takes the form of the democratic demand for rights. It puts into question the established order.

The republic is not an institutional form fixed once and for all; it is *symbolic*, representing the political aspect of any social structure. Julliard's 'new politics' neglects this symbolic dimension, as do the propositions of Lyotard and Ferry. Lefort's political theory of democracy does not reduce politics to action within a fixed institutional frame. Democracy is the symbolic relation which a society, and social individuals, establish to the dimensions of power, law and knowledge. These three symbolic relations are constitutive of any society. Totalitarianism conflates them, and identifies them with the body of society itself; democracy separates them from each other and from society. Other political forms are also possible. Democracy is not a permanent achievement; it does not depend on real social, institutional or material conditions.[25] In France, democracy was instituted when the French Revolution overthrew the absolute monarchy. 1789 did not inaugurate capitalism; it began a political adventure which was threatened from the outset not so much by the economic domination of a few but, more fundamentally, by the temptation to find a new incarnation of the King in the form of *le peuple*. From this point of view, socialism does *not* constitute a symbolic break with the universe of the Ancien Régime; democracy *is* that crucial rupture. The confusion of the two goals under the heading of the Republic has bedeviled French political history in the imaginary guise of 'Jacobinism'.[26]

Two aspects of the experience of Socialist power have changed the perception of the political terrain. The first was identified correctly by Julliard: socialism is no longer able to claim theoretical purity; it no longer defines the Idea which unifies diverse societal demands. This need not result in that fragmentation of society whose necessity is made a virtue by deconstruction. The diverse social interests legitimated negatively by the lack of a '*grand récit*' are given a *political* place by a second aspect of the socialist experience. The 'austerity politics' practised after the devaluation of 1983 was forced to appeal to a new character among the traditional actors in French politics: the entrepreneur. A paradoxical result of the Socialists' realisation of their political dream of speaking for all was the necessity of legitimating the interested behaviour of each. This paradox would remain anecdotal were it not for a further paradox, due this time to the politics of the right in opposition. The Constitutional Court established by the Fifth Republic followed the historical pattern in minimising access to its jurisdiction to questions defined by the institutional forms of politics. Interests, and their juridical form as rights, were excluded. The right reacted to the nationalisations by the Socialists by appealing to the Constitutional Court, where their appointees were a majority. Because they were a minority in Parliament, they continued this practice. The unintended result was a new legitimacy acquired by a politics of rights. The canny François Mitterrand showed a practical awareness of the new situation when he appointed his Justice Minister, Robert Badinter, to be the head of the Constitutional Court when the Right returned to power in 1986.[27]

The French Socialists' behaviour in opposition – or in 'cohabitation' – has not drawn the radical conclusions from the new situation that its experience of power has created. They have tended to go on, as if the Fifth Republic would endure, and as if their old goals were to be realised by the same political means. Indeed, taking the advantage of the decentralisation instituted by the Socialists, whose *Weltanschauung* seemed to prevent them from capitalising on its implications, the Right has temporarily captured the momentum established by the politicising of rights. That Right, which the French call 'neo-liberal', and which Americans would call neo-conservative, will not be able to conserve the old order, despite its intentions. The Fifth Republic remains a republic; but it is now mined by the demands of democracy. These 'demands' are not focused around the kinds of issues presented by the Socialists' '110 Propositions'. Their status is *symbolic*; their reach cannot be circumscribed, for each achievement opens on to new demands. Contrary to Julliard's more prosaic assertion, the Socialists did not complete at last the French Revolution; they have returned to the questions posed by that Revolution. They have made possible a return of the political.

## Notes

1. The answer proposed by Mitterrand prior to the March 1986 Parliamentary elections was to reintroduce the system of proportional representations in place of the 2-round, winner-take-all system of the Fifth Republic. The victorious coalition of the Right has returned to the old system, strengthening its hand with a little gerrymandering *à la française*. These are not the kind of institutional questions that concern the political theorist, however important they may be in the short-term.
2. The critique of totalitarianism by Castoriadis and Lefort is not a belated discovery of what had been developed by American Cold War scholarship; nor is it reducible to a critique of the 'jacobin logocentrism' of the Germanic 'master thinkers', as the new philosophers would have it. The latter were significant as a sign of the times, no more but also no less. Whether the assemblage of theories paraded through this paragraph represents a coherent evolution need not occupy us here. I will return to this issue with reference to the critique of what has been baptised 'la pensée 68' at the appropriate moment below.
3. Pierre Grémion's *Paris-Prague, 1968–1978* (Paris: Julliard, 1985) is a brilliant reconstruction of the manner in which the French left reacted to developments in Prague: to the Dubcek reforms, to the 'normalisation', and to the birth of the Charter 77. It is also a depressing document, showing the stubborn influence of ideological blinkers on the left's ability to understand what was in fact taking place in Czechoslovakia. Anyone who attempts to understand French left politics cannot neglect Grémion's account – nor can anyone seeking to understand what a new Left politics might be neglect his lucid analysis of the Czech developments themselves.
4. The party name, SFIO, speaks already of its dogmatism: it means 'Section Française de l'Internationale Ouvrière'. Some background on the internal composition of the new Socialist Party is presented in 'Socialism and Modernization in France'. The Mitterrandist centre of the party is flanked by the CERES group led by Jean-Pierre Chèvenement, which is more orthodox in its Marxism, and the 'second left' led by Michel Rocard, which questions the centralising and top-down inheritance from both the Socialist and the French Jacobin traditions. The Socialists control no trade union organisation, although the CFDT, led by Edmond Maire, was at first sympathetic to the 'second left' orientation before internal problems led to return to the insistence on the non-political, strictly trade union tasks.
5. I use this example to illustrate a more general argument because the distance from which the analysis was conducted could have provided the speakers with the chance to argue directly, without fearing what the 'enemy' might do with their candid evaluations. The speakers were candid; and their arguments are the more revealing for that.

   The theme of the Conference, which drew some 2500 visitors over three days in April was 'Resistance, Rebellion, and Revolt!' The Conference included some 166 panel discussions and plenaries, open to all points of view. Organised by the Democratic Socialists of America

(DSA), its goal was to celebrate the '100th Anniversary of the Haymarket Riots, 75th Anniversary of the Triangle Shirtwaist Factory Fire (which helped galvanise the women's working class movement here in New York City), the 50th Anniversary of the great sit-down strikes which helped found the CIO, the 50th Anniversary of the Spanish Civil War, and the 30th Anniversary of the Hungarian Revolt'. The meeting was also to commemorate 'the millions who have fought and died in the real socialist struggle, the continual revolt from below'.

The ecumenical, and explicitly political, orientation of the Conference is mentioned here because, although I am concerned with one specific panel here, I think that the issues raised there apply more generally to the questions raised by the Conference, namely, the relation between socialism and scholarship.

The two participants in the panel on 'France and Socialism under Mitterrand', Mark Kesselman and Daniel Singer, have published papers elaborating their positions in *New Politics*, vol. 1, No. 1, 1986.

6. Compare this argument to that of Nicole Questiaux, the Socialist Minister of Solidarity, who justified her resignation from the Cabinet on the ground that she would not take responsibility for administering declining social benefits.
7. Some would call the 'second left' *lib-lib*; others identify it with its trade union carrier, the CFDT, led by Edmond Maire. For the details, see, Hamon et Rotman, *La deuxième gauche* (Paris: Ramsay, 1982). The source of the label seems to be Michel Rocard's speech at the 1977 Socialist Congress at Nantes, which identified two cultures within French socialism: a self-management and a Jacobin or centralist orientation. Rocard has since gone several times to Canossa in order to keep his credibility within the party, at the cost of sacrificing any claim to represent a different sensibility within the Party. He remains highly popular in opinion polls, but cannot seem to decide to break with a party practice which condemns him to constant compromise.
8. *Intervention*, No. 1, novembre–décembre, 1982, pp. 87–102; translated in *Telos*, No. 55, Spring 1983.
9. *Intervention*, No. 15, janvier–mars 1986.
10. Citations from *Pour Marx* (Paris: Maspero, 1966), pp. 12, 13.
11. This 'work' has taken place largely in Britain, where Althusser's influence was strongest longest. For a summary and critique, see Laclau and Mouffe, *Hegemony and Socialist Strategy* (London: Verso, 1985). The critiques of Althusser have neglected generally that other typical deconstructionist task which, following Nietzsche, asks not what but *who* is speaking, and from *where*. In Althusser's case, the speaker is an unreconstructed Stalinist; his discourse is at the service of the Party. For a devastating critique, see Claude Lefort, *Un homme en trop* (Paris: Seuil, 1986), pp. 78ff.
12. Theories of 'mass society' which were so popular in the 1950s have disappeared from the sociological and political discourse. Instead we have the so-called 'culture of narcissism'. The French rediscovery of Tocqueville, and of Constant, may suggest a different, and potentially more fruitful, reading of the often pertinent observations of Lasch and

his following. The 1950s critique of mass society, like its critique of totalitarianism, is uninteresting if it is taken *only* as sociological description of what supposedly *is* the case. From the standpoint of political *philosophy*, both concepts have more to say.

13. Published as *Les fins de l'homme. A partir du travail de J. Derrida* (Paris: Galilée, 1981). See the critical essay on these themes by Nancy Fraser, 'The French Derrideans: Politicizing Deconstruction or Deconstructing the Political', in *New German Critique*, 33 (Fall, 1984).
14. The exaggerated version of this is of course Richard Rorty's embrace of a post-analytic, post-hermeneutic, post-critical theory which, when it comes right down to it, is homespun American pragmatism, at least in Rorty's own eyes. See, for example, his discussion of 'Habermas and Lyotard on Postmodernity', reprinted in R. Bernstein, ed., *Habermas and Modernity* (Boston: MIT Press, 1985). Rorty's position, by the end of what begins as a clever, and yet lucid critical analysis, is its own *reductio ad absurdem*, insisting among other points that philosophy represents only an 'idiosyncratic need' which may amuse some people but in no way serves society. Rorty adds, without further comment, that his theory 'thus has links with the antirationalist tradition of Burke and Oakeshott, as well as with Deweyan pragmatism'.
15. An English translation of *Au juste* was published by University of Minnesota Press, 1985. The theoretical elaboration of Lyotard's position, combining an appropriation of analytic philosophy and a peculiar reading of Kant's theory of the sublime, is found in his major work, *Le différand* (to appear from University of Minnesota). Lyotard's attempt to appropriate analytic philosophy, like Habermas' variant, goes beyond my competence, and my interest. None the less, their common fishing at the same pond would bear exploring.
16. Despite the American attempt to press it to the cause, French deconstructionism is not equivalent to post-modernism. Self-referential, self-grounded judgement is characteristic of modernism . . . since Descartes, or at least since Kant's essay 'What is Enlightenment?' On the recent Kant debates, see my Note on the recent Conference, 'In the Wake of Kant', in *Telos*, No. 67, Spring 1986.
17. This is of course not strictly true, since the *Critique of Judgement* treats also the teleological judgement of nature. This notion of a natural teleology could be used, as suggested by Lucio Colletti, to make less determinist the Marxian theory of a teleological history. One can see how this would work by comparing Kant's very 'Marxist' arguments in 'The Idea of World History from a Cosmopolitan Point of View' with what these same arguments become in the mature formulation, e.g. in 'Perpetual Peace'. On all these technical details, see my *From Marx to Kant* (Albany: SUNY Press, 1985).
18. *Not* a neo-conservatism, which reintroduces absolutes; deconstructionists cannot be (consistent) neo-conservatives. Conservativism is built on the notion that society is 'too complex' to be meddled with by well-intentioned reformers deluded by the simplicity of their philosophy (or science). Complexity implies the impossibility of democracy, or its limitation to inoffensive spheres, as in the infamous Trilateral

Commission proposals that seek to 'save' democracy by limiting its reach.

19. See, Luc Ferry et Alain Renaut, *La pensée 68* (Paris: Gallimard, 1985). The disappointment experienced when reading this volume, which followed the work of which I will speak in a moment, suggests that there are problems with the theoretical basis of the critique. Ferry and Renaut present first a highly schematic categorisation of the interpretations of the May 1968 experience. This is followed by often justified critiques of the 'French' version of Nietzscheism, Heideggerianism, Marxism and Freudianism in the works of Foucault, Derrida, Bourdieu and Lacan. The 'anti-humanism' which unites these thinkers is guilty of an irrationalism based on their absolutising of one or the other of the antinomic poles. Ferry and Renaut conclude with the 'return of the subject', after 'naïve and traditional' humanism is correctly criticised. Their argument is based on the observation that it is a strange regression for post-modernism to replace Kant's ideal of 'nature subordinated to a will' by the pre-modern idea of 'a nature to which the will is submitted' (pp. 24, 285). But the story told in the intervening pages, although formally coherent, is only formal. The philosophies they criticise are taken out of context, as if they were a set of positive statements and not part of an ongoing dialogue which makes philosophy political precisely because it operates in the interrogative mode. If one is to talk about a *political* philosophy emerging from *La pensée 68*, the 'lib-lib' orientation of the 'second left' cannot be simply neglected.

    A more positive evaluation of Ferry's earlier work, and its relation to the recent theories of Habermas, is found in my *Philosophy and Politics*, Occasional Paper, Center for Humanistic Studies, University of Minnesota, 1986, reprinted in *The Politics of Critique.*

20. Volume 1 of *Philosophie politique* treats the issues raised by the Straussian critique and seeks to give them their place. See my essay 'Philosophy and/or Politics'.

21. Lefort expresses the dilemma when he asserts that 'There is no institution which, by its very nature, can guarantee the existence of a public space in which the questioning of right is propagated. But, reciprocally, that space supposes that distinct institutions articulate the image of its own legitimacy, and that the actors within those institutions exercise their political responsibility.' Ferry and Renaut do away with Lefort quickly in *La pensée 68* by treating him as a 'phenomenologist', who is thus assimilated under one of the antinomic poles. This is unfortunately typical of the schematic style of their polemical text.

    Lefort's discussions of the rights of man are found in 'Droits de l'homme et politique', in *L'invention démocratique* (Paris: Fayard, 1981), and 'Les droits de l'homme et l'Etat-providence', in *Essais sur le politique. XIXe-XXe siècles* (Paris: Seuil, 1986). The passage cited in the text is from the former, p. 74; the above citation is from the latter, p. 57. A fuller discussion of these arguments, and of Lefort's work in general, is found in my *The Marxian Legacy*, whose second edition (Minneapolis: University of Minnesota Press, and London: Macmillan,

1987) contains a lengthy Afterword which deals with these issues in detail.

22. See, *Le différend* (Paris: Editions du Minuit, 1983); English translation forthcoming from University of Minnesota Press.
23. *Intervention*, no. 7, novembre–janvier, 1983–4, pp. 50–58.
24. Ibid., p. 57.
25. Totalitarianism is not simply the opposite of democracy; it can also present itself as its completion or realisation, as in the Marxist attempt to replace formal democracy by 'real democracy'. Totalitarianism is not simply a more efficient form of despotism or authoritarianism; these classical political forms represent a different articulation of the relations among power, law and knowledge and their relation to society. Totalitarianism comes about only in the conditions established by democracy, whose lack of foundation can become the basis of a self-doubt which seeks a 'real' foundation.
26. The critical historian of the French Revolution, François Furet, captures this situation partially when he asserts that 'The history of the French 19th century in its entirety can be considered as the history of the struggle between the Revolution and the Restoration across episodes dated 1815, 1830, 1848, 1851, 1870, the Commune, the 16th May 1877. Only the victory of the republicans over the monarchists at the beginning of the Third Republic marks the definitive victory of the Revolution in the depths of the country: the lay teacher of Jules Ferry, that missionary of the values of 89, is a symbol more than the instrument of that long victorious battle. The integration of the villages and the peasantry of France into the republican nation through the principles of 89 would thus have taken at least a century.' Furet corrects the partiality of his description when he adds that the victory was not definitive, for the idea of 'the' Revolution has lived on as the twentieth-century socialist project. (*Penser la Révolution Française* (Paris: Gallimard, 1978), pp. 16–17.)
27. See Michael H. Davis 'The Law/Politics Distinction, the French Conseil Constitutionnel, and the U.S. Supreme Court', in *The American Journal of Comparative Law*, vol. 34, no. 1, Winter 1986, pp. 45–92. Davis succeeds, against most French and American opinion, in showing remarkable similarities between the two institutions. The basis of his argument, however, is his rejection of the attempt to draw a firm distinction between law and politics. That distinction is shown to be difficult to justify empirically; its foundation is a metaphysics which Davis proposes to 'deconstruct' with the aid of Derrida. The upshot of Davis's position is that the Conseil Constitutionnel, like the US Supreme Court, erects a barrier against democratic participation.

    Davis's arguments can be interpreted differently within the framework proposed here. The 1958 Constitution of the Fifth Republic strengthened immeasurably the Executive against the unstable legislative branch whose weaknesses undermined the Fourth Republic. The Conseil Constitutionnel was designed to interpose its decisions against any parliamentary law which impinged on the prerogatives of the Executive. The 1974 extension to legislators of the right to bring cases before it began to shift the weight of the institution. Politics accelerated the shift. When the Socialists came to power, the legislators of the right began to use this new right, which at first seemed to block socialist measures. The Socialists railed against an antidemocratic 'normocracy' controlled by men appointed by the old power. Yet some of the Conseil's decisions began to reaffirm the rights of the legislature against the Executive, for example in the case of planning in 1982. Although Davis's article was written before the advent of 'cohabitation', his recognition of the role of politics in the development of institutions should have warned him against the simple pleasures of critical deconstruction. One lesson of the Socialists' exercise of power is the demythification of direct popular sovereignty, which seems to be Davis's only positive recommendation. A second lesson is the need to avoid the reduction of politics *or* law to simple empirical questions of who gets what when and how. The transformation of the Conseil Constitutionnel in the sense of the US Supreme Court is no panacea, as Davis's critical presentation of the latter shows well; but it does mark an innovation in the sense of French politics, which Davies' empiricist deconstructionism cannot see.

# 11 France, Germany and the Problem of Europe

## 1. INTRODUCTION

Jean Monnet's hope that economic necessity would produce a European political unity in spite of the parochial concerns of national politicians has failed. The economic downturn has not pushed the politicians any more than the rising tides that preceded it pulled them toward unity. The increased membership of the Common Market has rendered it more quarrelsome and bureaucratic. The fulsome rhetoric that accompanied the Spinelli proposals in 1984, and the apparent French enthusiasm during its six-month presidency, have ebbed. The admission of Spain and Portugal consecrates the already existing two-tiered structure of the community's core-and-periphery economic relations without changing the political checks by which national interest can paralyse communal action. Symbolic gestures, like the recent creation of new passports bearing the title 'European Economic Community', are nullified by the national reality expressed on those same passports by the larger letters inscribing the bearer's country of origin.

There was reason to be more optimistic about the European future in 1984. On the economic front, United States tariff policy was imposing restrictions necessitating a united European reply. Domestic policies in a shrinking world economy forced the formerly dominant heavy industries to take account of their former rivals who are, after all, also neighbours. Soviet assertiveness in Afghanistan coupled with the emplacement of the SS-20s and the repression in Poland was not simply forgotten by the American basing of Pershing and Cruise missiles within the NATO arsenal. The US failure in Lebanon, and its over-aggressive activity in Central America, suggested the need for an independent European diplomatic capacity, backed ultimately by the potential for military action. The core nations of Europe had to recognise their economic and military-diplomatic impotence. The result was the quest for cultural identity which appeared, for a moment, capable of being translated politically.

It is hard today to find a politician or commentator who believes seriously that a European initiative is possible. The European

Parliament in Strassburg may protest the budget submitted to it by the Executive in Brussels; yet all know that Strassburg is a place for the early retirement of politicians who carry no weight on the home front. Jacques Delors' departure from the Finance Ministry in Paris for the direction of the European Executive in Brussels appears to some as the harbinger of an initiative that would centre around the development of the European currency unit (the ECU) into a true money, thereby forcing the national governments into economic co-ordination at a broader level. Yet Delors has maintained a staff in Paris, where another political future may await him. Talk of an extension of the French national deterrent beyond the Rhine has not been concretised by the conventional military co-operation that necessarily would accompany such measures. Europe, in short, remains the subject for Sunday speeches by politicians whose bread-and-butter is elsewhere.

There are, however, reasons to think that despite the behaviour of politicians, movement is possible. Whatever else they may say, politicians seek office. In France and in Germany – perhaps in Italy as well – the socialist politicians face situations which may keep them from office for a long time. The French Socialists are in power, for the moment; the Germans are in opposition. Neither has a programme capable of mobilising support in the upcoming elections. The French came to power with an ideal; three years of austerity government have destroyed its credibility. The Germans experienced more than a decade of social democratic government before the present conservative regime came to office. Although the Socialists have established a 'Commission on Fundamental Values' in preparation for a doctrinal renewal, oppositional initiative has been seized by the new Green Party. The difficult domestic prospects for the Socialists in both countries suggest that a European initiative from the left is possible in both cases. Its details are unclear, save that it would almost certainly entail the explicit creation of a two-tiered Europe centred around the original Six who signed the Treaty of Rome nearly three decades ago. This is not the place to speculate about details such as the shape of the proposed 'Eureka' co-operation as an alternative to the US 'Strategic Defense Initiative'; my contention is only that the initiative is possible, and desirable, from both sides of the Rhine. *L'intendance suivra!*

## 2. FRANCE, GERMANY AND THE IDEA OF EUROPE

The French Socialists who have come to govern alone for the first time in their long history seem to have traded in their old ideology for geo-politics, *realpolitik*, and French history. Necessity has not proven to be the 'mother of invention'; socialist theorists are instead trying busily to make a virtue out of the necessities they belatedly have recognised. In foreign policy, Mitterrand adviser and former Gueverist theorist Régis Debray has lent his pen to the new cause, praising *La puissance* and excoriating *les rêves* of naïve if generous socialists.[1] His President, however, was less successful in teaching his German socialist comrades this same lesson: Mitterrand's December 1982 address to the Bundestag in support of the installation of the Pershing and Cruise missiles made no converts among the opposition. Meanwhile, Mitterrand continues to do his best to justify the Russians' support of his conservative opponent of 1981, keeping the cause of *Solidarnosć* alive while insisting that the 'Yalta' division of Europe cannot be considered final.[2] The appearance of a French Atlanticism is as surprising as its correlate, Socialist Atlanticism. Its explanation is at once geo-political, *realpolitisch*, and quite French. This policy puts into question many unspoken assumptions about socialism; the ideology that had served well in opposition is challenged by a modern world from which it had been insulated for a century.

The German left has been the most irate critic of the French revision of socialist doctrine. France's support of the unpopular 'double track' decision to deploy the American missiles is only part of the explanation. The German Left itself has been the chief object of (at times offensively self-righteous) French socialist criticism. The French claim that the German peace movement is politically naïve about the nature of Russian communism. The mass appeal of this movement is said to be based on a 'politics of fear' or a 'zoological politics' which puts life before the Good Life. What politics the French do discern among the German left are identified with a revival of (political and/or economic) nationalism covered over by appeals for *détente* with the East. The polemics can become quickly self-justificatory, aimed more at domestic consumption than at initiating dialogue. Attempts at reasoned analysis and dialogue have made little progress toward consensus.[3] The grounds of the disagreement are ideological; their implications are practical, for the Germans, the French . . . and for Europe.

Precisely because they are quite French in their socialism, and pragmatic in their politics, Mitterrand's government will have little choice in the 1986 parliamentary elections other than to play the Europe-card. They did not do so in the June 1984 elections for the European Parliament, partly because they were still allied with the Communist Party, partly because of divisions in their own ranks. The departure of the Communists and the surprising success of the far-right National Front (which nearly equalled the declining Communists' 12 per cent with its slogan '*Les Français d'abord!*') have changed the political field. Replacement of the old-style Prime Minister Pierre Mauroy by the well-bred technocrat and Mitterrand loyalist Laurent Fabius was the first step. The next one is suggested by two features which de Gaulle built carefully into his tailor-made Constitution of the Fifth Republic. The President remains independent from his political party, appealing over its head to '*La France*'. Further, the Gaullian President has chiefly concerned himself with foreign policy, consistent with that '*certaine idée de la France*' with which de Gaulle begins mysteriously his *Mémoires*. Mitterrand's '*idée*' emerges from the particular experience of French socialism.

Jean Monnet and the founders of 'Europe' worked from the functionalist assumption that a series of gradual steps toward economic integration would create a *de facto* unity which eventually would be recognised *de jure*. Monnet's aphorism is famous: 'I don't give a damn about coal and steel, what I am after is European union.'[4] European union foundered on the issue of military unity and the attendant need to define a common foreign policy. The Treaty of Paris proposed by Prime Minister Pleven in 1950 was defeated finally by the French Parliament in 1954. The arguments of the time are not without contemporary significance. Then Prime Minister Mendès-France defended the Treaty with the suggestion that 'The most significant advantage is in my opinion that the EDC [European Defence Community] will bind and tie the Federal Republic of Germany to the western world.'[5] His opponents could appeal positively to the easing of East–West tensions that followed the 1953 death of Stalin. Negatively, the defeat at Dien Bien Phu, and difficulties with the Mediterranean colonies suggested that France's essential concerns were not East/West but colonial or southern. After the defeat of the EDC, NATO amended its Charter to admit the Federal Republic, satisfying Dulles' fear that without a strengthened European contribution to its own defence, Congress would reduce NATO funding. The French too were satisfied; the 'German threat' was integrated into the West. De Gaulle's move toward *détente* and his 1966 withdrawal from the NATO military command followed logically. The functional integration of the European economies did not have the political consequences predicted by the logic of Monnet and his co-workers.

If the French vetoed the military, and therefore political unity of Europe thirty years ago, the German Left threatens informally to do the same today. The old animosities between the two great European powers have not been lessened by the greater functional integration of their economies. A curious reflection of this situation is the smooth functioning of the tandem Giscard–Schmidt, and its repetition by the new leaders, Mitterrand–Kohl. Opposites seem to attract, as if ideology were of no importance. Yet it is. The Socialist Party which brought Mitterrand to power is no more similar to the old socialist orthodoxy of the SFIO of Guy Mollet than is the Fourth to the Fifth Republic. The experience of opposition, and now the lessons of power, have created a new socialist synthesis, which is not without its own contradictions. The German Socialists, for their part, have been seriously divided by the peace movement; even a hypothetical alliance with the Greens does not promise them an early return to power. If their divisions are to be overcome, a German Socialist version of the Europe-card will have to be invented. Dialogue instead of polemic with the French could have positive consequences – or at least, avoid choices whose implications for Europe would be negative.

## 3. FROM FRENCH POLITICS TO DEMOCRATIC SOCIALIST THEORY

As expected, French Socialist domestic and foreign policy has reversed the direction set by the previous regime. The difference, however, is that the governments of Valéry Giscard d'Estaing and Georges Pompidou acted in what generally would be called a 'socialist' direction. Social peace was purchased by social gains and clientelistic practices. More important than wage benefits were the forms of social security and job tenure which increased the redistributive role of the state while discouraging initiative by independent entrepreneurs. The result was that the French Socialists came to power faced with serious domestic economic problems, to which they replied – as one right-wing critic admits – by doing what the capitalists themselves did not have the courage to attempt.[6] Their foreign policy, too, is the inverse of the old regime's priority on détente and trade with the Soviet Union. While not falling into the pattern of seeing the hand of

Moscow behind all the disagreeable developments abroad, the French Socialist government has been critical of the tendencies of the Nicaraguans or Palestinians to implement communist forms of organisation whose totalitarian results it fears. If the previous regime tended to worry more about the Americans, the Socialists tend in the opposite direction. The cardinal rule remains France First; but if tilt there must be, the Socialists feel safer in the democratic embrace.

The Party is not entirely unified around these orientations.[7] The Socialist Party's Marxists – the CERES, Centre d'education et de recherches socialistes – take a different tack. The CERES presented a counter-project at the party's Bourg-en-Bresse Congress in October 1983. It warned against the economic liberalism and the return of the market that it says are being imported under the pretext that France must become internationally competitive. It condemned the so-called realism that simply 'administers' a crisis-ridden economy instead of challenging the crisis itself by mobilising the working class(es). The CERES proposed a nationalist voluntarism whose economic measures are expected to awaken the political enthusiasm necessary to rekindle the Socialist experience. France is said to need '*un grand projet*', which liberalism, realism or modernism cannot offer. A 'competitive devaluation' accompanied by protectionism, and a new 'saint-simonian alliance' (i.e., industrial restructuring) are the *projet* which they believe will stimulate greater productivity in adversity while bringing voters to the defence of the courageous but beleaguered Party. The logic behind these proposals is very French if not particularly Marxist. Revolutionary images of *La patrie en danger* are evoked by this very Jacobin appeal . . . with its Gaullist overtones.

The CERES' analysis is revealing because it correctly insists that it is only restating the platform which brought the Socialists to power. This fact highlights a neglected aspect of French-style socialist politics. Although the Socialist party had led coalition governments in the 1940s and 1950s, participating in almost all of the Fourth Republic's waltzing coalitions, the PS was only a linchpin which could bring others a majority; it did not rule the country. French Socialism had never confronted the difficulties of governing alone, except for one brief moment of glory in 1936. Absolute powerlessness, like absolute power, corrupts. The victim loses touch with reality. He lives in a dream world where anything is possible. The political result is the voluntarism and nationalism that were apparent in the first year of Socialist government. Socialist Keynesianism accompanied by nationalisations superbly ignored France's place inthe world economy. The same ideological voluntarism expected the enthusiasm of the working masses to pay for the new social measures gaily voted. But the masses acted like good consumers, spending their new benefits on goods which the depressed French industry could not produce. Inflation increased as the trade balance worsened and the franc weakened. This was not anticipated by the Socialists' theoretical plans.

French Socialism has been a culture of opposition since the foundation of the Third Republic more than a century ago. This explains the ideological passion that characterises French politics. The cultural attachment of the '*peuple de gauche*' is electorally crucial. This century-old tradition explains some of the incongruities of Socialist politics, for example the maintenance of Pierre Mauroy as Prime Minister despite shifting policies, or the abortive educational reform that was the proximate cause of the recent cabinet shuffle. The Party majority attempts to prove (at least to itself and its faithful electorate) that it has maintained its Socialist 'essence'; its austerity policies are considered a 'parenthesis' due to a 'conjunctural' accident. When the Communist Party withdrew its Ministers from the government, the Socialists tried to maintain symbolic continuity and connection to the '*peuple de gauche*' by returning the CERES Ministers to the government (with Chèvenement taking over the Education Ministry as a sop to the traditionally socio-communist FEN teachers union whose programme for secularising education had brought a million people to the streets of Paris, uniting the political right and toppling the government. The secular reform was promptly abandoned by the 'Marxist' Minister). This ideology and its symbolic political translation clash with the reality of Socialist practice. Some means of resolving the contradiction must be found; in the Fifth Republic, foreign policy is the logical place to search.

The simple fact that the Socialists are now in power means the symbolic demise of a century of French history which nurtured the Socialists' culture of opposition. It marks the end of the ideological passions that dominated French history, despite lingering sentimental or cynical attempts to rekindle them. The situation is classically dialectical: the ideology that served for the conquest of power is no longer relevant once power has been achieved. The question of a substitute emerges, and with it another paradoxical effect of French history. The identification of French nationalism with the revolutionary tradition of 1789 (or 91, or 93 . . .), and with the *Résistance* provides a kind of *ersatz* ideology which, as ideologies will, creates strange bedfellows. The quasi-unanimity in favour of the French version of deterrence – which some support from anti-Americanism, others from anti-communism, others for idiosyncratically French reasons – is an obvious illustration. Enthusiastic support for *Solidarnosć* is another. The ideological vacuum and vacillation are broken only by one general agreement among the contending versions of socialism: that *the* enemy is 'Totalitarianism'.[8]

Americans are surprised to hear Mrs Kirkpatrick's distinction between totalitarian and authoritarian governments in socialist mouths. Their reasons are not hers, for the French experience is not comparable. They begin from the fact that ever so many of 'the best and the brightest' went through the communist party. This suggests to them that the totalitarian temptation is not an accident of personal psychology. Manichaean anti-communism is insufficient for understanding either the Soviet Union or the possible domestic consequences of communist politics. When the French socialists talk about the Soviet threat, they refer to something more than de Gaulle's *realpolitische* concern with the geographic entity he persisted in calling 'Russia'. When they hedge their aid to Nicaragua because of its internal evolution, they are not acting as loyal agents of Atlanticism. They have tried to distinguish between East/West and North/South relations (encountering difficulties, however, when it comes to their own traditional Franc-zone partners).[9] Their critique of totalitarianism is not reducible to the simple anti-communism whose we/they discourse is incapable of seeing either the greys or the possibilities of change. Poland's experiment with freedom, and its crushing by the *coup* of 13 December 1981 were experienced in France as confirmation both of the nature of totalitarianism *and* of the possibility of change within the *glacis*. Nicaragua's precarious balance between a multi-party and a simple party-state expresses the other side of this analysis. Totalitarianism is an omni-present threat *from within*; democratic politics has to take this tendency into account.

The French experience of the totalitarian temptation – either personally, or for politicians like President Mitterrand, from the necessity of dealing with the Communist Party – suggests that even democratic societies cannot avoid the totalitarian potential. The Polish example illustrates the obverse, that societies which have experienced totalitarianism tend to be immune from it. The French quickly wax philosophical on these matters, but the point is simple enough. Modernisation destroys the traditional life-patterns of millions. It generates material as well as psychological insecurity. The welfare state, socialist or capitalist, comes to the rescue.[10] The danger is that its intervention creates a class of dependent persons addicted to the aid received. This danger is magnified when – in totalitarian societies, or those on their way – the state acts by means of a party which dispenses security and ideological identity in order to keep itself in power. The more familiar leftist critique of Welfare State capitalism and the rejection of totalitarianism go together. Their intellectual result is expressed in the rediscovery of Tocqueville's America.[11] Democracy becomes the key political concept for analysing their own and foreign societies. It is possible to be an *anti-communist leftist*. The *ersatz* that replaces ideological socialism is the concept of democracy.[12]

French Socialism has always been more French than theoretical. The practical imperatives imposed on socialist theory by French history provide the ideological justification for many of their domestic political decisions. Nationalism, voluntarism and the appeal to the '*peuple de gauche*' brought the Socialists to power in 1981. The exercise of governmental responsibility has made it imperative to reformulate the ideology which served so well in a culture of opposition. This is where foreign policy makes its influence felt. The analysis of democracy's weakness suggests a different understanding of Soviet strategy. The French Socialists are not worried about the Soviet military buildup for reasons determined by national security policy. Their concern is political. As they see it, the Soviets are attempting to play upon the insecurity of western democracies. The USSR's goal is not to march physically across the Fulda Gap; Western Europe is not Afghanistan. The goal is what Montaigne's friend La Boétie described 400 years ago: self-willed servitude, or what we moderns call Finlandisation.[13] This was already the case in their relations with West Germany in the Berlin Deadline Crisis of 1958–9, and again in the Berlin Aide-Mémoire Crisis of 1961;[14] the same attempt was made this past year in the debates leading to the implementation of the 'double track' decision. The French Socialists interpret the Soviet goal as the encouragement of a neutralism in the Federal Republic which would divide NATO and make impossible any common European action, either within its territories (East and West) or abroad (for example in Lebanon). The uniqueness of this strategy is that it is to be *freely chosen* by the democratic voters in the West. This interpretation of the goals of Soviet policy and the specific type of danger it poses to democracy as such permits the

French Socialists to replace the ideology of socialism and its nationalist *ersatz*, which got them elected by selling the politics of austerity to the public as the inevitable result of France's involvement in world politics.

Geography, economics and history provide only part of the explanation of the French Left's adopting a politics different from that of the Germans. The theoretical development of an anti-totalitarian politics is the crucial missing link. It clarifies some downright silly arguments that one hears from them – defending Reagan's Grenada adventure, or his rearmament race, for example – and some more sophisticated ones – supporting the NATO double decision, or putting new pressures on Nicaragua. It is also part of the explanation for the decline of the French Communist Party to its present 12 per cent of the electorate. It may explain the newfound discretion of Culture Minister Jack Lang, whose anti-American bombasts served Fidel Castro better than they did the French public. (There is of course much that it does not explain; and not all actions whose justification is presented in these theoretical terms were in fact motivated by theory.) Most importantly, the critique of totalitarianism and the primacy of democracy explain the massive reaction to the declaration of martial law in Poland on 13 December, 1981. Poland seemed to the French a vibrant experiment with precisely those concepts to which their own development had driven them. They were shocked when the assassination of Polish freedom was not met with equal outrage elsewhere – particularly among the members of the German peace movement. Along with their own internal economic problems in facing the world economy, this silence has forced them to a new set of reflections centring on the role of Europe.

## 4. GERMANY AND THE CONCEPT OF EUROPE

Although Franco-German differences are nothing new, the acrimony of the debate concerning what the French insist on calling 'pacifism' has reached a point where dialogue is nearly impossible. In these polemics, the French anti-totalitarian premise hardens to an absolute first principle which does resemble that of Mrs Kirkpatrick, despite the fact that the concept was framed to account both for the temptation of *and* the immunisation to totalitarianism. Meanwhile the German quest for an alternative politics, in which the issue of nuclear arms is only one part, is transformed into a nearly caricatural pacifism sometimes tinged with a utopian longing for unilateral measures that would reunite Germany. The May 1984 publication in *Le Monde* of a 'Memorandum to the French Left' in which the Germans invited the French to a public debate in Mannheim is illustrative of the problem. The well-intended letter was couched in schoolmotherly scolding and facile psychologising whose self-righteousness hardly encouraged any but a formal party-political response.[15] The result was that the Socialist Party sent its official foreign policy delegate, Jacques Huntzinger, whose officious explanations were greeted with predictable disdain. Psychology aside, the lack of debate can be explained by the memorandum's analysis of the Soviet Union. Refusing a 'moral' condemnation of Stalinism as the basis for its politics – but of course condemning Stalinist practices – the Memorandum argues geopolitically that the Soviet Union is no threat. A comparison of the Soviet Union's threat to the West with the pre-war Hitler regime's *Drang nach Osten* forms the basis of this judgement. But this comparison is a German, not a French illustration.

The French have one strong *political* argument, restated in various rhetorical turns of phrase. They reject what Castoriadis has called 'zoological politics', suggesting that since the Greeks politics has concerned itself not with the preservation of mere biological life but rather with the quest for the *Good* Life. Beyond that, the French political rhetoric verges quickly toward the psychological – for example Paul Thibaud cites Clausewitz to the effect that 'A conqueror is always a friend of peace. He would be happy to enter your State without opposition.' The Germans reply most significantly with arguments that the French do not understand the implications of the newest advances in counter-force weaponry. The authors of the Memorandum stress the different geographical situations of front-line, divided Germany and sheltered nuclear France. The Germans admit that their movement has raised the 'national question' which had lain dormant during the years of atonement. They propose a potential political solution for 'going beyond Yalta' and eliminating the block-system without resorting to unilateral measures. But then they too turn toward the psychological, as if they were unable to understand otherwise why their rational arguments would not convince.[16]

Psychology is no more irrelevant than history or conjunctural political imperatives to the explanation of national behaviour. The shift in German opinion and behaviour (begun under the socialist government but continued and accelerated practically under the conservative leadership) *is* remarkable. As in the case of the development of French democratic socialist theory, the national history in which a political phenomenon is nurtured provides the first steps toward understanding. Hans Morgenthau has pointed out that the eventual unification of Germany under Prussian domination to the exclusion of Austria is an excellent illustration of the political strategy which later took the name 'Gaullism'.[17] The inability of the German bourgeoisie to transform 1848 into a truly national revolution is legendary. The often-proclaimed internationalism of the pre-War Socialist Party broke apart on 4 August, 1914. The Weimar democracy that followed the war-and-revolution years brought Hitler legally to power. The Federal Republic created by the occupying powers in 1949 is the longest German experience with democratic institutions.

The Western founders of the new Republic, as well as its first Chancellor, Konrad Adenauer, sought to avoid historical repetition by binding their creation tightly to the West. It is as if they feared that Germany on its own was incapable of the requisite self-control. This orientation coincided with the Allies' needs, and fit the pattern of a Cold War whose outlines had been sketched implicitly at Yalta. It also coincided neatly with the extremely powerful Chancellor's intentions.[18] Adenauer's only pre-war experience in international politics had been a brief participation after the First World War in the *Rhinebund*, an attempt to separate the more liberal Rhenish provinces from the militarist and Junker-dominated Prussian East. After the Second World War, and with the help of the Western allies, this goal was *de facto* realised: what had been Prussia was now the Eastern or German Democratic Republic.[19] From this point of view, *Ostpolitik* was not a radical departure, as its continuation by Adenauer's self-anointed 'nephew', Chancellor Kohl, makes clear. Although it may have other intentions, *Ostpolitik* is based on the explicit recognition of a distinctly Western Germany whose culture, economy and political forms differ from the formerly Junker-dominated, authoritarian and relatively more backward Eastern regions. The détente guaranteed by *Ostpolitik* is the contrary of the dream of reunification; détente can exist only between partners recognised as independent and equal.

Adenauer's political genius was to recognise and to exploit the difference between a military and a political alliance. He was able to play on the Allies' military insecurity at the outbreak of the Korean war in order to achieve what was, for him, a political goal: the recognition of the Federal Republic as a sovereign and equal state. His intention was recognised by those French who feared the military and political weight of their hereditary enemy. These generally conservative politicians provided the final weight that permitted the 1954 veto of the proposed European Defence Community which would have consecrated Adenauer's achievement. When, nearly a decade later, it became impossible to dismiss the political reality of German economic might, de Gaulle quickly established direct and privileged *political* relations with Adenauer. These institutions endure, and could function as a kind of counterweight to American *military* presence within the Atlantic community.[20] But the psychological side of the relation cannot be neglected. It is as if Germany, the economic giant of Europe, cannot speak alone in its own political voice. Mitterrand's Address to the Bundestag in December of 1982, advocating installation of the Pershing and Cruises, was rubbing salt on a wound which many had forgotten. Not only what Mitterrand said, but the fact that he would come before the Bundestag to teach them a lesson in *realpolitik*, could only be an affront to Germans generally. This aspect of Mitterrand's intervention points to a further result of German history: Germany is not only divided; the Federal Republic is not fully a sovereign state. Its occupation by American, British and French troops (whose 'tripwire' function is put into question with the replacement of massive retaliation by graduated response strategies) cannot be neglected.[21]

The question of political sovereignty has been raised anew by the massive German peace movement whose *raison d'être* is not just the *fear* that its critics condemn as irrational (or, in the French case, as apolitical). One need only look at a map, read some of the more foolish verbiage from Washington, or think through the logic of flexible response to see that the fear is not the product of paranoia. What needs to be explained is why this fear arose when it did, and in what conditions its spread became possible. This is where the question of sovereignty plays a role. 1979 was not only the year of the NATO double decision; it marked also the height of German economic power, and the possibility of its translation into *political* influence. The anti-democratic means that had been used in the struggle against the terrorism into which a part of the student movement had degenerated were no longer necessary; *Ostpolitik* had brought new prestige abroad, and the role of the governing SPD within the Second International (in the Spanish and Portuguese transitions, and in Latin America) gave further prestige to Helmut Schmidt's governing

Socialists. The Edition Suhrkamp chose to celebrate its thousandth volume with a series of essays commemorating the fiftieth Anniversary of Karl Jaspers' attempt to understand the 'Spiritual Situation of the Times' as Weimar democracy was agonising.[22] The slogan that reappeared frequently in the essays was '*Wir sind wieder wer*', we are again someone. But they weren't. Helmut Schmidt, the so-called *Weltökonom*, was unable to translate Germany's strength into internationally accepted political power and projects. *That* was the beginning of the end of the social-liberal coalition in Bonn and the precondition for the fear's emergence, and not vice-versa.

The unity of the fear and the question of sovereignty in the broadly-based peace movement need not be interpreted as containing the potential for a revived German nationalism.[23] History and psychology alone do not explain the present potential of German democracy. A third component is the radical cultural change which leaped to public attention in the 1960's phenomena of student rebellion and alternative culture. More important than the headline-gathering demonstrations or the attention-creating vestimentary regalia is the institutionalisation and spread of so-called '*Bürgerinitiativen*', popular initiatives on issues that concern the citizen in all or any aspect of her daily life, from crèches to nuclear power plants, from public transportation to pollution control measures. This participatory orientation is coupled with a quite 'un-German' suspicion of the state which culminated in 1983 in the cancellation of the mandated national census on the ground that it would interfere with the individual's right to privacy. Its better known manifestation, of course, has been the rise of the Green party, whose choice of a parliamentary role should be stressed against those who see in it the danger of a return to the atavistic longing for the Teutonic forests.[24] These phenomena are the precondition for – not the result of – the massive protests against the stationing of the missiles.

The historical and psychological mixture that created the new movement-politics explains also its undeniable ambivalence. The very term, 'movement', conjures up memories of fascism, which claimed to represent the good of the Whole against the democratic parties which are, by their very nature, partial.[25] When elements within the present movement began to address the national question, these memories became nightmares. There is ground for worry, and reasons for caution; and yet, it is also true that the 'national question' – whether in the form of unification or in the form of limited sovereignty – cannot be ignored nor left to the Right. The most tempting approach for many in the movement is also fraught with difficulty. It begins from the idea that Germany is not 'really' part of the West: Germany (East and West) belongs to that geographic sphere known as *Mitteleuropa*. The term is thought of sometimes in a cultural framework, indicating something that is neither impressed by the Tsarist knout nor left simply to the competitive egoism and raw vulgarity of upstart American pragmatism. Its political translation is an anti-Americanism (tempered usually by anti-Sovietism or Russophobia) and a yearning for neutrality between the blocs. Its military translation is something like a return to the old Rapacki Plan (which, it should be recalled, was offered during the debate over German integration into NATO as a kind of Soviet bait tempting the Federal Republic to remain outside). The image of *Mitteleuropa* is emotionally satisfying, but it is not without practical difficulties.[26]

The visions of an independent and neutral *Mitteleuropa* has been suggested as the solution both to the German problem and to the anxieties of the Germans. It is a political slogan which appeals to different threads of German character and culture. Its chances of success are limited by the same German history that suggested it. From the point of view of the other hypothetical *Mitteleuropaens*, the slogan is a veil for renewed German domination. It is hard to imagine Czechs or Poles forgetting their unhappy history of German domination. On the other side, for the French, it conjures up visions of a new *Reich* whose economic power would be coupled with a new military potential. Both fears were reinforced by the impressive silence with which the German peace movement greeted the imposition of martial law in Poland on 13 December, 1981. Already during the movement that began at Gdansk (Danzig, as the Germans insist still on calling it), well-intentioned Germans, showed a condescending attitude toward the Poles who were seen as again yielding to their romantic impulses whose disastrous results would again have to be set right by stolid German wisdom.[27] The gradual reconciliation between the Federal and German Democratic Republic which has been based largely on economic measures, might have taken on a new dimension had the Soviets not finally prevailed upon Honnecker to 'postpone' his scheduled September 1984 visit. (Tolerance of the Rumanian visit later that year is not surprising if one accepts the notion that it is the creation of an eventual *Mitteleuropa* that bothers the Soviets.) The Western, and especially the French, reaction to the potential *Mitteleuropaïsche* solution has been muted thus far since the project's unlikelihood demands nothing more for the moment.[28]

Clearly, opposition from East and West do not bode well for the creation of *Mitteleuropa*.

## 5. DETERRENCE AND DEMOCRACY

The German concern with the implication of deterrence for its national sovereignty (and survival) need not be antithetic to or incompatible with the French preoccupation concerning the implications of democracy for socialist practice. The French discussion of democracy leans heavily on Tocqueville's *Democracy in America*. Tocqueville's concept of democracy is sociological, not ideological. Democracy is founded on equality. Political liberty can be threatened by the effects of this social equality. The 'democratic tyranny' feared by the nineteenth-century Frenchman has parallels with the twentieth-century French analysis of totalitarianism. Paul Thibaud has drawn the contemporary conclusions.[29] *Deterrence is a contradiction in terms for a democracy.* Deterrence demands that the nation be prepared to go to war; it relies on constant mobilisation;[30] it sacrifices the present and the individual to the future and the collective. Deterrence is a military strategy whose domestic political consequences necessarily destabilise the foundations of democracy. The costs can be hidden for a time, but their danger is always present. Mass pacifism, Thibaud concludes, is inherent in the Western democracies which rely on deterrence. (One might add that since nuclear deterrence puts the power of war and peace in the hands of a single actor, its anti-democratic character increases.)

The situation of Europe, between the strategic stockpiles of the super-powers, is particularly delicate. Henry Kissinger's *Nuclear Weapons and Foreign Policy* noted already in 1957 that the American umbrella could not protect Europe once the Soviet Union had acquired strategic vectors. De Gaulle drew his own conclusions; his theorists (Gallois, Poirer, Ailleret) developed the notion of 'deterrence from the weak to the strong'. But, as Thibaud points out, French public opinion has not quite understood this – or has misunderstood it to its own psychological and political advantage. The average Frenchman conceives of deterrence as 'sanctuarisation'.[31] This misinterpretation may explain the lack of a pacifist movement in France. It may also explain why its neighbours show a lack of enthusiasm if not a suspicion of French intent when it speaks of the need for a European defence policy. If France is, or thinks that it is, truly a sanctuary, its support for NATO rearmament or common production of conventional weaponry appears simply as a projection of egoistic national interest. A French political initiative toward Europe would have to take into account this perception abroad, and the misperception at home.

The difficulty cannot be resolved by a renewal of *détente*. The positive as well as the negative or defensive formulation of this approach are based on the unstated assumption that the sides to the agreement share common values. The positive formulation – that *détente* leads to *entente* and co-operation – depends on the co-existence of common interest imposed by economic necessities; the negative-defensive version presupposes a common perception of military-political dangers that both parties seek to avoid. Only such convergent interests make possible a non-zero sum relation between partners in negotiation. The French Socialist analysis of Soviet society as a specific kind of totalitarianism denies the existence of such commonalities; it accepts neither an economistic convergence theory nor a 'zoological' priority on mere life. The Soviet Union can neither be tamed (Kissinger) nor marginalised (Brzezinski). Nor can the Yalta division of Europe be treated as final. The Russian reading of the Helsinki Accords as the confirmation of Yalta[32] must be confronted with the possibilities of democratic renewal that the Poles or the Charter 77 have read into them. But how? There is no generally accepted agreement on the concretisation of these basic premisses; Mitterrand's June 1984 visit to Moscow broke no new ground, succeeding only in avoiding the *gaffes* made by Giscard at his 1979 Warsaw meeting with Brezhnev just after the invasion of Afghanistan. One option would substitute a concept of 'extended deterrence' for the present limited and anti-cities based French doctrine; another suggestion focuses on the European implications of the recent creation of a conventionally armed French Rapid Strike Force. One notion that has *not* been suggested is the return of France to the NATO military command. Whatever policy does come to replace the *détente* pursued by the previous regime, the Germans' attitude and eventual co-operation will be crucial.[33] The legacy of Franco-German enmity, and the geopolitical difference in their situations, is made even more complex by the different attitudes of their domestic constituencies toward the politics of deterrence.

The German Socialists' response to the breakdown of superpower détente has been twofold. They, as well as the Christian Democrats now in power, and even the Christian Socialists of Franz-Josef

Strauss, have attempted to continue their own process of *détente*, especially with the German Democratic Republic. On the other hand, they have to worry about the effects of a renewed 'mansfieldism' which would involve an even more radical decoupling than the nuclear one that Kissinger invoked at Brussels in September 1979. This issue was brought to a head by Gunther Gaus, former representative of the West German government to the East, at the decisive – and divisive – Social Democratic Party Congress in Berlin in November 1981. Gaus's speech was a deliberate provocation[34] which received the reply he desired. Yes, said then-Chancellor Helmut Schmidt, flexible response means that the Americans will not sacrifice Chicago for Hamburg! Gaus's point was clinched: the only protection for Europe would be a return to the doctrine of Mutually Assured Destruction (MAD). As that is not possible, he concludes, there is no reason for Germany to remain in a NATO Alliance dominated by the wishes of the United States. Gaus's position is not atypical, nor is it illogical, so far as it goes.

It is less difficult to criticise NATO than it is to formulate concretely a system of European defence, either with the French extended nuclear deterrence or by conventional means.[35] The historical legacy of Franco-German relations leads to the suspicion that the French are seeking only to create a condominium in which the Germans will pay the economic costs of the arms which will turn their own country into the first battlefield of a new, if not necessarily atomic, war. Self-interest points the Germans in a different direction: toward *Mitteleuropa*! If the fractious independence of the sovereign NATO member-states prevents the development of a common policy, could not the Germans turn East? A nuclear-free island of peaceful trade could implant itself securely between the two super-powers whose strategic arsenals hold each other at bay. The desire for survival, and the mutual benefits of trade, appear as the solid material foundations for this return to an age-old pattern.[36] Germany could then become 'someone', independent of vulgar American and autocratic Soviet culture and politics. As for the French, they would go the way of their former colonial rival England, or perhaps envisage a Mediterranean solution in alliance with the Socialist regimes in Spain, Portugal and perhaps Papandreou's Greece!

The *mitteleuropaïsche* solution for Germany is not politically realistic nor economically wise. The differences between the super-powers are not only military. The Soviet economic potential is limited, and the Soviets are fully aware that the difference is not only quantitative. The treaty the Soviet Union signed on 4 May, 1984 with Poland asserted that Solidarity arose because Poland had become dependent on the Western economies. The Soviets undertook to grant aid as a way of breaking this dependence. Such aid has limits; the Soviet Union does not have the technological goods or organisational abilities that could bring its zone to equal standing with the West. In these circumstances, *Mitteleuropa* would be dominated by the economic power of a united Germany. Worse, it would draw the East bloc satellites toward its economic orbit. The Soviets could not tolerate such a situation *even* on the hypothesis that *Mitteleuropa* were neutral or pro-Soviet in its political orientation. On the other hand, the Soviet Union needs the anti-Americanism of the peace movement because (despite the French analysis of the attractive force of totalitarianism in democratic societies) it has lost the attractive power and potential fifth column that the Communist ideology once assured it. The precedent of the 1950s, and the present frustrated apathy in the German peace movement, suggest that without some attractive issue around which to unify positive support, the protest energies that arose from a moment's fear and refusal will wither or encrust into sects. The Soviets therefore must encourage some hope for an independent European solution. Yet, Soviet rhetoric of a 'revanchist Reich' conceals a well-grounded fear whose nature is *not* military but economic.

Creation of an independent *Mitteleuropa* would not only weaken the NATO alliance and threaten the economic base of Soviet domination of its satellites; paradoxically, the hypothetical new political zone would be itself weakened economically as well. The correlate to 'Finlandisation' is what Andrew Arato calls 'Hong-Kongisation'.[37] The East represents a potential market with which the Germans traditionally are familiar, and which could represent a solution to their present economic difficulties. The political reversals that have seen Franz-Josef Strauss and Helmut Kohl champion such economic relations are not surprising. The unanimity with which the Germans earlier rejected Reagan's proposed oil pipeline boycott has the same roots. The Eastern trade could make Germany the engine of European recovery; it could save its heavy industry from the ravages of the Rustbelt countries of the West. But at what cost? Finlandisation is the political form of that 'self-willed servitude' to which the French have found democracy to be prone. 'Hong-Kongisation' suggests its economic form. André Gorz makes the argument succinctly. Gorz calls those heavy industries whose future

Germany could salvage by turning its economic attention to the East 'second wave' industries; they represent the past, not the technological and electronic future in which that socialist dream of a society no longer based on the exploitation of labour-power becomes materially, if not yet politically, possible.[38] By turning East, Germany would sacrifice its long-term development to the immediate benefits of a trade which preserves its present prosperity without assuring its future.

The source of the difficulty is that neither deterrence nor *détente* make sense for the democracies of a Europe whose unity is only geographical. 'Europe' is a concept whose political reality is as contradictory as the zoological politics that the French socialists criticise for putting life before the Good Life. Both arguments make the same formal error. Of course, life is the real precondition for there being a Good Life at all; similarly, the reality of an independent Europe is arguably the precondition for the independence of any of the sovereign nations which compose it. But one should not confuse real causal priority with logical priority – or what Aristotle distinguished as 'First in the order of Things' from 'First in the order of Being'. Less abstractly, the protection of life and the creation of European unity and independence depend on conditions which make political action not simply possible or desirable but practical. The abstract logic of deterrence, unilateral or multilateral disarmament, or massive moral refusal by the citizenry will convince only the convinced. The existence of 'Europe' in its art, religion and philosophy is beyond doubt for those who happen to dwell in these realms. But a practical, not a categorical imperative is necessary for the realisation of what is abstractly and logically possible. The initiative could come from France's Socialists whose idealism is exhausted, but whose pragmatism will force them to take a domestic initiative in the European arena. If the German left can break free of its own form of self-righteousness and its ideological socialism – if it can be politically pragmatic, concerned with power and not prophets bearing a message to the world – it may be able to transform this French Socialist opportunism into a German and European opportunity.

## 6. SOCIALIST IDEOLOGY AND THE EUROPEAN OPTION

Although the commentators agreed unanimously that the June 1984 elections for the European Parliament were decided on national, not

European issues, the French case was somewhat different. The three opposition parties had joined together to present a list of candidates headed by the popular Simone Weil, well-known as the former President of the European Parliament. Granted, the case for the national character of the French choice is made by the low score of the Communist Party, but the surprising 11 per cent received by Le Pen's right wing National Front (*'Les Français d'abord!'*) may have been a rejection of the united opposition's European orientation as much as it was a xenophobic reaction to the economic crisis ravaging France. The unification of the opposition around the candidacy of Simone Weil had a symbolic value. The opposition wanted to seize 'Europe' as its issue. Attempts to counter this by forming a centre-left 'European' party, supposedly with the tacit aid of the Elysée itself, got nowhere. This failure[39] should not prevent the recognition of a significant electoral possibility for the 1986 Parliamentary elections. A centre-left coalition, united by the power of the Presidency and excluding the nationalist extremes on the Left (the CERES Socialists and Communist Party) and the Right (the National Front and Chirac's RPR) is a real possibility, especially if the Socialists take seriously the implications of their 1981 campaign promise of not only increased decentralisation but a return to proportional elections. Such a coalition could play the European card. The modernising economic policies already put into practice under 'austerity' would make it an appealing partner to a 'third wave' Germany. Arrangements for the new marriage could be made under the guidance of former French Socialist Finance Minister and now European Commission head Jacques Delors. But such a coalition would need a theoretical justification if it were not to appear as sheer opportunism. Most importantly, it would have to find a way to appeal to the electoral remnants of the ideological '*peuple de gauche*'.

A 'Europe' capable of mobilising domestic French support would have to be integrated into the conceptual framework suggested by the evolution of socialism from an essentially economic ideology to a democratic politics along the lines suggested by the French critique of totalitarianism. The Europe outlined in the Treaty of Rome's Common Market would not suffice. That Europe has no place for the institutions – even for the consideration – of a common defence policy whose necessity is made evident by the nature of the Soviet threat and the need to found the European edifice on a Franco-German accord. The Common Market is simply a market for the redistribution of already produced goods.[40] Just as the French

Socialists' redistributionist ideology got them into trouble in the first year of their government, so would a mere common *market* be unable to draw its members toward policies for the necessary modernisation of their economies. The European Parliament as presently constituted does not have the power or the tools for such a task, while the European executive is ultimately dependent on arrangements at the regular meetings of the heads of state whose leader changes every six months. Mitterrand's June 1984 speech to the Strassburg meeting of the European Parliament and his support of the Spinelli proposals that tend toward wider integration suggest that he is testing the waters; the manner in which he dominated the June 1984 meeting of the EEC chiefs at Fontainbleau show that he is keeping his options open. His initiative, however, will not come within the institutions of the Common Market, where he has little leverage and no constituency. The initiative will have to be domestic; and de Gaulle's institutions are made-to-order.

Mitterrand's nickname during the Fourth Republic, when he served as Minister in some 11 cabinets, was 'The Florentine'. He reconstituted his political virginity by vigorous opposition to the Fifth Republic which he denounced in the title of a 1964 book as 'the permanent *coup d'état*'. He has since found that the suit de Gaulle knit fits him well; the Florentine has reappeared in presidential robes. The Gaullian President is not bound by the party whose support brought him to power. His appeal is to the nation, directly; and this means that the vehicle of foreign policy is readily available. Realistically, of course, the President must consider the opinion of his party. The sharp evolution through which the rhetoric of socialism has passed since the Socialists came to power in 1981 has left the general public confused, apathetic or negative. Mitterrand could make a virtue of necessity. The first steps toward a new Europe would not be formulated in terms of economics, let alone socialist ideology. They would be justified by the need to defend democracy against the Soviet threat *and* the slippage of Germany toward *mitteleuropaïsche* dependency. Even on the optimistic assumption that the economy begins its upturn before the 1986 parliamentary elections, the Socialists will need to mobilise two quite different group of electors – their own '*peuple de gauche*', and a floating centre which is socially and also economically 'liberal'. A good dialectician knows that this can be done only by moving to a level higher than each of the opposites. Such a '*grand projet*' is possible only for a Socialist President for whom that '*certaine idée de la France*' can coincide with a vision which transcends the hexagon and who, because of the evolution of socialist theory, can identify French democracy with the need for constructing a democratic Europe. Its realisation is prepared by ideology and by politics. Its success would consecrate the end of the socialism of the Third Republic; it would inaugurate a new vision of democratic socialism.

Will he do it? The idea is in the air.[41] It is generally agreed that Mitterrand will have to act in order to avoid disaster in 1986. Some of those who suggest the centre-left option argue in terms of the ideological evolution of French socialism. Others are more cynical in suggesting that the Florentine will turn to the Europe card because there are no more trumps in his deck. No one has suggested, as the above analysis proposes, that the 'Europe card' could be more than simply a domestic tactic. Consideration of the evolution of Germany, as in the case of the 1961 *rapproachement* undertaken by de Gaulle, will give this tactic a strategic dimension whose consequences may not have been intended by the actors. The internal political necessities confronting the Florentine take place in an ideological climate quite different from the parliamentary jousts of the Fourth Republic. The politics of austerity by which the Socialists are attempting to make a virtue out of necessity has been justified by the fact that the future of France depends on relations outside their borders. What was at first only the rationalisation of policies imposed on the Socialists can become the ideological weapon permitting the 'dialectical' reconciliation of the opposing poles of their electorate. Yes, I think Mitterrand will try it.

Will it succeed? This is not the place for electoral arithmetic.[42] True, whether Mitterrand's Socialists manage to find a workable parliamentary majority or not will be important for the future of the institutions of the Fifth Republic. The President will remain in power until 1988, regardless of the composition of the Parliament returned in 1986. Victory by an anti-Socialist opposition could lead to a constitutional crisis. There is, however, no reason to expect that some compromise solution will not be worked out; France does remain a democracy. The 'success' of the Europe-card will not be measured in the coin of national political power; the key to 'success' lies outside of France. The Europe-card will be perceived as a real option in France only if there is some expectation that there is German support for this choice. That support can come only from the German socialists (and the parliamentary Greens), since the economic *Mitteleuropa* option has been taken over by the CDU-CSU regime.[43] There is, alas, no ground for expecting that this socialist support will be forthcoming. If the signatories of the Memorandum to the French Left could justly feel that the lack of dialogue between the lefts of the two countries is harmful to both, the same could be said to the Germans by those French who see the European option as the only choice not only for French Socialism and France, but for Europe and socialism generally. No, I don't think it will succeed!

## Notes

1. *La puissance et les réves* (Paris, Gallimard, 1984). As the proofs of this text go to press, Debray – now no longer a Mitterrand adviser but member of the Conseil d'Etat – has come out with yet another tome: *Les Empires contre l'Europe* (Paris: Gallimard, 1985). While *Le Monde*'s editor André Fontaine writes generally approvingly of its thesis as 'the last Gaullist', Pierre Hassner notes cogently the difficulties that come from a simple equation of the US and the USSR as 'empires'. Hassner's points are well-taken. Both articles appear in *Le Monde*, 25 June, 1985.
2. Mitterrand's position should not be confused with the recent revival of this theme by Ronald Reagan. André Glucksmann has condensed the French reasoning in a simple phrase. 'Yalta today is proving to be a second Versailles' (*La force du Vertige*, Paris: Grasset, 1983), p. 136. It creates the conditions from which a third World War could emerge, just as the Versailles reparations pointed toward a second World War. Glucksmann does not, interestingly, suggest the correlative reading of 'Versailles' as a betrayal demanding *revanche* (by whom?).
3. Much of the public dialogue has been initiated by the journal *Esprit*, which has returned frequently to the subject. See, for example, the issue of juillet, 1983, 'Raisons et déraisons du pacifisme', with articles by P. Hassner, N. Gnesotto, Sigrid Meuschel, Paul Thibaud and Dick Howard. See also the reports by Thibaud and Howard on a meeting of French and Germans concerning the importance of the Polish question, in the January, 1983 issue. Pierre Hassner has written numerous analyses of the issues raised by this misunderstanding, including an important contribution to the collective volume, *Pacifisme et dissuasion*, edited by P. Lellouche (Paris, IFRI, 1983). A different analysis is suggested in my 'Franco-German Misunderstandings', *Cross Currents*, vol. XXXIII, no. 4, Winter 1983–4. (Also printed in *Thesis Eleven*, no. 10/11, 1984/85, pp. 236–41.)
4. Cited in Hans A. Schmitt, *European Union, From Hitler to de Gaulle* (New York: Van Nostrand, 1969), p. 62.
5. Schmitt, op. cit., p. 142.
6. The pseudonymous Caton, *De la reconquête* (Paris: Fayard, 1983), p. 155, argues that 'We spent our time putting off the moment of truth.

Now the socialists will be forced to act aggressively.' Caton is severely critical of the preceding Giscard government, subtitling his polemic, 'In order to defeat the left it will be necessary to get rid of the right.'

7. The domestic side of the present French situation, and its historical development, are treated in my 'Socialism and Modernisation in France', in *Telos*, no. 61, Winter 1984, pp. 113–20, reprinted above.
8. The so-called 'Solzhenitsyn effect' on the French intelligentsia has perhaps been overrated. Its roots, in all events, predated the publication of *The Gulag Archipelago*. The most important influence, spreading slowly during 25 years, was the group which began in 1949 to publish the journal *Socialisme ou Barbarie*, and whose best-known figures are Cornelius Castoriadis, Claude Lefort and Jean-François Lyotard. Their ideas were popularised and vulgarised widely in the late 1970s by André Glucksmann and then by Bernard-Henri Lévy's 'new philosophers'. They have been developed further by others, particularly in the journal *Esprit*, which has provided the practical link to the political actors known as the 'second Left'. As to the French critique of Marxism itself, the author of a 1979 study aptly titled *Le marxisme introuvable*, Daniel Lindenberg, has recently suggested that 'one might say of Marxism what Malreaux said of marriage, namely that no one cares about it any longer save a few priests' (in *La Quinzaine Littéraire*, août 1984, no. 422, p. 10). See also the excellent study of the background of this attitude, traced to the disillusionment with Euro-Communism that came with the Russian invasion of Czechoslovakia in 1968: Pierre Gremion, *Paris-Prague* (Paris: Julliard, 1985).
9. The attempt by the former Minister of Co-operation, Jean-Pierre Cot, to at once justify the regime's policies and yet explain his own positions which led to his departure is a generally disappointing mixture of middle-range theory interspersed with incomplete anecdote. (Jean-Pierre Cot, *A L'épreuve du pouvier. Le tiers-mondisme, pour quoi faire?* (Paris: Editions du Seuil, 1984).)
10. The best illustration of this 'rescue' as both material and psychological is Jürgen Habermas' *Legitimation Crisis* (Boston: Beacon Press, 1979). Habermas does not, however, apply his analysis to so-called socialist countries.
11. A similar logic may explain the popularity in France of the rather turgid novels of Alexander Zinoviev.
12. One could be quite sarcastic in describing the *passe-partout* utilisation of this concept of democracy, but self-congratulation is hardly called for from our side of the ocean. It is, however, worth noting the near-adulation with which left-leaning intellectuals are now treating Raymond Aron, in whose journal, *Commentaire*, they are flattered to write. Former socialists tend nowadays to identify themselves as 'lib/lib', liberal libertarians. The socialist concern with *égalité* has been replaced by a flirt with *liberté*. One finds Hayek accompanying references to the yet-untranslated Rawls and Nozick (sometimes identified) on the pages of 'left' journals. 'Liberalism' has become as confused and confusing a label as Marxism once was.
13. The best development of this argument is André Gorz's 'Security,

Against What? For What? With What?', *Telos*, no. 58, Winter 1983–4, pp. 158–68.

André Glucksmann illustrates the extremes of this position with suggestive interpretations of recent Soviet behaviour. For example, Soviet willingness to take the blame for downing the KAL 007 flight is said to aim at frightening the West with a show of bellicosity. The Soviet choice of quantity as opposed to miniaturisation in its nuclear armament is explained as due not to their backwardness but again to a desire to frighten western opinion (in op. cit., pp. 79–80).

14. See, for example, Alexander L. George and Richard Smoke, *Deterrence in American Foreign Policy. Theory and Practice* (New York: Columbia University Press, 1974).
15. The Memorandum begins from the reminder that 'The military prestige of a national state has always been an instrument in the hands of those in power whose victories over an external foe were thus at the same time victories over the internal political opposition of democrats and socialists.' It then suggests that the earlier pro-communist experience of many French intellectuals has led them to a 'new irrationalism' which makes the Soviets into a demonic force. It points out that 'Munich' is a French experience, and that the support for Reagan's arms policy may be a belated compensation for what was not done against Hitler prior to the Second World War. It even compares the French attitude to that of the Israelis whose 'preventive strikes' against the Arabs are supposed to prevent a 'second holocaust'. One could, however, turn this psychological game against the authors of the Memorandum, who note that 'whomever, as a conscious German antifascist, takes upon himself the responsibility for this bitter inheritance of German national history [i.e., for Nazism and the war and terror it brought], comes easily to the conviction that precisely the Germans must lead Europe in opposition against the means of mass annihilation.' (Translated from p. 3 of the German typescript of the Memorandum whose signatories include Heinrich Albertz, Peter Brandt, Oskar Lafontaine, Jo Leinen, Alfred Mechtersheimer, Michael Theunissen, Ernst Tugenhat and Werner Vitt.)
16. Most of the important theoretical position papers on these issues have been translated into English in the journal *Telos*. See especially no. 51, Spring 1982, and subsequent issues.
17. Hans Morgenthau, 'Charles De Gaulle. The Grand Design', in *Truth and Power* (New York: Praeger Publishers, 1970), p. 112.
18. Arnulf Baring, *Im Anfang war Adenauer. Die Entstehung der Kanzlerdemokratie* (Munchen: R. Oldenbourg Verlag, 1969) explains well Adenauer's role and the institutional anomalies on which his power was built. In the early years, occupied West Germany was certainly not a sovereign state. There was no Ministry of Defence, nor was there a Foreign Ministry. This structural gap explains the massive power that Adenauer was able to centralise in the Chancellor's office.
19. Adenauer was inadvertently helped in this policy by the ineptness of the nationalism of Kurt Schumacher's revived Socialist Party which insisted that reunification was the first and foremost socialist task. The

SPD had to shake off this legacy before it could become a party which could be trusted with the reins of government. This transformation may have been more important than the ideological abandonment of Marxism in the Bad Godesberg Programme of the SPD in 1959. There are echoes of the Schumacher-SPD position in the Memorandum to the French Left from which I quoted above.

20. The history of these relations has of course its psychological side as well. The strange cross-party relations that brought together Helmut Schmidt with Giscard d'Estaing have continued in the seeming *entente cordiale* of Mitterrand and Kohl, whose most recent achievement gave the 'German' seat in the EEC Brussels administration to the French austerity Finance Minister, Jacques Delors. This decision will certainly play a role in the eventual elaboration of a Franco-German European politics.
21. This is *not* to say that the Federal Republic is in the same dependent status with regard to its allies (or protector) as is the German Democratic Republic in relation to its side! Too many within the German peace movement draw this conclusion without reflecting sufficiently on the difference between what might be called having an empire (the US case) and *being* an empire (the Soviet case). This is where the French analysis of totalitarianism is important. Sovereignty is an attribute of state power which permits it to guarantee the political freedom of its citizens. The degree of political freedom in the Western and Eastern German states can hardly be compared. As Mitterrand puts it, there are missiles in the East, pacifists in the West. As if to confirm Mitterrand's analysis, the Kremlin's pressures finally forced East Germany's Erich Honnecker to 'postpone' his long-awaited September 1984 visit to the Federal Republic.
22. *Stichworte zur 'Geistigen Situation der Zeit'*, edited by Jürgen Habermas (Frankfurt-am-Main: Suhrkamp Verlag, 1979).
23. This thesis is familiar to readers of the *New York Times* whose John Vinocur became the *bête noire* of more than just the German pacifists. Now stationed in Paris, he returned to the theme in a comparative essay in the 'Sunday Magazine', 6 May, 1984. The point is made more systematically, and from a left political perspective by Sigrid Meuschel, 'Neo-Nationalism and the Peace Movement', in *Telos*, no. 56, Summer 1983, pp. 119–30.
24. The Greens have been much misunderstood, not to say maligned, by friend and foe. The most balanced recent account is that of Andrew Arato and Jean L. Cohen, 'The German Green Party', in *Dissent*, Summer 1984.
25. This point has been stressed by the respected French commentator, Joseph Rovan, in his *L'Allemagne du changement* (Paris: Calmann-Levy, 1983). It should be noted that Rovan's previous book on Germany, *L'Allemagne n'est pas ce que vous croyez*, was written in 1978 in order to defend Germany against the left's charge that the campaign against Terrorism was the beginning of a new fascism that ultimately would be a threat to French national security.
26. This view of *Mitteleuropa* is not that 'Central Europe' about which

Milan Kundera has written so elegantly, most recently in *The New York Review of Books* (26 April, 1984 and 19 July, 1984). Kundera's 'Central Europe' is emphatically a unity *in diversity*, whose origin lies in the old Austro-Hungarian monarchy, and whose independence was to be preserved between the poles of German and Russian cultural influence. If one can judge from their reading habits, the French who speak of a *Mitteleuropa* have the same object as Kundera in mind. The failure to achieve a dialogue concerning this option has cultural roots, to which I will turn in a moment.

27. This attitude is evident in conversation, for example among the participants at the Paris colloquium mentioned earlier. The most subtle illustration is found in the essayist, Peter Bender, whose frequent contributions to *Die Zeit* are a model of his solicitous realism. See, for example, 'Polen fühlt sich alleingelassen', in *Die Zeit*, 29 Juni 1984. From the other side, one should note the comments of Cardinal Glemp at the Assumption Day festivities at Czestochowa in 1984, criticising the German ethnic minority in Poland for its failure to integrate itself into the Polish nation and for looking still to Germany as its true Fatherland (*New York Times*, 16 and 18 August, 1984).
28. From the point of view of the German peace movement, the French are in fact already reacting. The American journalist, Diana Johnstone, whose reporting for the left weekly, *In These Times*, is a model of partisan selectivity and self-righteous, lesson-giving 'socialism', has addressed the issue in a special issue, 'La Gauche en Question' of the French journal, *La quinzaine Littéraire* (1–31 août, 1984, no. 422). Johnstone suggests that the French Socialists' anti-sovietism is accompanied by a selective anti-Germanism – selectively against the left! She sees the French as 'beneficiaries and gendarmes of "Yalta"' whose nuclear umbrella serves to maintain Germany's subordination. As Johnstone has close contacts to the German peace movement, one suspects that her analysis is not idiosyncratic. Her acceptance of it is, however, typically foolish.
29. Paul Thibaud, 'Pacifism and its Problems', in *Telos*, no. 59, Spring 1984, pp. 151–62, originally in *Esprit*, novembre 1983.

Tocqueville's own discussion should be recalled. At the end of Book I, Part II, Chapter V, Tocqueville considers how American democracy deals with foreign affairs. He cites Washington's farewell warning to stay out of European politics, and adds Jefferson's admonition to ask nothing from others lest they insist that we return the favour. These foundations of American isolationism do not depend simply on geography. They reflect an implicit recognition of the disadvantage democratic societies confront in foreign affairs. Democracy, notes Tocqueville, 'can coordinate only with difficulty the details of a great venture, fix a plan and then obstinately follow it through despite all obstacles. It is little capable of planning secret measures and awaiting patiently their result.' Thus, the chapter concludes, when the Revolution broke out in France, it took the prestige of Washington to prevent the impetuous democracy from leaping generously but stupidly into a situation from which it could not benefit. The protests against the stationing of the missiles in recently democratic Germany would not have surprised Tocqueville.

30. This is a psychological, not a real personal mobilisation, and from this point of view deterrence fits perfectly the ethos of a commercial democracy from which the notion of democratic citizen participation is absent.
31. An illustration of the widely accepted French attitude can be drawn from a comparison of the French Bishops' pastoral Letter on nuclear weapons with the conclusions drawn by their American colleagues. See the debate on this matter between Stanley Hoffmann and Pierre Hassner in *Esprit*, février 1984.
32. *Tass*'s reply to President Reagan's insistence that Yalta is not a final division of Europe confirms the French position. *Tass* insisted that 'No one has the right to call into question the decisions of the Yalta conference *or of the 1975 Helsinki Accords that confirmed the borders of Eastern Europe*' (*New York Times*, 19 August, 1984, my stress).
33. Helmut Schmidt's 28 June, 1984 speech to the Bundestag suggests that the notion of 'extended deterrence' would be the most desirable outcome, but his views seem not to represent a majority in a situation where the German socialist position is only beginning to be articulated. The position of the government is constrained by the demographic fact of declining birthrates, and the economic difficulty of increased costs. (See Christopf Bertram, 'Die Armee auf dem Marsch in durre Zeiten,' in *Die Zeit*, 31 August, 1984.)

    One longer term set of French considerations should be mentioned. André Glucksmann's provocative *La force du vertige* is not only a sustained criticism of pacifism. It contains the germs of a philosophical reevaluation (in Chapters VI and VII). Glucksmann sees parallels between the warring violence and psychological insecurities of the seventeenth century and the constant threat that characterises our own. As the seventeenth century gave rise to the nation state and to a system of international 'law of peace and war' (Grotius), so our twentieth century must emerge from a 'state of nature' to found international relations anew. And, the parallel suggests, the new system of international relations will not be a 'world state' where harmony rules. The sovereignty of each state means that its citizens can choose whatever forms of the 'good life' suit them. They will relate to other states as competitive equals in a framework of rules which takes into account their ultimate sovereignty.

    The parallels between Glucksmann's suggestions and the socialist concern with reconceptualising democracy are obvious. See my discussion in Chapter 14, 'The Republic and the International Order.'
34. Gaus explains himself in the published version of the speech, to which he added a postscript 18 months later. I will be referring to this in the text. See Gunther Gaus, 'Schöner ist der Friede nicht zu haben', in *Kursbuch*, no. 71, Marz 1983.

    Theodore Draper singled out Gaus's speech for criticism in a broader discussion of the problems of the Alliance in 'The Dilemma of the West' (1982), reprinted in his *Present History* (New York: Random House, 1983).

Gaus's four-page postscript contains some surprising assertions worth noting. He speaks of Germany as a de-statised nation (*entstaatlichte Nation*) which has been factually united by the peace movement's realisation that the first battlefield will be all-German (*gesamtdeutsch*). He then turns to some simplistic psychology to explain how, after their defeat, the Germans took over American values and lost 'their own identity'. Granted, they did not take over all of America's values – yet, he asks, where else is there a society without communists, save in the USA? where else is one so much the architect of his own fortune? This loss of identity, Gaus suggests, will be the German theme *par excellence* in the next decade – 'if the time remains'.

35. An interesting comparative study by the French journalist T. Garçin, *Les impératifs de la défense* (Paris: Economica, 1984) combines technical arguments with representative interviews to give a feeling for the spread of a common *attitude* which has yet to find its adequate institutional translation.
36. The debate concerning the need to upgrade the railroads in the Federal Republic pointed to the fact that existing railways move from West to East, not in the South to North direction that the economy of the present-day Federal Republic would have dictated. To be fair, it should be noted that at the Mannheim debate on the German 'Memorandum' to the French left, the Germans spoke of 'denuclearisation' while the French continually translated this as 'demilitarisation'. There is a difference!
37. See Andrew Arato's remarkable essay, 'Empire vs. Civil Society, Poland, 1981–1982', in *Telos*, no. 50, Winter 1981–2, p. 47.
38. The argument is developed in Gorz, op. cit. with regard to the German choice. The general thesis has been presented in Gorz's two recent books, *Adieux au prolétariat* (Paris: Galilée, 1980) which argues that the classical industrial proletariat of Marx can no longer be taken as the 'agent of revolution', and *Les chemins du Paradis* (Paris: Galilée, 1983), which develops the argument about the possibilities opened by the micro-electronic technologies. Translations of Gorz's books have appeared as *Farewell to the Working Class* (1983) and *Paths to Paradise* (1985), both published by South End Press. (The term 'second wave' is taken from Alvin Toffler.)

    A somewhat different perspective is offered in Theodore Draper's essay, 'The Western Misalliance', in his op. cit. Draper sees the Soviets seeking to buy high technology goods, and ultimately the technology itself, through its trade with Western Europe. He expects that the dependence on this trade with the Soviet Union will encourage docility from Western Europe with regard to Soviet actions elsewhere in the world.
39. The failure should not be surprising. After a first attempt by Maurice and Edgar Faure, a list of candidates was constructed under the direction of a former Giscardian Minister (Stirn), the former presidential

candidate of the Ecology Movement (Lalonde) and a little known centrist politician (Doubin) – earning the label LSD ticket. The clearly opportunist manner in which this grouping was assembled doomed it from the start. See, for example, Eric Hintermann, 'Après l'échec de l'ERE' in *Le Monde*, 7 juillet 1984.

40. There is one exception to this, as Pompidou's former Foreign Minister and Mitterrand's former Minister of Commerce, Michel Jobert has recently argued. The apparently irresolvable and certainly frustrating disputes over a common agricultural policy blurs over the real fact that this is the one domain where the member nations are actually dealing with the problems of production of goods. Jobert insists on the need to take seriously the *positive* results of the common agricultural policy (especially in bringing French agriculture into the modern world). He also suggests that the next step toward progress will come when the European Currency Unit (the ECU) becomes a true money, not simply a unit of accounting (in which function it remains dependent on the value of the dollar). See, Michel Jobert, *Vive l'Europe Libre!* (Paris: Editions Ramsay, 1984).
41. The suggestion was made immediately after the European elections by Jean-Marie Colombani, 'Faire oublier Valence', in *Le Monde*, 4 juillet 1984, and by Jacques Julliard, 'Un socialisme à l'heure de 86', in *Le nouvel observateur*, 6 juillet 1984. It has been evoked, and criticised as a typical betrayal by the American 'Leftist' journalist, Diana Johnstone, in *In These Times*, 8–21 August, 1984. In Germany, Roger de Weck's 'Mitterrand in der Schusslinie. Nach dem Abschied der Kommunisten, der Prasident will die politische Polarisierung uberwinden' (*Die Zeit*, 3 August, 1984) sees it as necessitated by internal political considerations.
42. On French internal politics, see my essay, 'Socialism and Modernisation in France', in *Telos*, no. 61, Winter 1984–5, pp. 113–20, reprinted above.
43. One could imagine that the FDP, which has been steadily losing electoral clout and political unity since it switched alliances and sunk the coalition between itself and the SPD, might try to stop its seemingly unavoidable disappearance by pursuing this option. The return of former European Commissioner and former head of the London School of Economics, Ralf Dahrendorf, might point in this direction – although Dahrendorf's actions as head of the FDP's Friedrich Naumann Stiftung have given no concrete evidence that this is his goal, nor has he been particularly active in the debates leading to Martin Bangemann's replacement of Graf Lambsdorff as Finance Minister and second-in-command in the FDP. The FDP seems for the moment to have chosen to represent upper middle class professional interests, assuming that this will keep it above the 5 per cent barrier needed to maintain political life in Parliament. A triumph of political opportunism!

# Part III

# Origins of the Political

## A. The Genesis of Theoretical Questions

# 12 Enlightened Despotism and Modern Democracy

## 1. HISTORICAL GENERALITIES AND CONTEMPORARY PARALLELS

Leonard Krieger knows that the past is no guide for the present, and that the task of the historian is not the edification of the public. Yet, his *Essay on the Theory of Enlightened Despotism* has a contemporary and political aim. Krieger explains the motivation of his investigation by noting that Enlightened Despotism has become 'a permanent category, a continual option, and a recurrent choice in our politics' (x).[1] 'Many of us,' he concludes, 'still practise an Enlightened Despotism that we have not the honesty to preach' (90). The *Essay*'s intended reader seems to be the democratic citizen whom Krieger addresses on his final page: 'Let the voter beware' (91). But that same page asserts that 'all modern despots have been, in theory, Enlightened Despots' (ibid.). Enlightened Despotism is presented as a privileged moment in which the quintessence of the modern state is at once revealed and concealed. The phenomenon presents a unique object for historical investigation. Its empirical study runs constantly the risk of saying too little or too much, weighing too heavily the social effects by reducing them to their material cause, or underestimating political novelty by a realistic concern with institutional effect. If the apposition of 'enlightened' and 'despotic' is legitimate, the theory of this new formation will have political implications, then as now.[2]

It might be suggested that eighteenth-century Enlightened Despotism corresponds to twentieth-century institutions like the Welfare State or Socialism. These contemporary political structures prove equally vague and frustrating to the analyst and the participant citizens. Were future historians to look back at them, their results would be as indeterminate as those accumulated by studies of Enlightened Despotism.[3] That research was begun by an international commission of historians in 1928, following a series of questions posed by L'héritier; its research was published regularly until the War. Fritz Hartung summarised the results in 1955: rather than clarification, he concluded, they simply multiplied confusion. The phenomenon was stretched in time and space, from the Italian Renaissance back to Marcus Aurelius, Pericles, and finally to wise Solomon himself. Even when limited temporally to the eighteenth century, and pinpointed spatially to France, Prussia, Austria and Russia, the concept lacks precision. Were the Enlightened Despots different from the Absolute Monarchs they succeeded? How absolute were their regimes? How practical and real were their reforms? In what sense were they themselves 'enlightened'? How was their theoretical enlightenment expressed practically? The historian is frustrated, the concept undefined.

It is tempting to look back to the eighteenth century with the eyes and experience of the twentieth. Early signs of the triumph of the bureaucratic institutional logic that dominates today's state can be detected. Liberal or socialist, the bureaucracy finds here witness to its necessity, titles of progress, and testimony to its rationality. The *philosophes'* critical efforts were offered to the service of the reforming Monarchs; the new Cameral and Physiocratic sciences were put to the service of Kings modernising their states while extending their beneficent control over greater areas of their subjects' lives. These developments can be viewed sceptically; the *philosophes* let themselves be used, and the culmination of their ideology, the French Revolution, realised only the equality of capitalist entrepreneur.[4] A more positive evaluation shows a vast progress in public enlightenment due to developing public education coupled with a freer press and the spread of a philosophical scepticism accompanying the growth of individualism. The increased role of the state entailed a recognition of its responsibilities to a citizenry whose demands on it became the basis for a new political public created by the top-down reformism of the enlightened authorities. Liberal or socialist, the bureaucracy whose outlines can be seen in the eighteenth century may wonder whether history holds lessons for it.

The difficulty in defining the political institutions of the eighteenth and twentieth centuries appears more sharply when attention is turned to the nature of political action. Compared to the seventeenth and nineteenth centuries, the eighteenth and twentieth manifest a fundamental theoretical indeterminacy. The seventeenth century could borrow from Nature to justify its action without confronting the uncertainties of history; the nineteenth could use History to dominate the otherness of nature. In both cases, a common theoretical principle founds action and sets goals for politics. The appeal to Nature or to History as the principle and reality which gives sense to appearances makes these phenomena homologous to the theoretical and political arms available for their solution. This was not the case in the eighteenth century, any more than Marxism or liberalism can be twisted to restore harmony in the twentieth. Krieger introduces two concepts to explain the problem. The static theory inherited from the seventeenth-century rationalists increasingly imposes a *distortion* on a changed reality swimming outside its nets. From the inadequacies in the theory which this distortion revealed emerges a *deflection* of the theory itself as it tries to rectify its aim. The eighteenth century actor had the choice of remaining faithful to the general theory at the cost of distorting the facts; or he could cling to the facts at the risk of deflecting the purity of the theory.

Eighteenth-century practice was unable to bring together rationalist theory with empirical attentiveness to fact. Theory and practice were stretched between these two poles. Theory sought to integrate a sense of existing change with a felt need for such change; its only tool was a reflection on the past whose natural unity had been, somehow, broken. The French Revolution brought the theoretical waverings to a head. From the Terror to the Empire to the Restoration, it gave the nineteenth century a new device for thinking the political: History. As nature was the fully immanent determinant of political thought in the seventeenth century, History was to be the principle of the nineteenth. This was no longer the natural history to which the pre-revolutionary eighteenth century had turned in vain. That history was externally necessitated and rational; it could be presented as a *tableau* in a unified space-time frame. Kant's 'Cosmopolitan History', can be seen as the theoretical turning point that parallels the practical shift inaugurated by the French Revolution. The novelty of the nineteenth-century formulation is the immanentisation of History as the theoretical and practical basis of the political.[5] This provides the theoretical foundation of liberalism and of Marxism; the need to deny its primacy led, for the first time, to the explicit formulation of conservative theory.

*Mutatis mutandis*, the twentieth century faces the same problem defined by the distortion and deflection which confronted the eighteenth. Although it was perhaps the fulfilment of one of the strands of nineteenth-century Historical Society, the Russian Revolution was the child of a War which destroyed the theoretical power of History just as the Lisbon earthquake symbolised the demise of all-powerful Nature. The Cameralists and Physiocrats of the eighteenth century have contemporary counterparts. As the former rationalised from the top down, the latter sought integration from the empirical and the natural. The similarity of their political conclusions was based on their shared theoretical distortion. They decomplexified politics, eliminating chance, accident, and history. As Rousseau noted, their theory is 'very good for the dwellers of Utopia; it is worth nothing for the children of Adam'.[6] Similarly today, organisational theorising at the service of a supposedly universal state-power is charged with overcoming the recalcitrance of the real. It too imposes a distortion on the empirical world, at the cost of a deflection which puts into question the foundation of the theories which supposedly govern its action. This is why the twentieth century is defined by its 'crisis of legitimation'.[7]

The theoretical foundation of the legitimation crisis shared by the eighteenth and the twentieth centuries can be defined broadly at this first level of comparison. The task of the political is to conjure away, to cloak or occlude, the divisions which haunt society, threaten its unity and its ability to conceive of itself as a coherent totality. The political dimension of social reality is ambiguous; it aims at closing and covering over; yet, because it is political action *on* the social world, this very movement opens the possibility for social critique. Krieger's concepts of distortion and deflection clarify this structure for the eighteenth century. The breakdown of the seventeenth-century synthesis through Nature puts theory into question because of the distortion imposed on it by its attempt to integrate awkward facts. The resulting deflection of the theory means that it must be repaired continually, renovated, embellished even. Theory becomes *active*; if the facts criticise theory, it can preserve itself only by changing these facts. The constant interplay is explicit because these problems of theory were also those of the monarch's practice. This is why 'Enlightened Despotism' is not an illicit combination of a theoretical programme with a political practice; it points, rather, to a style of theory-as-praxis whose analysis permits the historian to develop a theory of *the political*.

## 2. THREE APPROACHES TO THE FRENCH REVOLUTION

If theory comes to distort empirical reality, the pragmatic temptation is to stick to the facts. Such was the radical tactic of the *philosophes*, whose encyclopedic project constructed no new theoretical edifice. The French Revolution was not the product of their theory; it grew within the Old Order as a material force which burst through the absolutist shell. The Absolute Monarchy's attempt to assure and to consolidate its own position led to the socioeconomic development that eventually undermined it. Monarch and young bourgeoisie united against the feudal remnants and Church interference. Colbertism was the economic correlate of this alliance. A standing army was created; centralised taxation was introduced to feed it. The results brought changes which eroded the old superstructure and its legitimations. A modern state was created. The French Revolution was either its expression or its consummation. But the French Revolution poses a double challenge: to explain its possibility, and to account for its incompleteness. Can a single theoretical orientation, based on scrupulous attention to empirical reality alone, do both?

The Marxist approach, building on the radical choice of the *philosophes*, claims to be able to explain both the origins and the further development of the Revolution. The elimination of the constraints of the hierarchical political order opened the field to the egoistic spirit of capitalist venture which had grown within the Ancien Régime. This explains why, of the slogans inscribed on its banner, the Revolution achieved only a legal equality which, in the end, was nothing but the Enlightened Despots' own goal. Aware that the interests of the state demanded the growth of modern industry, they had encouraged it.[8] But this makes the Revolution an *ad hoc* reaction, an accident due to the Enlightened Monarchs' inability to carry through their reforms quickly and efficiently. The Revolution is then *nothing new*; quantity does not become quality; the *sociology* of the Same replaces the *political* thought of the New. 1789 appears as a 'revolution' only from the retrospective point of view of a nineteenth-century theory of an immanent directionality to History.

If Marxism were only a sociology of the same, the dimension of political practice would be lost. The Marxists have established that the initiative for economic development came from the Monarchs. If there is a political class struggle between a rising bourgeoisie and a feudal nobility, the state and the classes in presence are treated simply as economic forces. Politics becomes a question of economics, a dependent variable or accident without inherent significance. While there are good grounds for such an approach, it neglects too much.[9] In France, for example, from the Fronde to the opposition to the Revocation of the Edict of Nantes there was a qualitative shift in the perception of the political. The Monarch, whom Bossuet had justified as a Father, came to be perceived in different colours. The anonymous author of the Huguenot pamphlet, 'Les soupirs de la France esclave', followed by La Bruyère and later Bayle, reintroduced the *political* notion of despotism. When Montesqieu popularised the term, his reference to its oriental form was intended to condemn the lack of *both* social and political freedom. The *Lettres Persanes* is not a critique of the regime of Louis XIV from the standpoint of a rising bourgeoisie demanding economic equality; it is a critique of the (classical political concept of) corruption which interferes with the exercise of *freedom*. This is *new*; it is the demand which gives the Revolution its radical political character. A Marxian theory would have to find a place for political liberty.

Another perspective on the radical nature of the Revolution is suggested by Henri Brunschwig's *Enlightenment and Romanticism in Eighteenth-Century Prussia*.[10] Brunschwig presents a detailed tableau of the everyday mechanisms by which the philosophical and socio-economic aims of the Enlightenment were spread. He traces its educational reforms, its officialdom, its press and the growing numbers of reading clubs sharing information and ideas. Already confronted with internal difficulties inherent in the social renovation of a 'backward' land, the Prussian Enlightenment had to cope with a series of new problems, many of which were its own unintended offspring. With increased prosperity came demographic growth and population shifts; the new middle strata educated by the Enlightenment found a fully staffed civil service and few, or ill-paid, opportunities to exercise the professions they had learned. After the death of Frederick the Great, Frederick Wilhelm II and his aggressively orthodox Minister, Wöllner, began a systematic fundamentalist attack on the radicality of the Enlightenment.[11] In this context, the young found themselves emotionally and socially separated from society, with no outlets for their energies, enthusiasms and reforming passions. The logical result was an intellectual romanticism and the popular attitude that Brunschwig documents as the 'mentality of the miraculous'.

Brunschwig provides the complement to the Marxist's one-sided reduction of the political. Opting like the Marxist for the empirical deflection of theory, he suggests that the everyday life of the Enlightenment provides the *material* base for understanding an intellectual movement which cannot be treated in terms of the History of Ideas alone. He does not, however, develop the implicit *political* dimension of the romantic choice as a manner of unifying the chaotic, warming the inhospitable, if enlightened, world. Comparison with the Marxist shows the difficulty in recognising the political dimension. The Marxist priority of economic equality neglected the political dimension of liberty and fraternity. Although Lenin built his revolutionary theory on the basis of the difference between immediate trade union consciousness and 'political' class consciousness, his Marxist state was used as an economic force, remodelling the society and fructifying the field for economic development. The missing element in his Marxism is suggested by the Prussian romantic reaction to the French Revolution. After hailing the political innovation, they found themselves incapable of concretising it in their own circumstances, and turned eventually to a mythical inwardness that solves problems by transferring them to literary fields where illusory battles can be fought and wonderous glories safely won. Where the Marxist sociological reduction of the political is strong, there the romantic is weak; where the romantic concern with liberty and fraternity comes to the fore, sociological concretion is lost.

The inability of the Marxist and the romantic to recognise the specific autonomy of the political can be explained by their concentration on what Krieger called the empirical *deflection* that destroyed the unitary foundation of the Ancien Régime. Both describe a process of delegitimation without being able to explain the emergence of a new form of political legitimacy. The 'formation of a bourgeois public' described by Jürgen Habermas would be one expression of a positive political unification of the economic and the political that began already under the Ancien Régime. But Habermas neglects the implications of this public sphere for political theory; the 'changing structure' that he analyses sociologically follows a declining path toward the kind of massification characteristic of contemporary societies.[12] Reinhart Koselleck's *Kritik und Krise* presents an account of this same development which stresses its place within the orientation that Krieger called the theoretical *distortion*.[13] The one-sidedness that Koselleck describes complements the equally particular approaches to the French Revolution; it completes the preliminaries to the investigation of Enlightened Despotism by making explicit the place of the political.

Koselleck argues that the formation of the Absolutist State in the seventeenth century was based on a division between morality and politics which had to be established and consecrated by theory to avoid a return to the Wars of Religion. The split between morality and politics, consistently maintained in the theory of a Hobbes or a Locke, as well as in the practice of the renewed English monarchy, made possible the private development of a moral theory and practice based on individual judgement (or on that peculiar British notion of 'taste' which spread across the Continent). The new morality of individual judgement was, in the best sense of the term, bourgeois. Its individual and private grounding in autonomous rational choice undermined the legitimacy of the Absolute State, which had been erected in separation from this sphere over which it was dominant but which it left, like religion, to establish its own self-rule. Economic development increased the weight of this new bourgeoisie, but its political thrust emerged only negatively, in the form of a generalised moral consciousness which was all the more dangerous to the prevailing order as it did not, and could not, express itself in a properly political language. Koselleck analyses the Free Masons and the social Clubs which were formed under the Ancien Régime. He shows how, gradually, the individual moral stance led the members to take political positions which judged the present from the standpoint of the universalised moral individual. The resulting empirical distortion made a clash inevitable. To exist, morality must be universal; where politics clashes with it, morality must either renounce or undermine the legitimacy of the political. Whereas Brunschwig's incipient romantics reacted by transcending the immediate, Koselleck's rising bourgeoisie universalised the inner moral court, politicising morality in a culture of opposition.

Morality could become political because the Enlightened Despots had led the way. Following an economic mercantilism, incapable of dealing with the remnants of feudal privilege in the countryside, their educational and administrative reforms limited by resistance and inertia, the eighteenth-century monarchs were unable to practice what they preached. But preach it they did! Frederick the Great insisted ostentatiously that he was but the 'first servant of the State'. Joseph II of Austria abolished the legal obligation to kiss the hand and bend the knee before the monarch on the ground that all are equal before God. More extreme was Joseph's brother, Peter Leopold of Toscany, whose proposed Constitution expressly noted that his rule was based on conquest, and declared the return to the citizens of their natural freedom in order that they should freely contract to restore their state. These may have been simple 'jeux d'esprit' and monarchical caprice, as Georges Lefèbvre argues, since along with the rhetoric, each monarch also stressed that the contract had in fact been constituted already (and Peter Leopold never instituted his new Constitution). None the less, the rhetorical distinction between King and Kingdom elaborated by Bodin was fully accepted by Louis XIV, who never equated himself with the state but, on the contrary, said on his deathbed, 'I am going, but the state will remain.' As Goethe concluded, while himself in the service of the enlightened Saxon court, such self-justifications led ultimately to 'sans-culottism'. In seeking to legitimate themselves morally, the monarchs contributed to their own delegitimation just as the moral court of individual conscience had to find a political outlet if it were to remain self-consistent.

Koselleck's moralists did not bring to fruition the crisis, any more than Brunschwig's romantics did. But where the German romantics appear as an *expression* of the crisis, the moralists contributed to its creation *as a political exigency*. Although unconscious of their own political thrust, Koselleck's bourgeois organised lodges and clubs, debated issues along rigorous logical lines from the viewpoint of the individual conscience. Their organisations in a sense prefigured that political liberty, equality and fraternity for which the Revolution would be made. Their formal moral imperatives acquired a social content. At the same time, however, this moral absolutism made the clubs a *particular* party, earlier for the Masons than for those who became the Jacobins after 1789. A political action appearing to be dictated by rational necessity led to the particularisation of its agents; the acquisition of content brought the loss of élan. Theory became simply one empirical particular among the many competing particulars which the delegitimated political sphere could no longer integrate. The same phenomenon is described in Hegel's *Phenomenology*, where it serves to explain the passage from 1789 to the Terror. The paradox can be explained by Krieger's notion of theoretical *distortion*. That proposal makes explicit the positive place of the political, which emerges in Koselleck's account only as an unintended negative consequence.

## 3. KRIEGER'S REHABILITATION OF THE POLITICAL

Krieger's concept of 'Enlightened Despotism' does not refer to what the Monarchs did, nor even to what they said. The term is justified by its 'synthetic function', its ability to express a unity in diversity. The distinctive lack of unity of eighteenth-century political theory is the key to its politics. The problems for its theorists, and for its historian, were the dilemmas confronted by the era itself.[14] Krieger defines Enlightened Despotism as a 'schema' in the Kantian sense. It is both 'signs and symbol . . . more than its immediate context. It is allusive to, not representative of reality' (33). It is a mediation between the empirical and the categorial, organising a manifold of data under unifying concepts. 'As schema, it extends to every theoretical and practical situation where there was a recognised and inherent dissonance between the tendencies of the political instruments at hand and the nature of the social goals to be achieved by them and yet where some linkage was nonetheless strung up between instruments and goals' (34). This description accentuates the 'active theorising' which Krieger attributes to the practice of the age. Enlightened Despotism serves to centre a decentred reality, bringing into focus a constantly changing structure. The Kantian synthetic categories express the practical reality of eighteenth-century political life.

The historian following the active theorising of the political has to find adequate concepts for its description. Switching his Kantian categories, Krieger asserts that,

> Like the state of nature, the social contract and the general will, Enlightened Despotism existed neither as a general political fact that could be indicated nor as a logically necessary philosophical truth that could be demonstrated. Like them, it existed rather as an idea of reason – that is, as a conditional principle whose truth stemmed precisely from the hypothetical necessity of assuming it if any sense was to be made of a political existence that was contradictory in itself and of theoretical dualities unbridgeable in themselves (89).

A theoretical account with practical implications, Enlightened Despotism speaks in the 'conditional mode', expressing 'a unifying reality inseparable from the facts of political life but yet existent on a different plane, operative at once behind them and through them . . . the expression of a political principle in the special language of political action' (84). This is why Krieger takes his descriptive categories now from the Kantian 'Dialectic'. Such an approach permits the treatment of the arguments of the theorists as prime historical data for understanding the practice of the times.[15]

If enlightenment refers to the seating of reason in the individual's critical faculties, its combination with despotism seems contradictory. The individual ought to be left alone to seek happiness according to self-chosen precepts. Of course, some state authority is necessary in cases of conflict. That authority must be itself enlightened. But this 'enlightenment' no longer refers to critical judgement; it designates a specific kind of knowledge: the knowledge of the natural laws of social intercourse. The existence of conflict indicates that those laws are not functioning. The state must intervene to set them into action. But the only way of knowing whether the intervention is successful is through its results, measured in terms of happiness. This is why the prophet of utilitarianism, Bentham, could admire the Enlightened Despot for his ability to prevail over any 'constitutional . . . obstacles . . . when he has the force of truth and power on his side' (43). The result is a shift in the 'locus' of the political principle (38). The political is no longer a transcendent legitimation of social structures; it is justified by results. This means that the political is open to critique; its representatives must legitimate themselves. This shift implies further that 'hypostatized discordance rather than unity' is now 'the fundamental constellation of 18th century politics [, making] the management of discord rather than the application of unity the function of political principle' (34). The function of the political as conjuring away and yet legitimating social division could not be more explicit.[16]

The management of discord by the creation of institutions safeguarding the individual's welfare and happiness has to take into account the active striving of these same individuals who, although not yet enlightened, are assumed to be in the process of becoming enlightened. At an institutional level, this gives rise to the 'Constitutional Increment'. 'In general,' writes Krieger, 'when the emphasis was on the *activity* of government, its unconditioned power was brought to the fore; when the emphasis was on the *being* of government, it was defined in terms of its constitutional structure.' (68) The activism of the Enlightened Despots brought a shift in the meaning of constitutional theory from its traditionally descriptive historical character to the accentuation of its normative and prescriptive functioning. The constitution now constitutes the body politic. This 'constitutional increment' was brought about by three factors.

> The political surge of the aristocracy undermined its constitutional position as a conduit of monarchical power; the emphasis on natural rights and individual utility undermined the natural definition of absolute political sovereignty; and the increase in the force available to the instrumentalities of the state dislocated the

> familiar balance between what was and what was not subject to political power (74).

This change was to lead to the notion that constitutionalism is essentially opposed to absolutism. The eighteenth century was not yet able to make that move because of the *explicit* divisions on which it was based, and the lack of an *immanent* principle permitting their elimination. The nineteenth century discovered such a principle in the immanent historicity of society.

Paradoxically, the constitutional limits placed on the monarch in the name of individual liberty increased his absolute power. Krieger describes a 'shift in the axis of constitutional thinking' which occurs as the state assumes social tasks that fell previously outside its sphere (76). The particular, moral and private realms are generalised, naturalised and rationalised. United in a single political order, social and political life are fused. As the supposed expression of natural laws, government becomes unlimited in scope.[17] Correlatively, Krieger describes a 'shift in the plane of constitutional thinking' whereby the distinction between what is and is not amenable to collective control is abolished, and the justification of the monarch rests now solely in his ability to know and to plan the future. These two 'shifts' in the approach to constitutional thinking define the political structure within which monarchical and popular politics could become autonomous.

Krieger describes the specificity of the eighteenth-century form acquired by the political structure of society by comparison to the seventeenth- and nineteenth-century forms.

> Whereas civil constitutions had been traditionally descriptive of existing governmental structure and would later be prescriptive for the distribution of power within the state, and whereas the constitution of nature had traditionally been prescriptive of divinely authorized moral norms and would soon be deemed categorically distinct from the constitution of the state; at our eighteenth-century transfer point what is descriptive in the constitution of nature became prescriptive for the constitution of the state (77).

The result was that the constitution served as a weapon for reform, not simply in the abolition of the feudal remnants but also, in Turgot's words soon to be popularised by Rousseau, to 'shackle men for their happiness' (78). Plans for political participation, for example in Turgot's reform programme, were based on the paradoxical argument that enlightened citizens were necessary to the monarch's ability to make rational decisions, *and* that the monarch should have the foresight to work for enlightenment in order to strengthen his own power. The functional concern with welfare explicitly poses the state as *totality and totaliser*, at once setting it apart from society and yet stressing its dependence on that society. Both in and of society, the state is strengthened and rendered more vulnerable. Social division required the creation of absolutist politics, but these politics can work only through social individuals who, in assuming their political role, become at once the sharpest critics and the staunchest allies of the state.

This interpretation of constitutionalism points once again to the role of the political in conjuring away the very social divisions on which the possibility of politics depends. The changed 'constitutional axis' takes the social divisions up into the political sphere where they can allegedly be dealt with rationally since the radical opposition of power and individual happiness is reduced to a common denominator. The changed 'constitutional plane' deals with the social division by extending the political into the very heart of individual life, eliminating the division by finding a common denominator. Enlightenment of the citizen by the state serves this latter function insofar as the rationality according to which the state operates and the one it teaches the individual are identical in principle; the enlightened individuals simply become agents of the state in the sphere of private life. Both shifts in the axis and in the plane are necessitated by the hypostatised discord from which eighteenth-century theory begins. They are made possible theoretically by the assimilation of rationality to nature which permits the political sphere to claim as its task the unification of society. At the same time, the affirmation of the explicit political task reaffirms *nolens volens* the social division. This is why, finally, Krieger's account can breathe life back into the eighteenth century by returning to it the indetermination which is the very possibility of the creation that is history. Because he does not explain *away* the complexity, his *historical* account is also a *theory of the political*.

## 4. HISTORIOGRAPHY AND POLITICAL THEORY

Krieger's use of Kantian categories is explained by his description of the practice of Enlightened Despotism. It reflects an 'ambivalence of reason, manifesting both the structure of the actual world and its transcendence [which] was connected with the relationship . . . between nature and politics: what was descriptive of the laws of nature became prescriptive for the laws of the state' (64). This is why Enlightened Despotism is an 'historically representative contradiction'. 'In the sociology of culture, the proponents of Enlightened Despotism may indeed be accorded a mediatory role between the collective mentality of the mass and the high culture of the philosophes' (90). An historical positivism which recounts the facts, confronts them with theory, and judges their correspondence is inadequate. The historian's task is to capture that 'conditional mode' of the everyday, to portray 'political reality in an active key', as Krieger titles his concluding chapter. History is the search for sense. Its criteria of validity concern what Krieger calls 'qualitative fidelity' (ix). Historiography is description that is itself theory; it describes the creation of sense. The sense of *social* phenomena in flux is given by a *political* theory.

Krieger does not treat the eighteenth century as a prelude to the French Revolution because his goal is to understand 'relations of unity and heterogeneity in eighteenth-century life by acknowledging the indefeasible reality of both' (32). This insistence on unity *and* heterogeneity refutes any reductive explanation; there is no single solution which can bridge the 'hypostasised discord' which poses the political problem. Politics strives for synthesis, but at the cost of destroying the very base on which it rests. Krieger is analysing *the political* space which makes possible such a politics. This is why he speaks of political reality as actionable, open and conditional. He confronts the 'problem of composing a language of action from linguistic components designed to communicate knowledge of the existing world' (85). The political structure defined by Enlightened Despotism does not have that fixed, substantive reality. Its analysis demands the 'restatement of indicative assertions about reality as hypothetical conditions of action in such a way as to recast the real relations between fundamental principle and factual appearance into the practical relation of a fundamental quality of an existing agent who can realise himself only by acting in accordance with it' (84). This principle makes the world a function of the projected action; 'the definite subject becomes an open-ended agent and principles of reality become practical postulates' (85). Only thus can the contradictory positions of the proponents of Enlightened Despotism be described: expressing reality, bound to it, and yet recognising that, alone, they are incapable of changing it, they are forced to develop a rhetoric based on contradiction.

The shifts in the plane and the axis of constitutional thinking described by Krieger point to the *tendency* of the modern state to become total and, ultimately, totalitarian. Classical nineteenth-century liberalism with its myth of progressive history never brought this tendency to fruition. That remained the task for twentieth-century bureaucratic society which is the outgrowth of premisses shared with that liberalism. The eighteenth-century romantic solution turned backwards, to a religious obscurantism and a metaphysics of nature; the absolutisation of morality as a political principle reached its culmination in the Terror of the French Revolution. Krieger does not cast doubt on the promises, power or enlightenment of the despot; he forces us to appreciate the *logic of the political*: its paradoxes, risks, and the conditions of its functioning. He shows the danger of the mirage of totality which comes from the conflation of the social and the political. If the political is founded by the attempt to bridge social divisions, the analysis of Enlightened Despotism's instable articulation demonstrates that only when the division is consciously recognised as 'hypostatised discord' does the modern political form of *democracy* acquire its full sense. But this same recognition of social division makes possible also the idea that reconcilation is possible by absolutising one or the other pole of the divided society. This is the lesson of the twentieth-century totalitarians. The same structure that makes possible democracy can also lead to its overthrow. Democratic participation does not imply only formal *social* equality; *political* liberty and fraternity are also at stake.

Krieger's warning to the citizen tempted by an enlightened despotism is only apparently based on the lessons of twentieth-century politics. He insists that 'the abiding relevance of history [is that] it restores our consciousness of those things in our lives that have sunk beneath the level of consciousness' (xi). This seems to fly in the face of his stress on the 'active key', which adapts the Kantian theory to the demands of historiography. His goal was the restoration of the historical object to its open, actionable, conditional state. This determination of his object, not the method he applied, explains the success of his analysis. The nature of his object makes possible Krieger's unification of historiography, political theory and political practice in a single essay. But Krieger did not define *the political* as the object of his concern. I introduced that definition because of the insufficiencies of the Marxist, Romantic, and Individual Moralist interpretations. Krieger juxtaposed his Kantian categories, making indiscriminant use of the productive schematism (in the form of politics in the 'active mode') and the dialectical idea (which explains his advice of 'caution'). He is not to be blamed for this; Kant offered the same syncretic approach in 'The Idea of World History from a Cosmopolitan Point of View'. That theory, whose fourth and seventh Theses proposed a solution in terms of a Cunning of Reason, added a ninth Thesis which introduced the contribution of the enlightened philosopher to the realisation of Nature's plan. Although the sixth Thesis had posed the problem of Enlightened Despotism,[18] the upshot of Kant's 'cosmopolitan history' was a nineteenth-century logic of Historical Immanence. This explains the inadequacy of Krieger's warnings to the twentieth century.

A different reconstruction of Kant's theory permits an elucidation of Enlightened Despotism from the point of view of the contemporary problem of the political. In the first *Critique*, the schematism is the temporal structure of the knowing subject which unifies the concepts of the understanding with the deliverances of sensible intuition. Kant's inability to resolve successfully the phenomenon–noumenon dualism from which the *Critique* began drove him to the notion of practical reason in the second *Critique*. Practical ethical striving by the noumenally free subject was postulated, but the 'ought' remained empty and formal, like the individual in 'What is Enlightenment?'. The problem was taken up again in the *Critique of Judgement*, which advances the notion of genius whose *creative* function brings forth the unification. A product of Nature, genius does not simply reproduce nature; the art work is the creation of the *new*. Although Kant retreats from the radicality of this assertion, its identity with the temporal schematism of the first *Critique* suggests the transcendence of the formal linear frame of time as simple progression which was canonised by the nineteenth century's concept of immanent History. *Historical time is the continual creation of the new*. This philosophical argument has political consequences. The seventeenth-century formulation of the political as determined by Nature, and the nineteenth-century attempt to conceive it through an immanent logic of History define the task of the political as *putting an end to history as the creation of the new*. The impossible harmony of the eighteenth-century distortion and deflection explain why the political emerged there *as a problem*. The twentieth century goes to the opposite extreme; it imagines the possibility of a *solution which would eliminate the problem*.

The twentieth century rediscovers the political as the theory of a revolution which would restore to history its dimension of radical novelty. The project is confused by the difficulty in understanding the French Revolution. Contemporary politics is articulated in order to conjure both social division and historical novelty by displaying them openly, eliminating the political as a common problem while making politics a technocratic speciality of the scientists of the social. This inversion of the eighteenth century 'hypostasised discord' does not change the terms in which the political problem is manifested. The contradictions are present, known to all, debated freely; otherness is integrated into a social pluralism where division appears natural and even rational. More than simply the multiplication and fragmentation of social interests, the twentieth century thrives on novelty. Novelty serves to domesticate the historically new. The twentieth century relates to History as the eighteenth century related to Nature: its choices are the theoretical distortion of the facts, or the empirical deflection of its (liberal or Marxist) theories. Where the eighteenth century posed the problem of the political, the twentieth century refusal of Revolution must deny its existence by eliminating the threat of the radically new. The political is socialised, and thereby opened to the control of technocrats who cannot be given a political name. This *ad hoc* solution renders conflict potentially more explosive by denying the existence of the political, even in the 'conditional mode'.

Krieger's 'conditional mode' and 'active key' led him to a politics of caution because he remains in a nineteenth-century orientation to history. The difficulty is apparent in his conclusions.

> In addition to the way this world looks when it is contemplated and the way this world looks to one who is preparing to act upon it, there is the most common perspective of all: the way political reality looks when we perceive it to be actionable – by somebody else. Small wonder that we have patented the eighteenth-century invention of enlightened despotism (90).

Krieger does not explain the political conditions which produce this 'most common perspective' that leaves politics to 'somebody else'. His argument is sociological. We too, he says, have had despots, 'rulers who brook no limit, save of their own devising, upon measures covered by the national security and the general welfare, and who brook no definition, even of their own devising, of the national security and the general welfare' (90). Krieger has forgotten the lesson of Montesquieu. Politics is transformed into the exercise of social domination. This does not square with the Enlightened Despots' need for legitimation. A historian looking back on this account of the twentieth century could not write its *political* history in the way that Krieger captured the problems of the eighteenth century. Krieger's twentieth century is not new; its citizenry is not democratic.

The reality 'perceived as actionable by others', and the attitude which will 'brook no limit' on its power are means for coping with social resistence. They are debased modes of the political; the one takes for granted its distortion and abandons itself to the bureaucracy, the other makes a virtue of the deflection of theory to avoid the need for legitimation. Neither admits the existence of demands which cannot be integrated, or reduced to the language of technique. These can be recognised only against the backdrop of 'Revolution' as expressing the possibility of the radically new. This explains the political force of the analysis proposed by Ernst Bloch's *Spirit of Utopia*. Bloch's *summum*, *The Principle of Hope*, finds radical political demands in every corner of daily life, from the dream and fairy tale to work and religion. They are demands for liberty and fraternity which cannot be fixed institutionally. The historian need not be blamed for neglecting Bloch's claim that these are an ontological definition of the human condition. But he cannot neglect the implications of the French Revolution for the object of his investigation, or for the contemporaries whom he is addressing. The political definition of an epoch expresses the manner in which its risks and hopes are conjured, rationalised or integrated. 'Revolution' introduced a dimension of radical temporality to the eighteenth-century definition. When the denial of the new is understood as the political structure of the twentieth century, it reveals the 'limits' power must accept because they constitute a reality 'actionable' only by *our* politics.

The result of this excursion into eighteenth-century historiography occasioned by Krieger's essay is a critical theoretical programme. The historical record, as well as the contemporary scene, must be studied in an 'active key', aware that it presents a 'rhetoric based on contradiction'. The ruses by which it seeks to legitimate itself must be uncovered, explained and analysed. These ruses exist on the broad plane of political theory; but they have ramifications in individual existence. As with the practitioners of Enlightened Despotism, this theoretical programme is not simply contemplative. Practice is not guided by a 'despotic' theory. Theory permits an always already ongoing practice to understand itself within the horizon formed by the question of the political. The specificity of the twentieth century is defined by the democratic political project, inaugurated when the French Revolution broke the spell of Enlightened Despotism's self-legitimations, but stifled by the nineteenth century's immanently progressive History which destroyed the radicality of the new. The democratic revolution was made possible by the realisation of the political as a specific domain whose temporal horizon is determined by the problem of 'Revolution'. Had he seen this, Krieger's cautiously pessimistic conclusion could have been reformulated in a more optimistic vein.

**Notes**

1. Numbers in parentheses refer to Leonard Krieger, *An Essay on the Theory of Enlightened Despotism* (Chicago: University of Chicago Press, 1975).
2. Krieger does not say that such modern despots are the totalitarian offspring of a Marxist theory whose concentration on the economic logic of civil society prevents it from understanding the proper place and function of the political. The relation between the democratic revolution and the advent of totalitarianism is not his explicit theme. None the less, the ubiquity Krieger attributes to the phenomenon, and the philosophical formulation which he proposes as its explanation, suggests that he would not reject such an interpretation.
3. For the following, see Fritz Hartung, 'Der aufgeklärte Absolutismus', in *Historische Zeitschrift*, 180, 1955, pp. 18–19, and Krieger, pp. 18–19. The singular difference between the two investigations is suggested in the title of Hartung's article. The term Enlightened Despotism was coined only after the fact, by the nineteenth-century German historians Roscher, Treitschke and Koser. Diderot used it only once, in his correspondence. Raynal used the term in his widely read *Histoire philosophique et politique des établissements et des commerce des Européens dans les deux Indes* (1770), but withdrew its positive connotations from the book's later editions.
4. The first accusation was the sad recognition of Voltaire after his stormy break with Frederick, and of Diderot after his failure to influence seriously the *Nakaz* of Catherine. One of the most serious of contemporary scholars, Robert Derathé, actually argues that the goal of the *philosophes* was to become what C. W. Mills called the 'power elite'. ('Les philosophes et le despotisme', in Pierre Francastel, ed., *Utopie et institutions*, Paris, 1963, p. 170.) The second accusation is of course the familiar Marxist reading of the French Revolution, to which we will return.

5. This movement is illustrated by Habermas's essay, 'Hegel and the French Revolution', in *Theory and Practice* (Boston: Beacon Press, 1973), which argues that Hegel de-radicalised the threat carried by the notion of Revolution insofar as he made radical historical change the *principle* governing his entire system. Hegel thus preserves the revolution by eliminating the place of the revolutionary who would make it.
6. Rousseau to Mirabeau, 26 July 1767; cited in Derathé, op. cit., pp. 74–5.
7. The 'crisis of legitimation' is thematised by Habermas's *Legitimation Crisis* (Boston: Beacon Press, 1975). The common 'organisational' orientation of contemporary political theories is developed brilliantly in Sheldon Wolin's history of political theory, *Politics and Vision* (London: Allen & Unwin, 1960).
8. Thus, for example, the Enlightened Despot, Joseph II, supported the publication of a brochure entitled 'La verité ou tableau comparatif des changements projetés par l'empereur et des points arrêtés par l'assemblée nationale en France' in which the identity of these goals is asserted forcefully. Similarly, the Prussian minister Hertzberg argued that the French Constitution of 1791 was in no way superior to the gains being accorded Prussian citizens. Perhaps hypocritical, such arguments were not implausible.
9. Marx was not the first, or the only, theorist who traced the economic roots of the shifting class arrangements within the Ancien Régime. He was preceded by Hegel; he acknowledges his own debt to Guizot; he was succeeded by Tocqueville. The first major twentieth-century re-evaluation of the Marxist orientation was proposed by Francois Furet and Denis Richet in *La Révolution Française*, 2 vols. (Paris: Hachette, 1965–6). Claude Mazauric proposed immediately a Marxist critique in 'Réflexions sur une nouvelle conception de la Révolution Française', in *Annales historiques de la Révolution Française*, juillet–septembre, 1967, pp. 339–68. Richet replied in 'Autour des origins idéologiques lointaines de la Révolution Française: Elites et despotisme', in *Annals Economie–Société–Civilisations*, janvier-février, 1969, no. 1, pp. 1–23. (Since this chapter was written, Furet has also replied to Mazauric and the Marxists, while spelling out his own original conception in *Penser la Révolution Française* (Paris: Gallimard, 1978).)
10. The original French title was more specific: *La crise de l'état prussien à la fin du XVIIIe siècle et la genèse de la mentalité romantique* (Paris, 1947). The English translation (Chicago: University of Chicago Press, 1974) includes a separately published article on 'The Struggle of the Jews for Emancipation in Prussia' which, although intrinsically interesting, has little to do with the main argument of the book.
11. It was Wöllner, for example, who censured the aged and honoured author of 'What is Enlightenment?' for his *Religion within the Limits of Reason Alone*.
12. Habermas has not permitted an English translation of his *Strukturwandel der Oeffentlichkeit* (Neuwied: Luchterhand, 1962). A short summary of his arguments is available as 'The Public Sphere', in *New German*

*Critique*, no. 3, Fall, 1974, pp. 49–54. I have tried to explain Habermas's inability to thematise the political as such in *The Marxian Legacy*.

13. Reinhart Koselleck, *Kritik und Krise*, 2nd edition (Frankfurt am Main: Suhrkamp, 1973; 1st edition, 1959). Habermas criticises Koselleck as belonging to the tradition of the 'counter-Enlightenment' in 'Zur Kritik an der Geschichtsphilosophie', in *Kultur und Kritik* (Frankfurt am Main: Suhrkamp, 1973), pp. 355–64. Whereas Habermas's 'enlightenment' standpoint wants to continue the struggle to realise the 'bourgeois public sphere', Koselleck shows why that effort is doomed to fail.
14. This explains Krieger's method. He cites frequently, à tort et à travers, passing from regime to regime, major to minor theorist. His justification is that just such a patchwork as he presents must have been the structure of political discourse at the time. That reformer and monarch, French and German, Cameralist and Physiocrat, can be used in this way is not Krieger's capricious ordering of the facts but the image, and the self-image, of the times.
15. Krieger does not distinguish between these two uses of Kantian categories. The schematism in the *Critique of Pure Reason* gives sense to the manifold of data united by intuition and unified by the categories. Kant can explain its functions only as 'an art hidden in the depths of the human soul'. In the *Critique of Judgement* the notion returns as the 'genius' whose natural creation of sense is explicitly distinguished from the categorial unification of the first *Critique*. The sense created is the *new*; it is not simply a readjustment of the already-given parts. In this sense, the schematism articulates the task of the political: creating and covering over the new. (See Kant, *Werke*, V, paragraph 49, esp. pp. 317–19.)

    The transcendental dialectic serves the historian who, like the philosopher, attempts to reconstruct the antinomies, paralogisms and conditional forms which synthetic reason treats as if they were absolute. The unity between these two moments of the Kantian philosophy was recognised by Fichte, for whom it founds the inaugural moves of his *Wissenschaftslehre*. I will return to the implications of Krieger's conflation of the two approaches.
16. A similar point is made in Richet's defence of his and Furet's interpretation of the French Revolution. Richet details the debates among the nobility in the seventeenth century concerning the question who shall be considered a peer. This reflects a social process which will have political implications insofar as these debates express the need to assure homogeneity in the political body, and to set up a barrier before the 'barbarians' (op. cit., p. 4). The recognition of otherness and the need to create a political body of free, equal brothers is *constitutive of the political debate* which, in Furet and Richet's telling phrase, was 'telescoped' into the French Revolution. Krieger's neglect of the French Revolution will be seen to explain the contemporary conclusions he draws from his analysis.
17. Krieger does not mention the implications drawn by Koselleck from this structure, namely that government is weakened and undermined by

the very shift that extends its field of action because its responsibilities grow beyond its ability to deal with them.

18. The thesis is implied by the assertion that 'man is an animal who needs a master . . . But this master will also be an animal who needs a master.'

# 13 The Revolution in the American Revolution

A nineteenth-century American historian once commented that the more a Frenchman, German or Englishman knows his national history, the more French, German or English he is. What of the American? How can he know himself? Is he the product of the Revolution which created his country? But in what sense was it a revolution? The assertion rings true, at least for the nineteenth century; for the modern era, which sweeps away identities while relativising political certainties, it serves only to introduce a series of more general reflections about political theory and about political societies. Revolutionary origins seem to have a different status than the traditional sociocultural definitions of society because they reflect a conscious choice. They pose the question of the place of the political in modern societies.

The victorious war against the English coloniser created a Confederation of thirteen sovereign states founded on political principles elaborated during the period 1763–76, which led to the Declaration of Independence, and on institutions created during the struggle to realise that independence. The Confederation consecrated in 1783 by the Treaty of Paris was an unstable political entity, paralysed by the incompatibility of the principles of 1776 with the institutions adopted by the sovereign states. The resolution of the crisis gave birth to a new politics translated by a truly national Constitution elaborated in 1787. The new national government was a federalism founded on a new understanding of the nature of political representation.

Was it a revolution or was it a continuous process which began in resistance against the Constitution of England, the most free country in the world? A revolution or a process which developed through constitutional experience in a country at war which was transformed in and by the new conditions of peace? A revolution or a process which concluded with a Constitution which remains in force two centuries later? Are there reactions, as well as qualitative leaps forward? Should each phase be analysed on its own before the attempt to totalise them under the concept if revolution is proposed? With what right does the philosopher subsume under the category of revolution actions whose basis was economic, others which sought to defend traditional and pre-modern freedoms within a liberal Empire in the process of modernisation, and still others whose motivation was religious or idealistic?

Some may answer by referring to Marx, others to Locke or Montesquieu, while still others play on theories of natural law. Some see a continuity in motivation where others discover a learning process replete with anticipations and regressions. Some distinguish the 'good' revolution and its results; they denounce the confiscation of their work in later times. Others are proud to have opened a new epoch whose horizons extend to the infinite. All are wrong. In its own way, the revolution continues in the practice (if not the theory, which has withered since that heyday) of American politics. But if the revolution is neither completed nor betrayed, one can still ask whether it has ended. The question is surprising only to those who identify 'revolution' with 1789 or 1917. For just that reason, the question is not without interest.

## 1. WHY THE QUESTION?

The evident failure of socialist, social-democratic and other Welfare States has led today to a new interest in liberal politics. I stress liberal *politics*, because it is these political institutions – which include the competitive market – and not the liberal economy in its capitalist form – whose relevance today needs to be rethought. Some think that liberal institutions explain the social and economic successes of the societies which have been able to acquire them. The different possible forms of political liberalism seem to explain the relative degrees of civil freedom and/or social equality present in such societies. The paradigm case of 'liberalism' is assumed to have produced – or perhaps to have been produced by – the American Revolution. But society is not an abstract will which can select institutions from a constitutional supermarket. The authors of the Constitution of 1787 took their cue from Solon, who claimed to give the citizens not the best constitution but the best one that they can accept.

Since 1789, the political transformation by which a society changes itself has been called 'revolution'. This suggests that the French Revolution was truly a revolution, whereas the events that took place in North America were the result of a quest for independence with no intention of changing the local political institutions (save by dropping the reference to the King) much less altering socioeconomic relations. This American model, which was to be sold to the ex-colonial nations that became independent in the 1950s and 1960s, is supposed to be based on the demand for political freedom whereas the French Revolution sought to create – indeed, to impose – social equality. This would explain why the American Revolution was decentralising while the French remained Jacobin even after the elimination of the Jacobins. In a word, the American Revolution is supposed to have been satisfied by political transformations which left a free field for private initiative (or egoism) whereas the French sought to change society in its most profound as well as its everyday foundations. The concept of 'revolution' thus signifies a total transformation of society and of the individuals who constitute it. Politics is the means, society the end.

The thesis opposing the two revolutions was formulated explicitly by the translator of Burke and future Secretary to Metternich at the Congress of Vienna, Friedrich Gentz. His *Comparison of the American and French Revolutions* was translated immediately into English by the son of President John Adams. It was to serve as a weapon in the elections of 1800 which opposed Adams to Thomas Jefferson. Gentz's thesis was intended to serve the European reaction; its function in the United States was broader, although it was also useful in a partisan context. At the time of the Declaration of Independence, contemporaries did not hesitate to speak of a 'revolution' in their country. The French historian, Claude Fohlen, points out that contemporary Frenchmen too spoke more frequently of an 'American Revolution' than of a 'War of Independence'. The French changed their vocabulary as their own Revolution was canonised retrospectively. In North America, doubt grew early, as history seemed to put into question the victories of yesterday. For some, the revolutionary rupture was sealed by the Declaration of Independence. This meant that the revolutionary process was defined by that struggle against English tyranny that took place between 1763 and 1776.[1] For others, the important moment was the conquest of independence, crowned in 1783 by the Treaty of Paris which recognised a *new* nation. Revolution was thus the armed struggle which forged the unity of thirteen independent colonies.[2] But then, at the time of the debates on the ratification of the new Constitution of 1787, both partisans and opponents could appeal to the 'principles of the revolution' to support their arguments and to attack the 'betrayal' of their enemies. Yet the question posed by the American Revolution is not simply partisan; it is a question of principle, a challenge for political philosophy.

The principles on which the different American opinions were based were generalities inherited not only from the English colonial experience but gleaned from the entire political history of humanity. During the long period from 1763 to 1787, the Americans had shown themselves devout collectors of political truisms. Words like 'republic' and 'freedom' – not to speak of pejorative concepts like the frequently abused notion of 'tyranny' – could cover meanings which were not simply different but frankly opposed. The reader cannot but be impressed by the flowering of serious political analyses which mixed syncretically concepts aligned with Newtonian pride yet animated by an appeal to the transhistorical experience revealed by the Greeks, the Romans and the Bible and given contemporary relevance by the English experience. The Americans could lend faith to this style because they were at once pragmatic and yet fiercely logical in their arguments. They used whatever came to hand; the lessons of History could serve at will, since what was important was the demonstration.

At the same time, and especially during the phase which led to the Declaration of Independence, it was above all necessary to develop popular support. Bernard Bailyn shows how this strategic need explains the remarkable, if not pedantic, insistence on logic which characterises American writings at the time. The same need explains the often-overestimated role of Locke's thought. It proposed no institutional solution, but the importance it gives to tacit consent could be transformed into an appeal for active participation. This is why the natural law to which the Americans appealed could combine with the freedom of religious conscience present already at the beginnings of colonisation in an explosive mixture.

The general orientation which developed during the confrontation with England was thus the unstable result of a combination of elements. The defensive unity preserved by the presence of the enemy could not last; it combined elements too diverse. Peace brought new problems, and new possibilities. The independent Confederation was composed of 13 institutionally distinct independent units; regional differences, opposition between larger and smaller states, and boundary problems made more acute by the new wealth on the frontier put into question the foundations of the republic. New political principles were necessary if the new nation was to survive.

The adoption of the federalist Constitution of 1787 did not put an end to the revolution's self-doubt. The supporters of that Constitution were accused of being counter-revolutionaries and potential tyrants who wanted to overthrow the noble principles of the Declaration of Independence. The national system which replaced the decentralised Confederation was perceived as a confiscation of the rights not only of the states but also of their citizens whose voices would be submerged in a vast sea surrounded by institutional dikes. The acceptance of the foundations of the new unity can be explained by a variety of material factors. Crucial was the certainty that the first President would be the 'Cincinnatus' who had retired to his lands after directing the victorious army. The national President and his government would not reintroduce that monarchical tyranny, with its associated corruption, from which independence had been won. But the preparation of the first elections after Washington's departure was coloured by the existence of parties, a political institution which the Constitution had not foreseen. The victory in 1796 of John Adams of Massachussetts, with the Virginian Thomas Jefferson as his Vice-President, revealed an opposition whose principled or 'philosophic' character was made clear by the support of the Jeffersonians for the French Revolution whose 'democratic excesses' were severely criticised by the friends of Adams. If the object of their dispute was the French Revolution, its subject was the nature of their own Rcvolution.

The partisan vote in favour of the Alien and Sedition Acts in 1798 gave to Adams's government the right of censorship over the press and public opinion. At Jefferson's direction, Virginia and Kentucky passed Resolutions which attributed to their states the right to annul federal laws which they took to be contrary to the Law of the Land. This proposed principle of nullification, and the correlative argument for 'states' rights' would weigh heavily as the Civil War approached. In the meanwhile, the Americans realised another first in political history. Jefferson won the election of 1800, and power was passed peacefully from the hands of one party to its radical opponents. The Jeffersonians called their victory 'the Revolution of 1800'.

The political system which seemed to be finally ratified by the transfer of power in 1800 was none the less constantly put into question during the ensuing 60 years of expansion which preceded the ultimate test of civil war. Despite the warnings against involvement with Europe in Washington's 'Farewell Letter' a war opposed England and its former colonies in 1812. The war did not enjoy wide support, even after the conquest of the capital – now called Washington – and the burning of the White House. A Convention of the New England States at Hartford threatened to secede in 1815. In 1824, a child of that region, himself the son of a President, was installed in the White House. But John Quincy Adams was not re-elected; he was defeated by the new spirit (and the new economy) of the West, incarnated by Andrew Jackson, hero of the battle of New Orleans.

Jackson presented himself as a son of the people; his inauguration was a popular feast which was intended to express the return of the people to power. The revolution was again on the order of the day. But this time it took clear socioeconomic forms, for example in the epic struggle of Jackson against the National Bank. Beneath this struggle lay a more serious threat. The South defended slavery at the same time that the movement toward the West created new states. Were they to be slave or free? As long as the South and the West were tied by a certain economic reciprocity, the problem did not become explosive. But the railroad and the new world commerce of the industrialising North put the old relations into question. The material struggle was fought, of course, in the language of political ideology, from which the antagonisms of 1800 were no more absent than those of 1787 or 1776.

The bloody Civil War (or War of Secession) which freed the slaves and saved the unity of the nation could be understood in terms of the frame created by the experience of the Revolution. Lincoln's address on the battlefield at Gettysberg, memorised by American school children to this day, began with the phrase: 'Four score and seven years ago, our forefathers founded . . .'. Calculating, one sees that Lincoln dates the foundation of the Republic to 1776, the year of the Declaration of Independence. No doubt, he had in mind the Preamble to that Declaration: 'We hold these truths to be self-evident, that all men are created equal, that they are endowed by their Creator with certain inalienable rights.' But Lincoln was not the only person to refer to the experience of the Revolution. The Southerners could evoke the nullification resolutions proposed by Virginia and Kentucky under the leadership of the author of the Declaration. They could insist that, after all, the colonies had revolted against the oppression of England, and that the Declaration affirms the right of revolution as one of the basic rights of man. What is more, as the iconoclastic Marxist historian Eugene Genovese observes, the Southern 'cavaliers' could claim to be the heirs of those republican values which egoistic and exploitative Northern capitalism was destroying.

The 'Reconstruction' of the South after the war was forgotten in the new expansion toward the West. The question of the Revolution was reactualised in 1893, this time by an historian whose thesis played on the American memory at the same time that it pointed to a rupture which would transform the Revolution into an object to be understood more than a subject in which Americans still participated. The historian's argument was founded by a theory of the uniqueness of the American Revolution. Frederick Jackson Turner's essay on 'The Significance of the Frontier in American History' began from the recognition that the conquest of the continent had ended. But the passing beyond the 'frontier' had been constitutive of the American character. The always open space had meant that the young republic was not going to repeat the classical political cycle in which a virile nation conquers an empire before its new wealth puts it on the dangerous slope of 'corruption'. America had been saved from that classical death in time by a continuous spatial movement beyond the frontier. The America of 1893 was becoming an urban, industrial power directed by venal politicians under the control of the 'robber barons'. Some drew the conclusion that the expansion had to continue by the opening of new frontiers; that became the politics symbolised by Theodore Roosevelt which led to the conquest of the Philippines and Cuba while opening the doors of China. This was the beginning of an American imperialism which claimed to be civilising.

At the same time, another orientation developed a militant political populism which dreamed of a return to an America founded on the individualist principles of the Declaration of Independence and which rejected support for the economic trusts and overseas expansion. Although these populists were defeated, their cause remains present in the American mind even today. Its popular form may be demagogic and inward, isolationist internationally and anti-minoritary in domestic affairs. Whatever its concrete manifestation, its appeal is still to the Declaration, and to the dilemmas of the republic. Its presence, against the background of the myth of a frontier which must constantly be recreated, suggests again that the question of the American revolution remains actual. When the historian's research and a popular social demand come together, the result gives the research a philosophical dimension; history is open-ended, presenting the self-interrogation of American society.

## 2. THE REPLY OF THE HISTORIANS

'Scientific' history was imported to the United States from Germany at about the same time that the frontier was closed and the continent began to understand itself as an empire. Although the new frontier lay ever more to the West, towards Asia, and its proponents were generally anti-European, the first generation of American historians were concerned to reinsert America within the European state system. They attempted to understand the Revolution from the point of view of the English. After all, the United States were becoming an empire; the difficult demands of that new position had to be understood. It was necessary to learn how English institutions were transformed when they were transplanted into a new world and a virgin society. The historians tried to explain how the Americans had misunderstood the needs of the empire after the victory in the Seven Years' War brought a reorientation of the European world from the Mediterranean to the Atlantic. The English measures against which the Americans had protested seemed justified and, all things being equal, moderate. It seemed that the Americans had lost more economically than they had gained from the break with the mother country. The culmination of this orientation is found in Lawrence Gipson's multi-volume *The British Empire Before the American Revolution* (1936ff) which is described by a recent commentator as 'nostalgically imperialist'. If the American Revolution was inevitable, it was because of geographical differences between the colonies and England, and changes in English institutions when they were transferred far from the motherland. The idealist image of the American Revolution as the realisation of a new freedom was rejected as an illusion.

The populist movement gave rise also to an historical reading of the American Revolution. Carl L. Becker's *History of Political Parties in the Province of New York* (1909) asked the basic question: was the issue 'Home rule, or who shall rule at home?'. Becker's assumption that the 'real' issues concerned domestic power became the basis of the progressive school of historians. The revolution was not made for moral or idealist reasons; the actors were practical men who knew their own interests. These interests were, in the last resort, economic. For example, Arthur Schlesinger Sr. traced an intra-colonial panorama in *The Colonial Merchants and the American Revolution* (1919) to show that the merchants who supported the first demands against the English withdrew from the fray when the crowds they manipulated began to go beyond their limited demands. Schlesinger argued that a dialectical relation of popular participation and merchant interests explains, for example, the relative moderation of the movement between 1770 and 1773 when the merchants left the battle because they thought they had the support of the English mercantile interests for a peaceful settlement with Parliament. The synthesis of the progressive orientation was proposed in 1926 by Franklin Jameson's lectures on *The American Revolution Considered as a Social Movement*. As his title suggests, the progressive school questioned the political nature of the Revolution. When it did speak of politics, its model was suggested by the title of John C. Miller's study, *Sam Adams, Pioneer of Propaganda* (1939).

The best-known work of the progessive school is Charles Beard's *An Economic Interpretation of the Constitution* (1913). Beard was not a Marxist; he proposed simply 'an' interpretation. His analysis of the making of the Constitution suggests that the truth of the Revolution lay in the principles of the Declaration of Independence and in the practice of the Confederation. Applying the progressive method, Beard sought the true interest which must have motivated the authors of the Constitution. He analysed the social composition of the Philadelphia convention. The members were urban lawyers, bankers from the coastal cities, merchants, industrialists and slave owners. They held government debts and were involved in frontier land speculations. Their interests pushed them to strengthen the central government against the states where the *vox populi* could impose inflationary laws and debtor protection. The Constitution they wrote reflected their concerns; it assured the rights of private property above other interests.

Although Beard's position would change later,[3] the progressive orientation dominated historical research until the 1950s. The new history that replaced it can be understood historically. The victory against fascism could be understood in terms of a neo-Whig theory. The Revolution returned to the agenda; a Whig politics which had made England the land of freedom before the inevitable corruption of the empire passed the flag of freedom to the colonies. The democratic nature of the Revolution had to be demonstrated, proving the validity of the political institutions which still incarnated it. The new 'consensus' historiography could be self-congratulatory; but it could also be the basis for a critique of abuses. The choice depended on the historian. This ambivalence led to a rediscovery of the philosophical dimension, for a choice had to be justified.

The new history of the post-war period presented two conservative variants. The social analysis of Kathleen and Robert Brown, as well as J. R. Pole's long-winded comparative portrait of England and America, sought to show that the colonies, and thus the United States, were a 'middle-class democracy'. This meant that the revolution was not a revolution. If there was a revolution, it transformed a deferential society in which politics only reflected the existing hierarchy into a society where political suffrage became increasingly important even though it elected the same representatives whose choices now depended on local instead of national or republican concern with the general welfare. Such arguments could be criticised empirically, for example by the work of Jackson Turner Main. More important, they made the revolution into a movement seeking to conserve a society threatened by the new mercantile interests of the English empire. The Revolution is treated as an anti-modernist reaction by corporative colonies seeking to preserve the status quo.

A second conservative interpretation could be developed from similar premisses. The 1950s were the decade described by Daniel Bell's famous thesis concerning the 'end of ideology'. Daniel Boorstin's *The Genius of American Politics* (1953) suggests that pragmatism, the rejection of ideology in favour of consensus, makes the American Revolution unique. The 'genius' of American politics is articulated in the Constitution of 1787, whose theoretical foundation is found in the *Federalist Papers*. If 1776 connotes the Revolution, 1787 denotes its success. To reintroduce the passions of 1776 would be to adulterate the pragmatism of American politics and to threaten the republic. The danger would be the identification of politics and morality, both of which are said to pose absolute demands which threaten a pluralist society. But of course, the decade of the 1950s was followed by the birth of a 'new left'.

Two other interpretations of the American Revolution in the 1950s sought to explicate the 'consensus' which formed the basis of American political life. This consensus was said to be articulated by a pluralist liberalism characteristic of the social life of the country. Richard Hofstadter first painted this picture in broad strokes in *The American Political Tradition* (1948). He applied that synthesis in a series of studies attempting to understand the basis of the deviations that threaten the consensus. Thus, the contemporary polemics collected in *The Paranoid Style in American Politics* (1964) are unified by the argument that liberal society is threatened not by class struggles but by battles over social status to which threatened groups reply by an irrational, if not paranoiac behaviour. Hofstadter analyses not only the right wing politics symbolised by Goldwater but also nineteenth-century populist movements which, in paradoxical ways, prefigure his rise. For Hofstadter, the American consensus is threatened by the right and by the left. Similarly, Hofstadter's study of *Anti-Intellectualism in American Life* (1962) attempts to find the roots of a messianic, anti-modern and fiercely independent spirit which re-emerges periodically in American life. Hofstadter's thesis sums up the consensus position; the liberal intellect is pragmatic, dry and fearful of the imagination, of hope and utopia. The reader finds himself often feeling like an 'anti-intellectual', proving perhaps the veracity of Hofstadter's account.

Whereas Hofstadter remains at the social-psychological level, Louis Hartz's *The Liberal Tradition in America* (1956) is based on a political analysis which recalls Tocqueville. Hartz proposes a positive inversion of the Trotskyist thesis of combined and unequal development which explains why America escaped the moment of feudalism to be 'born liberal'. It had no frustrated middle class confronted by aristocratic institutions with which it must break. It had no established Church, so that the Revolution did not have to be anti-religious. With no monarchy, the new nation did not have to centralise its power to protect itself; nor was it caught in a love/hate relation with power. Because a liberalism that is realised without struggle cannot recognise its own theoretical foundations, the only ideology that could arise in liberal America was nationalism. This nationalism became a 'Hebraism' imagining itself to be a chosen people; American national pride depends on a legacy and not on a consciously attained political goal. The Revolution could not give rise to a Christian universalism seeking to spread its message like the French of 1789, but only to a proud and chosen separatism accompanied by an isolationist fear of external contamination. Whereas European liberals sought to master nature and to transform their traditions, American liberals acted like European conservatives in worshipping nature and organic tradition. This is why the United States has had no prophetic leaders; politics does not tempt American intellectuals. The agonies of Europe encouraged magnificent dreams whereas the free and prosperous Americans could look prosaically and soberly at reality, producing a pragmatism in philosophy and a willingness to compromise their interests.

Just when the theory of the liberal consensus seemed to eliminate finally the question of the Revolution, the issue was sharply posed anew by the birth of the civil rights movement in the 1960s, and by the American war in Vietnam. The 'revisionist' reading of American history had three choices. It could return to the progressive orientation to show that the benign appearance of liberalism hid an interested and therefore unjust politics. It could return to the principles of the Declaration of Independence and appeal to the need to realise at last the 'truths' proclaimed by the Founders. Or it could study the history of those 'without voice', but without whom there would never have been a revolution nor its results. None of those options was satisfactory, because each posed the question wrongly. The progressive orientation corresponded in fact to the realism of the authors of the Constitution who sought to preserve the gains of 1776 by taking into account the reality of social interests. That politics is interested does not mean necessarily that it is unjust. The return to the principles of 1776 does not explain why they would be heard more clearly in 1976 than they were two centuries before. Such writing of history is simply a moral and moralising tactic. To replace such an idealism by the realism that returns the revolt to its true agents ignores the fact that these actors could not find the institutional forms which would have permitted the political success of their actions. Revolution and revolt may have come together for a moment, but the success of the result depends on the institutionalisation of the revolution.

The question of the American revolution is not historical; it is above all philosophical. That is the way it was lived at a time when, as Douglas Adair demonstrates convincingly, history was above all the search for those universals which constitute the social life of men. The colonists read history as philosophers; their political principles were drawn from a history which provided them with their theoretical legitimation. Contemporary historiography since the pioneering work of Bernard Bailyn and Gordon Wood has developed this colonial orientation in what is called 'the republican synthesis'. Bailyn follows the political logic expressed in the pamphlets published during the debate which led to independence. He explained the theory behind his analysis in an article published several years after his major work, *The Ideological Origins of the American Revolution* (1967). Basing himself on the ethnography of Clifford Geertz, Bailyn argues that the political logic he had studied became an ideological framework through whose lens any English action could appear only as an aggression. The republican ideology of the colonists explains why reconciliation became impossible and the crisis deepened between

1763 and 1776. But while an ideology can unite disparate strands, its stability is not assured in a changing society.

Gordon Wood's monumental analysis of *The Creation of the American Republic, 1776–1787* follows the fate of the republican ideology when it attempts to give itself institutional form in the new independent nation. What was valid for interpreting the actions of others is no longer useful in a country where popular sovereignty is the foundation of political institutions. The republican appeal against monarchical sovereignty needed to acquire its own positive forms. The essence of an ideology is to veil experience; its refutation takes time. Wood traces the gradual awakening of the Americans to their new experience, at the national level and within the governments of the sovereign states. He claims that the Constitution of 1787 is the expression of a new politics which overcomes the republican ideology. But other historians – most notably J. G. A. Pocock in *The Machiavellian Moment* (1975) – insist on its continuation into the nineteenth century. Some see that same ideology still present today.

The American Revolution and its historical development must be understood in terms of its republican ideology, which precedes and determines the actions undertaken. It is not the product of a society in revolt, seeking to give itself a legitimacy or a political reflection. It begins from a political theory which discovers social relations, is transformed by them, and transforms them in turn. Pauline Maier illustrates this relation in an aptly titled study, *From Resistance to Revolution* (1972). She presents the process through which the crowd, manipulated at first by the anti-English merchants as initially analysed by Schlesinger, becomes aware of its power and its political capacity. That mutation made of a group of artisans and workers a force capable of picking up the slack in the movement when the merchant interests were inclined to accept a compromise with Parliament. And these new citizens adopted and adapted, as their own, political concepts which had served the merchants only as rhetorical slogans. In the new hands, this ideology became a reality and a political power. American republicanism came to express a popular philosophy which could claim to define the American character.

## 3. PHILOSOPHICAL ARMS

The development of the American political system shows one striking characteristic: the lack of a true opposition to the Revolution. This is not the result of the fact that the Americans were all united around a project for the future, or that their society was so homogeneous that conflicts of interest could not arise. On the contrary. The Revolution was violent; it did not hesitate to act against its real or supposed enemies; it seemed to some to go too far and to others to stop too soon. The leaders of one phase lost their influence and their positions later, when energies freed by the break with the old habits went beyond the deferential framework which had provided them direction. The historian who studies the revolution in one city, region or state finds all the forms of personal, economic, social and political conflicts which appear in other revolutionary situations. He finds vanguard parties, a polemical press, coalitions which do not distinguish personal interest from adherence to the common cause; he finds personal conflicts masked by political verbiage, military men seeking to acquire civil power, financial and land speculation. And he notes too that the Revolution did not benefit everyone, and that those whose interests were hurt did not simply react passively. None the less, he does not find a true opposition.

This lack of opposition is explained by the Americans' shared ideology, even when they accentuated one or another aspect of its realisation. The republican synthesis grew gradually. Its roots were of English origin, but its general formulation was sufficiently broad to permit the addition of ideas taken as well from Antiquity as from the Bible, from the French Enlightenment and from the scientific revolution. The English matrix of the American ideology is called 'Whig thought'. It was constituted above all by a philosophy of History based on a progressive evolution which presents the slow triumph of freedom against a power which seeks constantly to expand its reach. At the beginning was the Norman conquest, which destroyed the ancient freedom of the Saxon peoples. Progress begins with the *Magna Carta* won from the King in 1215. First the Lords, then the Commons, progressively take back their freedoms from a monarchy whose power is based on the control of the Executive, concentrated in the Court, and spreading its power by means of the 'corruption' of society. In its political translation, Whig thought is founded on the opposition of freedom, incarnated in the legislature, against power, represented by the executive. The early absence of an American opposition is explained by the fact that resistance was based on the right of self-government against a royal English executive seeking to expand its power.

The Americans could appeal to Whig thought to justify their

famous slogan, 'No taxation without representation.' But things were not so simple. Ideology cannot neglect its own social evolution. Seventeenth-century English history was marked by two Revolutions, one of which cost the head of a King before establishing a republic. But that first series of events, beginning in 1640, seemed to prove the dangers inherent in the Whig conception of the realisation of freedom. The republic itself was undermined by more radical currents; democracy seemed to have briefly been established before tyranny was reborn – exactly as the classical political theorists since Aristotle and Polybius had predicted. Whig thought had to be modified; the simple dichotomy between power and freedom had to find an equilibrium permitting the establishment of a government at once just and stable. The so-called Glorious Revolution of 1688–9 created the conditions for this new government in England; the administration of Walpole in the early eighteenth century realised the desired stability. As to justice, the success was less encouraging; its partisans, who expressed their demands in the famous journals of Addison and Steele, *The Tatler* and *The Spectator*, criticised mordantly the court and the aristocracy in the name of a rising bourgeoisie. They were called, apparently without intentional irony, the 'polite Whigs'.[4]

To call the realisation of the Whig system a republic is an anachronism justified by the American experience. The republic was certainly not the preferred category of the times; the Americans did not use this term either before 1776, but after that date, they made of it a passe-partout which has to be analysed carefully in order to understand their debates and their political choices. Tom Paine's 'common sense' intuition, that a republic is simply a government without a monarch which aims to realise the common good, offered no help for the creation of free institutions. A country strongly influenced by the sobre Calvinist religion could not count on the optimism that assumes that men are already virtuous, and that corruption is due only to bad institutions. The American concept of the republic had to contain not only guarantees of freedom but also incitations to virtue. The republic had to be able to protect itself from its own evil inclinations. The conquest of independence could not be assumed to complete the Revolution that would inaugurate the republic.

The republican model was built at first from the English system whose theory and practice the Americans knew well. But just that familiarity explains the confusion of their analyses, which amalgamate syncretically principles drawn from sources as different as Montesquieu and Locke, Harrington and Hume, natural right and its positive form elaborated by Blackstone. Although his thought did not play a crucial role in America, its premise was that of Rousseau – that 'any legitimate government is republican'. But the Americans had to draw the implications of Rousseau's definition of the republic as 'any state governed by laws, under whatever form of administration: because only then does the public interest govern, only then is the public thing something'. What form would the republican institutions adopt? The independent states chose differently; and the Confederation adopted another principle still. A further premise from Rousseau was implicit in their dilemma. The American conception of popular sovereignty corresponded to Rousseau's general will. A first difficulty is suggested by Rousseau's conclusion that 'to be legitimate, the government cannot be identified with the sovereign; insofar as the government is simply the minister of the sovereign, the monarchy itself can be a republic'. John Adams was to make a similar suggestion in his *Defence of the Constitutions of the United States* (1788). The Jeffersonians did not agree. They called themselves Democratic Republicans, and they might have recalled Rousseau's rejection of the idea that the general will can be represented. The English roots of the American experience suggested a different way out of the dilemma.

The American whig concept of the republic includes three moments whose political implications became manifest gradually during the Revolution. The republic was first of all the *res publica*, the shared and public concerns of the community. As opposed to private affairs where individual interest dominated, the republic was the sphere of the political where freedom dictates its law. In this sense, John Adams's influential *Thoughts on Government* (1776) defined the republic simply as a government of laws as opposed to a government of men. But that general formulation does not specify the institutional means which permit the elaboration of political laws. It leaves aside the question of virtue, which cannot be presupposed but which is necessary if private interest is not to replace public freedom. Such a republican government as Adams proposed could be either monarchical or aristocratic; the government of laws could even oppose a self-managed participatory democracy insofar as that form makes the people both judge and participant in political affairs. The proponents of this first republican position had to explain the legitimacy of the representation of those 'aristocratic' elements of society which claim to obey republican objectives; and they had to show how these elements work toward the discovery of the common good through the formulation of laws.

A second definition of the republic furnishes the beginnings of a reply to these difficulties. England did not have (and still has not) a written Constitution. What was called its Constitution was its social structure, which combined and unified organically the three components of society in the political functions of monarchy, Lords and Commons. The Roman correspondence of the *res publica* and the structures of society was coupled with a neoplatonic image of a society functioning like an organism. The political structure of the republic thus depends in the last instance on the structure of the society that it is to govern. When the Americans became aware that their new world was peopled by new 'democratic' social structures, they could no longer accept this second definition of the republic. But the weight of classical theory, and the English Revolution of 1640, made the adoption of democracy an ideological impossibility.

The Americans' attempt to adopt these first two models of the republic can be understood as a reaction against the modernity represented by the new commercial and mercantile English empire. One of the empirical 'causes' of the Revolution is certainly the fearful reaction of provincials confronted with the rationalisation which modernity demands. When they based their demands on the 'rights of an Englishman', or on natural or divine right, the Americans were appealing to a premodern tradition. This difficulty has to be borne in mind in evaluating the novelty of their political solutions.

The third American formulation of the republic begins from the recognition of the social transformations that put into question the organic correspondence between the social and the political. Basing themselves on the simple definition of the republic as a government of laws, and defining the common good simply as freedom, this orientation returns to the original vision of the Whigs. It defines the republic as the institutional form capable of preventing the excesses of a power which seeks to aggrandise itself at the expense of freedom. That freedom, however, remains to be defined. A double slippage took place in America. On the one hand, the freedom of religious conscience had become the model of virtue. But that freedom is private, and the virtue it defines may also be privatised. On the other hand, the tendency toward privatisation goes together with a democratisation of society brought about by the rupture with the monarchy and the elimination of the artifical divisions created by its politics. The republic becomes the political form which guarantees private freedom, including the freedom of socioeconomic interests. Privatised virtue no longer has a place in the political sphere.

The problem posed to Americans for the past two centuries by these developments remain our own: that of the compatability between a republican politics founded on public virtue and a commercial society based on the private interest of the abstract and isolated individual. This was the question which the so-called 'progressive historians' of the early twentieth century reformulated after the closing of the frontier: is the creation and the freeing of the capitalist economy the normal completion of a political revolution? To this question must be added, however, another: if the capitalist economy, with all its faults, is the product of a political revolution, should one also seek to remedy its evils by political means? If so, by what political means?

## 4. WHERE PHILOSOPHY LEADS

This reconstruction of American history could be mistaken for what is called today neo-conservative thought. That approach distinguishes society from its political representation; the resulting depoliticisation of society serves well the established order. To treat the political as an independent variable seems to imply at the same time the refusal to permit society to transform itself. The quest for justice is relegated to the private sphere. The end of political ideologies is justified by the same move. The political participation characteristic of democracy is replaced by a technocratic governance which cannot call itself by its own name because it thinks that it is founded by the eternal laws of a market which it wants to 'liberate' from the grasp of a providential State. The immediate moral demand for justic is confronted by a reply which appeals to the complexity of problems and their rootedness in a long secular history. Private virtue is supposed to be the foundation of this antipolitics.

Retrospectively, it is not obvious that the role given by the Constitution of 1787 to the multiplicity of particular interests did not facilitate or even encourage the domination of the political by the economic. The political institutions which were supposed to make scientific use of human nature in order to dominate over its evil tendencies proved incapable of giving society a direction. As Hegel once said, it appears that the United States never really became a modern nation-state; the political 'administration' in Washington has not shown itself capable of truly governing the country. But in this case, the neo-conservative argument based on the separation of the social and the political is not valid. What exists in the United States as political life would be a perpetual self-transformation of economic society, a kind of permanent revolution guaranteed by constitutional mechanisms which, in good Whig fashion, guarantee that none of the branches of government can claim to incarnate the popular will.

These two interpretations of the contemporary problems of the United States are in fact based on a single principle: the American revolution institutionalised the division between the political and the social; and it is the latter which dominates even when the analysis tries to privilege the political. American politics reproduces the structure of the economic market, with all its distortions, but also with all its advantages. The social associations in which Tocqueville saw the political salvation of the country become lobbies representing corporative interests. The famous thesis of Robert Bellah which suggests that a civil religion occupies the place left empty by politics has recently been questioned by Bellah himself, who sees in the multiplication of sects and religious denominations an attempt by the churches to cope with the demands emerging from an increasingly fragmented society.

We come back finally to the comparison of the French and the American Revolutions. Hannah Arendt's *On Revolution* (1963) tried to show that the French Revolution was undermined by its orientation toward the social whereas the American was saved by its ability to institutionalise the political space. The preceding analysis suggests that the inverse is the case. Jürgen Habermas proposes one explication when he distinguishes two notions of natural law. For the French, natural law was an ideal to be realised, which had to be imposed by force if necessary; for the Americans, natural law was a real state of affairs which political intervention could only distort. From this point of view, it is not surprising to find the critic of the rationalist pretentions of the French Revolution, Burke, taking the side of the American colonist in their conflict with England. The American Revolution would be thus a conservative restauration whose ethic was basically antimodern and antipolitical. The true modern revolution would be the French, which sought to impose a single and unified will on a disparate society. The American freedom, as opposed to French equality, would be an archaic form for which modern society has no place.

This conclusion does not explain the economic modernisation of

American society since the Revolution. How can that modernisation be explained within the frame of the 'political' institutions created by the Revolution? Are those institutions in fact modern? and in what sense?

Treating the French Revolution as the model of a modern revolution neglects a fundamental lesson of the American experience. If a revolution is a transformation operated by society on itself, the mediation by which society appeals to what it is not – the political – to realise its goals must be explained. When the political instance is treated as distinct and external to society, the imperative of modernity is violated. A modern form – be it political, aesthetic, scientific, or even religious – is characterised by its immanence. A real political instance, be it monarchy, theocracy, or technocracy, recreates the structure that was imagined by the Whig theory's vision of a struggle of freedom against an already existing power. In the case of the French Revolution, the structure is different, but the principle remains the same. The monarchy, which incarnates the will of the nation, and thus its freedom, struggles against the intermediary powers which prevent its self-realisation. The Revolution changes only the actors, not the basic structure. Whether we are dealing with a struggle of the will against power or that of freedom against power, changes nothing in the institutional logic being analysed.

The American Revolution began from the Whig theory and ended with its radical inversion. Rather than protecting freedom against power, the sovereign and independent nation found itself obliged to invent institutions in which freedom could be incorporated. But at the same time the plural society which changes itself by setting up these institutions cannot claim to be incarnate in those same political institutions. The people in its plurality – the Preamble to the Constitution of 1787 declares, 'We, the people . . . ' – is the foundation *and the limit* of political action. This plural people reserves and preserves its political judgement. It does not claim to speak in the name of some principle nor to dictate eternal truths; in particular, it does not claim that this plural people can be *really* unified in a single class, interest or institution. The political instance, the Constitution, is treated as a norm; it is neither a reality nor an actor on the social stage. The society which appeals to the political instance to transform itself relates to the political as a symbolic mediation which permits it to understand itself in its specificity and to define the goals that it pursues. This non-real, *symbolic* status of the political explains why the American Revolution has no end, in both senses of that term.

If this revolutionary structure that emerged from 'pre-modern' political demands is adequate to the imperatives of modernity, the inadequacies of its present form must be explained. This is not the place to repeat the usual criticisms of contemporary American society. We are concerned with the political. From the point of view of institutional norms, nothing prevents the society from transforming itself by means of an appeal to the political. But that appeal should not be conceived on the model of the French Revolution. The problem is not one of governmental intervention but of the action of society on itself by means of the symbolic mediation of the political. Change is prepared when two demands appear together: that for a universality, presented at first by law and in the last instance by the Constitution; and that of a particularity which permits the social articulation of that universality. That is what we experienced, for example, during the Civil Rights movement when social actions like the sit-ins showed the contradiction between positive law and the Constitution. Such a movement is liable to two sorts of failures: when social action neglects the level of universality, and when the appeal to constitutional law tries to get along without the support of a social movement.

The American Revolution is modern in the specific sense that it results from, and it invites, the action of society on itself. This is the sense in which it is a political revolution and that the politics it institutes remains modern. But this structure is not without theoretical and empirical problems. Is it necessary that the economy dominate the society, as it tends to do in capitalist societies? How can the political instance permit society to give itself another set of norms? It seems to be the case that the political institutions create the space within which capitalist relations take form. But if these political institutions have a symbolic status, how can one understand and put into practice social transformation?

## Notes

1. For example, John Adams answered his own question in a letter of 1815 to his former enemy Thomas Jefferson: 'What do we mean by the

revolution? The war? That was no part of the Revolution; it was only an effect and a consequence of it. The Revolution was in the minds of the people, and this was effected, from 1760 to 1775, in the course of fifteen years before a drop of blood was shed at Lexington. The records of thirteen legislatures, the pamplets, newspapers of all the colonies, ought to be consulted during that period to ascertain the steps by which the public opinion was enlightened and informed concerning the authority of Parliament over the colonies.'

2. For example, the revolutionary Doctor, Benjamin Rush, argued in 1787, at the moment of the framing of the new national Constitution: 'The American war is over: but this is far from being the case with the American revolution. On the contrary, nothing but the first act of the great drama is closed. It remains yet to establish and perfect our new forms of government, and to prepare the principles, morals, and manners of our citizens for these forms of government after they are established and brought to perfection.'
3. For example, his book, *The Republic* (1943), sees the Constitution as the only alternative to a military dictatorship; his general *History of the United States* (1944) sees in the system of checks and balances a protection against despotism whereas in 1913 he treated it as a means for defusing popular energies. At the end of his career, Beard was a nationalist and an isolationist. For the logic of this development, and for a general treatment of American historiography in this period, see David W. Noble, *The End of American History. Democracy, capitalism, and the metaphor of two worlds in Anglo-American Historical Writing, 1880–1980* (Minneapolis: University of Minnesota Press, 1985).
4. For the sake of completeness, it should be noted that the influence of Shaftesbury, and of Scottish moral philosophy, played a role here. The Scottish theory of moral intuition, for example in the writings of Thomas Reid, had an important influence in the colonies because, among other things, of the role of the President of Princeton University, Joseph Witherspoon. Witherspoon was a delegate to the Constitutional Convention; but more important is the fact that among his students are numbered a President, a Vice-President, 21 Senators, 29 Congressmen, 12 State governors, 56 State legislators, and 33 Judges, of whom 3 sat on the Supreme Court. Garry Wills has attempted to document the influence of Scottish thought in America's institutions in a series of studies, including *Inventing America* (1978) and *Explaining America* (1981). Interesting, his analyses are not convincing.

# 14 The Republic and the International Order

The French translation of Stanley Hoffmann's *Duties Beyond Borders*[1] put the book into a political context of which its author could have been only partially aware. The book was written before the Socialists came to power in 1981; before the Left, and even the Right, began to discover the virtues of a certain liberalism; and before a Euro-pacifist movement had shaken the foundations of the standard views of socialist foreign policy, at least in France. Hoffmann's arguments could be used differently by different partisans. The attempt by the 'second left' journal, *Intervention*, to pose the questions that underlie present socialist practice suggests a more theoretical approach. This orientation is justified by Hoffmann's own arguments, even though he only hints at the philosophical issues which concern me here. The contrast between American-style liberalism and a European variant best described by the concept 'republican' casts theoretical light at the same time that it has practical implications for classical political theory, whose problems are not so dated as they may seem.

A quarter of a century in the United States explains in part the psychology, and some of the tics, in Hoffmann's provocative and yet frustrating book. The author was born in Vienna and educated in France, where he was a student of Raymond Aron, a critic of the 'blocked society' that hindered French modernisation, and an interpreter of the new Gaullist phenomenon. This background explains that he has not forgotten the lessons of *realpolitik*, or the permanent tension of an ethic of responsibility and an ethic of conviction. He knows how to turn theory against supposed pragmatists while brandishing a tactical realism in the face of utopian *naïveté*. The Harvard professor, on the other hand, is more relaxed. Although he refers frequently to Kant, he dialogues mainly with his contemporaries, whom he supposes well-known and worthy of attention. Ethical questions are not addressed in a classical form; they are approached through replays of the debates between Rawls, Walzer, Beitz, Falk & Co. The relaxed style permits logic to give way to example, argument to illustration, recommendation to prudence. After all, we are warned at the threshhold of the final chapter, Hoffmann's project is not philosophy but 'applied morality' (189). But the European had begun his presentation by opposing the 'applied morality' which he attributed to Walzer. His stated goal was to be a 'political scientist' whose analysis is to be 'an attempt at uplifting politics' (1–2).

The European would not have written so provocative a book; the American would not have tried. Hoffmann picks apart repeatedly the American attempt to save moral good conscience by means that are finally only differing forms of hypocrisy founded on the denial of the real effects of their professed good intentions. He is ironic in his criticism of professors who become 'the adviser of the prince': 'I have enough colleagues who have professionally been doing this, with results which are the best evidence ever given for the merits of ivory towers' (28). The European repeats frequently the phrase: the enemy of the better is the best. Americans' moralism simply can't play the international game. Theirs is an attitude which is not only naïve but, worse, manichaean and antipolitical. Its domestic consequences – for example, after the 'loss' of China in 1949 – need not be overstressed. Hoffmann's critique of the antipolitical *naïveté* of such moralism, for example in the case of the Rawlsians, is more important. The abstract ethical demand to give aid to the poor of Bangladesh before taking care of the poor in the Appalachians excludes discussion of the tactics that might permit one to reach goals which, although moderate, are at least realisable (155). The philosophical moralist replaces political judgement by the brutal affirmation of a universal 'ought'. Such a tyranny of good intentions destroys the efficacy of a politics which would like to be anti-tyrannical.

While criticising American moralism, Hoffmann also denounces the complementary moralism more familiar to the European. This position insists on the specificity of politics and the unique responsibility of the State. For example, Third World states demand aid from wealthier former colonisers, yet they refuse to give the grantors any control over its utilisation, balking at questions of human rights or the introduction of democratic institutions. The arguments Hoffmann uses to criticise the claim that such control would amount to an interference with 'sovereignty' are formally identical to the ones he used against the American moralists. The separation of politics from morality is no more satisfactory than their identification. Similarly, Hoffmann's discussion of distributive justice denounces remedies for underdevelopment which share an absolutist premise. Whether they begin from the simple denunciation of exploitation, or the asymmetry of centre and periphery, or forms of neo-imperialism (with or without the collaboration of the multinationals), these absolutisms make the determination of a politics which has a real chance of success impossible. However Hoffmann's own proposals are disappointing. To speak of 'the necessity of eclecticism' (175) or an 'equilibriated view of things' (183) or 'a certain modesty' (184) is hardly a counterproposal.

## 1. LIBERALISM, AMERICAN STYLE

Hoffmann defines his politics as liberalism, American style. 'To be a liberal,' he writes, 'does not mean necessarily to believe in progress, it means only to believe in a limited and reversible perfectibility of man and society, and particularly in the possibility of devising institutions based on consent that will make society more human and more just, and the citiziens' lot better.' (8) Such a liberalism, he continues, is built upon and preserves a morality based on the individual, not on the class or the nation. Its political implications are reformist, not revolutionary. But, 'This does not mean that I believe revolutions to be necessarily evil or even avoidable. They are often inevitable, and sometimes beneficial, given the alternatives.' (9–10) Since Hoffmann is not playing 'adviser to the prince', he might have explained this attitude toward social change by reference to his favourite philosopher. Kant was troubled by the same dilemma when confronted with the French Revolution, whose results he supported although he could not find a place in his philosophy for a *principle* of revolution.[2] But Kant was a *republican*, not an American liberal. Hoffmann's liberal takes from him only the argument that any action said to be moral must also be realisable. A moral imperative which cannot be realised is a contradiction in terms. This insistence is important; it suggests that Hoffmann is seeking more than just an abstract moral standpoint.

For the American liberal, political action is structured by a double relation. It must take account of the relation of the individual to the state, and that of the state to the world order. Individual rights can exist only within a sovereign state.[3] What, then, is to be done to a state which violates the rights of individual citizens? The problem of intervention brings together the two horns of the double relation defining political action. The liberal can find grounds for justifying intervention, or for condemning its practice. Hoffmann's discussion of the Turkish intervention in Cyprus, or the Somalian involvement in the Ethiopian Ogaden illustrate his conclusion that moral politics is an art of execution, not a system of formal but abstract principles. The dual political relation permits the justification of intervention insofar as the sovereign state is itself bound to the existence of a world structure in which reciprocal rights and duties are recognised. When that world structure is threatened, the state itself – and therefore the individuals within that state – suffer consequences. This justifies the use of force against an aggression that threatens the very principles of a structured world order (although it may pose empirical problems as to the seriousness of the threat; and it may confront value judgements in conditions of civil war). However, this justification of the use of force does not work in one crucial case. The paradoxical logic of nuclear deterrence depends on the reality of the threat to unleash a blow which would end all human order, destroying both states and individuals.

The dual logics which relate the state and the individual on the one hand, the state and the world order on the other, are built on the liberal premise of the primacy of individual rights. This provides the basis of Hoffmann's moral theory. His first chapter examines the place of ethics in international relations. He plays out the objections to utilitarianism and to a political realism based only on the notion of the national interest. A moral politics has at least the advantage of giving some direction to the actors, as well as to those trying to understand their action (43). The basis of Hoffmann's argument here is a commonsense Kant. He begins from the distinction of the noumenal ethical world, where freedom and morality hold sway, and the phenomenal domain of experience, where causality and determinism permit a calculation which, although formally certain, is useless because it takes place in the realm of mere appearances. This permits a critique of any politics based on good intentions alone, since one cannot know that these intentions will be followed by the desired effects. It permits also the rejection of a utilitarian politics whose calculations in the phenomenal world cannot be certain. In international politics, which deals with a plurality of actors who are as much subjects as they are objects on whom each seeks to act, this assertion did not need to be formulated in Kantian jargon to be accepted. If Hoffmann's liberal morality can in fact provide a guideline removed from the world of appearance, its political implications are not yet evident at this first stage.

Liberal morality has to be shown to be compatible with the need to act politically. The utopian satisfactions of the empty goodwill do not suffice. Hoffmann turns to the dilemmas posed by the need to legitimate the use of force. Although the old doctrine of the Just War is no longer applicable in the secular modern world, it still provides methodological guidelines. Hoffmann applies the notions of proportionality, hierarchy, and especially the 'double effect' rule (concerning potential costs to civilians) to contemporary historical examples. The guidelines prove useful, to a point; they permit the refinement of sub-categories of forceful intervention. But in the process they move toward a kind of utilitarian casuistry. The extreme to which this kind of reasoning is forced appears in the discussion of the neutron bomb, which seems to fit the Just War categories. Hoffmann rejects it because of the 'symbolic' implications of breaking the nuclear taboo. Rather than develop this concept of 'symbolic implications', Hoffmann takes a different tack, as if he recognised the dangers of simple casuistic enumeration. He reformulates his premisses, suggesting that morality is not situated at the level of the means to *make* war; morality concerns the ways to *avoid war*. The citizen enters at this point, but only briefly, in order to provide a transition to the discussion of human rights in the third chapter.

The liberal recognises that the avoidance of war depends on domestic as well as international conditions. A theory of the Rights of Man has to begin from the question of their nature: are they political or social, acquired or inherent, negative freedoms from or positive freedoms for? Hoffmann rehearses the well-known arguments from each of these standpoints, attempting to avoid conclusions which would force him into the Cold War trap of defining his Western liberalism by opposition to the Eastern forms of socialism. He escapes this facile temptation by insisting on the individual foundation of both aspects of the dual political relations. The result is to be a 'modest' politics which tries to integrate political and economic rights according to a doctrine whose major criterion is 'coherence'. Unlike the previous shift to avoid war rather than to moralise about its means, this move does not change the terrain of the argument. The illustrations offered seem closer to the Just War casuistry, formulated this time on the basis of the primacy of an asserted 'world order' perspective whose relation to the liberal individual is not spelled out. As if he saw the difficulty, Hoffmann concludes that violations of the Rights of Man are manifestations of deeper structural problems, to which his fourth chapter turns under the heading of distributive justice.

Perhaps because he is admittedly not a technical economist, Hoffmann's presentation of the dilemmas of global economics is the most succinct section of his book. His conclusion is that 'science' in this domain is merely pretext; the prescriptions of the various authors determine their diagnostics. It follows that the discussion of distributive justice cannot be left to the technicians. As in the critiques of utilitarianism and realism in Chapter 1, morality again finds its place as a guide to practical inquiry. But this solution retreats from the major premise of Hoffmann's liberalism, which insisted on the dual relation between individual and state on the one hand, state and world order on the other. Instead of presenting a new politics, Hoffmann's concluding chapter offers 'An Ethics of World Order'. This title suggests the transition from an individualist liberal ethics to a political morality which would not sacrifice that individual whose place is fundamental for the liberal. Yet, despite the proposed primacy of the 'world order', nothing new emerges. Just as the shift from morality in the use of force to morality as avoiding its use became a casuistry founded on the 'coherence' of a human rights politics, so here the new conceptual terrain opened by the logic of Hoffmann's argument is closed quickly.

## 2. LIBERALISM, EUROPEAN STYLE

Another reading of the material analysed by Hoffmann can be suggested. It can be called 'European' when we recall the American liberal's willingness to accept revolutions which have taken place even while hoping that a reformist path to the same ends can be found. That was the position of Kant's *republican*. A contemporary reformulation is suggested by Hoffmann's insistence on the primacy of the World Order, which is a *decentring* of the type made popular by contemporary French philosophers. This decentring puts an end to any political philosophy conceived in terms of a 'constitutive subject' whose action totalises the empirical world and gives it sense. The decentring refutes a political theory based on the primacy of either the liberal individual or the liberal state, let alone the proletariat, or the Third World. This is consistent with Hoffmann's dual political logic which cannot be reduced to a linear model of cause and effect. Hoffmann's Kantianism suggests calling the new stance a 'Copernican Revolution'. The result is not that the state is abolished, any more than the liberal individual is eliminated. Hoffmann's insistence on the sovereignty of the state as necessary to the protection of individual rights remains valid. The decentring occurs on a second level. It takes the form of a co-existence of multiple cultures, values, ways of living a common world. A 'European' politics is not identical with the actions of the 'Common Market'.

Hoffmann's American liberalism does not draw the republican conclusions implicit in the structures he describes.[4] A recent study of the French republican tradition suggests a manner of concretising the Kantian morality.[5] Whereas the liberal model postulates a negative or limiting relation between the national order and the individual, republican thought seeks to establish structures of participation. In the context of the decentred world of international relations, this would mean that the relation between the world order and the nation states is not defined by exclusion. A 'world republic' would establish a positive interaction between the two logics of political action which, as Hoffmann has shown, define the space for a moral intervention into politics. This would explain the transition to a world-order-ethics; it would permit Hoffmann to clarify the transitions between his chapters without falling back from the new terrain to the older casuistry. For example, the discussion of human rights concluded that 'a human rights policy is a kind of first timid step, *faute de mieux* – an oblique way to handle political change as an international issue' (139). This American liberalism is a defensive stance which at best can give direction to a reactive politics. The 'European' republican position should permit the elaboration of a positive politics which creates new relations among and within states.

This republican orientation can be deduced from Hoffmann's account in a more philosophical formulation. The discussion of modern arms, planetary technology and economic disorder, and the assertion that the 'world order' is in fact a powder-keg full of 'Austria-Hungaries' (201) poses a classical philosophical problem: *how to create cosmos from chaos*? Traditional political philosophy asked how to explain the leap from a state of nature to an organised political state. From the standpoint of the individual, this philosophy encounters an apparent vicious circle: if obligation is to exist, there must already exist the very order which this duty is obliged to create and preserve. From the standpoint of the state, if perpetual peace among states is to exist, there must exist already ordered and legitimate relations among states. In Hoffmann's own words: 'The aim of a human rights policy is to establish a moderate, livable world order, and yet the precondition for success, for the effectiveness of a human rights policy is that the world already be moderate . . . that there are not too many states or governments depending for their very life on violations of human rights' (139–40). Kant's solution to these classical dilemmas was new. His 'Idea of World History from a Cosmopolitan Point of View' explained how men come to constitute a 'civil society under law' by recourse to international relations. Hoffmann refers to these passages. 'It was Kant,' he notes, 'who predicted that nations would move toward peace not because of the moral will and virtue of human beings, but because of the terror of modern weapons and because of greed – people being dragged by the horror of modern war and by material need' (37). But Hoffmann's liberalism does not draw the consequences of this philosophical insight.

## 3. REPUBLICANISM AND CLASSICAL POLITICAL PHILOSOPHY

We are living a crisis of the political models and theories on which the modern nation state was founded. International politics renews the classical questions on which these old theories were built. The war of all against all from which a sovereign state was to emerge by means of a bargain between individual freedom and personal security returns at the level of relations among states. Hoffmann's analyses of the role of force, of human rights and distributive justice were intended to point to a modest, realistic and reasonable linear path to the creation of order. The frustrations and contradictions in his analysis are due to his forgetting the classical vicious circle on which his liberal political theory is founded. When he does see the necessity to shift to a new terrain to deal with new problems, he fails to get beyond the objective description because his analysis is limited explicitly to the standpoint of the state and the statesman (9). Such an analysis remains at the constitutive level; it does not draw the 'Copernican' implications from the decentring that his own dual political logic describes. Rather than develop the 'symbolic' significance of the neutron bomb, he seems to draw back at the logic of nuclear deterrence as if the choice were between the Anglo-Saxons, Hobbes and the more modest Locke. But his own internationalist decentring forbids either alternative.

The republican translation of the classical dilemma of political philosophy was formulated by Kant as the question, 'What is Enlightenment?' The French republicans were more practical; they were concerned with public or civic education, which they called a 'demopedagogy'.[6] This education is explicitly *political*. Hoffmann's Kantian ethical guideline does not help here; it is a priori and noumenal whereas politics is a posteriori and phenomenal. Morality as a priori cannot be taught or learned. Hence, when Hoffmann has to make practical recommendations, he 'phenomenalises' his morality; it becomes a 'feeling' of 'obligation' which did not exist 50 years ago (157, 102), or an 'incipient cosmopolitanism' (95), a 'fragile sense of duty' (165) which must somehow be reinforced. Since Hoffmann has correctly insisted that a duty which cannot be realised is not a duty, the slippage from the a priori to the a posteriori seems to entail the return of a utilitarian casuistry of costs and benefits. This calculation is the ratiocination of a constitutive subject, state or individual; it neglects the imperatives imposed by the dual political logic Hoffmann had shown to be necessary in international relations.

The republican 'demopedagogy' concretised by Kant's 'Cosmopolitan History' was developed in a remarkable analysis by the German historian, Otto Hintze.[7] Hintze's comparative study of the origins of the representative constitution shows that the diplomatic relations established among the Italian City-States during the Renaissance distinguish Western developments from all others. The practice of diplomacy presupposes the impossibility of a world-empire or a unified international state; it depends on the existence of a plural world-order in which state sovereignty is preserved and individual rights (eventually) protected. The world of sovereign states creates structures of space and time which make possible a representation of the way we live together in society. Such representations differ from the unreflexive shared everyday attitudes and interests of the citizen within a single nation state. The plural structures of such a world order create the conditions for the dual logic of political action defined by Hoffmann's liberalism. The space-time on which diplomatic relations depend is not the same as the one that structures the all-or-nothing world of the moralist, the utopian or the manichaean. It is based on the *decentring* which diplomacy presupposes and reaffirms constantly. This distinction between the space-time of the world-order and the non-reflexive space-time of domestic political life makes possible a Kantian form of the republican 'demopedagogics'.[8]

The decentred structures of international relations point to a further contribution of Kant to a republican politics. Concepts such as modesty, moderation, prudence recur frequently in Hoffmann's discussion. Although these sometimes give the impression that the author has turned casuist, he himself suggests a different view. Moderation, for example, 'entails simply taking into account the existence of moral claims of others' (33). Kant could not have said it better. 'All the precepts I advocated,' continues Hoffmann, 'suppose a great deal of public discussion, a very limited amount of secrecy, a very limited possibility of cooking up Machiavellian schemes in the dark' (36). The author of 'Perceptual Peace' expected that just such public discussion would guarantee his proposed Treaty establishing it. The foundation of Hoffmann's agreement with Kant is suggested at the conclusion of the analysis of distributive justice, which warns that progress is 'more prudential than moral' (184–5). This 'prudence' is what the Greeks called *phronesis*, and what Kant called 'reflective judgement'. Prudence, as opposed to morality, can be learned. It is the philosophical formulation of the aim of the republican demopedagogy.

As opposed to ethical and scientific reason, which subsume particulars under pre-given, a priori universal laws, reflective judgement begins from the particular to search for its specific kind of lawfulness. When I affirm that a painting is beautiful, I affirm that you, too, must find it beautiful. My assertion is not based on a physical law or a moral a priori; nor can I presuppose that we share inherent values or a common culture. I say, 'put yourself in my place', after I have put myself in yours in making the judgement. I insist that a public discussion without preconditions will bring us to agreement. The same conditions define a political judgement which avoids the temptations of a technocratic scientism and a moral absolutism. The analogy between Kant's aesthetic judgement and republican political judgement is founded by their common concern with representation. The Kantian republic was to guarantee a framework in which individuals had constantly the freedom to exercise publicly their political judgement. Domestic republican institutions are made possible by the new space-time that emerges with the necessary co-existence of sovereign states in a world order from which the formation of a unified world-state is excluded. The 'republican' world-order, conversely, is made possible by the autonomy of the individual within these republics whose quest for a moral politics demands the affirmation of the sovereignty of each.

The crisis of established political theory is due to its inability to break with the subsumptive judgement which reduces the particular problems of politics to simple instances of a general lawfulness. This orientation is based on a constitutive theory which privileges either the individual or the state as the subject of politics. The decentring made necessary by international relations brings the issue to a head. International relations are not simply the macrocosmic formulation of the classical liberal problem of the origin of the state. Hoffmann insists rightly on the dual logic governing international relations. But he neglects the *symbolic* nature of these logics which is underlined by the Kantian theory of judgement. Not every object can be called beautiful; not every moral sin demands political retribution. Why do only some particulars call for the reflective political (or aesthetic) judgement? The *de facto* international republican order affects domestic political choices; the necessary imbrication of states within the world-order transforms technical or moral issues into political problems. It operates a *mise en scène* which de-realises the apparently obvious choices. The domestic implications of Hoffmann's intuition concerning the symbolic importance of the neutron bomb must be generalised. This is not an affirmation of the old *Primat der Aussenpolitik*; our 'Duties beyond Borders' make possible our political *judgements* at home. The 'international republic' imposes symbolic mediations within the domestic republic. These can become the basis for a theory which redefines the political domain.

**Notes**

1. The French edition was published by Editions du Seuil; the English by Syracuse University Press, 1981. Pages indicated in parentheses in the text below refer to the latter edition
2. See my essay, 'Kant's Political Theory: The Virtue of His Vices', in *Review of Metaphysics*, vol. XXXIV, no. 2, December, 1980, pp. 325–50, reprinted in *The Politics of Critique*, for the problem; and *From Marx to Kant* for a proposed solution.
3. The most powerful demonstration of this argument, not cited by Hoffmann, is found in Hannah Arendt's *The Origins of Totalitarianism*, whose chapter 9 illustrates abundantly 'The Decline of the Nation-State and the End of the Rights of Man'.
4. The book's concluding lines are that 'it is not necessary to hope in order to act, nor to succeed in order to persevere'. This is presumably Hoffmann's secular reading of Kant, since it falls under the sub-heading 'Some reflections on cosmopolitanism and the art of governing'. Kant's 'cosmopolitan' theory of history would permit other arguments, as I shall show in Part 3, below.
5. See Claude Nicolet, *L'idée républicaine en France* (Paris: Gallimard, 1982). One central theme in Nicolet's extraordinary study concerns the difference between liberalism and republicanism. Although the book, alas! has no index, cf, pp. 108, 137, 256, 342ff, 357, 397, 417, 451, and 467ff. Nicolet only alludes to Kant in passing, as his philosophy

influences the tradition described. The influences can be traced back to the very origins of French republicanism, in the attempt to set up a correspondence between Kant and the Abbé Sièyes!

6. Cf. Nicolet, op. cit., p. 295. A more concrete formulation of this 'demopedagogics' could be suggested by drawing on one of Stanley Hoffmann's (unmentioned) Harvard colleagues. Hoffmann stresses the plurality of traditions and cultures which make moral judgement in international relations difficult. Lawrence Kohlberg's social psychology suggests that rather than concentrate on the specific contents of moral theory we should analyse the level at which moral argumentation occurs. A 'demopedagogy' would be concerned with the development of a theory of learning how to make moral or political judgements. Such learning depends on a symbolic mediation by means of which a not-yet existing ideal draws empirical actors into the process of its own realisation. In this sense, Nicolet cites Gambetta's acceptance of the less-than-perfect forms of the Third Republic in 1875 on the grounds that 'the form will carry with it the content'. Such a learning process is described in Kohlbergian terms by the critical theorist, Klaus Eder, in *Geschichte als Lernprozess. Zur Pathogenese politischer Modernität in Deutschland* (Frankfurt: Suhrkamp, 1985).
7. Hintze's essay is translated in Felix Gilbert, ed., *The Historical Essays of Otto Hintze* (New York: Oxford University Press, 1975). Hintze himself does not refer to Kant; I have developed the argument suggested here in *From Marx to Kant*.
8. I cannot treat here the French republican version of this doctrine, which – despite Nicolet's optimistic account – degenerated to the form of a simple republican pedagogy teaching a kind of lay catechism. One contributory element in this decline was the conception of the republic as *one*, a unity in which all tended to be(come) alike. This neglects the necessity of social plurality which the irreducible sovereignty of states makes unavoidable at the level of international relations.

# Part III

# Origins of the Political

## B. The Practice of Normative Theory

# 15 The Political Origins of Democracy

## 1. POLITICS AFTER 'THE' REVOLUTION

The heading under which I introduce these remarks points toward the conclusion at which I will arrive. It also suggests some of the premisses from which these reflections begin. First of all, I am bothered by the abuse of the concept of democracy which assimilates it simply to the interest of the so-called free world. This refusal of simplification for political ends holds for another abuse of the concept of democracy which has taken root recently in France, especially among an intelligentsia seeking to make amends for its former sins of philocommunism. To awaken from the dream of happy tomorrows and to uncover everywhere the seeds of totalitarianism is not a politics. But these twin abuses are not without significance. Claude Lefort, who cannot be accused of either deviation, suggests an orientation for further analysis when he subtitles *L'invention démocratique* 'The Limits of Totalitarian Domination' instead of opposing simply a 'critique' of totalitarianism to a praise of democracy.[1] Democracy and totalitarianism are not simply antithetical. The analysis of their relation has to pass through the mediation by the *political* structure of modern societies, which I will define as republican. As a political form, democracy expresses a society's self-understanding, its vision of the good life, which cannot be fixed by a simple formula or procedure. It is not a fact but the expression of the *sense* of social action. Its relation to totalitarianism makes clear that this sense must be constantly reaffirmed if it is not to degenerate.

I was going to begin these remarks under the heading 'post-revolutionary politics'. Aside from the fact that I dislike the modish application of 'posts' that has gained public favour recently and that serves to cover over the need for analysis, such a title would have led to confusion because I do not intend to talk about what should be done once 'we' have 'taken power'. The implicit assumption made by 'revolutionary politics' in fact separates power from politics; it introduces a pre-modern image in which the political sphere is conceived as if it were a thing or place that could be occupied and whose command could bring about social transformations which would, ultimately, permit the political state to 'wither away' because society would become capable of self-government. I speak instead of politics after 'the' revolution to indicate the refusal of the idea of a transparent society which has become, finally, reconciled with itself and in which, as Engels put it, the government over men has been replaced by the administration of things. That representation of 'revolutionary politics' ignores the symbolic role of the political and denies its difference from other social facts. But to give up on 'the' revolution does not imply the acceptance of the established order. It is necessary to conceptualise here the philosophical *origin* of this attitude whose empirical foundation is no doubt the fact that we are living 'after' the totalitarian revolution. But totalitarianism itself must also be explained. Its *origin* is found in the political structure of democracy itself.

My introductory title suggests another premise of the argument. That dichotomy of politics and power which I reject is founded on a representation which imagines political forms as if they were things. 'Democracy' is opposed to 'totalitarianism' as if each were a fixed essence which is unchanged by any relation into which it enters. Beyond the methodological criticism of that representation of politics, I want now to draw from it a positive implication. At the time of the American Revolution – which, it should be recalled, *was* a revolution – many people spoke of 'the democracy' as a thing, or rather as a threat which weighed on the newly independent state. 'The democracy' was the masses, the populace, or what philosophical jargon calls 'civil society'. The threat that it represented should not be reduced to its simple economic consequences; the threat was political, symbolic, endangering the meaning of those actions by which the colonists had become a free people. The American Revolution, it will be recalled, claimed to be republican; it felt itself threatened by the mercantile spirit for the same reason that 'the democracy' was a threat: the *res publica*, the public thing, had to be protected against private interests, be they majority or minority interests. This republican argument can of course be demystified by a progressive or a Marxist historian; but the reductionism supposed by that demystification is not a politics. The politics I propose to consider here will take as its premise the development of that American Revolution which realised, in its way, the republic.

One last premise needs to be mentioned. When 'the' revolution is not identified with the Bolshevik Revolution, it is often conceived in terms of the French Revolution. But the French model poses problems of its own. Was it the work of 14 July? The night of 4 August? Or the more 'radical' moments which continue in a linked process up to the fall of Robespierre, if not beyond? If I introduce the French Revolution into these reflections, it is not in order to return to the famous thesis of Hannah Arendt which suggests that the American Revolution succeeded because it knew how to remain at the political level whereas the French Revolution was undermined by the contradictions imposed on it by the social question. That dichotomous formulation is too simple for the historian, too exclusive for the philosopher. Once again, politics is not reducible to a thing, whose essential nature can be opposed to another fixed identity called society; politics is concerned with the way in which a society makes sense of itself by means of an appeal to what it *is not* and can never fully become. Because politics expresses the symbolic dimension of society, it is always confronted by its own inherent historicity. I introduce the French Revolution into my premisses because its analysis by François Furet, in *Penser la Révolution Française*, permits me to treat the question of democracy without falling into a manichaeanism which distorts the nature of the political. The origin of that manichaeanism explains why politics is inherently symbolic and historical.

## 2. THE MODERNITY OF REVOLUTION

What is one trying to explain when one analyses a revolution? Attention can be directed to its objective causes, the material necessities which explain why things had to take the course that they did. But the existence of these causes does not explain the modality of action, the process by which men and women become conscious of those so-called material necessities. The problem comes from the separation of the subject and the object. Thus, Furet shows how Tocqueville's analysis of the Ancien Régime has to be completed by the study of the new modes of political behaviour by new actors described by Cochin. But the problem remains: how is one to conceptualise the unity of that juxtaposition of the two approaches? The concept of 'thinking' (*penser*) in the title of Furet's study has philosophical resonances. 'The' revolution is neither what existed before, nor what came to exist after. The historian wants to reproduce the unity of the material foundation and of a mode of action. But that unity no longer exists. 'The' revolution is known only from its manifestations; it expresses the symbolic sense of an historical action.

The Before and the After can be represented; but 'the' revolution has to be thought as its own origin. Conceived in this manner, the revolution inaugurates *modernity*.

This identification of a revolutionary origin and modernity has to be elucidated. When we speak of a science or an art, an institution or a state, as modern, we are affirming that the structure being analysed is autonomous and self-legitimating. We are saying that its *genesis* and the *norm* which legitimates that institution are *immanent* to it. From this point of view, the two moments which are unified in 'the' revolution can be conceived of as that of its genesis and that of its normativity. This is why the revolution can be called 'modern'. But we know that the path that began on 14 July 1789 was tortuous; we know that Thermidor was followed by a succession of regimes whose conclusion was the Empire and its defeat; indeed, Furet affirms that, in a certain sense, the entire history of modern France (which was perhaps concluded in 1981) can be conceived of as the vain pursuit of that promise which I am calling the entry into modernity, and which Furet calls the Republic.[2] The categories of genesis and normativity can explain what Furet calls the 'skids' (*dérapages*) in the path of the revolution. These skids, in turn, permit me to make more clear what I mean by the concept of origin.

Without going into the historical details, one can say that there is a skid in an originary structure when the constitutive tension between genesis and normativity becomes either too loose or unbearable for its actors who are driven to break out of it. The result can be a politics in which genesis determines normativity; an example would be the Jacobin moment in which the appeal to *le Peuple* results in the elimination of all constitutional protections for real people. The result can also be a politics in which normativity determines genesis; an example would be the politics of the Directory which was so concerned with assuring its own legitimacy that it made the established institutions inoperable. Other forms of this skid away from the originary revolutionary unity are possible. What served as a genetic principle can invert itself and function as a norm; an example would be the appeal to *la Patrie en danger*. Similarly, what served as a legitimating norm can be inverted to serve as an animating principle of society; an example would be the abandonment of its role by the Constituent Assembly in favour of the Convention. Because they function within an originary unity, genesis and normativity are related to one another as *reversible*.[3] This reversibility is not an empirical fact; it operates within the domain of meaning; it is political.

These brief allusions, which could be developed, describe a structure which reappears, for example, in the art forms called modern, but also in a politics which claims to be revolutionary. The debate between reformists and revolutionaries, between Social-Democrats and Bolsheviks, could be replayed in these same terms. Reformists appeal apparently to the genetic pole while revolutionaries insist on the normative demand. But Rosa Luxemburg was a 'genetic revolutionary' who defended the need for democracy against Lenin and against the Bolshevik seizure of power; and Karl Kautsky's radical orthodoxy became the basis of a reformist strategy for which acting before the structural logic of capitalism had prepared its downfall was giving in to a provocation by the enemy. The result of these necessarily fruitless theoretical jousts, condemned by the one-sidedness of their empirical options, returns us to that other revolution, the American, whose republican institutions pose the question of democracy. Before doing so, let me again insist on the fact that an originary structure, defined by the co-presence of genesis and normativity, *is* revolutionary *and* modern to the degree that it is constituted in a manner that avoids the 'skid' toward one or the other of its constitutive poles. 'The' revolution, which wants to go beyond that constitutive dichotomy by replacing, for example, formal or political democracy by its real or social incarnation is to be rejected just as is 'the' revolution which would come into being in order to realise the Laws of History or of Science.

This is the point at which the analysis of totalitarianism can be introduced briefly. As opposed to the classical forms of despotism or tyranny, totalitarianism is specifically modern. Like democracy, it is born of the revolution that breaks with the Ancien Régime which was formed as a *political society*. The destruction of that unity of society with its political representation produces a political state which is both separate from and yet dependent on society. The space opened between the two poles makes possible the practice of democracy; but the same democratic space expresses the tension defined by the originary structure of 'the' revolution. Democracy is constantly threatened by the 'skids' which are built into its very structure. The totalitarian temptation is built on a critique of the inherent instability of democracy and the necessary empirical incompleteness of its realisation, which can be only symbolic. The totalitarian move can take the genetic form of a demand for 'real democracy', eliminating the difference between state and society; or it can take the form of a normative appeal (to the Science of History, but also to the Nature of the *Volk*) to overcome the artificiality of the public space. In both cases, the constitutive unity of modernity is destroyed by the attempt to eliminate difference and to efface the threat of the new by realising it in the here-and-now. Democracy is *par excellence* historical; totalitarianism seeks the end of what Marx euphemistically called 'pre-history'. An unsatisfactory or incomplete democracy can be changed from within; the 'limits to totalitarian domination' take the form of a return of the suppressed pole which restores the conditions for democracy by returning to society the possibility of political action which the empirical 'realisation' of Natural or Historical Law claimed to produce.

## 3. THE MODERN STATE AS REPUBLICAN

I insisted on the fact that the authors of the American Constitution of 1787 feared equally 'the democracy' and private mercantile interest. Their republic was intended to control what since Hegel has been called 'civil society'. In the Remark to Paragraph 258 of his *Philosophy of Right*, Hegel criticises the politics for which the protection of the individual and his interests would determine the activity of the state. The state is not to be confused with civil society; its specific end is not 'the security and protection of property and personal freedom'. Hegel's state can be said to be republican despite its monarchical moment; it determines the 'true content and the goal' of the individual. Hegel explains why the 'principle of the modern state' has such an 'incredible strength and depth' in Paragraph 260. Its secret is that it permits 'the principle of subjectivity to realize itself as an *autonomous pole*', and at the same time to '*return it to the substantial unity* in which it is preserved'.[4] This Hegelian argument could be interpreted as recognising and seeking to give form to the original structure I have described. But if Hegel's state can be called republican, it is hardly democratic. Marx's path begins from the demystification of the 'political illusion' which he finds in Hegel. In our terms, Marx criticises Hegel for being simply a normative philosopher. The 'substantial unity' engulfs the 'autonomous pole', eliminating the tension constitutive of democracy by treating the symbolic nature of the political as a really realised or '*objective*' spirit. But Marx's solution is based on the representation of a civil society and a proletariat which would be the genetic foundation of a true politics which would not need to refer at all to a state for its unification. Like Hegel, but by a symmetrical error, Marx breaks the constitutive tension of modernity; he too wants to 'realise' the political.

Before returning to the Americans through this brief detour into the culmination of German Idealism, it should be noted that it is Kant who provides the philosophical basis from which a modern democratic theory could be derived. His critical theory attempts to maintain the duality of genesis and normativity; it explains the peculiar but necessary 'dialectic' which constantly threatens to explode the tension and lead it into skids. Working from his own form of the constitutive tension furnished by the first two *Critiques*, Kant analyses the critical activity itself in the *Critique of Judgement*. The theory of reflective judgement formulated there is crucial to any attempt to think modern politics. Kant's last writings, which address questions of politics, confirm this orientation. For example, the essay 'On the Common Saying: "This may be true in Theory, but it does not Apply in Practice"' (1793), criticises the error committed by the revolutionaries. They have not understood the implication of the form of reflective judgement. They assume that the 'social contract' *really* took place; their revolutionary goal is justified as the realisation anew of a real achievement which they assume has been perverted by power. This theoretical justification of practice is rejected at the same time that Kant none the less insists on the practical relevance of properly understood theory. The key to that theory is the distinction between the subsumptive universalising judgement which eliminates particularity and the reflective judgement which begins from particularity in order to propose, in public communication, a universal form adequate to it. The beautiful is affirmed explicitly as the 'symbol' of the concrete ethical life (in Paragraph 59) while the teleology of nature revealed to the reflective judgement is given an explicit political form by its comparison to the French Revolution (in Paragraph 65).

In his great 'post-Jacobin' proposal for 'Perpetual Peace' (1795), Kant remains still a supporter of the French Revolution, whose foundation he attempts to understand. The reflective judgement affirms the republican solution and rejects the attempt to found a 'real democracy' which would identify the executive and the legislative branches. That kind of democracy would leave no public space in which political judgement could be formed. The crucial role of the reflective political judgement is said by Kant to be an 'affirmative and transcendental principle of public right', whose formulation is that 'All maxims which *require* publicity if they are not to fail in their purpose can be reconciled with both right and politics.' Only in the republican form is this publicity guaranteed. The Americans, in effect, anticipated the argument of the philosopher. But the philosopher of modernity offers the critical tools with which to understand the limits, and possibilities, of the American achievement which cannot be reduced to its material achievements or failings.

If the American Revolution is characterised by its republican spirit, and if that spirit is truly anchored in the Constitution of 1787, its *democratic* realisation provides a critical standpoint from which to analyse that Revolution. Although the historians still debate when the rupture with the revolutionary phase took place, all admit that the Founding Fathers would not recognise the contemporary manifestation of their new society. The obvious source from which to begin an analysis of the relation between this political form and its social realisation is Tocqueville's attempt to generalise from its lessons. Claude Lefort suggests an approach to Tocqueville which permits us to develop the implications of the structure of modernity by applying the concept of 'reversibility'.[5] In a word, Tocqueville's first volume seems to define democracy as a 'social fact' whose political, cultural and moral consequences he analyses. But Tocqueville is not an empirical sociologist; he is a political theorist. In Lefort's formulation, social equality is here the visible, political freedom is its 'invisible' correlate which Tocqueville is trying to understand. But things are not so simple; the relation can invert itself; apparently empirical liberty can become the visible foundation of an invisible equality which democratic politics attempts to realise. This second orientation dominates Tocqueville's second volume, whereas the primacy of visible economic equality characterises the first volume. Equality could be replaced here by 'civil society', and freedom by the 'republican' institutional structure. The two are inseparable, functioning alternatively as genesis and as normative legitimation; equality can engender forms of freedom but its isolated pursuit threatens them; freedom demands conditions of social equality but when pursued for the sake of private advancement it comes to threaten that equality. Tocqueville's conclusion returns us to contemporary politics: I like democracy, he says, not because of what it is, but because of what it makes people do (*fait faire*).

## 4. THE POLITICAL ORIGINS OF DEMOCRACY

Tocqueville sees the heart of American democracy in its rich associational life. The preservation of associational democracy is due to the fact that the goals of the groups are neither too great nor too insignificant; association becomes a habit, a mode of behaviour which is at once political and social. This median role incarnates the reversibility stressed by Lefort: democracy maintains itself by straddling the political and the social, correcting its skids as it attaches itself to the flesh of national history. But Tocqueville's description should not lead to an idealisation of democracy; the movement of self-correction is constantly threatened from within ; and the history of the United States can just as well be told in terms of its 'skids' whose amplitude is perhaps increasing! Democracy is not a thing whose essence is fixed; the constitutive tension by which it is defined explains also the possibility of its distortion. If the goals of associative life are too great, the attempt to realise them breaks with the symbolic unity of the democratic polity from the side of society, which seeks to make itself fully political; if the goals are too small, the symbolic unity is destroyed from the side of politics, which is left to the control of others. Once again, Tocqueville is offering an analysis of democracy as political; his apparently empirical illustration is not simply sociological.

The critique of 'really existing democracy' is not the property of the 'left'. Indeed, the notion of a 'left' needs to be rethought once the belief in a logic of History is jettisoned along with the faith in 'the' Revolution. Contemporary neo-conservative theory explains the need for a revision in our political definitions. It proposes a critique of a democracy whose excesses are said to threaten to make society ungovernable. For these neo-conservatives, democracy must be limited in order to preserve democracy. This solution explains why its proponents are called 'neo-*conservative*'; it also helps define a modern 'left'. When political options are conceived without reference to 'the' sense of History, conservatives and radicals can be distinguished by their attitudes toward popular participation. What bothers the worthy neo-conservative protectors of democratic society is the birth of what are called 'new social movements'. These movements are new in that they present themselves neither as the representatives of particular social interests, nor as political actors whose goals concern society as a whole. Their novelty can be understood in terms of the originary structure. They are the carriers of a practical critique of 'really existing democracy' insofar as that democracy leans either too far toward politics or too far toward particular social interests. That is to say, these movements carry with them a democratic civil society in the making.

This briefly sketched analysis suggests a 'post-revolutionary' definition of the distinction left/right in terms of their respective attitudes toward democracy. But that conceptual distinction does not yet found a politics. The new social movements are not born like mushrooms after the rain. To explain their *origin* demands a return to the problem of revolution, and to the republican politics proposed by Kant. Analyses as different as those of Habermas, Gorz, Ferguson and Cohen, or Laclau and Mouffe,[6] all run into difficulty when confronted with the question of the *origin* of democracy; they treat it as the reaction of a threatened *Lebenswelt*, as existential choice, a rational decision, or a discursive given. None of them is able to think the *political questions* posed by the new social movements conceived as a democratic civil society in the making. The result is that once the movement no longer moves, those who wish to remain active politically find themselves condemned to adopt diverse 'revolutionary' formulas from the past; the search for a new political subject occupies some, while others debate the demystification of the ill deeds of the interests. This seems to be the point at which the left finds itself today; but it is no more the last word than is the state of contemporary American democracy.

The 'post-revolutionary' politics that I am proposing can be conceptualised in terms of republican theory. What characterises that theory throughout the ages[7] is the concern to avoid the centralisation of power in the hands of a single person, group, interest, or even a political institution. This republican demand was well understood by the authors of the Constitution of 1787. *If* their republic has become a *social* democracy without at the same time losing its political soul, this is because the domination of one branch of government, one material interest, or one legal codification has been avoided – barely at times! The point is not to complain that politics has done too little, or that it has been kept out of the hands of its rightful possessors. These empirical facts are founded by a *political* structure which remains their 'invisible' corrollary. A radical politics whose aim is the restoration of the kind of participatory politics which Tocqueville described as American associational democracy has to make visible the political structure which frames the republic. This does not mean addressing 'the democracy', any more than it is possible to appeal to the (re)creation of 'the' proletariat or 'the' revolution. Republican theory, and the history of the American republic, suggest a different orientation.

American history suggests a mode of conceptualising the new social movements. They are not 'the democracy' feared by the Framers of 1787. The Americans had gone through an historical experience between 1763 and 1776, which led them to declare their independence in ringing tones of natural right; they had attempted to give institutional form to their political creed in 13 states and a Confederation; and they had come to see the dangers of a politics which ignores its own specific form and limits. The attempt to incarnate materially the popular sovereignty which independence had achieved led to theoretical paradox and practical confusion. The new Constitution, inaugurated by the phrase 'We, the people', recognised the plurality of interests among the people; the popular sovereignty it affirmed was to be present in each of its carefully checked and balanced branches of government. Because it was present everywhere, this popular sovereignty is incarante nowhere; it is symbolic and political, not empirical and social. If the Constitution can be seen as excluding the 'social question' from the political sphere,[8] its claim to represent popular sovereignty takes on its full sense in the light of the double lesson drawn from Kant. Reflective judgement prevents us from conceiving of politics as a science or an applied morality; his republican theory insists on the necessary existence and preservation of a public space in which that judgement can be practised. This republican politics also expresses the goals of the great French liberal who loved democracy for what it *fait faire*.

The ambiguous but really existing democracy in America, whose history has not ended, is founded by its republican political institutions. If we want to see the benefits of democracy extended at the same time that we admit that the civil society represented by the new social movements cannot be created from outside of that society, our politics must aim first of all at the realisation of the *republic*. Democracy is its result, not its cause. This does not change or make less necessary empirical struggles within society; but it does affect their political *sense*. Politics cannot be reduced to the question of who gets what from whom. The political is not defined by the social; on the contrary, politics defines those questions around which social action – that 'revolutionary' transformation which society exercises on itself – becomes possible. Modern societies, inaugurated by the rupture signified by the American and French Revolutions, are always already political. There is no reason why contemporary politics should exist only in the deformed mode of competition among existing social interests. A radical democratic politics which reactivates the normative republican institutional framework can be generated by the new social movements' ability to realise the implications of their own political existence.

## Notes

1. Claude Lefort, *L'invention démocratique. Les limites de la domination totalitaire* (Paris: Fayard, 1981). Lefort's analysis of the relation of totalitarianism and democracy can only be alluded to in the present context. For a fuller discussion, cf. *The Marxian Legacy*, and especially the Afterword to the second edition.
2. The parenthetical suggestion that the Socialist victory of 1981 may have ended this secular history of the Revolution is due to Jacques Juilliard. Cf. 'French Rhetoric and Political Reality', in this volume.

   Furet writes that 'The history of the French 19th century in its entirety can be considered as the history of a struggle between the Revolution and the Restoration across episodes dated 1815, 1830, 1848, 1851, 1870, the Commune, the 16th of May 1877. Only the victory of the republicans over the monarchists at the beginning of the Third Republic marks the definitive victory of the Revolution in the depths of the country: the lay teacher of Jules Ferry, that missionary of the values of 89, is the symbol more than the instrument of that long victorious battle. The integration of the villages and peasantry of France into the republican nation through the principles of 89 would have taken at least a century.' *Penser la Révolution Française* (Paris: Gaillimard, 1978), pp. 16–17. But this is only the victory of the principles of 1789; for the more radical, 'the' revolution could be identified with the Rousseauian–Jacobin dream which remained, or remains, alive in the dream of a socialist or communist revolution. On the implications of Furet's argument, see my essay on 'The Origins of Revolution', *Journal of the British Society for Phenomenology*, vol. 14, no. 1, January, 1983, reprinted in the *Politics of Critique* and Claude Lefort's 'Penser la Révolution dans la Révolution Française', in *Essais sur le politique* (Paris: Seuil, 1986).
3. The concept is elaborated by Claude Lefort's essay on Tocqueville, to which I shall refer in a moment. Its philosophical basis is formulated by Merleau-Ponty's phenomenological ontology. My claim is that this relation is specific to modernity, and that its elaboration depends on the presence of the political as the horizon which gives sense to this unity-in-difference.
4. *Rechtsphilosophie*, Paragraphs 258, 269. Translation mine.

5. 'Réversibilité: Liberté politique et liberté de l'individu', in *Essais sur le politique*, op. cit.; English translation in *Telos*, no. 63, Fall, 1985.
6. Habermas's position is articulated systematically in his *Theorie des Kommunikativen Handeln* and numerous articles; Gorz's in *Adieu au proletariat* and more recent articles; Ferguson and Cohen's in *On Democracy*; and Laclau and Mouffe's in *Hegemony and Socialist Strategy*. Habermas and Gorz's theories are analysed in the Afterword to the second edition of *The Marxian Legacy*; Laclau and Mouffe's in 'Another Resurrection of Marxism' in this volume. Ferguson and Cohen's is muckraking for the most part; theoretically its application of 'Rawlsianism' adds nothing to the political debate because its 'Kantian constructivism' operates still within the world defined by the first two *Critiques*.
7. Cf. William R. Everdell, *The End of Kings. A History of Republics and Republicans* (New York: Free Press, 1983). Everdell begins his analysis with Samuel and Solon and carries it through the Watergate affair. The popular, biographical and narrative form of his account does not invalidate its main theoretical argument. The abuses Everdell sees in the Nixon administration have recurred in the recent *débâcle* of the Reagan administration.
8. This is of course the accusation of the 'progressive historians', expressed classically in 1913 by Charles Beard's *An Economic Interpretation of the Constitution*. Beard tries to show how the Framers wrote a document whose defence of the interests of the minority was intended to protect private property from the hands of the citizenry who might revolt against *social* domination.

# 16 Ethics and Politics

This discussion attempts modestly to do three things. It seeks first to address the general topic, ethics and politics. It then proposes a contemporary illustration in order to show the implications of that theoretical question. Finally, it makes some theoretical proposals, drawn from my own recent work. The latter aspect of the essay is, I fear, too brief. I can only hope that my manner of confronting the first two issues at least arouses your curiosity concerning the conclusions.

## 1. THE RELEVANCE OF PHILOSOPHY

Had the title of this essay posed the choice, ethics *or* politics, the philosopher's task would have been simple. Either politics would be shown to be an 'art', if not a mere 'technique' – in all events, dependent ultimately on a rational ethics; or a neo-aristotlean rehabilitation of *phronesis* would have had to legitimate the philosophical dignity of politics while relativising the assertions of moral a prioris. Similarly, the disjunctive formulation of my title would have made things easier for the political thinker. Either politics is a 'higher' form of an ethics limited to individual rights and neglecting social duties; or ethics is an ultimately ungroundable value-choice which the responsible politician must but cannot ultimately avoid. In both cases, the conflict apparently set up by the disjunctive formulation is in fact avoided. A 'critical philosophy', in the footsteps of Kant and/or Marx, is not so shy, or so self-assured.

The problematic conjunction of ethics and politics is historically specific. Classical philosophy's foundation in natural law was destroyed by the advent of a *modernity* which Leo Strauss and his followers never tire of denouncing. The diagnosis is correct, although Strauss was hardly the first to encounter the problem. Jürgen Habermas's *Philosophical Discourse of Modernity* points to Hegel as the philosopher who makes the diremption of the moral and the political, the individual and the social, faith and knowledge, the immanent principle of systematic philosophy. We need only recall Hegel's early attempts to understand the tragedy of Greek *Sittlichkeit* or the paradoxical salvatory message of the Jew Jesus, and their transfiguration in the world-historical panorama of his *Phenomenology*. This Hegelian attempt to hold together both sides of the conjunction defines our modern age. Hegel's successors attempt to break out of this uneasy conjunction by emphasising one or the other of its constitutive poles. Habermas's political, and moral, imperative is that we must 'complete the Enlightenment' and realise the modern project. But no more than Strauss, Habermas does not explain the relation of his general description of modernity to its concrete forms. Its 'realisation' remains abstract, its relation to the Enlightenment (or its individual-philosophical form) is unclear.

Hegel's prescriptive power fell short of his diagnostic skill. The *Philosophy of Right* distinguishes between abstractly universal *Moralität* and concrete experienced *Sittlichkeit*. Within the latter, 'civil society' is based on a principle of particularity which seems to recall the imperatives of morality, but whose limitations make necessary the presence of a state.[1] Hegel stresses the specificity of the modern state, which 'has prodigious strength and depth because it allows the principle of subjectivity to progress to its culmination in the extreme self-subsistent personal particularity, and yet at the same time brings it back to the substantive unity and so maintains this unity in the principle of subjectivity itself'.[2] But Hegel does not explain the concrete origin and nature of this state which, it will be recalled, is only the first moment of a movement that engulfs it within intra-state relations before absorbing it into World History as 'the Court of the Last Judgement'.

The Hegelian state might be interpreted as the symbolic form of the classical conception of 'the political'. It is that moment in which a society represents itself to itself as different from its empirical givenness. Marx of course denounced the Hegelian 'illusion of politics' – but he did so on the basis of a shared premise: the primacy of civil society, which defines a problem for Hegel, presents a solution for Marx. Civil society is the real 'place' where ethics and politics are united, as a question for Hegel or an answer for Marx. The result is that social theory replaces both ethics and politics. The liberal contractualist, whose invisible hand provided Hegel the model for the Cunning of Reason, appeals to it as does the Marxist materialisation of this historical teleology. Philosophy, ethics and politics are simply variants of social theory – as the Marxist Habermas tried to show in *Knowledge and Human Interests*.

The autonomy of ethics and the specificity of politics emerge against the backdrop of the failure of social theory and of its liberal or communist incarnations. Totalitarian societies call forth an ethical response from the individual which acquires a political implication of which its agents may not have been conscious because the totalitarian system (in principle at least) conjoins ethics and politics. We might then choose to address our topic by asking what kind of a balance these societies could permit such that neither the ethical nor the political extinguish the other. The 'self-limiting civil society' of pre-coup Poland could serve as a case in point. Rather than speculate on what might have been had not the 13 December, 1981 intervened, I want to look at the example of a liberal society because it seems to illustrate the more frequently considered and intuitive *disjunctive* formulation of our topic. A closer analysis will show the philosophical importance of the *conjunctive* formulation.

## 2. A MODERN EXAMPLE: 1968–86

From 22 November to 8 December 1986 French students forced the government to withdraw its proposed educational reform. The shock was double: the reform was a rather modest attempt to adapt an outmoded system to a new society,[3] while the students' outraged reaction did not express the sociological attributes expected of their individualist, pre-yuppie generation. The commentators were quick to seize upon the contrast of the Winter of 1986 with the Spring of 1968: the former was said to be a movement based on ethics, the latter was thought of as the product of political demands. This comparison forgets that the students' movement continued to the *10th* of December, concluding with a demonstration commemorating the brutal death of a student at the hands of the police. The slogan of this final protest was '*Plus jamais ça*', and it was not without importance that the dead student was a *beur*, a French citizen of Algerian origin, with whom the students felt the need to show solidarity. The comparison further neglects the fact that, in withdrawing its educational reform, the government also cancelled the winter session of Parliament, annulling a series of other measures on its agenda.[4] But the comparison was true in one specific sense – in the political eyes of the government, which recalled that the 'excesses' of May were followed by a massive reaction providing victory for the '*partie de l'ordre*' in June 1968. This explains the brutal behaviour of the Minister of the Interior, and the use of 'agents-provocateurs' (identifiable to the TV-watching public by their yellow scarfs!) during the demonstrations.

The relevance of the 1968–86 comparison for the government, and its irrelevance to the self-understanding of the movement, suggests a theoretical distinction. The present government called itself liberal in its campaign against the Socialists in 1986, but it is composed, uneasily, of three distinct groups – neo-liberals (the PR), centrists (the CDS), and a hard right that can only be called the 'parti de l'ordre' (the RPR). It has constantly to worry about holding the 12 per cent of the vote that went to the far-right National Front; and its various leaders have to think within the perspective both of the present 'co-habitation' with a socialist President, and of the upcoming May 1988 presidential elections. This means that governmental politics have a double sense: to the everyday give and take of politics is added a *symbolic* dimension which means that each measure has a resonance beyond its immediate goals. Measures adopted aim not only at their immediate results; they seek to create a 'climate of opinion'. This was the case for the proposed privatisation of the prison system, for the reform of the nationality code, and of course for the educational reforms.[5] From this point of view, the students were not protesting simply against a measure that touched their personal concerns; they were not putting into question particular programmes (*la* politique) but the assumptions carried by, and implicit in, the overall politics of this regime (*le* politique). This does not make the students political 'revolutionaries', in the sense attributed by the commentators to 1968. The results of 1986 suggest, rather, that the 1968ers misunderstood the implications of their own actions for the same reasons that transformed the 'ethical' revolt of 1986.

The French students of 1968 can be seen as an inverted image of the coalition government attacked by their successors. They were a combination of political movements fused by the catalyst of the March 22nd Movement. The critique of the University, from which the movement began, turned quickly to the capitalist nature of the society served by that institution.[6] Once the Universities were engulfed, the premisses of the movement condemned it to political paralysis. Some, like the Maoists who were to become the Gauche Prolétarian, went so far as to leave the barricades of 13 May for the workers' quarters, from which alone theory taught that salvation was to be hoped; others, like the PSU and many autonomous leftists, were captivated by the idea that state power might be seized through a 'long' Revolution in which Mendès-France would play the role of

Kerensky in February 1917; others, like the communists, played the card of realism and reform against the 'anarchist provocations' of the students. With isolated exceptions, like the authors of *La Brèche*,[7] no one could conceive of the movement on its own terms – despite its own self-identification in graffiti and slogan, and its own practice which did, for many, *changer la vie*. It was as if the political premisses of the movement's actors blinded them to the moral implications of their own actions. But the movement did not end with the June triumph of the party of order, any more than the 'self-dissolution' in December 1986 marks the conclusion of the new struggle. 1968 became gradually what it had been all along: a moral and cultural mutation hidden by an imaginary political schema drawn from the past and needing a new political representation to understand its own future.[8] That 'political representation' turned out to be, in fact, 'ethical'.

The political agenda that emerged from May 1968 took first the form of the demand for workers' self-management. This orientation could be formulated within the framework of Marxism. This explains why, although condemning the invasion of Czechoslovakia in August 1968, the movement did not draw the ethical implication that this self-management is simply a form of moral autonomy. The 'socialism with a human face' that had been crushed in Prague was instead given the political form of 'Euro-Communism', which permitted the first steps toward a Common Programme of the Left that finally came to power in 1981. A different attitude was suggested by the critique of totalitarianism, rendered vivid by Solzhenitsyn and popularised by the so-called 'new philosophers'. Even the self-managed form of Marxism that was supposed to ensure that 'real democracy' replace the formalism of bourgeois institutions, was sharply challenged, in theory but also by events. When the Vietnamese victory brought the tragedy of the 'boat people', and Pol Pot's political enforcement of the true community proved to be terror, politics was condemned; it was reason run rampant, totalising particularity, destroying society. Only the individual moral stance – whose foundation is a value *choice*! – could stop this machinery. It was a short step to the consecration of this return of the *disjunction* of ethics and politics in the wake of 1968 in the form of the primacy of individualism as ethical value choice.

From this perspective, 1968 prepared the anti-political generation which 'logically' should not have emerged as a political force in the winter of 1986. The age of morality become the 'era of the void', the defence of particularity, the atomism of the solitary entrepreneur. The ruling Socialists' 1983 rejection of the national and republican mission of 'La France' in favour of an 'austerity' politics seemed to consecrate the replacement of politics by the administration of things; meanwhile ethics, in Foucault's phrase, turned around 'the care for oneself'. The *disjunction* of ethics and politics seemed ultimately to imply the demise of both in the 'liberal' inversion of their totalitarian conjunction. This conclusion was refuted *de facto* by the students of 1986. Its philosophical foundation, in the abstraction typified by Strauss's and Habermas's theories of modernity, is put into question at the same time. Philosophy need not abandon either itself or the concrete so easily.

## 3. A PHILOSOPHICAL EXPLANATION OF POLITICAL CONFUSION

The disjunction of a political 1968 and an ethical 1986 cannot be maintained. Nor is the modern attempt to explain their empirical conjunction by means of *social* theory adequate. Marx's rejection of the 'political illusion' is no more acceptable than his denial of ethical autonomy in his critique of the notion of the Rights of Man (in 'On the Jewish Question'). 68 and 86 are not defined by their empirical effects, or by their declared or imputed intentions; that is the point of view of the policeman (or that of the present French government). 68 and 86 – unlike the 'free schools' movement of 1984 – reacted to the *symbolic* implications of politics. As one provincial lycéen put it, they knew that they would not achieve full equality of their schools with the privileged Parisiens, but 'we have to fight for the principle'. In so doing, he continued, 'we lived what our parents experienced in 1968'. He described that experience as learning to listen to others, to debate with them and to take each other seriously. He didn't use the word, but what he was describing – at the level of principle and that of experience – is what the French are coming to know as *democracy*.[9]

The *conjunctive* framework of modernity is not determined by socio-economic conditions; nor does it presage totalitarianism. Marx's reduction of the political and the ethical blinded him to the radical novelty that Strauss and Habermas glimpsed, but only abstractly. The separation of ethics and politics is only possible within a constantly threatened unity conceptualised by Hegel's modern state.

Hegel's dissolution of that state into World History was not a conceptual error. Such a state cannot exist once and for all; that would be the dream of the party of order, if not of the totalitarian party. But that state does exist, *symbolically*; it is that which makes possible a democratic society in which politics and ethics are conjoined necessarily. Such a democratic society is *not* that empirically real 'society' to which Marxism and liberalism would reduce politics and ethics. Tocqueville's *political* liberalism suggests an approach to its philosophical (or phenomenological) description.[10] Volume One of *Democracy in America* describes democracy as a 'social state' (*état social*), determined by the conditions of equality found in the New World. Political liberty appears to be the consequence of this social equality. Volume Two inverts the perspective. Democracy is defined by liberty, yet threatened by the forces of equality which, in the earlier analysis, made it possible. This dilemma, which Tocqueville rediscovers in the foundations of the *Ancien Régime*, defines our modernity. Liberty and equality, morality and politics: in the language of philosophy, their relation is that of the visible to the invisible; neither is possible without the other, but neither has an identity which is determined apart from the other.

The movements of 1968 and 1986 were democratic movements which demonstrate the inseparability – and the '*reversibility*' – of ethics and politics. Their disjunctive contrast is misleading; it fixes them as eternally opposed essences, never to be reconciled. 1968, and 1986, refute the disjunction. This leaves open the question, why were these movements successful where others failed? Are there 'lessons' to be drawn from them? Have students replaced Marx's workers as the 'universal class'?[11] Or are we confronted here with types of 'new social movements' of which feminism, ecology or pacifism might also be illustrations?[12]

These empirical questions can be reformulated theoretically. What are those *particular* conditions which call forth the moral-political response of modern individuals? And what explains the *receptivity* of modern politics to these responses? Marx thought he had found the answer in the structure of capitalist civil society which produces the proletariat as its own grave-digger. This solution translates empirical reality into the language of principles. The movement of 1986 inverted this procedure; it began from ethical principles – and remained at that apparently modest level. (For this, it earned the undesired and misguided praise of its journalistic elders, who constantly marvelled at its 'maturity'.) This 'success' cannot be judged empirically, as the students knew in calling symbolically for an 'Estates-General' in the spring to re-evaluate the situation. Their success is measured also in the slogan of their final demonstration: *Plus jamais ça!* In the context of the proposed Spring meeting, this slogan poses ethics as a political *question* that can neither be avoided nor resolved once-and-for-all.

Tocqueville said of democracy that he loved it not for what it was but for it what *fait faire*. Democratic politics preserves the capacity of society to act, demanding now the increase of political freedom, now that of economic equality. The ethical and the political cannot be distinguished, assigned to one or the other pole. The democratic task is not Habermas's 'completion' of the Enlightenment and realisation of modernity. That goal rings still of the Marxian critique of the 'illusion of politics', to which it seeks to put an end in reality. Democratic philosophy has, rather, to return to Kant, to the philosopher who asked the question 'What is Enlightenment?' and to the political thinker whose 'Cosmopolitan History' postulated the *creation* of civil society as the greatest, and most difficult, task for humanity. These two Kantian themes point to the democratic realisation of the aim of the original 'critical theory', to put Reason back to her Throne without the sacrifice either of the ethical or of the political. The *conjunction* of ethics and politics transforms philosophy; Reason's throne is constantly in question, while Reason's necessity is constantly reaffirmed. This is why Kant's critical system ends with a theory of judgement.

## Notes

1. This necessity does not depend on the empirical problems encountered within the particularism of civil society. Hegel insists, in the Remark of Paragraph 258, that 'If the state is confused with civil society, and if its specific end is laid down as the security and protection of property and personal freedom, then the interest of the individuals as such becomes the ultimate end of their association, and it follows that membership in the state is something optional.' (Knox tr., p. 156) The nature of this 'state', which is different from the sort of 'welfare state' (the '*Not- und Verstandesstaat*') with which the discussion of civil society concludes, needs to be made explicit. I will return, briefly, to this question below. A more inclusive interpretation is found in my *From Marx to Kant* (Albany: SUNY Press, 1985).

2. Paragraph 260, Knox translation, p. 161.
3. France increased its mandatory school attendance age to 16 only in 1959. The percentage of high school students receiving the high school diploma permitting them to enter the university is still under 30 per cent. One proclaimed goal of the reform was to increase this to 80 per cent by the year 2000. At the University level, the system is divided into the elite Grandes Ecoles and the Universities, whose diplomas are in principle equal (as are those of all high schools). In principle, any student with a high school diploma can go to any University. In fact, the Universities are unequal, and their admissions are more or less open. The reform wanted to take this into account, making a virtue of necessity. It also proposed differentiated tuition rates (in a ratio of 1 to 2, or to 3) – a small matter in fact, given the low cost of tuition, and the benefits available to those holding student IDs. The importance of the reform was not its empirical content – although the students could at first protest only against this – but the political implications it symbolised within the broader framework of the right-wing government that came to power in 1986, as we will see.
4. The cancellation also showed weakness on the part of the government, which was immediately seized upon by various discontented groups which had heretofore felt too weak to push their demands in the form of strikes. The withdrawal was supposed to show the 'statesmanship' of the government; it remains to see whether it will continue this path in the face of the new agitations, or return to the disciplinary image it had adopted prior to December. The Paris correspondent of *Die Zeit* wrote with astonishment and disclaim that 'since the end of the War, no other Western democracy has capitulated unconditionally in the face of demonstrators.' (19 December, 1986)
5. It should be recalled that the proposed educational reforms of the socialist government, and particularly the attempt to move toward a fully secular system, met with massive opposition before being ultimately withdrawn. The 'liberal' government in turn was forced by electoral imperatives to please specific clienteles. Its tactics were overlaid with the rhetorical flourish of any 'party of order'. This explains its policies on naturalisation and drugs, as well as its reaction to the wave of terror bombings during the Fall. Beneath the rhetoric lies of course another reality, somewhat evident in the de-nationalisation of industry, less clear in the reforms of labour law (firing procedures, flexible hours, etc.), hidden in budgetary decisions. But before attributing these moves to 'capitalist machinations', one should recall that many of these proposals were made already by the Socialist government after 1983. If they are being pushed with such vigour now, it is for their rhetorical symbolism more than for their real effects. It is in this context that the assassination of a *beur* was felt so strongly by the students.

   In the case of the Universities, the Minister charged with the reform, M. Devaquet, was less subtle. He explained that his proposed law would increase the role of full professors in university governance because, having reached this stage in their career, they had more free time to devote to the institution than those younger persons still climbing the academic ladder. This is of course simply a cynical way of preparing what commentators called 'the revenge of the mandarins' against the liberalisation of the Universities begun in the wake of May 1968 (the Faure Reforms) and continued under the socialist Minister, A. Savary. M. Devaquet's political *naïveté* was apparent also in his statement that the Cabinet would decide on modifications of his bill depending on the size of the next day's demonstration . . . which of course was enormous!

6. This was clear already in the pre-May pamphlet, 'Pourquoi les sociologiques?' distributed by the March 22nd Movement at Nanterre, and reprinted in *Esprit*, juin 1968. The answer, of course, was that sociologists are there to regiment and discipline the working class.
7. Claude Lefort, Edgar Morin and C. Coudray (a.k.a., Cornelius Castoriadis), *La Brèche* (Paris: Fayard, 1968). This volume was published in June; Morin's contribution had already been published in *Le Monde* in May.
8. This is the theme of Dany Cohn-Bendit's new book (and television series), *Nous l'avons tant aimée la Révolution* (Paris: Barrault, 1986), which is a compilation of interviews with actors from the different movements of the 1960s. Cohn-Bendit seems to think that, while not giving up his ideals, he can understand now the need to realise them through a reformist, but *democratic* (his stress: constantly) politics. The argument is not convincing theoretically because its premise about the political nature of the movements separates the ethical from the political, distorting both. Interestingly, Cohn-Bendit does not seem to consider the American civil rights movement as part of the 1960s movements. His own perspectives come out more clearly in a recent article, 'Ich lebe da, wo ich verliebt bin', in *Die Zeit*, 12 December, 1986.

   It is worth noting here that at the moment when the demonstrations threatened to get out of hand, a group of 'ex-68ers' formed themselves into groups identified by their white helmets and intervened in order to preserve the success won by the 'maturity' of the movement in the eyes of the public. (See, *Le Monde*, 12 décembre, 1986).
9. I say 'coming to know', because the republican political tradition remains strong on the left, where Jacobinism and Marxism combine easily (as Lenin had noted already in 'One Step Forward, Two Steps Backward', and as those Ministers who opposed the 1983 austerity programme argued). The French are coming to know democracy through their concern with the critique of totalitarianism; and they are coming to know it through the sobering experience of the Socialist Party in power and now in 'cohabitation'. This explains in part why the right has reacted more as 'the party of order' than as the 'party of capital'. It also explains the hope for success of the Socialists' present electoral strategy: the re-election of Mitterrand in 1988 against a divided right, and the attempt to draw centrist deputies from the CDS toward a left government without calling for immediate parliamentary elections in 1988. The result would be that, by the 1991 parliamentary elections, a democratic left could win power on its own.

10. I am borrowing these remarks from Claude Lefort, who made clear the phenomenological underpinnings of this argument in a seminar on Merleau-Ponty offered at Stony Brook, Fall 1986. On Tocqueville, see especially his 'On Reversibility', translated by Martha Calhoun in *Telos*, no. 65, Spring 1985.
11. Under the title, 'Who will Dare Reform the Schools?', *Le Monde*'s Fréderic Gaussen proposed an analysis whose implications point toward the dilemmas of modern democracy (*Le Monde*, 11 décembre, 1986; see also Gaussen's earlier article of 25 novembre, 1986). The schools involve a vast public – parents, who are voters; teachers, who are unionised; students, with no representatives; yet this public is not linked to the political system by any 'transmission belts'. Politics, in the everyday sense of the term, becomes an impossible risk in these conditions. Yet political action is necessary because our modern societies make education the ticket to individual success. Individual pressure from below meets political imperatives from above. The result can only be explosive. It need not, however, be 'revolutionary'. Indeed, at the height of the December demonstrations, *Le Monde*'s front page (12 décembre, 1986) headlined first that 'Student Protest has Enlarged the Splits among the Components of the Majority', and in another article on the same page, 'The Paris Stock Market is in its Best Form'.
12. On the question of 'new social movements', see the issue of *Social Research* (vol. 52, no. 4, Winter 1985) edited by Jean L. Cohen, and her excellent introductory essay, 'Strategy or Identity: New Theoretical Paradigms and Contemporary Social Movements'.

# 17 A Renaissance of the Political in the USA?

The public seems more bothered by the moral fault committed by a President ready to barter for hostages than by its underlying political implications. Their President was unable to stand tall and alone; he yielded the rhetorical high ground of reborn America. Fearing such a reaction, the President's men provided him with a real-political or geo-political justification – a relative novelty during the Reagan years – which was badly received. This might explain the ensuing revelations of the diversion of funds to the Contras, characterised by the President as 'freedom fighters' in the tradition of the Founding Fathers. The Congress is divided on Central American politics. The Boland Amendment, passed in 1984 after the mining of Nicaraguan ports by the CIA, was repealed narrowly in 1986. But that Amendment was still in force when the first deliveries to the Contras took place. The White House may hope that Congress will concentrate on the juridical aspect of the affair, letting the moral indignation of the public cool down gradually. This would explain its declared willingness to co-operate with Congress. Meanwhile, its continued support for the Contras in spite of the unravelling of the secret network is consistent with the attempt to associate the national interest, the Presidency, and the moral initiative that has characterised Reagan's politics.

The White House is seeking to save the 'Reagan Revolution'. The President has not criticised his policies; he admits only that 'mistakes were made'. The Democrats, who took control of the Senate in November 1986, after a bitter campaign in which the President engaged his prestige, have to avoid personalising the affair while giving it a political translation that goes beyond its immediate effects. They remember the fate of Walter Mondale; and they know that the polls indicate that the President himself is more popular than his specific programmes. The greatest loser is Vice-President Bush. Candidates will multiply in both parties because the Presidency now seems a prize open to all comers. The Democrats seem fated to recapture that office, but success could well be only the kind of pyrrhic victory that brought Jimmy Carter to office after Watergate at the head of a party too divided to govern. It is not clear that the 'therapy of opposition' has given the Democrats a new sense of themselves and their political mission. The liberal creed canonised by the New Deal is exhausted; that, more than anything else, explains the triumph of Reaganism.[1]

The 'Reagan Revolution' sought a political realignment that would make the Republicans the dominant party. The Democrats had succeeded in identifying the New Deal with the national interest; Reagan used moral exhortation to identify the national interest with his party. This tactic can be called *anti-political*. Reagan did not invent it; Eisenhower's non-partisan posture inaugurated an attitude that the partisan Kennedy used for his own ends in his famous Inaugural appeal to 'ask not what your country can do for you . . .'; similarly, Carter's anti-Washington rhetoric only echoed Nixon's 1972 proposal for a 'New Federalism'. Anti-politics has dominated post-War American political life. At an institutional level, anti-politics explains the structures which permitted the Iran-Contra affair. As an ideology, anti-politics explains the self-destructive nature of contemporary liberalism which brought Reagan's triumphant rise to power. His fall from grace suggests that his moralistic nationalism did not overcome fully the antinomies of liberalism. The equation of nationalism with morality could not succeed in a democracy. Instead of realignment we may see a rebirth of (small 'd') democratic politics.

## 1. INSTITUTIONAL CONDITIONS

The 'anti-politics' that defines American political life took shape when foreign policy became vital to domestic politics.[2] That moment can be situated with the Maoist victory in 1949. In a climate of Cold War, which became 'hot' in Korea, McCarthyism could dominate domestic politics in the face of a Democratic party which trembled at the accusation of having 'lost' China. The situation was stabilised under Eisenhower, who administered to the nation while the Democratic opposition controlled Congress. Partisan divisions returned in the elections of 1960 when Kennedy appealed to a new patriotism while using the supposed 'missile gap' to attack Vice-President Nixon. No matter that Kennedy's information was false; his tactic has been appropriated by candidates down to Ronald Reagan, who preached that America must again 'stand tall', attacked the SALT II Treaty, and discovered a 'window of vulnerability' threatening American security. In the meanwhile, Lyndon Johnson had justified his engagement in Vietnam by a domino theory' which veiled thinly the fear of 'losing China' once again. Richard Nixon won the Presidency on the basis of a promised Plan to end that war. And Gerald Ford was humiliated by Jimmy Carter for having affirmed that Poland was a free nation. In short, anti-politics expresses the domination of the 'national interest' over the politics by which the republic articulates its goals. This is its first premise.

It is perhaps only normal that foreign policy play a key role in the domestic politics of a democracy. But what role, and under the direction of which actors? A recent study, *Our Own Worst Enemy*, explains the process by which anti-politics was institutionalised.[3] The authors underline first the arrival of new actors on the political stage. The Establishment, centred in New York around the Council on Foreign Relations, had always been able to send its lawyers and pragmatic businessmen to direct the State Department and the machinery of foreign policy. The Vietnam war divided the Council; the Carnegie Foundation funded a new and more liberal journal, *Foreign Policy*, to compete with the Council's *Foreign Affairs*. The withdrawal from Vietnam left *Commentary* to present a neo-conservative politics typified by Mrs Kirkpatrick's distinction between authoritarian and totalitarian governments. At the same time, the political scene moved from New York to Washington. The new centres were 'think tanks' like the Brookings, which became after 1969 a sort of 'government in exile' of the Democratic party, or the American Enterprise Institute which was its right wing counterpart. (Further to the right was the Heritage Foundation; further to the left, the Institute for Policy Studies.) This process is described as the shift 'From "Establishment" to "Professional Elite"'; its best known symbols are the ideological academics, Kissinger and Brzezinski.[4]

The new actors have changed the nature of the foreign policy debate. They are experts who have mastered a complex material which they translate into professional jargon. But they are also ideologues serving a cause veiled by their expertise. This double role exacerbates their quarrels and increases their differences to the point that they can no longer be mediated by pragmatic compromise. The new actors create a new game played by rules in which differences between Democrats and Republicans are unimportant; the ideologies hidden by expertise compete for the definition of the 'national interest'. A well-known example during the first Reagan administration was the guerilla struggle between the Under-Secretary of State, Mr Burt, against the Under-Secretary of Defence, Mr Perle, concerning strategic negotiations with Russia.[5] Other illustrations from the press and from within the enlarged staff of Congress – which Destler *et al.* call 'the new irresponsibility' – can be added. When Congress attempted to recapture its lost initiative in the wake of the weakened Watergate executive it engaged its own experts from the 'professional elite' which plies its trade between the Universities and Washington. The result was an ideologisation but also a fragmentation of the political sphere whose real stakes were hidden from a public whose only source of information is other members of the same elite who people increasingly the world of journalism. It is perhaps not surprising that it was a small Lebanese journal that disclosed the Iran arms for hostages affair.

The fragmentation that accompanies this transformation of the political scene calls forth a centripetal reaction which Destler *et al.* name 'The Operational Presidency'. Its roots are found already with Kennedy, who installed Harvard's McGeorge Bundy as his National Security Assistant with the task of revivifying the traditionalist State Department. The importance acquired by this new position under the direction of Kissinger, and then Brzezinski, is well-known; Oliver North was minted at this mill. The political question is how these creatures of the President could increase their role beyond their constitutionally limited spheres. The increased importance of foreign policy in domestic politics is a partial explanation; so is the political fragmentation engendered by the new expertise. More generally, Destler *et al.* argue that what they call 'the politics of foreign policy' shifted from a system of 'barons' enjoying a functional autonomy because of their Establishment connection to a structure dominated by 'courtesans'. The power of these courtiers depends on the President; their skills in turn permit him to increase the centripetal, and operational, tendency of the anti-political presidency. The Iran-Nicaragua affair symbolises the apogee of their power. The Secretaries of State and of Defence had opposed that operation, which was conducted from the White House largely without their knowledge. The increase of Presidential power can thus be seen as the effect rather than the cause of deeper transformations. Simple institutional reforms, as suggested in the conclusion of *Our Own Worst Enemy*, will not repair the damage; nor is the return of bi-partisan Establishment politics desirable. The Tower Commission's conclusion that the institution was undermined by rogue actors simply avoids the issue. The political question lies deeper, in the ideology which legitimates anti-politics.

## 2. IDEOLOGICAL CONDITIONS

Ronald Reagan's conquest of power can be understood as the culmination of an evolution of American *liberalism*. This apparently paradoxical thesis is defended by Frederick F. Siegel in *Troubled Journey. From Pearl Harbor to Ronald Reagan*.[6] The story begins in 1941. President Roosevelt had learned from the failures of his predecessors. Woodrow Wilson had made the American entry into the First World War in 1917 a moral crusade; certain of its own virtue, the country refused the diplomatic deals of the Versailles Treaty which were the price of the League of Nations. That same isolationist moralism governed the Republican 1920s which culminated in the Depression. After unifying the inward-looking, localist domestic scene around the interventionist social politics of the New Deal, Roosevelt had to mobilise opinion for an intervention in the name of the politics of the national interest. The war was won *both* by American democracy and by its superior economy (pulled finally from Depression by military demand). This dual character explains the continuation of American interventionism after the War, in the form of the Truman Doctrine *and* the Marshall Plan. Pragmatic rather than doctrinaire, Roosevelt and Truman did not hesitate to add a dose of moralism. The old-line isolationists, typified by Senators like Vandenberg and Taft, wanted to preserve American purity and virtue in the face of the corruption of the Old World. Converted to political interventionism by the war, these Republicans believed that they were remaining consistent with the old principles, proposing 'to maintain American purity, but now . . . by imposing a single standard of morality worldwide, with exemptions for friendly but right-wing nations like fascist Spain and Argentina'. But the *social* logic of New Deal domestic interventionism was not the same as the *political* foundation of the new foreign policy.

The two logics that founded the bi-partisan post-war foreign policy were not necessarily compatible. Eisenhower continued the foreign policy of his Democratic predecessors, creating a network of global alliances to support American interventions. But the isolationist temptation was not eliminated; the nuclear strategy of massive response which protected the security of the American continent reassured those who dreamt of retaining the virtuous peace of their ancestors. When President Kennedy, and then President Johnson, sought to return to the domestic New Deal, the conflict between the two logics of intervention became apparent. Johnson never explained the relation between his 'Great Society' and his intervention in Vietnam; seeking at once guns and butter, he left the Presidency in dishonour. The Vietnam war ripped apart what remained of a consensus among the Democrats. The anti-war 'New Politics' faction combined international isolationism with domestic interventionism while the Humphrey-Jackson internationalists were saddled with the weight of an unpopular war. On the Republican side, Nixon pursued that war for four long years at the same time that he practised *détente* with Russia and opened relations with China. The two logics were coming untied. Carter sought to return to the New Deal synthesis, refusing anti-Soviet single-mindedness while offering the world the benefits of American *social* politics.[7] Reality defeated that generous hope. Recognising that American liberalism could not have it both ways, Carter's social option left the state politically rudderless. His belated recognition of international realities produced a politics which, Siegel suggests, anticipated Reaganism, domestically (e.g. in deregulation and fiscal policy), and in foreign policy (e.g., in the wake of Afghanistan).

Reaganism is the culmination of American liberalism. It can attract the social isolationist while practising a *unilateral* interventionist politics justified by moralism. Its foundation is the renewal of an economy freed from the limits of the social State. This is the basis of Reagan's incantation, 'America's Back!' But free market capitalism denies that the state acts in the national interest at the same time that the Reagan state intervenes vigorously. The apparent success of this politics which refuses to call itself by its own name can be explained by demographic, economic and technological changes.[8] More important is the fact that Reaganism represents the end in both senses, *and* the culmination of a liberal politics torn between domestic social reform and external political intervention. It does both, without appearing to do either. This explains the incoherence of Reagan's politics; despite its rhetoric, this anti-politics is not guided by any political ideology! Politics is reduced to economics or moralism. Reagan wants to be ideological; but his can only be a moralism serving as an ideology without *political* direction. That subordinates feel authorised to undertake grandiloquent projects is no more surprising than the inconsistencies in domestic politics detailed exhaustively by David Stockman. That Reagan forgot about his European allies at the Rejkavik summit is par for the course. 'America's back' recalls the pre-war isolationist slogan, 'America First' and the post-war slogan 'America First Everywhere'. Its post-liberal consequences put into question the anti-politics that made possible the 'Reagan Revolution'.

Reagan's success goes beyond liberalism, whereas Carter's failure remained behind it. Carter publicly admitted his doubts in the famous 15 July, 1979 speech that followed his 'retreat to the mountain'. He had discovered that international politics is a zero-sum game, that history is governed by 'inexorable powers'; he bemoaned an 'American malaise' and 'crisis of confidence that strikes at the very heart and soul of our national will'. Such un-Rooseveltian histrionics are not for Ronald Reagan. He seems to incarnate a different tradition altogether, that of a magical monarchy, the daughter of Fortune. Did he not survive an assassin's bullets and triumph over cancer while winning economic bets against all logic? But this curious monarchy is post-liberal; it is based on a perpetual plebiscite. The Reaganite commentator who suggested this description[9] admits that the Iran-Contra affair has disastrous consequences for such a regime. 'The magic was blinding,' he says; but 'Now that it's worn off, his flaws are easier to see.' The new situation reveals a 'reality principle' which strikes more deeply into the American political system than any revelations expected from Congressional investigation. Post-liberal America is defined by a question which united the Socialist Norman Thomas with the Republican Robert Taft in opposition to US entry into the Second World War. Can a democracy pay 'the price of power'?[10] The question dates from the foundation of the republic; the Rooseveltian synthesis papered it over; the failure of anti-politics makes it again urgent.

## 3. DEMOCRATIC DILEMMAS

If the domestic role of foreign policy is not new, its implications pose problems which touch the essence of democracy.[11] The heights from which Ronald Reagan has fallen make the stakes clear. Tocqueville provides the classic definition of the problem that faced the Founders of the republic. On the one hand, 'democracy can co-ordinate only with difficulty the details of a large enterprise, decide on a plan and carry it out obstinately despite all obstacles. It is little able to work out measures in secret and to wait patiently for their result'.[12] On the other hand, the American Constitution had the wisdom to place 'the general politics of the Nation beyond the direct and everyday influence of the people'.[13] Thus, President Washington could prevent 'the generous but unreflected passions of his fellow citizens' who wanted to declare war on England at the time of the French Revolution.[14] The difficulty arises from Tocqueville's conclusion that 'The majority was opposed to his politics; now the entire people approves of his decision.'[15] Will every decision of every President show similar wisdom? Will the people be capable of recognising it? The 'reality principle' revealed by the fall of Reagan's monarchy argues in the negative; the President cannot pretend to incarnate the national interest any more than does Congress or even the people or its majority. The common good or national interest is nowhere incarnate; democracy is precisely the quest for a common good whose nature is nowhere prescribed and whose essence is not fixed.

A frequent argument of the neo-conservative ideologues close to the Reagan administration rejects the democratic basis of the national interest. Like Tocqueville, they argue that democracy is incapable of formulating a politics that represents the national interest. The problem is serious for a great power whose national interest is *ipso facto* international. The second volume of *Democracy in America*, which treats foreign policy in terms of war, makes clear the roots of the difficulty. 'Democratic peoples,' says Tocqueville, 'naturally wish for peace, and democratic armies naturally wish for war.'[16] This assertion is based on the character of that 'separate little civilisation' formed by the army within a democratic society.[17] Tocqueville's description of the army can be extended to the 'little civilisation' constituted by the new elites and courtisans. He asks 'What makes democratic armies weaker than other armies at the beginning of the war, and more dangerous when the war is prolonged?'[18] The answer is that 'the same passions which led them to consider peace as so important are redirected towards war'.[19] In the first volume, and for the neo-conservatives, these passions led to the belief in the existence of a real and permanent national interest defined by social interest in material goods. Such a national interest can be defined by geo-politics; the President's task is to defend this material reality. But this neglects those democratic 'passions' whose participation made a democratic foreign policy impossible, and which must now be mobilised in the national interest.

The second volume of *Democracy in America* seems to describe the post-War American political world; the first fits better the politics of the Reagan administration. Whereas an ambivalence in defining the national interest characterised post-war liberalism, the new nationalism wants to return to the Presidency of Washington in order to overcome the contradictions of liberalism's two logics. As if he anticipated the difficulty, Tocqueville sums up his intuitions in 'Considerations on War in Democratic Societies'. The political analysis regains its priority here. 'It is only the passion and the habit of freedom that can struggle successfully against the habit and the passion of well-being. I can imagine no situation so ripe for conquest in the case of a defeat than a democratic people which does not have free institutions.'[20] The reader is left with the task of finding the harmony between the presidentialist politics of the first volume and the democratic freedom which is at the basis of the second. The politician is left with the task of reconciling the national interest and the interest of democracy. The political philosopher and citizen is left the task of asking what political effects result from the confrontation of these two interests now that the 'reality principle' has revealed the political foundation of contemporary anti-politics.

## 4. DEMOCRATIC RENEWAL

The Democratic Party has been attempting to put itself back together since the failure of George McGovern in 1972. Since the conquest of power by its 'New Politics' wing, the party has been divided, incapable of uniting around a social project or even a presidential candidacy. It has retained to a reasonable degree its local roots and much of its power in Congress. The party machinery managed to impose its candidate in 1984, but Walter Mondale was beaten before the campaign began. His defeat was due in part to the 'magic' of King Ronald, but its grounds lie deeper. The Republicans mocked a divided party which tried to pay attention to each and all of the diverse constituencies it amalgamated. They could claim that they incarnated the single national interest itself. The power of this anti-political argument, more than its internal problems, defines the task of the Democrats in 1988. They can succeed only if they are able to make a political virtue of democracy; the plurality of interests which must have access to the public debate has to be identified with the national interest. There is good reason to doubt the Democrats' capacity to escape electoralist constraints. Should party unity emerge, it will be founded on a compromise that leaves minority interests voiceless; the result will increase the (already majoritarian) 'party' of abstention. Were the Democratic party to win the Presidency, it would be on the basis of a renewal of the old liberal compromise. The chance for political renewal would be put off, as it was in 1976.

The paths to change will not be discovered by the politics of the politicians. Whatever the investigation of the Iran-Contra affair reveals, public cyncism and political mistrust will only deepen. The 'reality principle' is not empirical; it puts into question the foundations of American politics. Because Reaganism marks the end *and* culmination of liberalism, its disgrace makes possible a basic reflection on *the political* as such, i.e., on the conditions of the possibility of politics itself. The ambiguity of liberalism covered over questions of political principle by stressing one or the other of the forms of interventionism. The neo-conservatives, after Tocqueville, have had the merit of uncovering the foundation of that liberal ambiguity in the very nature of democracy. The national interest *does* exist; the idea is not the invention of a ruling class seeking to justify, or to mask, its social domination. But the President does not incarnate the national interest. This does not mean that the Presidency should be made a simple administrator of Congressional decision, as suggested by the reforms that followed the Watergate affair or perhaps the Boland Amendment. That only reinforced the anti-politics of the new experts. The changes that follow the present affair will have to show democracy to be necessary to the national interest.

There are good reasons for pessimism; attitudes change slowly, institutions are weighed down by inertia, politicians want to preserve their positions. None the less, the question has been posed by the débâcle of Reagan's transcendence of liberalism. Easy solutions are ruled out. Democracy cannot be sacrificed on the altar of national interest; and the national interest cannot be incarnated by a person, a party or an institution. Nor does the simple equation of democracy with the national interest suffice. The national interest is that common good which founds the *res publica*; it exists in the *symbolic* mode. Its reality cannot be ignored; but its symbolic nature means that it cannot be realised definitively, once-and-for-all. It is the stake of a conflict of interests which must be able to show themselves in the public arena if they are not to be condemned to impotence by a politics which claims illicitly to incarnate *the* nation. The liberal triumph of the Welfare-State took the anti-political form the French call aptly the *Etat-Providence*. Political interests are condemned to the status of private cares.[21] Reaganism has eliminated that obstacle to democratic participation; unilateral political interventionism based on the social power of the private economy makes clear the political character of interest. The future will depend on the ability of a democratic politics to incorporate it without succumbing to an undifferentiated pluralism. Symbols are real, but they cannot be reduced to the materiality of private interest.

These theoretical questions will not be posed directly by the politicians or even the pundits. But they are not simply the philosopher's abstractions. The realignment of the major political parties that commentators have been predicting since the triumph of Nixon in 1972 is unlikely; continued fragmentation as the presidential primaries develop is more probable. That is not necessarily bad. Its implications were suggested recently in an article in the *New York Times* by Senator Moynihan. The former Ambassador to the United Nations argued against the unilateralist critics of American participation in that body by comparing his old job with his present Senatorial tasks. The representative of the large state of New York has to seek interest-coalitions, use parliamentary procedures, negotiate as an equal with representatives of tiny Rhode Island and underpopulated North Dakota. This is politics. The condition of its possibility is the *symbolic* nature of membership in a unity which must constantly define and articulate its common good. The national unity is a symbolic reality within which politics takes place. Everyday politics is of course about interests; but the 'Reagan Revolution's' overthrow of liberalism demonstrates that it is not only about interests. Recognition of the symbolic condition of the possibility of politics is the premise for any new politics which goes beyond the incoherence of the anti-political liberal synthesis and the plebiscitory monarchy which has temporarily replaced it.

American history is marked by it's inability to articulate the relation between politics and interest. Rebelling against a king, the federalist Founders of the republic solved this problem badly. The Civil War which resulted saved the symbolic national unit without assuring a reconstruction for the future. The Founders were confronted with the choice of representing interest in the form of wealth or interest manifested by numbers; they created a Senate where the states were equal, and a House based on population (including 'three-fifths' of the non-represented slaves). The debate was renewed after the Civil War; the democracy represented by number was 'crucified on a cross of gold' until the New Deal created a government which intervened to fulfill the *social* promise of democracy. War and the Truman Doctrine revealed the lack of a political foundation for this compromise. Truman's Fair Deal was forgotten; Eisenhower brought happy mediocrity to a society without political purpose; Kennedy sought a New Frontier whose conquest could renew the American spirit. It was to no avail; American liberalism remained social; no politics unified its coalition of heterogeneous interests. As it broadened its net it reduced its coherence. This made it possible for Reagan to invert the social agenda of liberalism by privatising domestic services from prisons to pensions, health care to housing. But the absence of a political agenda became blatant when he let foreign policy be 'privatised' by Iranian middlemen and Contra supporters. The anti-political logic of post-liberal politics was made clear when Under-Secretary of State Eliot Abrams asked with apparent sincerity, 'Is there something wrong with the Administration, having lost the vote in Congress, appealing directly to the people?'[22] This 'people' is not the citizenry but the *private*, and interested, plebiscitory mass!

Grounds for pessimism, but also for optimism, can be found in Tocqueville. A chapter in the *Ancien Régime et la Révolution* describes 'How the French wanted Reforms before wanting Freedom'. Tocqueville concludes his account with a resounding declaration which affirms the faith animating his entire work. '*He who seeks in freedom anything other than freedom is made to serve*.'[23] The context in which this passage occurs points to its contemporary relevance. Tocqueville is analysing the projects of the reforming economists, whose desire to ameliorate the *social* condition of their fellows led them to accept an Enlightened Despotism. Such a choice was explained in *Democracy in America* as the result of the 'constant opposition between the instincts born from equality and the means equality furnishes to satisfy those instincts'.[24] The political implication was drawn in a later chapter which explains 'That the Sentiments of Democratic Peoples agree with their Ideas in leading them to Concentrate Power.'[25] The twin paths to the *Etat-Providence* described by Tocqueville were realised in the United States by the liberal compromise. But Tocqueville was not pessimistic; he saw the vital role of associative life as a counterweight. Those associations today have become the representatives of material interests, whose 'rights' the courts protect as 'free speech' and 'freedom of association'. This travesty need not be the last word.

The associative democracy described by Tocqueville in the nineteenth century has not disappeared. The 'end of ideology' celebrated by liberal ideology in the 1950s gave rise to a 'New Left', whose demise in the 1970s came when it abandoned politics in favour of social change. The anti-politics of what Theodore Lowi calls 'interest-group liberalism' transformed a political movement into another social interest feeding at the trough of the providential State. 'It is one of the tragedies of our time,' summarises Lowi, 'that so many Negro leaders themselves took the War on Poverty as their own.'[26] But new movements have sprung up. Ecology, feminism, anti-nukes *can* become simply social interests seeking to privatise the political for their own purposes. But they cannot be *reduced* to social interests because they are the carriers of a political demand for a redefinition of the national interest. Freedom sought for its own sake, political freedom, is not separable from the social equality without which it cannot exist. But freedom cannot be reduced to social equality, nor is it the inevitable corollary of equality. The new movements have to recognise that their social demands have a political character which cannot be represented in either a renewed liberal coalition or a post-liberal plebiscitory presidency. It is not their numbers or the interests that they represent which make them political; their politics depends on their ability to influence the definition of the national interest.

If the political realignment predicted by the pundits in 1972 and again after Reagan's triumph in 1984 is ruled out by another scandal, a realignment of *politics* is possible in the wake of the Iran-Contra affair. Siegel is correct in seeing the triumph of Reagan as 'the last election of the 1960s'. The Democrats will not be able to restore the old politics. A period of uncertainty is in store. The associative, democratic movements are not a solution; they tend to remain single-issue interest-groups whose sense of the national interest is strongly isolationist. They have added little to the issues raised by the Iran-Contra affair. But that affair will not disappear; it poses the fundamental question of a democracy that seeks to avoid paying 'the price of power'. The *moral* outrage that greeted the Iran phase of the affair was correctly seen by the President's men as the real threat to his policies. The realignment of politics has to articulate that morality without creating a new anti-politics. The equation of nationalism and moralism destroys the political process as effectively as the reduction of politics to morality. The national interest, at home and abroad, provides the framework within which democratic politics is possible. Morality makes necessary that politics. Neither the national interest nor morality defines an absolute and really existing *thing*; each defines the other, in a process whose nature is *symbolic*. This structural framework should be kept in mind as the affair unfolds and the anti-politicians attempt to ply their trade as before.

## Notes

1. This argument is proposed by Fred Siegel in a review of the two more typical explanations of the triumph of Reaganism. Sidney Blumenthal's *The Rise of the Counter-Establishment: From Conservative Ideology to Political Power* (New York: Times Books, 1986) traces Reagan's success to the domination of policy formation by right wing think-tanks like the American Enterprise Institute, the Heritage Foundation and the Business Roundtable. Siegel suggests that this is 'like watching a chess game with only one set of pieces on the board'. On the other hand, the 'neo-Beardian' orientation of Thomas Ferguson and Joel Rogers's *Right Turn: The Decline of the Democrats and the Future of American Politics* (New York: Hill and Wang, 1986) proposes to 'follow the money'. The difficulty with this 'political market place' approach (which won James Buchanan his Nobel Prize) is that it implies 'that American politics has little to do with voters or popular sentiment . . . [and] masks the real politics of corporate manipulation'. I will return in a moment to Siegel's own position; the present arguments are found in 'The Political Marketplace', *Commonweal*, 27 February, 1987, pp. 113–16.
2. This generalisation ignores the often persuasive arguments condemning an anti-politics suggested by Theodore J. Lowi's *The End of Liberalism* (New York: W. W. Norton, 1969). Lowi dissects the politics of 'interest-group liberalism' which began with the New Deal before acquiring the status of 'the public philosophy' after the War. For the pluralists, the state becomes simply another interest among society's countervailing powers; process replaces political decisions, means become ends, bargaining eliminates the need for planning. But Lowi's proposed solution, which he calls 'juridical democracy', does not seem relevant in the Age of Reagan. His new study, *The Personal President* (Ithaca: Cornell University Press, 1985), develops one aspect of the earlier analysis, the theme of the 'plebiscitory Presidency' which is necessary to repair the dysfunctions of interest-group liberalism. His proposed solution this time, the creation of a multi-party system, comes closer to the analysis suggested here. It neglects, however, the dilemmas of liberalism dissected in the earlier study.
3. I. M. Destler, Leslie H. Gelb and Anthony Lake, *Our Own Worst Enemy. The Unmaking of American Foreign Policy* (New York: Simon and Shuster, 1984). The authors, who have all held positions of importance in the State Department, tend to idealise the period of bi-partisanship and the role of the Establishment. Indeed, Gelb was the co-author of an earlier work entitled *The Irony of Vietnam: The System Worked* (Washington, D.C.: Brookings Institution, 1979). I am making use of these arguments for my own purposes.

   Again, for those who want to analyse anti-politics in its domestic setting, Lowi's *The Personal President* points out that Nixon's second term began with an attempt to create structures similar to the ones described here in order to assure control through a 'Domestic Council'. Cf. op. cit., pp. 142ff.
4. Of course, both Kissinger and Brzezinski were long-time associates of

the old elite centred around the Council on Foreign Relations. Kissinger's reputation was first made by his Council-sponsored study *Nuclear Weapons and Foreign Policy* (1957); he and Brzezinski contributed volumes to the Council's 'Atlantic Policy Study' series (1965) which attempted to deal with the 'crisis' in the NATO Alliance brought about by Gaullism. I use their names here only because they are better-known than the legion of smaller fry – such as Michael Ledeen – whose names turn up in investigations like the present Iran-Contra affair.

5. The 'Battle of the two Richards' is described by Strobe Talbot in *Deadly Gambits* (New York: Knopf, 1984). The loser, Richard Burt, is now the American ambassador to West Germany.
6. (New York: Hill and Wang, 1984).
7. For example, the candidate Carter asserted in 1976 that 'in the near future . . . issues of war and peace will be more a function of economic and social problems than of the military security problems that have dominated international relations since World War II.' Cited in Robert D. Schulzinger, *The Wise Men of Foreign Affairs. The History of the Council on Foreign Relations* (New York: Columbia University Press, 1984), p. 230.
8. The expanding post-war economy was accompanied by a triple consensus which assumed 1) that although trading with other countries, America's economy would remain independent of international pressures; 2) the high-wage social contract of labour and industry made well-paid workers the essential market for American goods; 3) that technological change would not be too destabilising compared to the benefits it brought. None of these assumptions can be maintained today.
9. Morton Kondracke, 'The Case against Glee', in *The New Republic*, 26 January, 1987, pp. 16f.
10. This is the title of Charles Krauthammer's attempt to frame the implications of the Iran-Nicaragua affair in neo-liberal terms. A citation from a member of the right-wing libertarian Cato Institute makes the point clearly: 'Nearly four decades ago, opponents of foreign entanglements cautioned that America could not operate as an empire abroad and remain a republic at home. . . . Burdensome military taxation, the malignant growth of an imperial presidency, and the violations of civil liberties during the McCarthy era and the Vietnam War offered earlier testimony to the dangers arising from America's status as planetary gendarme.' (Cf. *The New Republic*, 9 February, 1987, p. 23.)
11. Foreign policy was at the root of the creation of political parties in the United States. The debate concerning the Jay Treaty with England in 1796 ripped apart the unitary republic whose Constitution had been defended by Madison and Hamilton in *The Federalist* before the two became the leaders of violently opposed political parties.
12. *De la Démocratie en Amérique* (Paris: Gallimard, 1961), p. 238f. A recent illustration from another domain of American politics was provided by Dr Gerold Yonas, former chief scientist of the Star Wars programme, who denounced the constant shifts of priority which 'make

you wonder if this country is capable of running a big, long-term programme'. (Cited in *The New York Times*, 10 March, 1987.)
13. Ibid., p. 236.
14. Ibid., p. 237.
15. Ibid.
16. Ibid., tome II, p. 270.
17. Ibid., p. 273.
18. Ibid., p. 281.
19. Ibid., p. 283.
20. Ibid., p. 290.
21. Lowi's *The End of Liberalism*, op. cit., is a sustained critical presentation of the logic, and the perverse effects, of the anti-politics.
22. Cited in *The New York Times*, 20 January, 1987.
23. *L'Ancien Régime et la Révolution* (Paris: Gallimard, 1952), p. 217, my italics. The passage is preceded by a sentence worth citing as well. 'What has in all epochs attached so strongly the hearts of certain men to freedom are its very attractions, its own charm, independently of its benefits; it is the pleasure of being able to speak, act and breathe without constraint, under the government only of God and the laws.'
24. Op. cit., I, p. 144.
25. Ibid., pp. 300ff.
26. Lowi, *The End of Liberalism*, op. cit., p. 248.

# Name Index

# Subject Index